Human Being
and
Citizen

Death is most fit before you do
Deeds that would make death fit for you.
                    Anaxandrides (a Spartan)

I chanced to meet a man who has spent more money on sophists than everyone else put together, Callias the son of Hipponicus. So I asked him (for he has two sons), "Callias," I said, "if your sons had been born colts or calves, we could find and hire a trainer who would take care to make them noble and good in the appropriate virtue, and this would be some groom or farmer. But now, since they are human beings, whom do you have in mind to take on as a trainer for them? Who is there who understands this kind of virtue, that of a human being and a citizen? For I suppose you have looked into this, since you have sons. Is there someone," I asked, "or not?" "By all means," he said. "Who," I asked, "and where is he from, and for how much does he teach?"

                                                    Socrates

Such is the nature of man, formed by his benevolent author no doubt for wise ends, that altho' he knows his existence to be limited to a span, he takes his measures as if he were to live forever.

                    Gouverneur Morris (an American)

Human Being
and
Citizen

Essays on Virtue, Freedom,
and
the Common Good

George Anastaplo

THE SWALLOW PRESS INC.
CHICAGO

Published by
The Swallow Press Incorporated
1139 South Wabash Avenue
Chicago, Illinois 60605

First Edition
First Printing

LIBRARY OF CONGRESS CATALOG CARD NUMBER: 75-21909
ISBN 0-8040-0677-6

To
MY PARENTS
who discovered
as Immigrants from Greece
how difficult it is for one to become
a Human Being
where one is not born
a Citizen

Contents

Preface

There is a curious custom in the British Navy: all the
cordage of the Royal Fleet, whether heavy or light, is
twisted so that a red thread runs through whole ropes,
by which even the smallest piece can be recognized
as Crown property.

J. W. von Goethe, *Elective Affinities*, c. 20

I happen to begin this preface under the immediate charm of *Death Comes for the Archbishop*, perhaps the most humane of American "novels"—most humane and yet confidently civic-minded. One can see there, in Willa Cather's story of two priests dedicated to civilizing a rugged land, what it means to be a citizen, something of what it means to be a human being, and how much (and in what ways) each depends upon the other. (She provides thereby a salutary corrective to the more talented Mark Twain, who is appalled, if not ultimately crippled, by the spiritual wastage he sees in the determined building of a new country by a new people.)

My first book, *The Constitutionalist: Notes on the First Amendment*, was devoted to "a consideration of American institutions and circumstances and what we can learn from them about both the human being and the citizen." That inquiry about both the human being and the citizen—an inquiry of particular interest to a "nation" of immigrants—is developed further in this collection of essays.

The human being is essentially unconcerned about his immediate circumstances: he reaches out to those virtuous men in other times and at other places who have thought as he has—to those, that is, who have thought. The citizen, on the other hand, is always rooted in a particular place: to him circumstances very much matter, as does the good of the country he chances to serve and for which he is prepared to sacrifice himself.

One can see, in the relation of human being to citizen, something of the relation of general to particular, of abstract to concrete. But one sees there also something other than the relation of whole to part—for in some ways the human being and the citizen are quite different people, oftentimes in tension with if not even mortally opposed to one another. Thus, Aristotle sees as a recurring political problem that of determining the proper relation of the good man to the good citizen. Thus, also, Marcus Aurelius Antoninus observes, "My nature is rational and social. My city and country, so far as I am Antoninus, is Rome, but so far as I am a human being, is the world."

The essays in this collection draw on ideas and principles which, however formulated here, are of enduring worth. The twenty-six talks and articles upon which these essays are based (and to which some residual diversity in "style" is due) were developed at the times and places specified in the note at the beginning of each essay. They were often set forth as constructive provocations—as efforts to suggest to partisans in controversial situations what should be said for the other side *and how*. Again and again, a neglected aspect of the dragon is pointed out to the engaged knight errant.

I have, as circumstances have changed, shifted my positions on men and issues when I have thought it salutary to do so. (A case in point is what I have been obliged to say *and to whom* during the past quarter century about the elusive Mr. Nixon.) In considering whether and how to speak on various affairs of state, I have been again and again reminded of Abraham Lincoln's prudent observation in 1862, "I am very little inclined on any occasion to say anything unless I hope to produce some good by it."

The affairs of state commented upon in these essays, from the perspective of law, political philosophy, and literature, extend back to the Second World War and even before. The comments themselves were made during the past decade—and are woven together in what is believed to be a coherent whole, with "theory" guiding "practice," with "practice" providing occasions for reconsidering "theory." There should be evident throughout these essays the intimate relation between my "deeds" and my "words": my career and my writings, for better or for worse, do go together.

The things I have done (and have had done to me) and the things I have thought (and have had taught me) do seem to bear upon one another. No doubt, natural temperament affects, for better *and* for worse, how I have conducted myself and what I have seen fit to publish. It affects as well my somewhat self-centered inclination to attempt to weave all these things together, to feel free (if not even eager) to refer the reader to what I have said and done elsewhere, and thereby to try to make sense of the many things intellectuals may happen to concern themselves with from time to time.

Thus, I have recently had occasion to say, in an article prepared for the *Political Science Reviewer*, "It is a curious fact that an occasional reader of *The Constitutionalist* somehow concludes that I believe 'principles must be given priority over consequences.' Perhaps this is because I once found it salutary to insist upon standing on a 'principle' which cost me my career at the bar. It is partly to correct careless misconceptions about my opinions on controversial issues that I have been obliged again and again to quote from and cite readers to various of my publications...."

On the other hand, the "liberal" reputation I have earned because of my Illinois bar admission experience *has* permitted me to speak responsibly (including, when that seemed advisable, as a "conservative") on controversial issues bearing upon the common good. That is to say, my exclusion in the 1950s from the practice of law and hence from a conventional academic career has licensed me to be (in my public statements) more respectful of prudence, as well as less concerned about personal consequences, than my much more ambitious contemporaries at the bar and in academic life can "afford" to be. (The Shakespearean Fool does come to mind.)

Intellectuals are today in particular need of prudent counsel, of a defensible common sense. Their unphilosophical partisanship and optimistic recklessness need to be moderated. Intellectuals all too often conduct themselves as if there should be no past from which to learn and no future to take account of. In this there is even a certain childishness—and this at a time when children can be most presumptuous in their romantic posturings. It is a time, after all, when talented children can conduct themselves with the callous imperiousness of a King Lear, even while they fancy themselves gentle Cordelias—without appreciating, by the way, what *can* be said against the respectable Cordelia and on behalf of her politically venturesome father.

It is often difficult today to stand for prudence without seeming vacillating and even unprincipled. It is always difficult to be independent without seeming simply rebellious and truculent, to stand for the proprieties without seeming simply rigid if not even obsessed. One must somehow be courteous and yet firm, steadfast and yet restrained. It is useful to respect old-fashioned civility and pieties, even as one recognizes their limits. One must recognize as well that a man who really knows what he is saying and doing may be misunderstood and ridiculed, especially by people who do not trouble to read carefully or who have not disciplined themselves to be aware of the evidence they lack in judging what is done or said by another. Be that as it may, a reconsideration of Plato's *Euthyphro*, as well as of his *Symposium* and his *Theages*, is certainly in order.

Thus, Socrates, in his toughminded gentleness, is the hero of these seventeen essays. He realized that his "self-centered" experiences and speeches were, in one sense, personal and daring, in another sense, points of departure for something radically impersonal and deeply sober. Critical to his way were consultation, inquiry, and discussion: those who confronted him with decisions which purported to bind him learned that he would continue to conduct himself as he believed he should— even at the risk of seeming self-righteous if not unfeeling to those closest to him, fellow citizens and relatives alike. Perhaps he realized that even his most vigorous critics would someday be grateful, once their passions were spent, that he had stood for a reasoned moderation (if only by quietly stepping aside) while others shamelessly catered to the prejudices and follies of the moment.

I continue to profit from my regular courses at Rosary College and The University of Chicago and from my annual seminars at The Clearing and The University of Dallas. My academic career has been particularly enriched by an intimate association in recent years with a law school teacher of mine of a quarter century ago, Malcolm P. Sharp, who has been serving since 1972 as the chairman of the Political Science Department of Rosary College. Also instructive has been my service the past year as advisor and research director to the Governor's Commission on Individual Liberty and Personal Privacy for the State of Illinois. (The dedicated chairman of the Commission, Bernard Weisberg, a Chicago attorney, defined my Commission duties from the outset as primarily those of a "gadfly.")

I continue to profit as well from my association with publishers (in this instance, Morton P. Weisman and Durrett Wagner of Swallow Press) who display that responsible competence which eases the burdens of seeing a complicated manuscript through the press. (George Malcolm Davidson Anastaplo and Theodora McShan Anastaplo have helped prepare this collection for the press.) It is particularly important, if instruction in careful reading and sensible conduct *is* to be conveyed, that disciplined writing should be permitted—and this does depend upon not only the forebearance but also the cooperation of publishers. The generous critical response since 1971 to *The Constitutionalist*, and especially to *its* notes (which take up half of its eight hundred pages), has been such as to encourage subsequent editors to permit an unusual amount of space to be devoted to my essay-like notes.

I trust that the essays in this collection can serve to guide the open-minded reader to reflections of his own upon the questions and problems touched upon in them—reflections which may help him determine what he should think and how he should live. Indeed, perhaps most important, these essays may contribute to the development in the reader of a useful understanding of "should" with respect to things both of the city and of the mind. It is well, in these troubled times, to be reminded of the "shouldness" of things, of the roots of the *should* in nature, and of the sense in which it can be said that to think and to act as one should is the fullest realization of one's freedom.

It is also well, in times that are particularly troubled for Americans —who see shortsighted foreign policies collapsing abroad (but not, however, without some enduring accomplishments) even while economic frustrations are endured at home—it is well to be reminded of the heartening salutation given by a Pope to Miss Cather's resourceful French missionary about to return to the consuming rigors of his challenging post in the Far West: *"Coraggio, Americano!"*

GEORGE ANASTAPLO

Hyde Park
Chicago, Illinois
April 23, 1975

Prologue

I. Dissent in Athens

An Invocation of First Principles

> The best guarantee that [Senator John F. Kennedy] is indeed the next President of the United States came tonight from a shrewd old Cook County politician, who said: "In all this figuring [about the possible effects of a recount in Illinois], which I must say is plausible enough, you have overlooked one law of American politics: when a vote is stolen in Cook County, it stays stolen."
>
> *Manchester Guardian,*
> November 21, 1960

It may seem ungracious of me, after we Americans have just been treated to a meal which it is impossible to consider in any way blameworthy, to dissent, as I am now obliged to do, from what has been said to us tonight in defense of the way the present Greek government conducts itself.[1]

It should be evident to all of you by now that I would have preferred, on this occasion, only to listen and thus to learn. But I cannot completely ignore the challenge we have just heard from our official host in his determined effort to induce me to say something to this gathering. An American, he complains, should not wait to say in Washington what he dare not say in Athens.[2] I therefore consent, despite the lateness of the hour, to comment on various of the things said to us this evening, as they now occur to me.

We have been reminded again and again that Greece and the United States have long been allies in defense of the free world. I need not dispute our host's observation that one form of freedom is that in which discussion appears. There is no doubt that we have had an opportunity tonight to exchange opinions, for us to ask questions, and for our host and his colleagues to give the answers of their government. But I must challenge his suggestion that this is proof that there is freedom of dis-

---

This is a reconstruction of an extemporaneous talk made in Athens, Greece, on September 20, 1968, at an official dinner given for the twenty-six members of a group from the Chicago Council on Foreign Relations visiting Greece on an archaeological and political tour conducted by the speaker. Some thirty Greeks were also present.

The talk was published in *Notes on World Events* (Chicago Council on Foreign Relations), May 1969, p. 1. It was reprinted in 115 *Congressional Record* E5156 (June 23, 1969).

cussion in Greece today. For the fact of the matter is that such a discussion as ours tonight is not now generally permitted in Greece. The only people who dare speak as freely in public as we have here are some members of the present government, a few other men with the famous names of old families, and visitors who hold foreign passports. Most Greeks dare not speak as we have except in the privacy of their homes and even there only with relatives and friends whom they can trust. All of you Greeks here tonight must know this. It cannot be forgotten that thousands of "enemies of the regime"—men and women of the Left, Center, and Right—are still held in Greek prisons without trial and without any prospect of trial.

We have been reminded that the American Constitution also followed upon a revolution. This is certainly true. But I hardly think that justifies the manner in which the constitution to be voted on in Greece next week has been brought forth. The Constitution of the United States was written by fifty-five men freely selected by the American people to represent them. Who these men were, why they were selected and by whom were known to everyone. This is not the case here. What those men produced in 1787 was discussed publicly and freely, for a year and more, in circumstances where no man was afraid of being officially penalized for the position he took in public. That is not the case here. Rather, we know that the most distinguished opponents of your proposed constitution—the politicians who we know have had large popular followings for years—have been for some time under house arrest and will not be released before next Monday, and only then in order to be able to vote the following Sunday on the proposed constitution. It has been made clear to them that they are not to speak publicly against the constitution. How can it be said in such circumstances that a genuinely free referendum is being held, irrespective of how the balloting itself is conducted or comes out? How can any ordinary citizen be sure that he will not be regarded as an "enemy of the regime" if he should be detected voting against the constitution proposed by his insistent government?[3]

Yet we have been told several times this evening that we are about to witness free balloting, that this is confirmed by the fact that some newspaper criticism of specific articles in the proposed constitution has been permitted. But we Americans know what a free election is. We know this from our own experience. We know what a free election feels like; we know what it sounds like; we know what it looks like. And we know this is not it.

Several of my fellow-citizens have this evening remarked on the fact that there are only *NAI* [YES] signs on display in Greece these days. Nowhere can one see *OXI* [NO] signs. In fact, I have the past week seen only one *OXI* chalked on a wall—and even it had been almost rubbed out. It has been suggested to us tonight that such signs are not significant, that Greeks will freely vote for what they "believe in." But does the government really believe that its monopoly of propaganda is inconsequential? Considerable money has been spent by the government on these signs, as well as on the press, radio, and film. They are intended to shape the opinions of many who can be moved by such things; and they constantly remind everyone of who is in control here and of what is expected of them. We Americans do know what to think when we see government resources and government personnel marshalled as they have been here in a massive (and no doubt successful) campaign to produce the desired result. This is no more a free referendum than similar exercises are free either in Spain or in Russia.[4]

And yet our host and his government have tried hard to persuade us that we are witnessing a genuinely free expression of the will of the Greek people. It seems important to them that Americans believe this. We Americans may not be informed enough about or familiar enough with Greek history and Greek affairs to be able to judge other claims of this government. But, as I have said, we do have the experience and the ability and the information to judge whether an election is truly free. And when we can see that this government claim about a free referendum, of which we have heard so much, is simply without foundation, what are we to think of all the other claims that we hear from the same government about what it has done for Greece, about what its motives are, about its innocence of deliberate torture of political prisoners, and about the imminent Communist danger from which it saved Greece by seizing power last year? Are we not entitled to judge what we may not know by what we can and do know?

We have been told several times this evening that Greek affairs of recent years required drastic medicine, that a doctor must sometimes prescribe harsh measures in order to save the life of the patient. But do we not all believe that an adult is entitled to select his own doctor and to discharge him when he chooses? By what authority does the presiding doctor prescribe what is necessary for Greece? How can the Greeks be said to have selected him, when they did not even know who he was? What diploma does he have as a doctor? What proof of his qualifications is there aside from his self-serving testimony about himself? Certainly, we cannot accept as indicative of public approval of his regimen the fact that an unarmed people does not resist a determined government that is heavily armed.

The republican precedent of the Roman dictatorship has been cited to us in justification of what has happened here since April 1967. But it should be remembered that the Roman dictator (usually a citizen of recognized merit) was given his authority pursuant to the constitutional processes of the Roman Republic—and this was done only after debate and deliberation. It should also be remembered that the Roman dictator held his power for a fixed term, a term clearly stated in advance of his appointment. We have also been cited, in justification of the suspension of civil liberties in times of emergency, the experiences of Great Britain and the United States during the Second World War. But it should be remembered that Mr. Churchill was repeatedly obliged during that war to submit himself to the will of an elected parliament. The Americans present tonight remember the difficulties President Roosevelt had with the American Congress, even in time of war. And in both cases, these wartime leaders were chosen pursuant to the constitutional processes of free peoples, despite the existence then of emergencies far more threatening than anything confronting Greece today.

I feel honor-bound to address myself, before I close, to the remarks made by our host about Eleni Vlachou, a lady whom he knows, from our conversation during dinner, that I respect. Every Greek here tonight knows that Mrs. Vlachou published, before the coup of April 1967, the most respected newspaper in Greece. You Greeks know that hers was a newspaper of the Right, that she was strongly anti-Communist (indeed, to my mind, too much so), and that she has repudiated the claims of the army officers who made the coup about the danger of Communism from which they "saved" Greece. You know that hers was the newspaper that most of you, and most of the supporters of the present government, once looked up to as the best in Greece. You know that your government made serious efforts for six months after the April 1967 coup to induce Mrs. Vlachou to resume publication of the newspaper she had immediately suspended upon being confronted by your press censorship, censorship that continues to this day. To disparage her as has been done tonight is simply unrealistic and even unbecoming. To honor her for the stand she has taken and the sacrifices she has made is to honor and to nourish and perhaps even to help revive the best in the Greek spirit. We will know that a significant measure of liberty has indeed returned to Greece when Mrs. Vlachou again publishes her newspaper freely, a newspaper in which I am sure there will be things with which I would be obliged to disagree. In any event, Mrs. Vlachou's exile, like that of your king, serves as a constant reminder that things are not right in Greece at this time.[5]

I have directed my remarks this evening to the question of liberty, to the question of whether liberty exists in Greece today. This is not the occasion to examine the advantages and the excesses of liberty, to examine the conditions for its preservation—all matters about which much needs to be said in Greece as well as in the United States. I must also reserve for another occasion my discussion of what has been happening under the present government to the Greek economy, of what has already happened to the effectiveness of the army that a handful of junior officers has usurped, of what Greece is supposed to have been saved from and saved for by this unconstitutional usurpation, of what has happened to Greek relations with its friends and allies in the West since April 1967, and of what has been happening the past seventeen months to the civil services, to the functioning of government, and to the quality of life in this country.[6]

We have been speaking tonight of liberty. Liberty is what we Americans do know something about. And when an American visitor, who respects both the truth and Greece, is confronted as we have been at such length, not only tonight but ever since our arrival in Athens, by the insistence that liberty is to be found in Greece today, he is obliged to dissent, if he presumes to speak at all.

If what Greek citizens have now is what you mean by "liberty," then we should all reconsider what we mean by "the free world."[7]

II. Human Being and Citizen

A Beginning to the Study of Plato's "Apology of Socrates"

> Just as others are pleased by a good horse or dog or bird, [Socrates said,] I myself am pleased to an even higher degree by good friends. . . . And the treasures of the wise men of old which they left behind by writing them in books, I unfold and go through them together with my friends, and if we see something good, we pick it out and regard it as a great gain if we thus become useful to one another.
>
> Xenophon *Memorabilia* I. vi. 14

i

S ocrates himself indicates to us the care with which his three speeches are to be read: even the most casual use of names cannot be taken for granted.[1] Names, which constitute at least an introduction to one's thought, are selected by Socrates with care.[2] Thus, we are meant to notice that nowhere in his principal speech of defense does he address the court as "judges," but rather as "men of Athens," or, on a few occasions, merely as "men" or as "Athenians." Meletus does address the court as "judges" when he is cross-examined (26d), but Socrates reserves this term for his final speech and uses it then only when he addresses that portion of the court which had voted against the death sentence.[3] Indeed, he then observes that only that portion of the court deserved an appellation which implied just action. (40a) Only he who judges rightly is truly a judge. (18a)

It is evident that Socrates, even on trial for his life, assumes toward the city and his fellow-citizens the attitude of a judge, the attitude of one who can pass judgment on their legal procedures, their use of language, and their standards of justice.

This essay was published in *Ancients and Moderns: Essays on the Tradition of Political Philosophy, in Honor of Leo Strauss,* Joseph Cropsey, editor (New York: Basic Books, 1964), p. 16.

Part One includes Sections i-iii; Part Two, Sections iv-vi; Part Three, Sections vii-xiii.

The citations in the text are to Plato's *Apology of Socrates*.

Socrates conducts himself before the people of Athens as a teacher before his pupils and as a ruler before his subjects.

ii

Another set of names catches our attention—those that are summed up in the accusations against Socrates.[4] There is, first, what the old accusers said of him: that "there is one Socrates, a wise man [a wise guy], a ponderer upon things in the air and one who has investigated everything beneath the earth and who can make the weaker argument the stronger." (18b) Socrates then puts these old accusers' slanders in the form of an indictment, to the effect that Socrates is "a busybody, investigating the things beneath the earth and in the heaven and making the weaker argument the stronger and teaching others these same things." (19c)

The substance of this "indictment" is similar to his earlier statement of the old accusers' slanders.[5] But the preface has been changed: "busybody" has been substituted for "wise man," and the count of teaching has been added. Perhaps we are meant to deduce that, from the perspective of ordinary citizens, there is something of the busybody about the wise man: that is, his concern to know all things means that he will meddle with things many regard as none of his business. We suspect also that it is the activity of teaching which converts private pursuits into social offenses, especially when this teaching seems to challenge that of the poets or the politicians.

It is this teaching that is reflected in the charge that Socrates corrupts the youth. Young men, imitating his examination of people who think they know something, manage to provoke those they examine into becoming angry with Socrates, whom they then charge with corrupting the youth. (23c-d) And when anyone asks in what way he corrupts the youth, they fall back on "the things that are at hand to say against all philosophers, 'the things in the air and beneath the earth' and 'not acknowledging the gods,' and 'making the weaker argument the stronger.'" (23d) Thus, the usual charges against philosophers provide the transition between the old accusations against Socrates and the new ones upon which he must stand trial. The prejudice that philosophers generally have earned is central to the sequence of accusations made against Socrates.

The official indictment, as Socrates states it, charges him with being "guilty of corrupting the youth and of acknowledging not the gods the city acknowledges but other new daemonic things." (24b)[6] The principal difference between the charges of the old accusers and the official charges of the new is that in the latter there is included an offense—respecting the acknowledgment of the gods of the city—to which legal sanctions attach. But even in this respect the two sets are related, since the improper attitude toward the gods can be said to follow from unrestrained (that is, busybodyish) inquiry into all things. Socrates had earlier reported the popular opinion that those who investigate the things in the air and under the earth do not acknowledge the gods. (18c) This is (as we have seen) a longstanding prejudice about philosophers, a prejudice which some men have an interest in employing against Socrates when provoked by the young men who imitate him. (23c-d)

Socrates' response to the old accusers' charges (as distinguished from his subsequent account of the genesis of the hostility that led to such charges [20c][7]) includes the observation that he had been mistaken for those interested in physical inquiries. As for the charge that he had been teaching "these same things" to others, he merely observes at this point that he does not teach for money (having first transformed the charge into one aimed at the man who does teach for money). (19c-e)[8] His evident poverty is a sufficient refutation of this transformed charge. (31b-c) The remaining count, that he makes the weaker argument the stronger, he passes over in silence.

His response to the official set of charges begins with the question of whether one person (rather than the many) can corrupt the youth. He suggests as an instructive parallel that horses are made better by horse-trainers and are harmed by the rest of mankind. (25a-c)[9] In addition, he doubts whether anyone would corrupt others willingly if he knew that he must associate with those who have been corrupted. (25c-26a) These points are made in the course of a colloquy in which Meletus unwillingly joins. This manner of response, which displays how Socrates can conduct an inquiry, may have seemed to much of his audience as indeed making the weaker argument the stronger.[10] Socrates' argument, insofar as it denies the possibility of any criminal corruption and, perhaps, even of any legitimate criminal law, seems to require the elevation in the city of persuasion and education over compulsion and punishment.[11] The politician is set aside as the poet and the philosopher are left to contend for political rule.

The charge that Socrates does not acknowledge the gods acknowledged by the city is transformed with the help of his poet-accuser into one of not acknowledging any gods at all. (26e)[12] Thereupon, Socrates can counter the charge of atheism by turning against it the concluding part of the official indictment, the charge that he introduces new daemonic things. (27a-e)[13]

It is evident that Meletus was eager to add the charge of atheism, that Socrates knew that he could be induced to do so. And yet the concluding charge of the official indictment could be turned against Meletus' amendment of that indictment.[14] One suspects that Meletus wanted to include atheism in the official indictment but that he was persuaded not to do so by more politically astute colleagues who recognized that the popular opinion of Socrates' daemonic thing fit in as poorly with the charge of atheism as the popular opinion of his poverty fit in with any suggestion that he taught for money.[15] But during the cross-examination, Meletus is free from his colleagues' restraint.

Meletus' insistence on the charge of atheism prompts the following speculations. To question the gods of the city must seem to one fully dedicated to those gods to be a questioning of all gods that make a difference—thus, in effect, of all gods. In addition, Meletus seems to have been skeptical about the daemonic thing with which Socrates was supposed to be visited. Perhaps it seemed to him similar to the divine inspiration that poets are popularly said to enjoy—and he, as a professional poet, knew better. (22c) That is, he may have had no experience of the divine which confirmed for him the possibility of that which Socrates was supposed to have had. In both respects, then, Meletus could be charged with being a poor poet—that is, in Socratic terms, no poet at all: his imagination, conceiving no dedication other than to this city, is limited; and the true poetic inspiration is missing. In any event, his harshness seems to belong to the politician more than to the poet.[16]

It is appropriate that a Socrates prosecuted by an aggressively patriotic poet should ask, as he prepares to conclude his appearance before the Athènian people, "What would any of you give to meet [in Hades] with Orpheus and Musaeus and Hesiod and Homer?" (41a)[17] That is, he holds out to them the prospect of meeting real poets for a change.

iii

Still another set of names deserves our attention, the names Socrates mentions in his second and third speeches. His second speech discusses the penalty appropriate upon conviction; the third speculates on the nature of death and on what awaits him after life on this earth. The reader notices that everyone Socrates refers to in the second speech is an Athenian and that all of the names (after his own is mentioned) in the third speech are of non-Athenians.[18]

This distribution of names—which is markedly different from that in the first speech, where Athenian and non-Athenian names are intermingled[19]—points up one of the underlying difficulties in Socrates' situation. He speaks in the second speech as an Athenian, as a man of a particular city, when he addresses himself to the question of the disposition that is to be made of him as a *citizen* convicted of a serious crime. But he speaks in the third speech as a *human being*, as a man free to range among cities and even above cities, when he addresses himself to the question of the disposition that is to be made of him when life on this earth is finished. Put roughly, one can say that Athens has jurisdiction, ultimately, over his body only, whereas his soul (during life as well as in death) falls under another jurisdiction. (30a-b)

This distinction is reflected as well in a conversation Socrates reports with a wealthy Athenian whom he had asked about the training needed to secure for that man's sons the virtue appropriate to them. Who, Socrates had asked, has knowledge of that kind of virtue, that of "a human being and a citizen"? (20a-c) Socrates opens his first speech before the court with the suggestion that the accusers had so conducted themselves as almost to make him forget who he really was. (17a) This observation should be taken as more than a playful comment on the rhetorical effectiveness of the accusers: the trial itself, if not the very life of Socrates as well, reveals the tension we see in him between the citizen and the human being and in Athens between the city and philosophy.[20]

iv

We do not have in the *Apology* the explicit constitutional arguments to which we are accustomed today. Thus, Socrates does not direct a challenge against the law requiring the citizen to acknowledge the gods of the city. However self-defeating it may have been to level such a challenge during the defense proper, there was little to deter him from at least making suggestions of radical law reform once the sentence of death had been pronounced.[21]

He limits himself, however, to the suggestion that Athens could well imitate those peoples (human beings) who require a capital case to extend over several days. (37a-b) The effect of such a reform would be to bring to the realm of the political something of the philosophical mode. That is, action would give way before deliberation. (35c) The philosophical manner is reflected as well in Socrates' defiance of the democracy when it "wished to judge as a body [rather than one by one] the ten generals who had failed to gather up [the slain] for burial after the naval battle [of Arginusae]." (32b)[22] That is, deliberation requires the drawing of distinctions. The rule of philosophy in the city would have been acknowledged if Athens had, instead of condemning Socrates, accepted his recommendation that such a man as he "be maintained in the Prytaneum." (37a)[23]

Socrates' failure to challenge the principal law under which he was indicted suggests to us that he thought that law justifiable, perhaps even necessary, for the typical city, whatever might be said about its application in a particular case. Indeed, Socrates indicates the usefulness to the city of the acceptance by its citizens of its gods. He announces that he will not try to influence the court by bringing in his family as others have done: if he were to do that, he says, he would be exhibiting the very impiety for which he has been indicted, insofar as he induced members of the court to disregard the oaths (sworn in the name of the gods) they had taken to render a just verdict. (35c) He implies that it is partly because of his belief in the gods that the typical citizen does his civic duty, or at least does it more faithfully than he otherwise would. Socrates explains even his own career, with its dangers, as pursued in obedience to a god's mandate. To strengthen further this influence of the gods and, perhaps, even to make the gods a better influence than the poets make them, he teaches that the gods do not desert good men and that they cannot lie. (41d, 21b)

Thus, civilization is not taken for granted: the gods are employed to reinforce what the city does to make men better than they would otherwise be. The city at its most primitive cares for the bodies of men, protecting them against the elements and against enemies and providing them with some comfort and leisure. The better city does something as well for the souls of men by inculcating the social virtues and affording at least the opportunity for that discourse and reflection which can lead to the full development of human reason. The claims of the city are acknowledged by Socrates in the duty he accepted to remain at the stations assigned by the generals at the battles of Potidaea, Amphipolis, and Delium, as well as in the duty he conceived he had to serve as a "gadfly" at the god's command. (28d-e, 30e–31b)[24]

The *Apology* can even be read as a judicious tribute to Athens. Socrates explicitly recognizes the special claims of a city upon its citizens, but especially of this city. (29d–30a) It should be remembered that Socrates narrowly missed acquittal, despite the peculiar turbulence of the times in which he found himself on trial and despite his unconcealed superiority.[25] It should also be remembered that the old accusers were a long time at work, that they had never resorted to an indictment, and that a full life had been permitted Socrates to do his work largely unimpeded. But even more significant is that democratic Athens was the city which produced, or permitted the production of, a Socrates, of a man who could make, and could be permitted to make, the kind of defense he did. There is no reason to believe that Socrates was any less fair than we can be in recognizing the merits of the city by which one is repudiated.[26]

v

The difficulties Socrates encountered were with the city as city, not simply with a particular city or regime. We are told that Socrates was obliged to stand firm against the demands of both democratic and oligarchic tyranny.[27] True, it is under a democratic regime that he met his death. But we learn that his earlier defiance of the oligarchic regime of the Thirty Tyrants would probably have led to his death had not that regime been overthrown (whereas nothing is said of anything having happened to the democratic regime to forestall retribution for his earlier defiance of it). (32d–e)

Oligarchy is characterized by an undue respect for wealth—and we notice that it is moneymaking which Socrates sees as the principal distraction (at least in Athens) from the proper concern in citizens for virtue. (30a–b, 36b, 41e) But, on the other hand, wealth permits leisure —and it is the wealthy young men with leisure who can attend upon Socrates, finding pleasure in hearing him examine people and in imitating him themselves. (23c) Still, it is under a democratic regime that that leisure is more likely to be left free for philosophical (among other) pursuits.

The limits of the democratic regime, with its reliance on public opinion, are suggested by the observation that the greater the reputation a man had for wisdom, the more deluded Socrates found him to be. (22a) It is the judgment, not the good intentions or even the moral rectitude, of the people that is called into question by Socrates. The humanity of the people is indicated by their repudiation of the illegal verdict against the generals of Arginusae, even though this repentance came too late to save the condemned. (32b) No such change of heart on the part of the Thirty is suggested: rather, Socrates saw their order (to him and others) to bring Leon of Salamis to his death as one of many deliberate attempts on their part to implicate as many citizens as they could in their crimes. (32c-e)

The moral rectitude of a people rests, in part, on their opinions about the gods, opinions for which the poets are principally responsible. But these old opinions remain inflexible, even when circumstances change— and an attempt to refine or qualify them is regarded with suspicion. Socrates hints that the principal offense of the Athenian generals at Arginusae was that of having failed to gather up the slain for burial after the battle. Nothing is said of the other offense, the failure by the fleet, intent on destroying the defeated enemy, to rescue the survivors on the disabled Athenian ships. He thereby reminds us (by his silence) of the religious implications of that prosecution, a prosecution which (among other results) helped cripple the military efficiency of the city and undermine its respect for the rule of law. Thus, religion can even undermine the city.[28]

But, on the other hand, religion itself is vulnerable. The doctrine attributed to Anaxagoras is that the sun and moon are stone and earth, not gods. Socrates assumes that the members of the court know that the books of Anaxagoras are full of such utterances. (26c-d) Athens is an open commercial city, enjoying abundant contact with the rest of the world. What is to become of the traditional popular opinions about the gods of the city if no refinement or qualification of them is permitted in the light of physical speculations and moral teachings that do not respect political boundaries?

The poets, who do not really understand their poems and the religious teachings they contain, have given men many "fine things." (22c) But these, like all good things, depend on virtue for their proper use by mankind. (30a-b) They depend, that is, on an understanding of the best defense available for the gods of the city against the discoveries of both the natural philosophers and the sophists.[29]

vi

The limits of political life in general are suggested not only by the fact that Socrates remained in an essentially private capacity whenever he could—he never volunteered for ordinary public service—but even more by the inability of even the most exalted politicians to defend themselves and perhaps even their city against searching inquiry. They do not really understand who they are or what they are doing. That is to say, such men are in danger of sacrificing to their political ambitions and pursuits the serious development of that reason which is distinctively human. They strive instead for another means of partaking in eternal things, and thereby securing immortality, by devoting themselves to the pursuit of reputation or glory.[30]

But, Socrates seems to suggest, glory or fame for its own sake is truly ephemeral.[31] The men who can be regarded as the two greatest actors in Greek political history are the only two mortals of any note who are not mentioned by name in the *Apology,* but who are otherwise clearly identified: the greatest warrior is recalled by reference to his immortal mother (Thetis) and to his vanquished enemy (Hector); the greatest leader, by reference to the army of equally anonymous men he led against a conquered city (Troy).[32] Such men are remembered not in themselves, but because of others.

Even more critical than the question of their memory is that of their self-sufficiency: they do not stand apart from or above cities. It is they who, it turns out, are most dependent on others, perhaps even enslaved by the city or by public opinion, if not simply by the poets who sing their deeds. Among the few things Socrates admits he knows is that it is an evil to have to live "in prison a slave to those who may be in authority." (37c) He is concerned, as few human beings and citizens are, lest he "do anything unworthy of a free man." (38e)

vii

Socrates seems to concede, if only by implication, the partial validity of the charges against him, at least those charges as they appear before they are transformed or corrected by him. Although he denies that he has done anything he should not have done, he would perhaps admit that there can be about the life of the mind something radically subversive of the ordinary city. Not only do questions about nature or the gods tend to undermine the accepted opinions about the gods and about the proper relations among men and between cities, but the life of inquiry stands as an independent alternative to the life of the men who take the city most seriously.

Although Socrates might on other occasions take issue with both the natural philosophers and the sophists, he does not openly do so here. (19c–20c) This may be not only because of an understandable reluctance one might have to save oneself by directing attention to the short-comings of others but also because, in the view of the city, the life of a Socrates and the life of these "intellectuals" are quite similar.

It is not surprising, therefore, that Socrates' accusers can mistake him for both a natural philosopher and a sophist. (18b-c, 19b-c) All of the sophists and natural philosophers whom he mentions are identified by him as foreigners. (19e, 20b, 26d) And like them, he talks with both citizens and strangers. (23b, 30a, 20b-c)) It is no wonder, then, that Socrates can be regarded as somehow not *of* his city. This is his first time in court, that is, before the people on his own behalf: he appears, even in his manner of speaking before them, as a stranger. (17c–18a)

We notice that Socrates' relation to a city—to eager youths and out-raged parents and relatives, for example—does not depend primarily on his peculiar oracle-guided history in Athens (of which he had made so much in explaining how prejudice against him had arisen): even now, and in a short time, he would expect to be in trouble in any other city to which he might go. (37c-e)[33] The city does not exist, except per-haps in thought, in which he would be fully at ease or truly safe.

The politicians, the poets and the craftsmen, on the other hand, live comfortably with the ways of the city. But, Socrates reports, these men are subject to the serious disability of being unable to explain and justify themselves under questioning.[34] His superiority to all of them is main-tained, except for the acknowledged skills of the craftsmen and the nature and divine inspiration of the poets. (22c-d) But Socrates, too, has his craft—we, to some extent, are among his products—and he can match as well the poet, for he has that daemonic thing which turns him from that which would harm him. (31d, 40a-b)[35]

The life that Socrates regards as preferable includes the constant examination of one's life. Without such examination, life is not human. (38a) The life he extols is characterized by an awareness of one's igno-rance. Socrates opens and closes his first speech, as well as the *Apology* as a whole, with admissions (in effect) of his ignorance. (17a, 35d, 42a) But it is ignorance of which he, in any event, is aware. We again notice how his life differs from that of the ordinary citizen: the citizen, and the city, must act as if certain things are known, even matters that are subject to the most decisive fluctuations. The slain enemy of the city today, for example, may have been its ally yesterday. The man executed today may be exonerated tomorrow on further examination of the evidence.

It is the fully human life—that life characterized by both an awareness of ignorance and a love of wisdom—with which the city and citizenship must ultimately come to terms.

viii

Does the examination of one's life require the examination of the lives of others? We are moved to examine with this question, how Socrates shifts from an explanation of his determination to learn whether anyone was wiser than he to a justification of his insistence upon exhorting others to virtue. This account, which serves as the public story of his life, displays in its legal rhetoric both skill and integrity. Socrates considers himself to have lived the life of a human being: we see here the model of how the human being should address himself to citizens.

Socrates begins with a report of the Delphic pronouncement, in answer to Chaerephon's question, that no man was wiser than Socrates. (21a) After being at a loss for a long time as to the meaning of the oracle of Delphi, he proceeds with great reluctance to investigate what the god meant. (21b) This investigation, which he interprets to be at the god's behest, permits him to conclude (after exposing the professions of those thought to be wise) that the god was merely using his name, as if he had said, "This one of you, human beings, is wisest who, like Socrates, knows that he is in truth of no account in respect to wisdom." (23b)

Socrates' assignment does not conclude with this discovery, however, for he reports that he has continued to make inquiries both of citizens and of strangers. This extended investigation is also said to be according to the god. (23b) He even adds that he helps the god by showing men reputed to be wise that they are not. (23c) Indeed, he can say (when he returns, after the colloquy with Meletus, to the account of his life) that the god had given him a station, with orders to spend his life in philosophy and in examining himself and others. (28d–29a)

The emphasis at this point could still be said to be on an examination that was concerned primarily with the pursuit of wisdom. But, in response to a hypothetical offer from the city to spare his life if he should stop investigating or philosophizing, he announces he must obey god rather than the city: he would not give up philosophizing, nor would he stop exhorting others to care for wisdom and truth and their souls more than for wealth and reputation and honor. (29c-e) If anyone denies that he does care more for wealth, reputation, and honor, Socrates will examine him to see if he has virtue, and rebuke him if he does not. (29e–30a) This, he says, the god commands him to do. No greater good ever came to pass in the city than this service to the god, this service of persuading everyone not to care for anything more than for the perfection of his soul. This persuasion includes the precept that from virtue all good things come to men. (30a-b)

Thus, the city's intervention—whether in the form of an "offer" or in the form of an indictment—obliged Socrates to justify his life in terms that the city respects. That is, he was prompted to portray himself as of service not only to the god but to the city as well. Indeed, Socrates can now describe himself as god's gift, as a gadfly assigned to the city. (30d-e) He is so much a gift from the god that he neglects his own affairs as he urges them to care for virtue. (31b)[36] Thus, the emphasis has shifted by this stage of the argument to the promotion of virtue, away from the concern for wisdom that marked the beginning of his career. He now describes incidents that reveal how he acted and how he can be expected to act (the trial of the generals, the condemnation of Leon of Salamis). (31c–32e) This is the public story of his life: we are not explicitly told, except as it bears on the prejudice that has arisen against him, the private story of his mind, what he has thought and learned over the years.

Socrates does return, after emphasizing both his efforts to promote virtue and the god's mandate for such efforts, to the obligation to examine those who think themselves wise—but the source of that obligation is no longer simply Delphi. Rather, he says he has been commanded to do so by the god through oracles and dreams and in every way in which any man has been commanded by a divine power to do anything. (33c) Indeed, he can speak (in his second speech) of his effort to persuade men to care more for goodness and wisdom than for other things without mentioning any divine agency. (36c) In his final comment on his own efforts, before he is sentenced to death, the emphasis on virtue (insofar as it can be distinguished from wisdom) remains explicit: he says that the greatest good to man is to talk every day about virtue and about the other things they hear him talking about and examining himself and others about. He does comment that to be quiet would be disobedience to the god—but he anticipates that his listeners will regard this comment as ironical on his part. (37e–38a) It is in this context that Socrates observes that the unexamined life is not human. (38a)

Why *does* the examination of one's life require the examination of the lives of others? Since all men in the city partake of one life—one life as a community—a man must, in order to examine his own life, examine the life of the whole, the lives of other men. That is, an understanding of one's life presupposes an understanding of its setting. Life would not be worth living among a people whose life is entirely unexamined: such a people would be little better than brutes. In the examination of others, furthermore, one learns what men are like, in what they differ from and in what they resemble one another—and this, too, permits the inquirer better to see and, if need be, to defend himself and to help them. He may even learn what other men know.

Socrates urges upon others that they do for themselves what he has discovered divine sanction for in his own life, the examination of one's own life. But the exhortation to virtue, as distinguished from the pursuit of wisdom, seems to be independent of any reasonable interpretation of the oracular mandate. Perhaps it is not that mandate, with its endorsement of the Socratic effort to secure wisdom, that dictates Socrates' concern for the moral virtues of others, but rather his duty as a citizen and his benevolence toward his fellow man.

It is, then, his concern for the virtue of citizens, not his love of wisdom, that can permit Socrates to justify himself in the eyes of the ordinary citizen. The god is useful in seeming to endorse such a dedicated concern on the part of a private man. The legitimate concern of the city for prosperity and self-defense and good government can lead to the glorification of wealth and life and honor, and even to the substitution of these for human virtue. Philosophy can help the city and its citizens distinguish between what is and what merely seems to be good.

Beyond the life of the citizen is that of the human being, the perfected human being, which the city must somehow divine as its ultimate goal and which may even be discernible in the gods that the city acknowledges. Mortal men need cities in which to carry out at leisure their inquiries—and some cities are better than others in this respect. There can be circumstances, then, in which the human being and the citizen, philosophy and the city, the philosopher and the gentleman, can become allies.

The speech of man testifies to the alliance in him of reason and natural sociability. Men are characteristically human, then, when engaged in conversation, in rational discourse, with one another. Socrates can lament upon finding himself estranged from his fellow citizens. (21e)

ix

The life of the human being, rather than of the citizen, would be continued by Socrates (he tells us) even in Hades—if there is a life after death (about which he does not claim to know). (40c–41c) Thirteen figures are particularly mentioned by him as being in some manner encountered in Hades. He reports an increasingly intimate relation with these men as he moves through Hades.

There are, first, the four just men. (41a) Nothing is said of their judging Socrates: perhaps they stand for his affirmation, even in the face of the injustice done him, of the principle of justice.[37] He speaks next of four poets, whom his hearers (he implies, not necessarily he) would very much like to meet: these may be poets liberated somewhat from the demands of particular cities, since they are honored by all the Greeks. (41a) The poets are, moreover, the means by which Hades (as a particular place) as well as the other nine characters in Socrates' enumeration are known to men.[38] There are then mentioned two men who were unjustly treated on earth, with whom he would compare his own experience. (41a-b) Three rulers are mentioned, men whom he would examine for their wisdom. (41b-c) We wonder whether he indicates the beginning even in Hades of that very cycle of inquiry we were told of in his first speech—political men, poets, and craftsmen.[39]

We wonder also whether we can determine the considerations that led to the selection by Socrates of the names he uses in this list and of the order in which he places them.[40] We are encouraged to speculate about these matters when we notice that the order of the four poets is that employed elsewhere by the comic poet whom Socrates refers to in his first speech, an order that probably reflects either the traditional sequence of the four or a deliberate borrowing from the comic poet.[41] Aristophanes, in a play produced with great popular success only a few years before the trial of Socrates, had put these words in the mouth of Aeschylus (*The Frogs* 1030–1036):

> Aye, such are the poet's appropriate works: and just
> consider how all along
> From the very first they have wrought you good,
> the noble bards, the masters of song.
> First, Orpheus taught you religious rites, and from
> bloody murder to stay your hands;
> Musaeus healing and oracle lore; and Hesiod all the
> culture of lands,
> The time to gather, the time to plough. And got not
> Homer his glory divine
> By singing of valor, and honor, and right, and the
> sheen of the battle-extended line,
> The ranging of troops and the arming of men?

We can again see the role of the poets, and of the gods of whom the poets sing, in the civilization and cities of men.

But we see also in this passage the movement from the suppression of early savagery, through the development of civilization, to the glorification and refinement of killing by civilized men. This reminds us of the question of whether the poets really know or control what they are doing. (20b-c) Socrates so places the names of the four poets that the name of Hesiod is central in the list of the thirteen figures in Hades: the activity around which he sees everything else revolving is the prosaic and most civilized art of agriculture, an activity that does not have the obvious attraction of Homeric adventures.[42]

Since the poet and the philosopher contend as to the best way of life, it is appropriate that the initiator of the prosecution of Socrates should represent the poets. An insignificant Meletus is made more of in the dialogue than the very influential Anytus. But it is evident that this representative of the poets is inadequate to his formidable task: we are tempted to suspect that he is merely the image of Socrates' much more serious critic, Aristophanes. The comic poet knew that the poet's way to defend the gods was to make poems, not indictments.

Socrates had found that the poets had made many "fine things" which they could not explain. The poets he had examined were "those of tragedies, and those of dithyrambs, and the others." (22a-c) Although he had mentioned Aristophanes earlier, he does not refer explicitly to comic poets as among those who could not explain what they had made. (18d, 19c) This is not the occasion for an open confrontation between Socrates and Aristophanes. But we do remember that the comic poet, unlike Socrates, is equipped, or at least willing, to move the people. (Cf. 36a.) Perhaps this prompts the comic poet to believe that this is because he understands better than the philosopher what the people need and what constitutes a threat to the city and its gods. Perhaps the poet also believes that he is better equipped than the philosopher to grasp these gods and all other things really vital to men. But we remember as well that Socrates perceived that the poets "thought themselves, on account of their poetry, the wisest of men in other things as well, in which they were not." (22c)

x

The list of names in Hades suggests further speculations. We notice that there can be said to be an intimate relation among the thirteen figures Socrates mentions. The four poets are, as has been noted, the principal source of what men know of the other nine and of such men (demi-gods and heroes). Two of the men are said to have been unjustly treated, with a consequent loss of life. But included among the parade are the very men who were instrumental in that unjust treatment.[43] Socrates, we can anticipate, will investigate both sides of these famous controversies: he will not settle for what the poets have labeled as the just and unjust parties.

Even Sisyphus, the wicked king who is reputedly consigned to eternal punishment, will be questioned. Perhaps it is his proverbial cunning that interests Socrates. But perhaps, also, Socrates refuses to accept without question the judgment of even the gods against Sisyphus: both Sisyphus and the four just men (three of whom, sons of Zeus, are the traditional judges of Hades) are available for Socrates' questions. He can pass judgment on the justice of the gods. Thus, we suggest, Socrates' inquiries can be of the most radical nature—and it is this that the more perceptive supporters of his accusers can be said to have detected.[44] The termination of the list with Sisyphus' name suggests as well the nature of the philosophical life: we remember that Sisyphus' punishment was one that required of him the endless repetition of a difficult task. Philosophy, too, especially if characterized by knowledge of one's ignorance, is Sisyphean in quality.[45]

Socrates had justified his supposedly onerous and allegedly impious career of questioning as one ordered by the god. Much is made of this divine mandate in the principal speech in defense, a speech whose manifest character is determined in large part by the nature of its audience. We, of course, must wonder whether the affirmative answer of the oracle to Chaerephon's question necessarily implied the mandate that Socrates took it to include. Indeed, some would even interpret the task Socrates undertook to be a *test* of the god's wisdom, rather than mere pious obedience to the god's command. We wonder, moreover, what it was that moved Chaerephon to go to the expense and trouble of an expedition to Delphi, what it was about Socrates that aroused such partisanship. We suspect that Chaerephon had already observed him as confounding others, as a man evidently without a match in Athens.[46] Just as the doings of his daemonic thing are analyzed by Socrates (40a-c, 41d-e), so the oracle of the god is examined. Nothing is taken for granted as man strives to understand. Even divine judgments are open to examination.

We learn from Socrates' projected adventures in Hades that he continues the life he led on earth. It is not there a "life" designed to make either men or cities better, or even to test a god's saying. Rather, he explicitly explains his inquiries in Hades (that is, beneath the earth) as pleasurable. (41c) His pursuit is one that he finds satisfying for its own sake. This satisfaction seems to resemble the pleasure the young men derive from imitating him. (23c, 33c) It is the pleasure of the human being, of the human being necessarily formed in the city but whose essential activity does not depend on the city but rather on that which is somehow his own, his reason.

The comparison of experiences with Palamedes and Ajax is anticipated as "not unpleasant"; the discussions with men reputed to be wise, as "the greatest pleasure" and as "immeasurable happiness." (41b-c) Socrates' concern in Hades, and thus eternally, remains more with wisdom than with virtue, more with words than with deeds. The people of Athens, on the other hand, honor deeds more than words. (32a)

The earthbound philosopher acknowledges an obligation to the city that permits him the truest pleasure of the human being. He does more than is required of him, and even more than is likely to be appreciated from him, to contribute to the well-being of his fellow citizens. He is not merely a just man: he is, despite his poverty, the greatest philanthropist.

xi

Nothing is said of any gods in Hades. Socrates does not anticipate meeting there any god, but at most the sons of gods. Whatever role the gods may have played in initiating or spurring on his inquiries or his way of life on earth, they seem to play no part now.[47] He had spoken of the god giving him an assignment to which he was obliged to stand faithful despite all dangers, just as he had been given assignments by the generals at Potidaea, Amphipolis and Delium. But the thoughtful Athenian remembers that those three battles had one striking feature in common, the death on each occasion of the Athenian commander. Can the god or gods, then, who had set or confirmed Socrates on the road he followed, also be said to have died? Was there something about the very activity of Socrates that led to the end, if only for him, of the gods of the city?

And yet he remained at his post, just as the soldier remains at his despite the death of his commander. In both instances, the dedication is to something greater than the commander: it is to that to which both the commander and his followers are dedicated. If Socrates can no longer acknowledge the gods of the city, it is through no voluntary misdeed, but is rather the almost inevitable result of the kind of life to which godlike humanity can lead man. Others, too, are led to disbelief: but it is the merit of Socrates that his disbelief is restrained, as he remembers the value to the city of religious belief. He discerns as well, in his effort to understand the world in which the human being finds himself, that to which such belief points, that which in the nature of things makes the poets' accounts plausible and which the poets somehow grasp.

We have seen that there are attributed to Socrates among "those things at hand to say against all philosophers," "the things in the air and beneath the earth." (23c-d, 18b) The inquiries implied here are such as those Anaxagoras carried on, which led him to call the sun stone and the moon earth. But we notice that Socrates assigns to himself in the *Apology* a version of this charge which is unique to him, that he investigates "the things beneath the earth and in the heaven." (19c) Only with reference to Socrates' inquiries is the word "heaven," rather than "air," used.

The words "earth" and "heaven" recall (in the Greek) Gaea and Ouranos—the parents and grandparents of the gods of the city—and this suggests, in turn, Socrates' concern with the origins, and hence the nature, of the gods. A refined parallel to this couple can be seen in Zeus and Hera, the only Greek gods Socrates invokes by name in this dialogue.[48] Zeus and Hera represent complete divinity, from which all other aspects can be generated. A blending of these two gods into one can be anticipated as the next stage of the development. But the many, it seems, require many gods—and poetry ministers to this need and may have thereby even prepared the way for philosophy. Were not the poets "the wise men of old"?

The tendency of Socrates' thought about the gods is further suggested by the manner in which he speaks of the Delphic oracle. Although he refers to the god of Delphi and his shrine, he does not use his name but speaks of him simply as "the god." And as the dialogue proceeds, this god becomes more and more general and impersonal. Indeed there is seen here a refinement, even an elevation, of the gods of the city, until they can be represented as divine intellect, as that being which is truly wise, as that being which is to be apprehended not by inspiration or revelation but by the reason of the free man. Was it not in this sense that Socrates could be said to have investigated the things in heaven?

It is with a reference to the unique wisdom of a god, a god who may be understood as that perfection to which the philosopher aspires, that the dialogue ends.[49] Socrates has just declared that no evil can come to a good man, either in life or after death, and that the gods do not neglect him. (41c-d) The gods of the city care for good men; the god of Socrates knows the truth.

xii

Socrates' case was entrusted to men who were not equipped to understand either the life they had come to review or what their city really needed.[50] One of the two men referred to by Socrates as unjustly treated is Palamedes: he was the victim of deliberate misrepresentations on the part of rivals jealous of his wisdom. The other man, Ajax, although he could be said to have been ruled against in a fair "trial," considered himself unjustly treated and committed suicide. Just as there is about Socrates something of Palamedes, so there is something of Ajax as well, since his conviction and condemnation could be said to have been permitted (if not, to some degree, courted) by him. He would not resort to the measures, such as a proposal of exile, that could have saved his life.

The measures that would have been necessary to win an acquittal are shunned by him as dishonorable. His sense of nobility is reflected in the urbanity, and even the irony, with which he faced his accusers and, as it turns out, his executioners. But, we are told, he is at an age when men's powers often begin to fail. (38c) He seems determined to be useful, not only to philosophy (and hence to himself, if only in the form of those like himself who will follow) but also to the city, in death as he had been in life. He does not seek this prosecution—but neither is it an unwelcome or chance event. (41d) He literally makes the best of it.

Unlike the sophists and the natural philosophers, Socrates realizes he is to some extent rooted in the city. He recognizes that he is "not born of an oak or a rock," but of humans—once again we see the significance of origins—and this basis, in the nature of things, contributes to his benevolence toward a particular city. (34d, 30a) He seems determined, that is, to leave behind an example, in word as well as in deed, of a lofty disdain of death that can only enrich and ennoble the life on earth of those who follow him. And he succeeds thereby in assuring the city, which tends to be dominated by the concern for mere survival, that those citizens are most useful to it who do not care the most for the sanctions with which it threatens or for the prizes with which it beckons. Socrates takes the opportunity to converse with his judges "while the archons are busy and before [he goes] to the place where [he] must die." (39e) It was thus with Socrates' lifework: he conversed while citizens were occupied with their affairs.

The success of Socrates' lifework is reflected in the respect he inspires from generation to generation even among those who would have been among his condemners. This is in part a tribute to the effect of poetry upon the many, poetry consecrated to the tasks to which a Plato happened to be able to turn it. Socrates modeled himself, he tells the court, on the son of Thetis as that warrior faced death. (28c-d) That young man remains the hero of the battlefield; an old man becomes the hero of life in the city.

Such heroism, which first appears to men in the accounts of poets, becomes even more significant when one considers what Socrates suggests about the goodness of life. The immortality of the soul remains an open question: to the extent it is acknowledged in this dialogue, it is on the basis of what is generally said, on the basis of unexamined sayings of the poets. (40c, 40e, 41a, 41c) The good things of which Socrates speaks are certain, to the extent that they are certain at all, only in life. For him, it had been a good life: he had had the "greatest good" that men can enjoy, conversing daily and examining himself and others about virtue and the other things he talked about. (38a) The efforts of his daemonic thing seem to have been directed, according to Socrates' report, to preserve an honorable life for him so long as that life could be effectively dedicated to philosophy. (31d–32a, 38c, 40a, 41d) There is no philosophy, nothing distinctively human, in that dreamless sleep that death may resemble. (40c-d) Indeed, such sleep depends for its appreciation on the awakened sleeper. The urbanity of Socrates cannot conceal the melancholy cast of his situation: his parting words reveal that he does not know whether it is better to die or to live, despite the encouraging inferences he has drawn from the failure of his daemonic thing to intervene. (42a) Since men are mortal, there are merely better and worse ways to die.

There is about the pursuit dictated by the divinity of one's humanity —by that reason which can be said to lie under a divine mandate to inquire into all things—something that is dangerous to human life itself. The Socrates who survived seventy years was endowed with that daemonic thing, that inarticulate, perhaps instinctive, thing with its respect for life that imposed a sense of moderation upon a radically immoderate pursuit.[51] What the daemonic thing did for Socrates he has to do for those who follow him, for the impulsive Chaerephons, for the young men who delight in questioning their elders, perhaps most of all for the philosophers and the sophists whose predecessors helped sow the crop of prejudice that Socrates harvested. (21a-b, 23c-d, 23d-e) Such men have to be restrained lest they bring on the destruction of others, if not of themselves. (39d) Self-restraint is necessary for the protection both of the city and of philosophy.

The *Apology* provides for the prospective philosopher a substitute for the daemonic thing Socrates happened to have. Indeed, the daemonic thing is transformed into the *Apology:* we should not expect to hear of it again.

xiii

Thus, the surface meaning and effect of the dialogue are intended for the city and its citizens, that they may be relieved of their fear and tempered in their envy. The decent, law-abiding citizen is provided sufficient grounds for siding with Socrates. In fact, the description of philosophy as service to the god may even conform to the citizen's conception of piety. (23b)

The more guarded meaning of the dialogue, which we have only begun to explore, is intended for the careful reader who may be prepared to succumb to the immoderate attractions of philosophy. Such a reader, tempted by the appeals of freedom, truth, or even a gesture of heroic self-sacrifice, must be reminded of the demands of mere existence, of the legitimate concerns and inevitable limitations of the city, and of the role of the philosophically-minded in the city. The state of our education today requires that this reminder be made more explicit than ever before.

The first long step in Socrates' political contribution (and his principal political contribution, considering the regimes of his and most cities)— the step to which he dedicated his public life—is necessarily cast in restraining, even negative, terms. He refused to desert the military posts assigned him; he questioned the men reputed to be wise; he rejected or refined many ancient opinions about the gods; he refused to acquiesce in the unjust actions demanded of him by democracy and oligarchy alike. Even his daemonic thing, as reported here, was limited to inhibitory commands.

This emphasis on negativity may strike some as perverse, even as irresponsible. (It can be said to be reflected in the charge that Socrates does not acknowledge the gods of the city.) But negativity is essential when the human being confronts the city with its perhaps inevitable reliance on received opinion, especially when changes in circumstances make fetters out of what have long been treasured as the people's staff and rod. For, as it has been observed, "What at first glance seems to be merely negative is negative only in the sense in which every liberation, being a liberation not only to something but also from something, contains a negative ingredient."[52]

Socrates liberates men from ignorance and vice, releasing them for that pursuit of wisdom and of virtue proclaimed by his words and sanctified by his example. To the extent that he repudiates the old, it is not in the name of the new, but of the eternal. His fellow citizens condemned as dangerous innovations what were essentially efforts to discover the unchanging.

Each of Socrates' three speeches invokes in its opening sentence the "men of Athens," as do the final passages of the first and second speeches. (17a, 35e, 38c, 35d, 38b) The absence of such a limitation at the conclusion of the third speech, and hence of the *Apology* as a whole, encourages us to consider him to have addressed the world at large, and especially those peoples engaged in self-government.

Socrates, insofar as he makes a place for the philosophical man in the city, suggests a constitution to which thoughtful men, both in public life and out, can aspire.

"Political Theory"

III. The American Heritage
Words and Deeds

> For this I can give you telling evidence, not words,
> but what you honor more highly, deeds.
>
> Plato, *Apology* 32a

i

My fellow-passengers on a ship that docked in New York harbor only this morning were for the most part immigrants from Greece and Italy. I wondered what America means to them, and—even more important—what it will mean to their children, to children who will be spared, more than their parents have been spared, the often crippling demands of mere existence. I wonder, that is, what can be said to be at the heart of the way of life brought forth on this continent almost two centuries ago.

One answer to this question is suggested by a conversation I had a few weeks ago during an extensive tour I was conducting for some of my students of archaeological sites on the Greek mainland. I had gone into a small town bank to cash a traveller's check and had been struck by a majestic photograph over the manager's desk, a photograph of a prosperous, self-confident, and vigorous businessman. (Of course, one expects in such circumstances something as well of the pompous and the self-righteous.) The manager, noticing my curiosity, took great pride in announcing (in Greek):

Manager: That is the greatest mind in Greece.
Anastaplo: Really?
M: Yes. He owns three bank chains, more than one hundred boats, and much valuable real estate. And he made most of it himself.
A: Where does he live?
M: In Athens; but he has homes all over the world—in Paris, London, all over.

This talk was delivered at the University of the State of New York, Binghamton, New York, August 26, 1963. It was adapted for publication as a review in 39 *New York University Law Review* 735 (June 1964).

The citations in the text are to Leonard W. Levy, *Legacy of Suppression—Freedom of Speech and Press in Early American History* (Cambridge: The Belknap Press, 1960).

A: Do you ever see him?

M: One can see him only in Athens—and even there it is very difficult.

A: Does he not ever come here?

M: Why should he come here? He has a thousand men to do his bidding.

A: But can they do his looking? What about the famous ruins you have here from ancient times—does he not come to see them?

M: I would not know if he came for that.

A: How do you know he is the greatest mind in Greece if you never talk to him?

M: By his deeds. You see, it is like America in this country.

A: In what way?

M: A smart man can make money and become very rich.

ii

The question—What is the meaning of America?—may have been easier to answer correctly a hundred years ago, or even fifty years ago. For we have enjoyed a progress in scholarly research which is forcing us to answer such questions in a way destructive to what has been generally believed—and which may even leave the field to the interpretation of my bank manager.

In any event, our understanding of the past is being continually corrected. We can be sure only that the scholarly hypotheses of today will likely be changed tomorrow. Things are not what they seem. Not even the most fundamental principles of the country are what they have seemed. We must, in the interest of scholarship, repeatedly correct them, repeatedly revise them.

And yet, a country depends for its vitality on what it accepts as its first principles, principles reinforced by the traditional account of how the country came to be. (Consider the relation between the Mosaic Law and the story of the life of Moses.) Thus, the scholar, as scholar, is inclined to undermine the tradition; the politician, to support, embellish, and employ it.

We, who reside in two worlds—the academic and the political—are, in principle, confronted with a hard choice, a choice between the truth and the common good, a choice between the goal of the scholar and the goal of the politician. There may come a time when the choice will, in fact, be much more cruel than it is now. For we are shielded from the consequences of this age-old conflict by the happy accident that, so far, the greatest American minds have been politicians, not scholars or even businessmen. It need only be shown (in defense of the tradition) that the revisionist conclusions of the scholars are not conclusive, that they are not as decisive as they and their colleagues seem to regard them. That is to say, we need only to see that the revisionists cannot be said to have understood the past.

The modern revisionist is a man who is both honest and thorough. He searches with avidity the most obscure archives, and he records with fidelity what he finds. But his very thoroughness makes him reveal more than he realizes—and he thereby arms the alert defender of the old faith.

iii

I am not speaking now of research into essentially secondary questions—such as how British constitutional history influenced the writers of the Constitution or who really started the Spanish-American War or what caused the Panic of 1907. No doubt these are important questions for some purposes—but not for the most important. Rather, I am thinking of such problems as what the American Civil War was really about. The revisionists have worked hard on this problem—and a presumption against the nobler account now seems to exist among the more respectable scholars. I suggest, on the other hand, that if you want to understand that profound constitutional crisis, you should study the speeches of Lincoln and listen to the songs of the North and the South. These go to the heart of the matter and suggest why it is that even the children of twentieth-century immigrants can be retrospectively caught up as partisans in that terrible struggle.

Perhaps I can most usefully develop my remarks by dwelling on a recent instance of the kind of scholarship I am talking about, a book by Professor Leonard W. Levy entitled *Legacy of Suppression*. The best introduction to the book for our purposes is provided by the author himself in his opening paragraphs:

> This book presents a revisionist interpretation of the origins and original understanding of the First Amendment's clause on freedom of speech and press. I have been reluctantly forced to conclude that the generation which adopted the Constitution and the Bill of Rights did not believe in a broad scope for freedom of expression, particularly in the realm of politics.

I find that libertarian theory from the time of Milton to the ratification of the First Amendment substantially accepted the right of the state to suppress seditious libel. I find also that the American experience with freedom of political expression was as slight as the theoretical inheritance was narrow. Indeed, the American legislatures, especially during the colonial period, were far more oppressive than the supposedly tyrannous common-law courts. The evidence drawn particularly from the period 1776 to 1791 indicates that the generation that framed the first state declarations of rights and the First Amendment was hardly as libertarian as we have traditionally assumed. They did not intend to give free rein to criticism of the government that might be deemed seditious libel, although the concept of seditious libel was—and still is—the principal basis of muzzling political dissent. There is even reason to believe that the Bill of Rights was more the chance product of political expediency on all sides than of principled commitment to personal liberties. A broad libertarian theory of freedom of speech and press did not emerge in the United States until the Jeffersonians, when a minority party, were forced to defend themselves against the Federalist Sedition Act of 1798. In power, however, the Jeffersonians were not much more tolerant of their political critics than the Federalists had been.

This has been a difficult book to write, because the facts have dictated conclusions that violate my predilections and clash with the accepted version of history. But just as my personal preferences as to current policy do not depend on what passed for wisdom in the eighteenth century, my views as a scholar do not depend on my civic convictions nor on historical convention. [pp. vii-viii]

The story that *had* been handed down to us was (in Lincoln's words) of a "birth of freedom" in 1776. But, we are now told, this was not the case. Rather, we are told in great detail of how Tories were ruthlessly suppressed during the Revolutionary War and of the severity and persistence of colonial and state legislatures in shielding government officials from public criticism. Indeed, we are practically asked to believe that it was almost inevitable that the Sedition Act of 1798 should have been enacted: the authors of that act were merely drawing on the legacy of suppression left by the colonial and revolutionary experience. Thus, the traditional account, we are informed, was inspiring, even noble, but simply mistaken.

iv

But are there not serious difficulties, on the other hand, with the revisionist account? The traditional account has been passed down for generations, seemingly without question. Was it accepted so early and so readily because it was true, or because it was salutary, or even because it happened to be both true and salutary? The revisionist account has, if anything, only the truth to recommend it—a recreated truth. But such truth is hard to come by: for there is something fundamentally arbitrary about an historian's formulation. And especially is this so when the *thought* of a distant period is being pursued. The evidence of old thought, except perhaps when one limits oneself to the understanding of a particular book, or of a particular author, is inevitably inconclusive. The historian gathers all the details he can muster—but who knows what will be turned up tomorrow in some unlikely attic?

In addition, the historian finds himself reduced to counting and weighing. True, he can acknowledge that one writer is more influential than another—but, since the scholar is primarily an historian and not a thinker, he tends to judge significance in terms others can test, by using measures and standards readily apparent to all. That is, he tends to be "realistic," to talk only about things he can see and number, and he is inclined to discount the spirit and mood that may survive primarily in unverifiable traditions.

Mr. Levy, for instance, concludes that there was, in late eighteenth-century America, an almost universal acceptance of Blackstone's common-law understanding of freedom of the press. Blackstone wrote in the 1760s that

> *The liberty of the press* is indeed essential to the nature of a free state; but this consists in laying no *previous* restraints upon publications, and not in freedom from censure for criminal matter when published. Every freeman has an undoubted right to lay what sentiments he pleases before the public: to forbid this is to destroy the freedom of the press: but if he publishes what is improper, mischievous, or illegal, he must take the consequences of his own temerity. . . . But to punish (as the law does at present) any dangerous or offensive writings, which, when published, shall on a fair and impartial trial be adjudged of a pernicious tendency, is necessary for the preservation of peace and good order, of government and religion, the only solid foundations of civil liberty. Thus the

will of individuals is still left free; the abuse only of that free-will is the object of legal punishment. Neither is any restraint hereby laid upon freedom of thought or enquiry: liberty of private sentiments is still left; the disseminating, or making public, of bad sentiments, destructive of the ends of society, is the crime which society corrects. [p. 14]

The almost universal acceptance of Blackstone is indicated, for Mr. Levy, by the overwhelming majority of the pamphlets, letters and other written remains he has, with impressive zeal, searched out and recorded.[1] The typical reader may even be persuaded that the Sedition Act enacted by the Fifth Congress in 1798 is really nothing to be surprised by, considering the circumstances. Indeed, one is almost surprised to learn that there should have been any objections on principle—and well-thought-out objections at that—to the critical section of that Act, which provided

> that if any person shall write, print, utter, or publish, or shall cause or procure to be written, printed, uttered, or published, or shall knowingly and willingly assist or aid in writing, printing, uttering, or publishing any false, scandalous, and malicious writing or writings against the Government of the United States, or either House of the Congress of the United States, or the President of the United States, with intent to defame the said Government, or either House of the said Congress, or the said President, or to bring them, or either of them, into contempt or disrepute; or to excite against them, or either or any of them, the hatred of the good people of the United States, . . . then such person, being thereof convicted before any court of the United States having jurisdiction thereof, shall be punished by a fine not exceeding two thousand dollars, and by imprisonment not exceeding two years.

The reader does learn, however, that there survive a few remarkable exceptions, from even before the Sedition Act of 1798, to the general acceptance of the Blackstonian formulation.[2] That is, there survive publications in which Blackstone is questioned or simply ignored, and in which there is found instead the disposition to insist that publication should be punishable only when it is immediately related to overt criminal deeds. These dissenters, for whom mere words did not seem to be punishable, even include a few authors of note. (See, e.g., pp. 116-121, 156, 164-169, 170-172.) The scientific historian, or political scientist, is obliged to count such men as merely a few among many. Otherwise he would be required to weigh subtle distinctions and consider factors that would make him rely much more than he does on the tradition that he wants to transcend.

What did the thoughtful men of 1791 think when the States ratified the First Amendment? Were they moved by the many repetitions of the usual Blackstonian formula by lawyers and judges who had been taught it in their monarchial youth? Or did they regard the formulation that dissented from Blackstone as one which fit in better with a republican regime? How does one assess the influence of the really talented writer? May not the thoughtful man, as well as the ordinary citizen, have found as attractive as we do the *political* implications of the preamble Jefferson wrote for the Virginia Statute of *Religious* Freedom of 1785? This preamble, which preceded by five years the writing of the First Amendment by Jefferson's fellow Virginian (Madison), declared these sentiments:

> that to suffer the civil magistrate to intrude his powers into the field of opinion and to restrain the profession or propagation of principles on supposition of their ill tendency is a dangerous fallacy, which at once destroys all religious liberty, because he being of course judge of that tendency, will make his opinions the rule of judgment, and approve or condemn the sentiments of others only as they shall square with or differ from his own; that it is time enough for the rightful purposes of civil government for its officers to interfere when principles break out into overt acts against peace and good order; and finally, that truth is great and will prevail if left to herself; that she is the proper antagonist to error, and has nothing to fear from the conflict unless by human interposition disarmed of her natural weapons, free argument and debate; errors ceasing to be dangerous when it is permitted freely to contradict them. [pp. 188-189]

We should further notice that many of the quotations, in which the Blackstonian position is endorsed, are evidently directed at others who had challenged it, perhaps even challenged it without troubling to learn its precise details. That is, one is obliged to ask what was the understanding of freedom of the press entertained by the ordinary citizen of the country, by the people who ratified the First Amendment.

It should be remembered that the Bill of Rights is said to have been written and adopted in conformity with public demand.[3] Mr. Levy discounts the extent of that demand, suggesting that the opponents of the Constitution thought the lack of a Bill of Rights could be "dramatically popularized," that they could use this omission as a stick with which to beat the proposed Constitution. (p. 227) But why could something thus be made of such an omission, why could it be dramatized and popularized, if not because the public had notions on this subject somewhat at variance with the Blackstonian supporters of the Constitution?

The nature of the popular attitude toward freedom of the press is reflected in the refusal of grand juries to indict and of trial juries to convict pre-War patriots whom British officials thought guilty of sedition. And, perhaps even more significant, the attitude toward freedom of the press is indicated by the number of respectable Americans who committed the offense of seditious libel during the reigns both of George III and of John Adams. That is, the offense was one that seems to have been condemned on the statute books but not by the moral consciousness of the community. When the better men in the community openly break the law, it is a law that is destined to be replaced, for it is already fading away.

It is by proceeding along these lines that one can turn against the revisionist much of the evidence that he gathers in his support.

v

We find, on the eve of the ratification of the present Constitution, a most devastating and sometimes unfair attack throughout the country on the then-existing constitution, the Articles of Confederation. Technically, this too was seditious libel under the Blackstonian view—but evidently no question was raised about the propriety or legality of such attacks. It seems to have been generally understood that it was up to the people to choose between alternative constitutions, an option guaranteed to the people by the Declaration of Independence. Indeed, we see in the people's discussion of such issues an analogue to the immunity traditionally enjoyed by members of the legislative assembly to discuss freely *and* without threat of subsequent penalty any matter before the assembly. The people, as sovereign in the new regime, are entitled to and require a like freedom of speech in the conduct of their *political* affairs. "The first born of American rights," a Virginia legislator argued in 1798, "was the free examination of public servants."[4]

It was this change of regime, in 1776, that undermined the Blackstonian or common-law approach to seditious libel and freedom of the press. For Blackstone's formula is most consistent with the British monarchical regime, notwithstanding the fact that a modified version of it retained American advocates into the nineteenth century. It is British constitutional theory that is reflected in sentiments such as those of the Massachusetts Legislature in defense of the Sedition Act of 1798:

> The president of the United States is bound by his oath, "to preserve, protect and defend the constitution," and it is expressly made his duty "to take care that the laws be faithfully executed"; but this would be impracticable by any created being, if there could be no legal restraints of those scandalous misrepresentations of his measures and motives, which directly tend to rob him of the public confidence. And equally impotent would be every other public officer, if thus left to the mercy of the seditious.[5]

A republican regime, especially one of such territorial scope and made up of such diverse elements as that in America, required (if it was to prosper) a national standard of freedom of speech and of the press which permitted (so far as the federal government was concerned, at least) a truly unfettered discussion of all public issues. This, it seems to me, was implied in the Constitution from the beginning, even before the Bill of Rights amendments were added. It is to this consideration of the nature of government, and especially of republican government, that one can direct the most fruitful inquiry. And it is to this, not primarily to an attempted measurement of the accepted opinions in the community, that American legislators addressed themselves when the constitutionality and the expediency of the Sedition Act were debated.

The statements that men such as Madison wrote in response to the Sedition Act, then, were not merely *ad hoc* political declarations—they *were* that, of course, as are all political statements—but they were even more the articulation of that which had been implicit in the American constitutional system from its inception. The decisive repudiation at the polls in 1800 of the political party responsible for the Sedition Act suggests that there may have been a deep public response to the interpretation by Jefferson and his party of the thought and experience of three decades. Thus, Madison argued, on behalf of the Virginia House of Delegates, in the 1800 *Report on the Virginia Resolutions,* that,

Some degree of abuse is inseparable from the proper use of every thing; and in no instance is this more true, than in that of the press. It has accordingly been decided by the practice of the states, that it is better to leave a few of its noxious branches, to their luxuriant growth, than by pruning them away, to injure the vigor of those yielding the proper fruits. And can the wisdom of this policy be doubted by any who reflect, that to the press alone, chequered as it is with abuses, the world is indebted for all the triumphs which have been gained by reason and humanity, over error and oppression; who reflect, that to the same beneficent source, the United States owe much of the lights which conducted them to the rank of a free and independent nation; and which have improved their political system, into a shape so auspicious to their happiness. Had "sedition acts," forbidding every publication that might bring constituted agents into contempt or disrepute, or that might excite the hatred of the people against the authors of unjust or pernicious measures, been uniformly enforced against the press; might not the United States have been languishing at this day, under the infirmities of a sickly confederation? Might they not, possibly be miserable colonies, groaning under a foreign yoke?[6]

The American legacy was not repudiated, however it may have been muted, by the war-time repressions of the Tories or by the peace-time persecution of one party by another. In these matters, the sentiments of men can be more important than their actions: for sentiments reflect principle, whereas actions are all too often the unfortunate products of passion.[7] It was the author of the Declaration of Independence who could, in his First Inaugural Address (of 1801) as President of the United States, rise to the occasion and speak authoritatively on behalf of what was becoming a prosperous, self-confident and vigorous country:

If there be any among us who would wish to dissolve this Union or to change its republican form, let them stand undisturbed as monuments of the safety with which error of opinion may be tolerated where reason is left free to combat it. I know, indeed, that some honest men fear that a republican government cannot be strong; that this government is not strong enough. But would the honest patriot, in the full tide of successful experiment, abandon a government which has so far kept us free and firm, on the theoretic and visionary fear that this government, the world's best hope, may by possibility want energy to preserve itself? I trust not. I believe this, on the contrary, the strongest government on earth. I believe it is the only one where every man, at the call of the laws, would fly to the standard of the law, and would meet invasions of the public order as his own personal concern.

vi

In his attempt to be realistic, and even scientific, the revisionist—whether historian or political theorist or archaeologist—discounts rhetoric. But it is in rhetoric—in the noblest of rhetoric—that the meaning of a people or of a country may be discerned. Indeed, rhetoric is of the very life-blood of politics. The modern revisionist is inclined to see self-interest as decisive in the pronouncements of men and to be suspicious for that reason of what he calls "rhetorical effusions." (p. 215) But is not a scholar's work also apt to be a kind of rhetoric, an *ad hoc* rhetoric usually considered "significant" only if he finds against the accepted tradition, not if he merely confirms it? If the scholar can be depended upon to rise above simple self-interest, why not the great men of a country as well?[8]

I have suggested what I believe are serious challenges to certain fundamental presuppositions of the revisionist approach to a study of American history and institutions. No doubt there are revisionists who *would* prefer to find what they call a libertarian legacy in American history. When they do not find it, however, they take comfort in the observation that we have progressed beyond the thought of olden times and that we have an "expanding democracy."[9] But their position comes down, ultimately, to an essentially arbitrary personal preference: that is, according to them, there can be for us no basis in the fundamental law of the land for any position we take. This attitude raises serious questions about the country's principles and the direction in which it is tending. In one sense, the typical revisionism is un-constitutional—that is, it does not take the constitution seriously.[10]

vii

The legacy left us by our great constitutional figures is not to be found by an interpretation of necessarily fragmentary records or by the reconstruction of ambiguous actions. Rather, the legacy worth reflecting on—and which we were *meant* to reflect upon—is that provided by

the great statements which have come down to us, in instruments such
as The Declaration of Independence, the Constitution of the United
States, the Bill of Rights, and the Gettysburg Address. Our most serious
concern should be with an understanding of these instruments, with the
principles that underlie them, and with the imaginative application of
these principles to the complex and sometimes novel circumstances of
our contemporary national life. We, too, can profit from the reminder
by the Virginia Assembly in 1800

> that a frequent recurrence to fundamental principles, is solemnly
> enjoined by most of the state constitutions, and particularly by our
> own, as a necessary safeguard against the danger of degeneracy to
> which republics are liable, as well as other governments, though in
> 'a less degree than others. And a fair comparison of the political
> doctrines not unfrequent at the present day, with those which
> characterized the epoch of our revolution, and which form the
> basis of our republican constitutions, will best determine whether
> the declaratory recurrence here made to those principles, ought to
> be viewed as unseasonable and improper, or as a vigilant discharge
> of an important duty. The authority of constitutions over govern-
> ments, and of the sovereignty of the people over constitutions, are
> truths which are at all times necessary to be kept in mind; and at no
> time perhaps more necessary than at the present.[11]

The patriot's duty is not to invent and construct but rather to discover and develop what has been given. Only thus can one approach
American constitutional government with the seriousness that it deserves. Indeed, it is here that we see the possibility of a truce between
the scholar and the politician. For the United States, perhaps alone of
all modern states, is to a surprising extent the product of human deliberation applied to political problems. Perhaps here, more than anywhere
else, the responsible intellectual need not feel estranged from the political
life of his country—if only because that country has been the child of
its finest intellects, and not so much, as are the other nations of the earth,
the result primarily of chance, of race, of class struggle, or of unrea-
soning faiths.

That is to say, America was the first country in modern times with
a meaning. That meaning—which we have only touched upon tonight—
is to be found in its fullness not in the reconstructions of historians but
in the writings of America's greatest men. That meaning *has* been
glimpsed, if sometimes crudely, in the popular tradition about American

deeds and purposes that has come down to us. The sacrifices the noble man makes should serve, in the eyes of his fellow-citizens, as pledges of the sincerity of what he says. In this way, deeds reinforce words.[12]

We are reminded that Lincoln, our noblest rhetorician, once proclaimed that the country and its institutions belong to the people. But a qualification may be in order in these days of thoughtless revision: the country and its institutions do belong to the people, but to the people who think about them—to the people, that is, who understand, refine, and, if need be, revive the heritage which has been handed down even unto this generation. That heritage is dimly but significantly reflected in the fact that an obscure eighteenth-century Virginia legislator could believe, *and* feel free to declare publicly, that he was as good a citizen as the President of the United States.[13]

IV. Natural Right and the American Lawyer

> "O brothers!" [Ulysses said,] "who through a hundred thousand dangers have reached the West, deny not, to this brief vigil of your senses which remains, experience of the unpeopled world behind the sun. Consider your origin: you were not formed to live like brutes, but to follow virtue and knowledge."
>
> Dante, *Inferno*, xxvi

i

A generation has passed since Professor Lon L. Fuller published his most important book, *The Law in Quest of Itself*.[1] Many of the arguments he made then were novel to legal readers nurtured on the doctrines of positivism and social science, however familiar and even elementary they would have seemed to lawyers and students of law a century earlier. Mr. Fuller stressed the importance of legal philosophy (or jurisprudence) for practical life, emphasizing the role of reason in the conduct of human affairs, even in the determination of moral standards. He argued, in that valuable series of lectures, for a doctrine of natural law that "denies the possibility of a rigid separation of the *is* and the *ought*" and that asserts that men's "conceptions of right and wrong are themselves significantly shaped by the daily functioning of the legal order."[2]

It was time for the beginning of such a shift in legal circles away from the engaging doctrines of positivism and its insistence (in the name of realism) that the just is simply the legal. The career of Nazism in Germany may have contributed to this development: the minds of decent men needed something more substantial than mere received opinion on which to ground their rejection of what was being done in the name of law in that most law-abiding country. Thus, Mr. Fuller was but one of several who looked to the natural law tradition for inspiration and guidance. But he emerged, because of the evident sincerity of

This review was published (with the title, "Natural Right and the American Lawyer: An Appreciation of Professor Fuller") in 1965 *Wisconsin Law Review* 322 (Spring 1965).

The principal book discussed here is Lon L. Fuller, *The Morality of Law* (New Haven: Yale University Press, 1964).

his concern, as the most distinguished spokesman of this school among legal scholars.[3]

By "natural law," writes another scholar (the leading student of this subject today),

> is meant a law that determines what is right and wrong and that has power or is valid by nature, inherently, hence everywhere and always. . . . The notion of natural law presupposes the notion of nature, and the notion of nature is not coeval with human thought; hence there is no natural law teaching, for instance, in the Old Testament. Nature was discovered by the Greeks in contradistinction to art (the knowledge guiding the making of artifacts) and, above all, to *nomos* (law, custom, convention, agreement, authoritative opinion). In the light of the original meaning of "nature," the notion of "natural law" (*nomos tes physeos*) is a contradiction in terms rather than a matter of course.
>
> The primary question is less concerned with natural law than with natural right, i.e., what is by nature right or just. Is all right conventional (of human origin) or is there some right which is natural (*physei dikaion*)? This question was raised on the assumption that there are things which are by nature good (health, strength, intelligence, courage, etc.). Conventionalism (the view that all right is conventional) derived its support in the first place from the variety of notions of justice, a variety incompatible with the supposed uniformity of a right that is natural. Yet the conventionalists could not deny that justice possesses a core that is universally recognized, so much so that injustice must have recourse to lies or to "myths" in order to become publicly defensible.
>
> The precise issue then concerned the status of that right which is universally recognized: is that right merely the condition of the living together of a particular society, (i.e., of a society constituted by covenant or agreement, with that right deriving its validity from the preceding covenant), or is there a justice among men as men which does not derive from any human arrangement? In other words, is justice based only on calculation of the advantage of living together, or is it choiceworthy for its own sake and therefore "by nature"?[4]

This passage raises several of the questions about both natural law and natural right that we propose to touch upon on this occasion.

ii

We rely on Mr. Fuller to explain what he is attempting to do in the four chapters of his most recent book, *The Morality of Law*:

> The content of these chapters has been chiefly shaped by a dissatisfaction with the existing literature concerning the relation between law and morality. This literature seems to me to be deficient in two important respects. The first of these relates to a failure to clarify the meaning of morality itself. Definitions of law we have, in almost unwanted abundance. . . . [T]he legal mind generally exhausts itself in thinking about law and is content to leave unexamined the thing to which law is being related and from which it is being distinguished.
>
> In my first chapter an effort is made to redress this balance. This is done chiefly by emphasizing a distinction between what I call the morality of aspiration and the morality of duty. A failure to make this distinction has, I think, been the cause of much obscurity in discussions of the relation between law and morals.
>
> The other major dissatisfaction underlying these lectures arises from a neglect of what the title of my second chapter calls "The Morality That Makes Law Possible." Insofar as the existing literature deals with the chief subject of this second chapter—which I call "the internal morality of law"—it is usually to dismiss it with a few remarks about "legal justice," this conception of justice being equated with a purely formal requirement that like cases be given like treatment. There is little recognition that the problem thus adumbrated is only one aspect of a much larger problem, that of clarifying the directions of human effort essential to maintain any system of law, even one whose ultimate objectives may be regarded as mistaken or evil.
>
> The third and fourth chapters constitute a further development and application of the analysis presented in the first two. The third, entitled "The Concept of Law," attempts to bring this analysis into relation with the various schools of legal philosophy generally. The fourth, "The Substantive Aims of Law," seeks to demonstrate how a proper respect for the internal morality of law limits the kind of substantive aims that may be achieved through legal rules. The chapter closes with an examination of the extent to which something like a substantive "natural law" may be derived from the morality of aspiration.[5]

Mr. Fuller discovers "a single, underlying disagreement" on his part "with the various schools of legal philosophy":

> The nature of this fundamental divergence may be expressed in these terms: I have insisted that law be viewed as a purposeful enterprise, dependent for its success on the energy, insight, intelligence, and conscientiousness of those who conduct it, and fated, because of this dependence, to fall always somewhat short of a full attainment of its goals. In opposition to this view it is insisted that law must be treated as a manifested fact of social authority or power, to be studied for what it is and does, and not for what it is trying to do or become.[6]

The decisive critique of this book was anticipated by its author. For he observed in an earlier work:

> Throughout these lectures I have been assuming that American legal scholarship suffers at present from the inhibitive effects of a positivistic philosophy. I cannot claim to have proved this thesis, nor shall I attempt to do so now. The tacit taboos imposed by a general climate of opinion are, after all, scarcely susceptible of demonstration, and I shall have to leave it to the informed reader to decide whether I have correctly sensed the prevailing bent of men's minds.[7]

These "inhibitive effects" may be detected in Mr. Fuller's latest work, for the positivist "climate of opinion"—which the sensitive scholar confronts among his readers and critics—does inhibit serious consideration of the problems and possibilities of natural law and natural right.

iii

The influence of positivism upon him may be reflected even in Mr. Fuller's use of the language of physical science. He speaks of a "moral scale," of an "invisible pointer" on that scale, and of "the pressure of duty." Also "scientific" is his discussion of competing aspirations in terms of marginal utility.[8] Related to this emphasis, but much more critical, is his discussion of fact and value: the aspirations he speaks of seem to be essentially subjective.[9] Indeed, Mr. Fuller can be said to have divined the necessity for natural law without really understanding it. This is a tribute to his instincts as well as to his common sense and fortitude, to say nothing of his good fortune.

The bleak catalogue that Mr. Fuller draws up of the alternative views to his of what law is should drive everyone to reconsider the modern rejection of natural law.[10] He is correct to insist upon regarding law as a "purposeful enterprise." He has, however, no substantial definition of that purpose.[11] He admits to a "modest indulgence in teleology"[12]—but nothing much seems to come of this. His common sense asserts itself when he questions the modern emphasis upon self-preservation as the objective most basic to man's activity; but he has nothing as attractive to offer in its place. His final chapter does include a few pages on the substantive aims of the law, but even there the concern is much more with process than with any goal. Thus, the value of communication is extolled, but little is said either of what is to be done with this communication or of what is to be communicated. His discussion of communication does not center, unlike comparable discussions among the ancients, upon the rational element in man's soul; rather, he elevates perception, feeling, and desire to the place once accorded to reason.[13] These disappointing conclusions, with their departure from the emphasis in classical political thought upon virtue and knowledge, are anticipated in disparagements by him of the practical relevance of the Platonic conception of excellence and perfection.[14] Mr. Fuller prefers to start from the bottom and to work "up," rather than.(as did the more sober Greek thinkers) to start from the top (or the goal) with some notion of the best man or the best city. Since he (in the modern tradition) grounds himself on the lowest, there can be no true goal, only the process of going "up," a direction that can mean little more than mere change unless some goal is in mind.[15]

The extent to which Mr. Fuller is the child, or rather the stepchild, of a positivist age is perhaps best reflected in his discussion of the relation of law and morality.[16] His distinction between the "morality of aspiration" and the "morality of duty" seems to lead to the assertion that the morality of aspiration (which seems to include most of the virtues) cannot be shaped significantly by the law. Our formulation here of his position must remain vague and tentative, since he himself leaves it that way. But it is an issue on which we need more light today, especially when confronted with the popular argument that morality cannot be legislated. Is not the truth rather that most of the moral code of any people has depended upon legislation, that it is difficult to establish a pervasive morality without the aid of legislation?

Two examples, ancient and modern, illustrate the relation between law and morality. Aristotle introduced the *Politics* as the means for securing the moral standards he had elaborated in the *Nicomachean Ethics:*

> But it is difficult to get from youth up a right training for virtue if one has not been brought up under right laws: for to live temperately and hardily is not pleasant to most people, especially when they are young. For this reason their nurture and occupations should be fixed by law; for they will not be painful when they have become customary. But it is surely not enough that when they are young they should get the right nurture and attention; since they must, even when they are grown up, practise and be habituated to them, we shall need laws for this as well, and generally speaking to cover the whole of life; for most people obey necessity rather than the sense of what is noble.[17]

Lincoln insisted again and again on the significance of the Northwest Ordinance of 1787 in determining whether the people of the Northwest Territory should stand for freedom or slavery.[18] He addressed an Ohio audience in this fashion:

> Pray, what was it that made you free? What kept you free? Did you not find your country free when you came to decide that Ohio should be a free State? It is important to inquire by what reason you found it so. Let us take an illustration between the States of Ohio and Kentucky. Kentucky is separated by this River Ohio, not a mile wide. A portion of Kentucky, by reason of the course of the Ohio, is further north than this portion of Ohio in which we now stand. Kentucky is entirely covered with slavery— Ohio is entirely free from it. What made that difference? Was it climate? No! A portion of Kentucky was further north than this portion of Ohio. Was it soil? No! There is nothing in the soil of the one more favorable to slave-labor than the other. It was not climate or soil that caused one side of the line to be entirely covered with slavery and the other side free of it. What was it? Study over it. Tell us, if you can, in all the range of conjecture, if there be anything you can conceive of that made the difference, other than there was no law of any sort keeping it out of Kentucky, while the ordinance of '87 kept it out of Ohio.[19]

It is no more reasonable to say that morality cannot be legislated, simply because there have been failures resulting from imprudent attempts, than it would be to say that disease cannot be controlled, simply because licensed doctors have made mistakes in diagnoses or prescriptions.[20] To the extent that Mr. Fuller seems to minimize the role of law in securing morality, to that extent he undermines the natural law tradition with which he has been identified.

It is characteristic of the great natural law teachers that they respect tradition. Even revolution is justified by them as a return to the best or to the traditional.[21] The traditional is most evidently incorporated in the terms that one generation passes on to the next. When Mr. Fuller speaks of a "morality of duty" and a "morality of aspiration," we suspect that he is distinguishing between justice and the other virtues; when he speaks of "the inner morality of law," he seems to be referring primarily to due process of law.[22] The reader cannot be certain of this, however, nor can he easily see why these linguistic innovations should be adopted. Confusion is created, novelty encouraged, and the centuries-old corpus of discussion and refinement of justice and of the other virtues as well as of due process of law is abandoned. One result is that the student is discouraged from consciously participating in a conversation which reaches back more than two thousand years. Instead, man is driven to try to remake his terms, and hence himself, every generation.

When Mr. Fuller's natural law is reduced to its essentials, it may be seen as almost entirely an insistence on due process of law. Indeed, the most valuable part of the book consists in the examination of the various elements of due process. Thus, he lists and examines in useful detail eight ways in which "the attempt to create and maintain a system of legal rules may miscarry":

> The first and most obvious lies in a failure to achieve rules at all, so that every issue must be decided on an ad hoc basis. The other routes are: (2) a failure to publicize, or at least to make available to the affected party, the rules he is expected to observe; (3) the abuse of retroactive legislation, which not only cannot itself guide action, but undercuts the integrity of rules prospective in effect, since it puts them under the threat of retrospective change; (4) a failure to make rules understandable; (5) the enactment of contradictory rules or (6) rules that require conduct beyond the powers of the affected party; (7) introducing such frequent changes in the rules that the subject cannot orient his action by them; and,

finally, (8) a failure of congruence between the rules as announced and their actual administration.[23]

And he adds:

A total failure in any one of these eight directions does not simply result in a bad system of law; it results in something that is not properly called a legal system at all, except perhaps in the Pickwickian sense in which a void contract can still be said to be one kind of contract.[24]

Mr. Fuller's concept of law bears on this argument: "The only formula that might be called a definition of law offered in these writings is by now thoroughly familiar: law is the enterprise of subjecting human conduct to the governance of rules. Unlike most modern theories of law, this view treats law as an activity and regards a legal system as the product of a sustained purposeful effort." He explains "that the purpose I have attributed to the institution of law is a modest and sober one, that of subjecting human conduct to the guidance and control of general rules."[25] It is just such a conception of law that makes possible the excessive regard we find in Mr. Fuller for the no doubt important role of due process. Compare the definition of law developed by Thomas Aquinas: "It is nothing else than an ordinance of reason for the common good, made by him who has care of the community, and promulgated."[26] It became the duty of the positivist Professor H. L. A. Hart to suggest that Mr. Fuller's "inner morality of law" is consistent with "very great iniquity."[27] Is not Mr. Hart correct in his suggestion that very great iniquity *can* follow at the hands of men scrupulous in adhering to the forms of Mr. Fuller's "inner morality"?[28] That is, there may have been good reason for including, in the traditional definition of law, the qualification, "for the common good." It is a qualification that induces the student of law to step behind the forms of law and to reflect upon what is best for man and for communities of men.

In any event, the legal positivist, with his strong sense of fact, points up the vulnerability of Mr. Fuller's formulation of law. But he cannot do so without speaking of "very great iniquity" and perhaps invoking (even if unbeknownst to himself) standards and a tradition that belie his positivist assertions.

iv

The lawyer finds it difficult to ignore or repudiate altogether his natural right heritage. When he speaks of iniquity, he is understood as many of his colleagues and fellow-citizens have understood such a reference for generations. When he works in and through the common law, he draws upon distinctions and nuances distilled from centuries of everyday notions of right and wrong.[29] He deals everyday, just as a millennium of English-speaking lawyers before him, with the unsophisticated assumptions about good and evil held by the laymen whom he must address as clients, jurors, and citizens. He may be a positivist in his study or even in the classroom: but it is a different story in the courtroom or on the public platform.

Since the lawyer must be, to some degree, a public man, he is shaped by and is obliged to try to walk in step with his great predecessors. Thus, in this country, the sentiments of our great statesmen and lawyers must be taken seriously: to disavow their moral and political dedication is to call into question one's own activity, purpose, and effectiveness as a political man.[30] Our very language, shaped as it has been in critical respects by the moral genius of Shakespeare, incorporates and helps perpetuate the natural right heritage.[31]

And then, of course, there is the founding document of the American heritage, the Declaration of Independence.[32] One aspect of the Declaration's influence is evident to all, the insistence upon the inalienability of certain rights. There was here a shift from the rights of Englishmen to the rights of men: the nature of things was appealed to.[33] But for our time, the more important influence may come from the invocation by the Declaration of one of those rights in particular, the right of a people to alter or abolish any form of government subversive of the ends of government. This doctrine of rightful rebellion strikes at the heart of the legal-mindedness of the positivist position: it reminds mankind of standards that are above any particular government or set of laws.[34]

But neither tradition nor hallowed documents can be much more than reminders of what may be known; they can be little more than incentives to recover what has been repudiated or, at least, weakened. We must still wonder: What is natural law? What is natural right? Indeed, what is the nature of nature? What are the significance and effects of such things? How does one learn about them? We must think about these questions in a responsible way, partly by returning to a serious study of what the best minds have known about them. We are obliged, even as we recognize the role of right opinion and of salutary myths for the country at large, to insist upon a proper education for the best among us if such opinions are to be preserved and properly employed.

v

A return to the serious study of the best minds is critical. One distinguished judge has been much praised for saying that

> It is as important to a judge called upon to pass on a question of constitutional law to have at least a bowing acquaintance with Acton and Maitland, with Thucydides, Gibbon and Carlyle, with Homer, Dante, Shakespeare and Milton, with Machiavelli, Montaigne and Rabelais, with Plato, Bacon, Hume and Kant, as with the books which have been specifically written on the subject. For in such matters everything turns upon the spirit in which he approaches the questions before him. The words he must construe are empty vessels into which he can pour nearly everything he will.[35]

But a "bowing acquaintance" can only mean that a judge's grasp of serious writers will be superficial. It is far better to know one great writer well—whether he be Homer or Thucydides or Plato or Shakespeare or Milton—or to have thought seriously about problems such writers confront.[36] Of course, there never was a time when many lawyers understood much of Plato, of Aristotle, of Plutarch, of Cicero, or of Aquinas. But there have been times—and this is not one of them—when the men who taught the lawyers had been significantly influenced by writers of this calibre.

We return, for an illustration, to Mr. Fuller's discussion of Plato. He reports Plato's position as dependent on "the assumption that we cannot know the bad without knowing the perfectly good, or, in other words, that moral duties cannot be rationally discerned without first embracing a comprehensive morality of aspiration." But he immediately observes that that which he designates as fundamental in Plato "is contradicted by the most elementary human experience."[37] We cannot, on this occasion, either analyze Mr. Fuller's interpretation of Plato or present an alternative. But we must marvel that Mr. Fuller does not pause to wonder that Plato should have failed to notice and reflect upon what Mr. Fuller considers "the most elementary human experience." He recognizes that Plato depends on some awareness of the perfectly good and seems to dismiss him on that account. But such a dependence may be discerned as well in many of the other great men to whom we may turn. Indeed, Mr. Fuller can speak of the "upward" without recognizing that, if he means anything other than mere change by this, he sharès the failing of Plato and his disciples.[38]

Contemporary lawyers and, even more serious, professors of law have been cutting themselves off from the great teachers of the West. The use made of such teachers and of the quotations taken from them by almost all legal scholars as well as the general attitude toward their teaching betrays a lack of genuine seriousness. The greatest works of the human mind are approached with a casualness that competent lawyers would find scandalous in the drafting of the most trivial deed or contract. The natural law tradition or even the common law—which may be understood as an everyday adaptation of natural law to particular circumstances—cannot be properly studied until this cavalier approach is reformed. The serious student must begin with the realization that certain thinkers know precisely what they are saying and why they are saying it.[39]

If the great teachers are not approached with the care appropriate to them, their teachings can lead to excesses, absurdities and misunderstandings of the kind that have been partly responsible for the disfavor that natural law and natural right have fallen into.

vi

The incentive to return to a serious study of natural right and natural law may be blunted somewhat by the use to which natural law has been put in some quarters. That is, natural law has been identified with particular doctrines which many good men reject as harmful. Curiously, then, natural law and natural right are often rejected on the basis of sentiments that themselves draw upon the unreflective man's awareness of what is by nature right.

Lawyers who remember the Supreme Court's decisions in the early 1930s are sometimes tempted to view them as instances of anachronistic, even destructive, applications of natural law theories to contemporary problems. But we must see such doctrines for what they were, the erroneous, even though well-meaning, identification of transient interests with the enduring core of the natural law teaching.

Another instance that disturbs many good men today is the teaching of the Roman Catholic Church with respect to birth control. If its prohibition of certain means of birth control were regarded by the Church as is, say, a requirement that meat not be eaten on Friday, that would be one thing—and, indeed, some restraints could even be salutary in some places, or at some times, if only to induce human beings to reflect upon the natural order of things and the role of sexual activity in it. But when the teaching is insisted upon (with an effect on public policy) as a universal and unalterable dictate of natural law—which would be binding on all right-thinking men and women, not Roman Catholics alone—serious problems arise.[40] We should not ignore here the authority and, even more important, the arguments of an Aristotle who could not only countenance rigid birth control but even (it seems) the exposure of defective infants.[41] Much of the Roman Catholic tradition on this subject can seem unreasonable, and even unduly sentimental, when viewed through ancient eyes.[42]

Thus, the Roman Catholic teachers who have done so much to keep alive the natural law tradition among us may, by their evident disregard of considerations of prudence, be inhibiting others, in a world beset by unprecedented population growth, from taking that tradition seriously.[43] But in another realm, which has to do with deliberations about the prospects and conduct of another world war, Roman Catholic thinkers seem to be among the leaders bringing to bear on a new problem some old teachings. Even notorious Marxists have praised papal statements on this subject. The question remains whether reasonable men of good will can work out accommodations and arrangements that will satisfy the legitimate aspirations and calm the unavoidable fears in all camps.[44] One difficulty grows out of our callousness in having learned to live with the problem. Thus, a newspaper article can report rather casually "the approach within the Pentagon" (which is, no doubt, also the approach within the Kremlin):

> The "Big War" will be an atomic exchange, probably an international holocaust, with half the northern hemisphere's population lost within a month. This would then be followed by a long war of attrition with more conventional weapons. The side with the largest atomic stockpile probably will "win."[45]

The population referred to here is that of North America, Europe, Russia, mainland Asia, as well as that of much of Africa. To believe that civilization can survive such a shock as is anticipated in this report is to be incredibly naïve about the nature of human communities. Even to bluff or threaten one another about such matters betrays an obtuseness which touches upon madness. One might have hoped that no leader of any nation advanced enough to be able to develop nuclear weapons would do anything to bring on such "an international holocaust." And yet, in the 1962 Cuban missile crisis, both the Russian and the American leaders took fateful steps the results of which we are given to understand they could not foresee. Thus, our Secretary of Defense at that time has been moved to reminisce:

> I do recall vividly that Saturday night, October 27, in the week of the Cuban crisis, when I was driving from the White House back ⁺o the Pentagon. It was a time when we were waiting for the Russian response, when the quarantine was a week old, when we had a huge invasion force poised.
>
> It was a lovely soft evening with a beautiful sunset and I found myself thinking that this might be the last evening I and the other people on the streets might ever see such a sunset again.
>
> One had the feeling of momentous events propelling us forward. This was the deepest sadness I have ever felt, for fear the Soviets ' would fail to realize the consequences of *their* actions. [Italics added.]

He went on to observe:

> In other ways the week of the Cuban crisis was the most satisfying week I've ever had in government. The responsible leaders worked very closely and very effectively, exchanging views, arriving at independent conclusions, considering alternatives, making a decision.
>
> Throughout it all, the President supplied the intellectual and moral leadership. He was the coolest and most perceptive man in government at the time. And the result was a triumph of reasonable men.

Thus, we are brought back to the question of what is indeed "reasonable" in such matters.[46] And this requires systematic reflection upon the nature of man and of his city, the best of which he is capable as well as the limitations which he must respect.[47]

vii

It should be apparent, as we prepare to close, why it is appropriate to salute Professor Fuller's contribution to the legal profession with a trib-

ute of another era: "His imperfections flowed from the contagion of
the time; his virtues were his own, the free gift of nature or reflection..."[48]

The lawyer, as lawyer, must play his limited but vital role in a world
beset by unprecedented challenges.[49] This role, which must sometimes
seem futile against the backdrop of momentous events, obliges him to
be competent and to know the extent of that competence. His role
also requires that moral character which bar association committees on
admission, discipline, and disbarment labor hard to insure but which
depends much more on the "general climate of opinion" among the
bar. It is to this that moralists address themselves—and here we are reminded of the limits of ordinary law—when they speak of the trusteeship, the burden of honor, that lawyers assume as members of their
profession.[50]

The sense of honor—that "sacred honor" with which the Declaration
of Independence concludes—is one everyday manifestation of the natural right teaching: it is the familiar version of "the sense of what is
noble" that emanates from the best of men. It is of honorable men that
an American diplomat wrote when he described the Department of
State "at the turn of the century":

> These men embodied that pattern of integrity of mind and spirit,
> moderation and delicacy of character, irreproachable loyalty in
> personal relations, modesty of person combined with dignity of
> office, and kindliness and generosity in the approach to all who
> were weaker and more dependent, which constitutes, it seems to
> me, our finest contribution to the variety of the human species in
> this world and comes closest to embodying our national ideal and
> genius. They were men so measured and prudent in their judg-
> ment of others, so careful to reserve that judgment until they felt
> they had the facts, so well aware of the danger of inadequate evi-
> dence and hasty conclusion, that we would be making ourselves
> ridiculous if we were to attend their memories and the evidences
> of their handiwork in any other spirit.[51]

The model described here is one that the American bar could with
honor aspire to measure up to.

In order for the lawyer's sense of honor to be more than merely
formal—in order that it not degenerate into empty or even callous
ritual—there must be somewhere in the legal profession the men who
have been properly taught by precept and example about the best

things. This is the concern reflected in the leavetaking several years ago of one former applicant for admission to the Illinois bar:

> [T]his entire [bar admission] controversy is itself but an image of a much more fundamental one which bears on the problem of the education and character of the citizen as well as of the lawyer. We must try to take seriously again the concern and conditions for virtue, nobility and the life most fitting for men.
>
> Petitioner, exercising the prerogative of one retiring from a profession, would advise the new lawyer that he learn well not only the tools of his craft but also the texts that have come to us from the ancient world. It is in those texts that one may find the best models, both in word and in deed, for the conduct of oneself in public as well as in private affairs. It is there that the better natures are most likely to be exposed to the accents and majesty of human excellence.[52]

V. Liberty and Equality

> We weigh what we undertake and apprehend it per-
> fectly in our minds, [said Pericles,] not accounting
> words for a hindrance of action but that it is rather a
> hindrance to action to come to it without instruction
> of words before. For also in this we excel others, dar-
> ing to undertake as much as any and yet examining
> what we undertake; whereas with other men ignorance
> makes them dare, and consideration makes them cow-
> ards. And they are most rightly reputed valiant who,
> though they perfectly apprehend more what is dan-
> gerous and what is easy, are never the more thereby
> diverted from adventuring.
>
> Thucydides, *Peloponnesian War*, II, 40.

i

The theme that runs through Professor Harry V. Jaffa's collection of essays, *Equality & Liberty*, is "the supreme importance of the Declaration of Independence as a statement of principles which not only did justify, but must ever justify, our existence as an independent people." (vii)[1] Mr. Jaffa continues:

> The declaration that all men are created equal has played a role in
> the American political experience not unlike that declaring the
> oneness of God, in the experience of the children of Israel. It is
> at once the cause and measure of our greatness and our tragedies.
> It has united us in those efforts which have demonstrated to the
> world civil and religious liberty beyond anything the world has
> seen elsewhere and has divided us in inner conflict, taking a greater
> toll in doubt and despair than in bodily destruction. The Civil War,
> I have written, is the most characteristic phenomenon in American
> politics, not because it represents a statistical frequency, but be-
> cause it represents the innermost character of that politics; it is
> the event in which the things that forever drive toward and hinder
> us from achieving our political salvation emerge in the sharpest
> and most visible confrontation.

This review was published in 41 *New York University Law Review* 664 (May 1966). It brought together several arguments generated by the Cold War during the preceding decade and even earlier.

The citations in the text are to Harry V. Jaffa, *Equality & Liberty: Theory and Practice in American Politics* (New York: Oxford University Press, 1965).

There is today a widespread notion—fortunately more widespread among political scientists than among lay citizens—that the principles of the Declaration are more to be considered an expression of "the thought of the time" than a serious teaching about man and his nature. Such mistaken sophistication, it seems to me, is the greatest stumbling block in the way of taking American politics with the full seriousness it deserves and requires. [vii-viii] [2]

It is this "full seriousness" that is evident in Mr. Jaffa's writings not only on American subjects but also in political science generally. Indeed, he may be the writer of his generation most worthy of study by the serious student of American institutions. The range of his talents and associations is such that one can say he contributed a voice of moderation to the Goldwater Presidential Campaign of 1964. [3]

His collection of essays serves to introduce readers to the range and depth of Mr. Jaffa's thought as he explores the confrontation in American thought between liberty and equality. [4]

ii

It seems generally true of enlightened Americans today that there is among them greater sympathy for "civil rights" than for "civil liberties." This seems to be true of Mr. Jaffa as well. [5] The general attitude is reflected, for instance, in the much greater emphasis placed since the Second World War, by courts and citizens alike, on attacking racial segregation than on maintaining the right of freedom of speech of unpopular political associations. Thus, although the Supreme Court of the United States could, for more than a decade, be depended upon to do no more than divide five-to-four or perhaps six-to-three for or against a political right claimed in circumstances where a question of Communism had been raised, that court could at the same time be relied upon to deliver a unanimous decision invalidating attempts by State governments to preserve segregation. [6]

How is this difference in attitudes to be understood? No doubt, the Cold War played its part in inducing Americans to "close ranks." Fear of "the enemy without" drove us to suppress, or at least discourage, any political expression which could be seen as that enemy's domestic subversion. At the same time, that international challenge prompted us to demonstrate to other peoples that the man of color finds in the United States a worthy ally. The Cold War, however, may have only hastened developments inherent in our way of life and our institutions.

There has been, from the earliest days of the Republic, tension between the demands of "liberty" and those of "equality." Thus, the political liberty of free men, culminating in the venerable "right of revolution," is defended in a Declaration of Independence which is itself grounded on the self-evident truth that all men are created equal. It is not difficult to conceive of instances in which the exercise of liberty by one man cuts into the right, or at least the demand, of another man to be treated as the equal of his fellows. One question that the American people must face in the decades ahead is whether the triumph of equality must mean disappearance of liberty and of the nobility liberty makes possible. Certainly, the age of equality has dawned.

iii

The call for "civil rights" is essentially a call for equality, a call for that form of justice that is seen in treating all men alike—in treating everyone as human. This insistence upon civil rights culminates in the rule of law: the emphasis is placed less upon what the law should be than upon the assurance that all should have applied to them alike the laws of the community. The rulers are left relatively free, so far as the advocates of equality are concerned, to do what they choose—so long as the government is compelled to apply the same rules to all. This requirement of uniformity of treatment is seen as a significant restraint upon rulers.

The advocate of liberty, on the other hand, tends to place greater emphasis on restraining government power, on limiting what the rulers may do: he often prefers to endure inequality rather than permit those restrictions on liberty that are designed to establish or protect equality. Indeed, he may sometimes regard simple equality—equal treatment for unequals—as unjust.

Obviously, there is much to be said for each approach—and, as circumstances change, even for the emphasis upon one or the other. This reflects the fact that there is rarely a position maintained by decent men which does not have something to be said for it. Surely there are times when exceptional men must be curbed and reminded of that which is due the common man, just as there are levelling eras when men of stature should be singled out, cherished, and emulated.[7]

Civil rights—which we may regard as incorporating an approach that aims at equality and, at its best, the rule of law—must rest, if they are to preserve a community of free men, upon a system of education that produces a ruling class qualified to be trusted with the vast powers of government. They rest, that is, upon an equality itself based on freedom of opportunity. On the other hand, the liberty-minded approach, since it restrains rulers and limits the government, leaves more power in the hands of the people at large: this approach rests, if it is to lead to a well-ordered community, upon a system of training which molds the citizen body, or at least a significant portion of it, into that inspiring spectacle of a community of self-governing free men. It rests, that is, upon the equality of citizens who know how to rule and to be ruled in turn.

The depreciation of liberty that we have witnessed since the Second World War may be in part due to an awareness among concerned Americans that something has gone wrong with the training and, hence, with the character and civic virtue of the prosperous American people. There now seems to be doubt in some quarters that the people can still be trusted to use liberty responsibly. On the other hand, our institutions may no longer be designed for the proper education of the rulers of an egalitarian community.[8] The legal profession, when dominated by competent men of integrity, has served heretofore to forestall such objections. This no longer seems to be the case.[9]

iv

Mr. Jaffa has exhibited in his writings a dedication to the proper education of the rulers of an egalitarian community. (28-29, 52, 64-66, 110, 189) His writings also reflect the depreciation of liberty evident in the concern (to which we have referred) whether the people can still be trusted to use liberty responsibly. This concern is seen in what Mr. Jaffa says about the attitude to be taken toward Communism, not only abroad but also at home. It has been the issue of the proper treatment of domestic Communism which has served, since the Second World War, to put to the test Americans' dedication to the cause of liberty.[10]

Thus, Mr. Jaffa is moved to equate Communism with Nazism, to see no essential moral difference between these two movements.[11] But even in his descriptions of Nazism and Communism, he includes distinctions the significance of which he apparently fails to notice:

> Both embody creeds calling for the proscription of individuals and groups innocent of any crime. The Nazis believe that one

so-called race, the Aryan master race, is so superior to all others that it has the right to treat other men as if they were animals of another species. They will not hesitate to exterminate masses of human beings as if they were plague-bearing rats, or to use their skin as parchment, as if they were cattle. And Communists differ morally from Nazis only in proposing a so-called class, the proletariat, instead of a race, as the sole subject of moral right. . . . The Nazis proscribe every social strain beyond the pale of their elite; and the Communists do the same with every class which they do not associate with the dictatorship of the proletariat. An American Communist is one who, if he knows the meaning and accepts the discipline of the party, would use power arbitrarily to deprive his fellow citizens of *their* property and liberty and, *if they resisted,* their lives. [180-181; italics added]

An examination of Mr. Jaffa's imprudent identification of Nazism and Communism could well begin with a consideration of the words we have italicized: the Jews, for instance, were indiscriminately killed by the Nazis, whether or not "they resisted." The examination could then move to a consideration of what "*their* property" means, keeping in mind such venerable precedents as that recorded in *Acts* 5: 1–11. The next question could well be whether Stalin's "bestiality" is as intrinsic to "the meaning [of Communism]" as was Hitler's to the Nazis. (189)[12] Indeed, one may then conclude that it is neither fair nor useful to treat Nazism and Communism as essentially the same morally.

Mr. Jaffa identifies "the central political issue of our time [as] the world-wide conflict between Communist totalitarianism and political freedom." (169)[13] He approaches the domestic Communist with the same attitude with which he would have us confront international Communism, with the result that he would permit official restrictions at home upon the political activities of members of the Communist party.[14]

He, unlike many admirers of Lincoln and unlike most partisans of the cause of the North,[15] has understood and appreciated Lincoln's insistence on a sympathetic view of the Southern slave owner even as he opposed the evils of slavery. That which can be said on behalf of the defenders of slavery and of the South, with the recognition that justice and self-preservation contended with one another, is said and said well by Mr. Jaffa. (47-49, 97-98, 110-113, 136-137, 150-152, 162) We presume to suggest that his appraisal of current American politics and prob-

lems would be more realistic, and even more useful, if the same detachment, moderation, and charity as are displayed in his Civil War studies
were employed in an attempt to understand the Communist.[16]

It is well to remember, for instance, that R. H. Tawney could speak
of Karl Marx as "the last of the Schoolmen."[17]

V

The proper appraisal of American Communism can begin with the
question: Has *justice* been done to the Communist and, by extension,
to his political association, the Communist Party? Has he been accorded
the protection and respect to which we insist all Americans are entitled from the government?

What does the Communist think he wants? Most sympathetically
stated, he wants social justice: he wants the Kingdom of God on earth,
without either king or god. In this he is doomed to disappointment, even
according to his own view, for the regime he anticipates and longs for
cannot be perpetual: it must end someday, at least when (if not before)
the earth disintegrates or falls into the sun. But while this regime en-
dures, there will be seen the full development of man's potentialities, the
proper distribution of the goods of life, and the most extensive peaceful
relations among men.

Stated this way, the Communist's objective is not unattractive. Certainly, it is no more preposterous, no more objectionable, no more dangerous than the objectives of many Christians. We might not share this
objective or approve of the means the Communist may *believe* himself willing to employ to attain that objective, but there are no doubt
other beliefs of our fellow citizens of which we vigorously disapprove
as well.[18] Still, do we really know what we do not like about the goals
or methods of the Communist? Do we know enough to justify legal
repression? It is hard to believe that Americans know much more about
the Communist's goals than they do about their own.

It might be objected, however, that we do know the most important
thing about the Communist's goals—and this is that they are the same
as, indeed they are determined by, the goals of the rulers of the Soviet
Union or perhaps of China (but not of Yugoslavia?). Should not
Americans be reluctant to consider this kind of argument conclusive?
The Roman Catholic, for instance, certainly does not want to be bound
and judged, as an American citizen, by the actions or beliefs of the
most eminent Catholic leaders elsewhere, at least as those actions or be-

liefs are reported to and understood by his fellow citizens of other faiths. Even if he should want to be so judged—and even if the Communist should want this—the question would remain whether our institutions permit such vicarious judgment. Should we not respect (and even begin our assessments with) what is distinctively American about the American Communist as well as about the American Catholic?

Are we able, in making everyday judgments affecting our fellow citizens' careers and liberty and property, to assess properly the significance of what is happening from day to day or from year to year or even from decade to decade in the Vatican or in the Kremlin? Must we not, in simple self-defense as well as for the sake of simple justice, insist upon restricting ourselves in our relations with one another to what is happening before our eyes and in our midst? The broader judgments about, say, the Soviet Union, its power, its intentions, and its activities, seem to be dependent on extended study and are most relevant to a determination of how our foreign affairs should be conducted. Domestic affairs should be kept distinct if we are not to bring into the domestic arena the attitudes and practises of the international struggle. One must wonder whether law and justice are really possible among nations—and, if not, whether an extension of international conflict into our domestic relations forecloses the possibility of justice in that one sphere where it is sometimes to be found.

Such considerations seem to lead to the conclusion that members of the American Communist Party should be judged by the traditional standards appropriate to and feasible in this country. One can grant the possibility that other approaches might have to be used elsewhere in dealing not only with the Communist but also, depending on the circumstances, even with the democrat or the Roman Catholic or the Protestant. Freedom, it has been noticed, is not the product of every clime.

The traditional standards referred to are reflected in the proposition that guilt should be individual and that it should relate to particular carefully defined acts. Does it really help in legal proceedings to fall back on the presumption Mr. Jaffa employs, "if [the American Communist] knows the meaning and accepts the discipline of the party"? (181) Indeed, there may be as much variety among Communists as among Senator Goldwater's speech writers, however "monolithic" such "conspiracies" may seem to outsiders.

It is hard to see what the American Communists who have gone to jail since the Second World War have done to merit punishment. They have not been imprisoned for espionage or for sabotage or even for the illegal possession of arms. They have not been imprisoned for taking or giving bribes or for failure to pay income taxes. They have not been imprisoned for any acts of violence or for any threat of violence. If one relies upon the announcements made by our government about the number of federal undercover agents in the Communist Party, one must conclude that this is the most spied-upon body of men in the history of the Republic—and yet surprisingly little in the way of ordinary law-breaking has been revealed about them. Indeed, they seem remarkably, even exasperatingly, law-abiding.

On what ground then have the leaders of the American Communist Party been sent to jail? They have been jailed, it seems, primarily because it is thought they may use force to overthrow our form of government. We are told that they have organized to teach that such force will have to be resorted to some day. All this, it seems to be admitted, is only in the talking stage: there are no guns, no troops, no secret armies. But, we are further told, there is in the Communist the willingness to resort to force if the occasion should present itself.

Of course, the American Communist is not without an answer to such accusations, an answer based on an expectation. The force he sometimes speaks of, he will say, is the force that will likely be needed in this country to overcome the forceful resistance of the present ruling class to the peaceful and constitutional rise to power of the Communist. Is this expectation unreasonable? Has not the treatment of the few Communists among us in our time anticipated the violent (and perhaps unlawful but not necessarily improper) resistance that would be offered to the emergence here of the Communist Party as a real political power? Is it not as unreasonable and unfair to prosecute and imprison Communists in our country for acknowledging this expectation or opinion as it would be for Communists to imprison anyone who believes that the right of revolution might someday be legitimately exercised against even a Communist government?

Presumably, the devoted Communist, upon his emergence from prison, continues the thinking and resumes the associations he had formerly had. Does he thereby at once commit again the crime for which he was originally imprisoned? If so, why is he not put right back into prison—or, even better, never let out? In short, is this really like other crimes of which we know—and with which our judicial institutions are equipped to deal?[19] Rather, have we not taken into the courts the legitimate and sometimes necessary opposition to Communists and Communism that is more efficiently and properly conducted in the political forum?

Finally, in this consideration of the justice of what has been done to the American Communist, we should again ask ourselves: What *is* it the Communist wants? In part, of course, he wants what his counterparts in the Republican and Democratic parties want: a role in the political life of his country. But, it must be admitted, he is more apt than his respectable counterparts to be unselfishly dedicated to what he conceives to be the general welfare. It is obvious that the Communist cannot be drawn to *his* position by the immediate prospect of public acclaim, or of lucrative contracts and appointments, or of political power. Rather, he must be prepared to be villified, to be deprived of employment and income, and even to be imprisoned—and all this in a country where there is every opportunity and encouragement, financial as well as moral, to abandon a despised cause.

We could do with such dedication among Americans generally, a dedication to what men think to be in the public interest and for the good of humanity.[20] Certainly there is something unjust about applying criminal sanctions in these circumstances.[21]

vi

But there is injustice all around us, much of it (from the very nature of things) that we have to ignore or learn to live with. Why should special attention be directed to this injustice? That is, what can be said about all this from the perspective of Americans who are dedicated to *the common good?*

It is not the least of the objections to the persecution of Communists among us since the Second World War that this campaign cannot really interfere significantly with the genuine threats posed by activities that every community is obliged to provide against, activities such as sabotage, espionage, and violence. There must be Russian spies in this country, just as there are American spies abroad. It is unlikely that the persecution of political opposition either here or abroad will curtail this form of cultural exchange. (Indeed, completely effective suppression of espionage today may even be dangerous if it should put powerful antagonists out of touch with [and hence make them more fearful of or careless about] each other.)

However unlikely it is that our campaign against the Communist Party has interfered with potential saboteurs or spies, it is certain that such campaigns *have* interfered with that which we should be most reluctant to interfere with, the essentially political activities of the Communist Party. This interference has had harmful political effects. Not only have we established precedents that may someday undermine our political liberties even more than they have been undermined already, but we have been deprived of the open partisan presentation among us of the Communist position.

The Communist, however crude he may be, has a significant view to offer us of the nature of modern industrial society and its problems.[22] What does he have? what makes for the appeal of his doctrine? is it correct? have we anything to learn from the Communist and Communism? what can the Communist learn from us? Our tendency has been to reduce the Communist position, both at home and abroad, to the simplest level, to substitute propaganda exchanges for discussion and to make it difficult, if not impossible, for the partisan of Communism to engage in public debate. For a community such as ours, which stands or falls on the possibility and usefulness of discussion of vital public issues, this is a dangerous state of affairs.[23]

The refusal to take seriously a major political argument has additional drawbacks. Not only does it reflect a loss of self-confidence, but the measures we have employed seem, in turn, to have made for even less self-confidence. In addition, the influence we have on others abroad suffers as a result: our material prosperity will long inspire both emulation and hatred; it is as the apostles of reasonable liberty that we must really stand or fall in the estimation of mankind.

But our "image" abroad should be the least of our concerns. Much more critical is the effect of the domestic campaigns against Communists on the tone of the public life of our country. The emphasis on "the Communist menace," which we have seen from time to time, leads to measures such as test oaths and loyalty programs intended to consolidate and extend the "gains" of prosecutions. Some citizens, non-Communists as well as Communists, will resent such measures; a few, quixotic or otherwise, will even refuse to conform to such demands. And, as the inevitable controversies proceed or the campaigns become more intense, definitions become less and less precise, with the result that anything controversial may become "Communist." Thus, a kind of war among ourselves develops and pushes out of the public forum searching inquiry into fundamental issues.

Much has been made of the domestic Communist menace in justifying the actions taken against American Communists. But we are sometimes warned by government officials that we cannot, even today, relax our vigilance over the Communist Party: for although that organization is reduced to a seemingly insignificant number, the members are now all "hardcore"; consequently, the Communist Party is more dangerous than ever before. This is a curious result of our campaigns of the last twenty years. If our prosecutions of the Communists have done this, if the deprivation of the privileges and respect that other associations are entitled to from the government has led to an increased threat to the country, there remains a simple remedy that the reader may be left to work out for himself.

Another curious result of the campaign against the domestic Communist menace is reflected in the emergence of the John Birch Society. Of course, there have always been fanatics of the right and left among us. No doubt there always will be. But there is something special here: the members of this society are not simply fanatics. Many seem to be respected and respectable, if somewhat disturbed men and women in their communities. They, like the Communists, are probably moved by a sincere desire to serve the public interest.[24] It is obvious to *them* that the measures taken against the Communists, however much these measures might constitute a departure from American tradition, simply have not been severe enough in proportion to the alleged threat. Compare, for instance, what would have happened in Nazi Germany or Communist Russia to the known leaders of a subversive organization dedicated to sabotage, espionage, and violence. The government has made much of the threat—and yet that threat is said, by officers of that very government, to remain as serious as ever. For some reason, the measures taken against Communists have not been severe enough. Does this not reveal the real power of the Communists? Does this not suggest that they continue to occupy high places in the government from which they are able to prevent the effective application of the measures really needed to make America safe for Americans?

The political implications of such fear and frustration can be serious. If matters become critical—either because of economic or racial disturbances at home or because of a widespread resort to arms abroad—such fear and frustrations will have even more impact upon our institutions and way of life than they have had already. Well-meaning and intelligent people are worried, and their anxieties and ignorance can be exploited. It is the duty of responsible men, both in government and

out, to correct misconceptions about the significance of the Communist Party in the United States and thereby help assure the calmness
and confidence free men are entitled to and need to derive from their
institutions.

vii

Mr. Jaffa provides us a thoughtful discussion of these institutions. His
thoughtfulness is a reflection of his capacity to look beyond the transitory political problems confronting citizens to the fundamental questions
that engage the human being. Thus he delves for the sources of Western thought in Greece and the Holy Land:

> The question (or any of the variants of the question), "What is
> human nature?" by its very form identifies the universal in man
> with the rational faculty and identifies the rational faculty with
> that which somehow perceives the universal. Yet the assumption
> upon which this question rests—in virtue of which all theory ancient
> or modern is legitimated—is not itself abstracted from experience
> in the way in which the answers to it may be. On the contrary, it
> seems to have been a unique experience, occurring in a particular
> culture [that of Greece], and one that has become general only
> by diffusion; that is, not by a repetition of the original experience but
> by its recollection. When we think how radically our understand-
> ing of human nature has been conditioned by our tradition and by
> the authoritative character of this question as an element of our
> tradition, the very idea of political theory must appear paradoxical,
> if not self-contradictory. A unique experience presents itself as
> inherently universal and becomes believable as such by becoming
> authoritative. This difficulty is the more acute for us, it seems to
> me, because there is another major element within the Western
> tradition—namely, the Bible—in which the identification of the
> universal with the particular is openly maintained and maintained
> in a manner that is not exposed to the objections [that may be]
> raised to the Socratic questions. . . .
>
> [T]he Bible, by insisting that the dependence of man upon God
> is radical, denies in effect that the divine nature—the heart of the
> mystery of human life—is knowable. Man's salvation is not, in
> principle, accessible to him by reason. The principle of the uni-
> verse, *the* universe *par excellence,* as it becomes accessible to man
> and therewith his guiding knowledge, is the activity of the living

Lord of the Universe. His actions are not vouchsafed to such as that offspring of wonder and of pride—Socrates. For Socrates, even in the consciousness of his ignorance, discerned the grounds of his superiority to every other man who lived. But Abraham, in his impotence (rather than ignorance), discerned the grounds of reverent submissiveness to a power higher than himself. Socrates' pride discerned within himself the grounds whereby an autonomous or sufficient human life might be lived. Abraham's humility made him a worthy vessel for the disclosure by the Almighty of the means by which helpless humanity might, like sheep, receive the all-encompassing protection of an eternal shepherd. [225, 228][25]

Is it not useful to see in Abraham and Jesus vital sources of our equality, and in Pericles and Socrates our liberty?[26]

VI. Law and Morality

The Kirk an' State may join, an' tell
To do sic things I maunna:
The Kirk an' State may gae to hell,
And I'll gae to my Anna.

Robert Burns, *Anna*

i

The State, Edmund Burke observed, is a partnership in every virtue.[1] Law depends on a sense of morality among citizens: the law, in turn, promotes morality. This is a commonsense notion with which many citizens would agree.

Yet it is often said that we cannot legislate morality. Is not the truth rather that most of the moral code of any people has depended upon legislation—that it is difficult to establish or maintain a pervasive morality without the aid of legislation? Our concern on this occasion, however, is not with that question.[2] Instead, assuming that we know morality can be legislated and enforced, we ask whether it should be.

It is fashionable today to answer this question in the negative. The immediate intellectual source of this negative answer may be found in John Stuart Mill's assertion of

> one very simple principle, as entitled to govern absolutely the dealings of society with the individual in the way of compulsion and control, whether the means used be physical force in the form of legal penalties, or the moral coercion of public opinion. That principle is, that the sole end for which mankind are warranted, individually or collectively, in interfering with the liberty of action of any of their number, is self-protection. That the only purpose for which power can be rightfully exercised over any member of a civilised community, against his will, is to prevent harm to others. His own good, either physical or moral, is not a sufficient warrant. He cannot rightfully be compelled to do or forbear be-

---

This review was published (with the title, "Law and Morality: On Lord Devlin, Plato's *Meno*, and Jacob Klein") in 1967 *Wisconsin Law Review* 231 (Winter 1967).

The books discussed here are Patrick Devlin, *The Enforcement of Morals* (London: Oxford University Press, 1965); Jacob Klein, *A Commentary on Plato's Meno* (Chapel Hill: North Carolina Press, 1965).

cause it will be better for him to do so, because it will make him happier, because, in the opinion of others, to do so would be wise, or even right.[3]

Thus, only that law is justified which protects the community and its members from attacks and impositions by others.[4] "[T]here must remain a realm of private morality and immorality which is, in brief and in crude terms, not the law's business."[5]

The problem raised here is, in part, that of determining what the proper attitude should be toward the satisfaction of any desires one may have, thereby raising the question of the proper relation of right, or pleasure, to duty. Or, put in other terms, it is the problem of the attractions of liberty placed in juxtaposition to the demands of order.[6] The currently fashionable intellectual position on this problem draws on a heritage much more venerable than that provided by Mill, a complex heritage we are reminded of by the works of Hobbes (whose way was prepared by Machiavelli and Bacon and whose teaching was domesticated by Locke) and of Milton.

It is in Hobbes that one finds an account of the self-preservation of citizens that justifies social restraint upon natural liberty. It is he also who has taught that in civil government it is "the law civil that determineth what is honest and dishonest, what is just and unjust, and generally what is good and evil." And it is in Milton that one finds a basis for the right of a man to govern his private affairs and thereby minister to his salvation (truly preserving himself?) in his own way:

I warn'd thee, I admonish'd thee, foretold
The danger, and the lurking Enemie
That lay in wait; beyond this had bin force,
And force upon free Will hath here no place.

We confront in Anglo-American thought a curious and sometimes uneasy alliance of these attitudes.[7]

ii

There are presented in Lord Devlin's lectures the opinions and arguments of a sober man of affairs who insists upon the intimate relation between law and morality.[8] The lectures in his book are described by him as stemming from

the Maccabaean Lecture and discuss[ing] different aspects of the relationship between law and morals that are suggested by it. The Maccabaean Lecture discussed the relationship between the moral law and the criminal law but was confined to those sorts of crime that can also be called sins. The second, third, and fourth lectures consider the moral law in relation to other branches of English law—the quasi-criminal law, the law of torts, the law of contract and of marriage. . . . The fifth lecture discusses the difficult question of how to determine for the purposes of the secular law what the moral law is. The sixth examines once again Mill's teaching, which, although as a whole it has never been adopted, is still the mainspring of liberal thought on this subject. The seventh, which is perhaps of interest only to controversialists, inquires what sort of doctrine, if any, is likely to replace Mill's.

The two themes in the lectures that have attracted most criticism are, firstly, the denial that there is a private realm of morality into which the law cannot enter; and secondly, the assertion that the morality which the law enforces must be popular morality.[9]

At the conclusion of the opening lecture Lord Devlin summarizes his argument:

> Society cannot live without morals. Its morals are those standards of conduct which the reasonable man approves. A rational man, who is also a good man, may have other standards. If he has no standards at all he is not a good man and need not be further considered. If he has standards, they may be very different; he may, for example, not disapprove of homosexuality or abortion. In that case he will not share in the common morality; but that should not make him deny that it is a social necessity. A rebel may be rational in thinking that he is right but he is irrational if he thinks that society can leave him free to rebel.
>
> A man who concedes that morality is necessary to society must support the use of those instruments without which morality cannot be maintained. The two instruments are those of teaching, which is doctrine, and of enforcement, which is the law. If morals could be taught simply on the basis that they are necessary to society, there would be no social need for religion; it could be left as a purely personal affair. But morality cannot be taught in that way. Loyalty is not taught in that way either. No society has yet solved the problem of how to teach morality without religion. So the law must base itself on Christian morals and to the limit

of its ability enforce them, not simply because they are the morals of most of us, nor simply because they are the morals which are taught by the established Church—on these points the law recognizes the right to dissent—but for the compelling reason that without the help of Christian teaching the law will fail.[10]

Can there be the division between private and public concerns that utilitarians assume exists? Do not the two concerns depend on one another? It should be recognized, Lord Devlin argues:

> What makes a society of any sort is community of ideas, not only political ideas but also ideas about the way its members should behave and govern their lives; these latter ideas are its morals. . . . For society is not something that is kept together physically; it is held by the invisible bonds of common thought. If the bonds were too far relaxed the members would drift apart. A common morality is part of the bondage. The bondage is part of the price of society; and mankind, which needs society, must pay its price.[11]

Thus, a "nation of debauchees would not in 1940 have responded satisfactorily to Winston Churchill's call to blood and toil and sweat and tears."[12]

"No one suggests," Lord Devlin concedes,

> that all private immorality should be punished by the law as a matter of course. You can grant that private morality is within the competence of the legislature in a free society and still advance many powerful arguments why the law should not try to punish particular vices in particular circumstances.[13]

The emphasis of Lord Devlin's position is on making sense of the law as it is—which is pretty much as most people, including his critics, want it to be. To make sense of the law, he suggests, it must be seen as dependent on and as enforcing morality, even when such morality seems primarily of a private nature. An effort can be made to rationalize in terms of social utility—a social utility that is not explicitly concerned with private affairs and private morality—practically everything any reasonable man should wish to see restrained by law. But is it not artificial and unrealistic to do so? English law did not, in fact, originate as the utilitarians think it did.[14] If one is to understand the law as its servants and the public have understood it for centuries, one must see it as drawing on an accepted body of moral principles of a private as well as of a public character and as dedicated to the reinforcement of those principles.

Is not the educational system sanctioned by the law of a community— both the formal aspect found in schools and the informal aspect reflected in customs and public opinion—designed, in part, to shape private morality? Should not youngsters continue thus to be taught by the community the right and wrong way to act in private as well as in public? Whatever the intention might be, does not an educational system (itself guided by law) in fact shape private morality?[15] The student is instructed in public morality, some may argue, and the law should enforce that and that alone. But surely the student is not told that he need not practice that morality in private as well. Rather, he is more likely to be instructed that he should apply to public affairs the morality he relies upon for private affairs. Usually, he will have no occasion to distinguish between the two: the citizen, unless incited to do so by the intellectual, makes no such distinction.[16]

To regard moral character as not a public concern seems, at best, unrealistic. Again and again we must as citizens rely upon the integrity of an individual in circumstances where what he does without possibility of supervision affects vitally both the public and the private interests of his fellow citizens. This fact is reflected in the public insistence upon testing the moral character of candidates for admission even to the private practice of medicine or law. If the community is entitled to examine one for such qualities—however perfunctorily it may act in most such examinations and however unintelligently it may act in others —is it not obliged to develop the characteristics for which it tests? Indeed, is not the very testing a way, indirectly, of developing and enforcing morality?

How the community may best achieve its objective with respect to private morality depends on prudential judgment. It may even decide to leave much of the task in particular circumstances to institutions not directly or immediately controlled by the community, recognizing that "the more we accomplish by opinion, the less we will have to do by law."[17]

iii

The merits of Lord Devlin's argument testify to the common sense of an experienced judiciary.[18] The limitations of that argument, on the other hand, are reflected in what he says about the determination of that morality he believes the law should enforce.

We have, Lord Devlin assumes, inherited democratic governments as the ultimate source of legitimacy.[19] It is to public opinion, therefore, that he considers us obliged to look for the morality he is prepared to have the law enforce. There is for us as democrats "no other tribunal."[20] Educated men can try to shape such popular morality: but public opinion is seen by him as decisive. Thus, Lord Devlin speaks only of the "advantage" of educated men in any contest to shape morality; he evidently does not consider them truly superior.[21] Nor does he seem to appreciate that to rely ultimately on public opinion, or for that matter on "history," is to rely, essentially, on chance.[22]

If one is not prepared to regard one view of morality as better than another, independent of what the public may happen to believe at any moment, why should one try to have any particular view of morality enforced or reinforced by law? Will not the community always have *some* moral code, some body of practices and "values," which it calls its own? Why should one be concerned with whether any particular body of values is protected? It can only be in order to promote one value—stability or moderate change. But whether that which has been inherited, including a desire for stability, should be preserved must depend on a judgment whether it is good—and that moves one beyond history and public opinion, however important these may be in determining the limits of what can be attempted and preserved at any particular moment.[23]

We find Lord Devlin emphasizing the passions, however, not judgment (and hence not reason), as decisive in social action:

> No society can do without intolerance, indignation, and disgust; they are the forces behind the moral law, and indeed it can be argued that if they or something like them are not present, the feelings of society cannot be weighty enough to deprive the individual of freedom of choice.[24]

May not what excites disgust and indignation in a community be also essentially a matter of chance?[25]

Disparagement of the role of reason in the determination of ends in human affairs is reflected as well in what Lord Devlin has to say about the right of revolution:

> Society cannot tolerate rebellion; it will not allow argument about the rightness of the cause. Historians a century later may say that

the rebels were right and the Government was wrong and a percipient and conscientious subject of the State may think so at the time. But it is not a matter which can be left to individual judgment.[26]

Compare this, however, with the Declaration of Independence's constitutional invocation of the old-fashioned proposition that there are standards outside and above the agreements and teachings of men and government—standards superior even to what "the people" might at any moment believe or choose. That is, the right of revolution implies reliance upon the supremacy of reason in the affairs of men.[27]

iv

Lord Devlin is aware of something valuable in the c ....non morality that it is necessary to protect, in a prudent manner, by law. But his ultimate reliance on public opinion rather than on reason concedes to his critics more than he realizes. His difficulty may be traced back to his insistence that the Anglo-American moral code in which he happens to believe is based on Christianity, and Christianity alone.

Much of what is in our moral code has indeed come to us through Christianity, but Christianity is not the originator.[28] Most of that code antedates Christianity or stands independently of it, however useful that religion (or some religion) may have been in establishing or preserving it.[29] To say that Christianity alone has thus far "ma[d]e a philosophy" for "the western world" is to overlook Greece and Rome.[30] To regard such institutions as monogamy as distinctively Christian, even in England, is surely mistaken.[31] To argue that there is no absolute authority outside of divine law with respect to right and wrong is to suggest that God does not reason.[32] On what are divine decrees supposed to be based, if not on an assessment of what is good and what is good for man? May not the believer, therefore, regard the ordinances of God as essentially reasonable?[33] Satan is rebuked by an angel loyal to God:

> Unjustly thou deprav'st it with the name
> Of *Servitude* to serve whom God ordains,
> Or Nature; God and Nature bid the same,
> When he who rules is worthiest, and excells
> Them whom he governs. This is servitude,
> To serve th' unwise, or him who hath rebell'd

Against his worthier, as thine now serve thee,
Thy self not free, but to thy self enthrall'd;
Yet leudly dar'st our ministring upbraid.[34]

If "God and Nature bid the same," reason can anticipate or endorse a
moral code supported by religious teachings. This means that we can,
whether or not we rely on divine instruction, usefully reason about the
nature of man and about the best life for him.[35] To aid us in this inquiry
it is only prudent to look to what the best minds have thought about
such matters. It is significant that the classical writers are hardly referred to by Lord Devlin: yet they have shown that he stands, in his
commonsense awareness of the relation of law to morality (as distinguished from his opinions about the ultimate sources of morality), on
a firmer foundation than he knows.

When Lord Devlin does refer to the classics, he misuses them:

> The State may claim on two grounds to legislate on matters of
> morals. The Platonic ideal is that the State exists to promote vir-
> tue among its citizens. If that is its function, then whatever
> power is sovereign in the State—an autocrat, if there be one, or in
> a democracy the majority—must have the right and duty to declare
> what standards of morality are to be observed as virtuous and must
> ascertain them as it thinks best. This is not acceptable to Anglo-
> American thought. It invests the State with power of determina-
> tion between good and evil, destroys freedom of conscience and
> is the paved road to tyranny. . . .[36]

The democratic majority referred to here is the very authority he
sees elsewhere in his lectures as sovereign with respect to private as well
as public morality among us. The problem with "Anglo-American
thought," as Lord Devlin interprets it, is that thinking is not an essential part of it. The "Platonic ideal," if it means anything, stands for the
role of reason, and of an understanding of the nature of man, in judgments about human affairs.

Lord Devlin endorses "the alternative ground" on which "the State
may claim . . . to legislate on matters of morals": "society may legislate to preserve itself."[37] What is lost sight of here is the cultivation of
the human being as the ultimate concern of even political life: in
effect, the State, or society, becomes for Lord Devlin the principal
concern. The natural right of self-preservation which Hobbes had seen
as fundamental only for man is attributed to the State as well.

It is revealing that Lord Devlin should follow his disparagement of "the Platonic ideal" with an endorsement of Justice Frankfurter's flag-salute language about the need for "the binding tie of cohesive sentiment." Was not that display of professional (not personal) callousness toward the sensibilities of those children, in the name of "the ultimate foundation of a free society," much more oppressive (in its pettiness) than anything found in the precepts associated with Plato?[38] To deny the superiority of reason and judgment in the affairs of men is indeed to make oneself the unwitting tool of tyranny.[39]

In his failure to study with the necessary care the best thought available to him, Lord Devlin shares the disability of the legal profession generally. Lawyers and judges, and even professors of law, find it difficult to explain what they do (and often do so sensibly), because there are serious flaws in their education. They have cut themselves off from the best minds and therefore must stand alone.

In trying to do too much, they do not do what they can.

v

It is partly because the art of reading great books has been lost that practical men of affairs, as well as modern intellectuals, no longer devote to such books the necessary care. They may sense that there is in them something exceptional but conclude that such old books depend too much on their own time to be truly relevant today.[40]

The man who reminds us of the lost art of reading with great care that which deserves so to be read is our benefactor. Professor Jacob Klein in his commentary on Plato's *Meno* does just that. One may even venture to predict that Mr. Klein's book is one of only a score of books of our time that will be studied by serious men centuries from now. Many other books may be useful for historians reconstructing current opinions, but this one stands independent of its time, at least in its subject matter and intention.[41]

Plato virtually begins in the *Meno* where Lord Devlin prematurely stops. The problem is that of virtue, what it is and how it is established. Only when the question—what is virtue?—is properly dealt with, may one truly know what one is saying when discussing the relation of law to morality. There is provided on the dust jacket of the book a description of it in which Mr. Klein's hand can be seen:

> In addition to Socrates, there are two heroes in the drama, a young Thessalian, Meno, who, as we know from other sources,

played a significant role in the rebellion of Cyrus against his brother Artaxerxes II of Persia, and the Athenian Anytus, a well-known politician who was one of the accusers in the trial of Socrates. Although the roles they played in "history" are supposed to be familiar to any reader of the dialogue, the roles they play in the dialogue are prescribed by nothing but the drama the dialogue itself presents. All three, Socrates, Meno, and Anytus, reveal themselves, in word and deed, as what they are—Socrates as the embodiment of *arete*, of human excellence, Meno as a man incapable of learning, and Anytus as the expression of an Athens that has lost its soul. Both Meno and Anytus are victims of their memories. The theme of memory, as opposed to recollection, is dominant in both parts of the dialogue. In the first, Meno personifies *amathia*, the state of ignorance, that is, the lack of learning; the second part presents—through Anytus—the sway of *doxa*, of opinion, as opposed to knowledge. A "digression" interrupts the running commentary of the *Meno* and explores the meaning of recollection in other Platonic dialogues. This helps the reader to grasp the full significance of the "exhibition" of recollection performed by Socrates on a young slave.

Mr. Klein proceeds step by step through each section of the dialogue. Throughout the book he stresses the dramatic quality of the *Meno* and other Platonic dialogues. The intent is to imitate oral instruction—each statement follows from the preceding one and leads to the one after—and to bring the reader into active participation in the dialogue. The author "expounds" the text, summarizes, explains, interprets all at the same time.

It is appropriate to emphasize here, as corrective of Lord Devlin's retreat from reason, that the question of virtue leads Socrates and Meno to the question of learning. Enduring virtue, it seems to be suggested, depends on knowledge: yet Meno is induced to wonder whether anything can be learned.[42] The geometrical demonstration with the slave boy is then advanced to assure Meno and us of the possibility of rebirth and of recollection—and hence of what we call "learning."[43]

There seems to be something innate in the boy, something that not only permits him to be prompted by Socrates—a dog or a horse could not be prompted in this way—but something that also enables him to judge between alternatives and to recognize now and then a difficulty and even an impasse. What is it that makes all this possible if it is not something eternally present in the rational animal, something so innate in human nature as to be of the quality that Socrates attributes to the much-born soul for which recollection (or, as we say, learning) is possible?

vi

A book of the calibre that Mr. Klein has endowed us with should not be reviewed but rather announced. Whoever is fortunate enough to know of it has both the duty and the pleasure of calling it to the attention of others who might benefit from it. The reservations expressed in such a brief notice as this are much more likely to reflect the assessor's limitations than those of the book, but they may nevertheless be useful for the legal reader who is induced by what is said here to turn to the book.[44]

The reader's interest in the dialogue is heightened by the dubious character of Meno. Mr. Klein is known for the provocative suggestion to a class at St. John's College that Meno asking Socrates how virtue comes to men is like Al Capone asking Gandhi whether a citizen should pay his taxes. A reviewer has noted that Mr. Klein "places considerable emphasis on the character of the 'historical' Meno and does not seem to consider seriously the possibility that Meno's responses to Socrates *show* that he is learning something about the nature of *arete*."[45] Indeed, one must wonder whether Mr. Klein's considerable scholarship sometimes gets in the way of a direct confrontation with the text and especially with the character of Meno.[46]

A commentary such as Mr. Klein's (as well as this notice) presupposes a "first reading" of the *Meno*—that is, the kind of reading that leaves one with an accurate summary of the "action" and of the ostensible teaching of the dialogue concerning virtue and its divine allotment. That summary is a necessary prelude and one which might well have been provided by Mr. Klein himself, if only because the ostensible teaching of this dialogue is evidently intended by Plato to suffice for most of his readers. It is this teaching that the acquisitive Meno leaves with at the end. It is this teaching that Meno is asked by Socrates to share with an indignant Anytus. But, it may be said, this teaching is precisely what the ordinary reader of the dialogue can be counted on to get for himself. Even so, why this should be the ostensible teaching remains a problem.

Mr. Klein's commentary can be considered a "second reading," a reading that takes every sentence of the dialogue seriously, that develops the thought of each passage as it bears on what is to come (for this the first reading is necessary) as well as on what has gone before. When one in this fashion reaches the end of a great work one is then equipped to go on—that is, on to the beginning. Mr. Klein does not go on to that "third reading": he points ahead to it and gives us hints of it, but he does not consider it necessary for his purpose to do more than that.[47]

I venture to suggest that there is more said in Mr. Klein's commentary about the personal and less about the political and even the moral dimensions and implications of the dialogue than one should expect.[48] Perhaps Mr. Klein would reply that he deliberately implies more and says less explicitly about political matters as his commentary on the dialogue progresses, thereby both empowering and liberating the reader to think for himself. Perhaps, also, he would regard as sufficient for his purpose such statements of the political problem as this:

> A human community, and especially a political community, has to protect its members in one way or another; it has, at least, to provide the minimal conditions under which the immediate needs of its members can be met. But it must also provide the conditions under which it itself may be preserved. It cannot dispense with institutions, customs, traditions. Whatever changes it may undergo, whatever "innovations" it may originate or accept, it lives by memories. Cities with their sanctuaries, public buildings, monuments, memorials, burial grounds, harbor memories of all kinds. Those of us who share, to whatever degree, in the community's memories are "at home" in it; those who do not, are "strangers" regardless of their legal status. One might well live in a city unaware of the intangible links between its present and its past and thus be merely its guest. On the other hand, the sharing of the community's memories may be quite "superficial," a habitual reliance on a shadowy past. This, in fact, is what happens to be the case more often than not.[49]

In any event we confront with Mr. Klein what he suggests is, for Socrates, "the ultimate political problem":

> [I]t can well be denied that the presence or absence of "teachers" of excellence decides the question of whether excellence is or is not teachable. But in the absence of genuine teaching—and learning—

of excellence the *polis* is bound to shrink: the mingled and mangled *mnemeia* [memories] of the *polis* will become its ghostly heroes.

To rely on "institutions, customs, traditions"—on the memories that happen to have been handed down from founders who may have known what *they* were doing—cannot suffice. Nor can mere hero worship. The community, if it is not to shrink spiritually, must have somewhere in it men who know what they are doing. Public opinion, however powerful it may appear to the democrat, is in its mindlessness and consequent changeableness much weaker than it seems.[50]

vii

Socrates leaves with Meno the salutary public teaching that virtue emanates from the divine. This teaching, which is reflected in Lord Devlin's opinions, recognizes the nature and hence the limitations of many men (including Meno) and of the community.[51] But recourse to authority—whether to the gods, or to precedent, or to constitutional rhetoric—can be trusted only if it is guided by reason somewhere in the community, by a reason that recognizes its own disabilities in directly confronting and shaping public opinion.

The legal reader touches upon the inquiry undertaken in the *Meno* whenever he speculates about the problems of education and of juvenile delinquency, about the causes of crime and of law-abidingness, about the uses and purposes of the law. But most of what he reads in current legal literature, to say nothing of the popular press, can do little more than suggest questions. He needs to be reminded of books in which there is the most serious discussion of these matters and he needs to be taught how to read such books.

On exhibition in Mr. Klein's commentary is his reliance on a principle of interpretation which lawyers should appreciate:

All depends not only on what, but on how, under what circumstances, where, and in what context something is being said.[52]

VII. In Search of
the Soulless "Self"

> It is hard to fight desire; what it wants it buys with
> the soul.
>
> Heraclitus, Fr. 85

i

I have been asked to consider what ought to be done with our knowledge of human behavior and with our ability to modify it. There is a short and simple prescription of what we ought to do about that "social control of human behavior" of which we hear so much today: we ought to think about it. That is, we ought to try to understand what it all means, especially the brain research (some of it startlingly fascinating) we have heard described for us here at Bethesda.

In order to begin to think about all this, we need to notice the questions apt to be overlooked, the questions critical for any proper exploration of the "ethical and social problems" with which research in "neuro- and psycho-biology" confronts us.

Consider, first of all, the questions that are perhaps avoided by the very use of the terms we have heard so much of here, terms that are included in our agenda and that do reflect the opinion of the day: "knowledge of human behavior"; "our ability to modify human behavior"; "the social control of human behavior."

What are the implications of the use today of that popular phrase, "human behavior"? It is in appearance more scientific, more "objective," more antiseptic, than would be, say, "the human being," to say nothing of "the human soul." Is not "human behavior" more artificial than the others, an attempt to isolate in the whole man a part of what men are or of what men do? Is its use something like what the surgeon feels he has to do in concealing from view everything but the very part of the body in which the incision is to be made? The term "human behavior" may be, I presume to suggest, indicative of an attitude toward human beings from which humanity and humaneness can very easily be abstracted.

This talk was prepared for a symposium, "Research in Neuro- and Psycho-Biology: Prospects and Social Implications," National Institutes of Health, Bethesda, Maryland, October 17, 1969.

The symposium panel included Hans Jonas, Gardner Quarton, and B. F. Skinner.

"Knowledge of human behavior" is made much of today. What do we mean by "knowledge"? Is *knowledge* of the transitory things that are the objects of current scientific research indeed possible? Or, more precisely, is knowledge of these things possible through the use of modern science? This may well be the most serious question we could examine, the question of whether modern science is capable of knowing anything, of knowing anything significant—but it is a question that transcends the purpose of this symposium. We are not equipped to examine it on this occasion. But I do venture the suggestion that this may underlie your concerns and our inquiries. This is related, I further suggest, to the question of the nature of the human soul and of its full development, to which I will return.

We have also heard "social control of human behavior" and "our ability to modify human behavior" spoken of in the course of this symposium. Does not "ability to modify," as used here, mean only "power to change" things? It would be difficult to deny that some men have power to induce changes in how other men act. Is this power "social"? Does society really "control" anything? Can it be said, that is, that the community (or, for that matter, anyone) governs what happens? Or is not chance decisive in what occurs with respect to these matters?

Notice how the question of what it means to know reasserts itself here: if there is to be any genuine *control*—by a man or by a community—there must be *knowledge* of what is being done, knowledge joined with effective authority. My suspicion is that the nature of our modern scientific enterprise is such that there is no longer any human "control," in the serious sense of that word, and that that probably cannot be altered in the foreseeable future. Indeed, modern science may have succeeded in putting permanently beyond our control the most important things we do. Thus, rather than having permitted us to "conquer nature," science may have subjected us in an unprecedented way to the vagaries of chance, including such chance events as who discovers what and who manages to persuade others to try it.

So much, then, for the moment at least, for the terms we happen upon in addressing the questions that are apt to be overlooked in considering "what ought to be done with our knowledge of human behavior and with our ability to modify it."

ii

What can I say about particular cases, specifically (in the words of our agenda) about those relating to "ideas and techniques in neuro- and psycho-biology, present and future"? Very little! I really know very little—even in the ordinary sense of "know"—about what you and your colleagues have been doing or about what you are likely to do hereafter. Certainly, I do not know enough to address myself intelligently and hence responsibly to specific cases and problems. But perhaps I can be of some use to you if I suggest what the more serious questions are for you to consider, for you to consider *whether* to consider—questions that may have been prematurely disposed of, or in many instances simply ignored or even avoided, in the development of modern science and the application of that science to human affairs.

One hears concern expressed about the implications of new techniques, of new discoveries. Perhaps there are *new* dangers awaiting us. But I must wonder if the most serious dangers have not already overtaken us and even settled down among us. That is to say, the fundamental questions relating to "the social control of human behavior" may be certain enduring questions that will continue to be inadequately dealt with, not new questions confronting us for the first time in our day. Our concern should be with what these perennial questions are, with why we do not regard them as genuine questions, and with what our "answers" to these questions have been thus far (insofar as we have tried to answer them) in our practical applications of scientific discoveries.

The perennial questions that have been improperly dealt with—that is, either ignored or disposed of prematurely or inadvertently—can be conveniently reduced for our immediate purposes to three:

(1) What is a good man?
(2) How does a good man come to be?
(3) What kind of man is likely to develop as a result of our present opinions and approach?

Similar, and related, questions may be asked about the good community and about the best possible community.

How have we dealt with these questions?

iii

I begin with the third question: What kind of man is likely to be produced by what we now believe and do? We tend to avoid this question by asserting that our intention is to leave each man *free* to become what he will. We do not realize that the most likely effect of this approach is to transform our precious *freedom* into mere *chance*, into whatever *happens* to move us. We depend on the "self" to "choose," without regard to what makes the *self* what it is.

The self that is liberated in this way is apt to be moved by the lowest and most common passions, those passions concerned with self-preservation and with the satisfaction of immediate bodily needs—and our scientific apparatus is apt to be recruited primarily in the service of the body, with "survival" being, of course, the great objective.[1] Indeed, it can be said that such notions as these of the *self* and *freedom* mean that man's last act of freedom has been to surrender his freedom and to give himself over to his passions.

Our second neglected question, "How does a good man come to be?" is obviously related intimately to the one we have just glanced at. This means that we ignore the things that make us what we are, that have perhaps already shaped us to be what we will be as long as our present technological competence survives. I suggest as an example the implications of contemporary television. The most troublesome problems relating to television probably have little to do with the calibre and intentions of the men in charge of the facilities but rather are intrinsic to the medium itself. One of its problems may be noticed in this auditorium today. It is even more difficult for me to know you than it is for you to know me—and thus it is virtually impossible for the most instructive conversation to take place among us, especially since we cannot proceed by question and answer. Television makes this even worse: conversation becomes impossible, and consequently so does serious learning, and yet the illusion of learning is created.

Notice also that the critical defects of television are beyond the ability of most families to avoid or to correct. Your children *will* watch it, either in your home or in the homes of friends—and additional problems are created by your efforts as parents (whether or not successful) to deny them what is generally available to others. This should remind us that the social dimension of the effort to produce a good man, of the effort to bring to perfection that which nature provides, is vital. We cannot depend only on particular families or particular individuals to produce good men. I add as my opinion that television has been, for us, a net loss—and that the only sensible remedy would be to abolish it completely. But I recognize that its enticements are overwhelming and that the sensible remedy of abolition is politically impossible, even though it may be instructive to consider total abolition—if only to guide our policies with respect to the regulation of the television (with its inevitable but spurious sense of intimacy) we are now saddled with.[2]

One is faced with similar impossibilities in any attempt to deal intelligently with other instances of scientific or technological "progress." I even dare to suggest that the anticipated "gains" in the conquest of disease and perhaps of death itself may seriously affect (for the worse) the quality of human life, of that highest life which not all men can have but in which all in a good community can in some sense participate. It will be virtually impossible, as long as the means are readily available by which the body can be served, to avoid an increasing glorification of the body and to preserve as our primary concern the cultivation of that which is truly distinctive to man.[3]

iv

Critical to the making of a good man, I have indicated, is the political community, not just the family or one's own volition. The political implications of our technology are far more serious than we appreciate, far more serious than even such potential misuse of technology as is seen in the power technology gives a handful of men to tyrannize their countrymen, or in the power it gives us all to pollute the earth and its atmosphere, or in the power it gives us to destroy all mankind in a nuclear holocaust. Yet these are not, for our immediate purpose, the interesting problems: these dangers are known; perhaps some of them can be corrected or provided against. Far more troublesome are what are considered the beneficial uses of technology, especially as they bear on the political community available to us.

One instructive way of considering how a good man comes to be is to ask, "What is the natural habitat of man?" I offer, for purposes of our discussion, the proposition that the natural habitat of man is a community of approximately 300,000, a *sovereign* community of 300,000 (give or take 150,000). A community much smaller than that is not likely to provide the variety of human material necessary for the consistent stimulation of the richest human activities. A community much larger than that makes impossible the intimacy necessary if men are to be guided, in shaping and governing one another, by what they know about everyone else—and serious citizenship, as well as full development of the human being, becomes more difficult. Mere private pursuits are more apt to become the order of the day in such circumstances.

Our technology permits us to have so-called communities that are much, much larger than the figures I have given. In fact, the satisfactions we derive from that technology *require* us to have such massive communities. Small communities cannot support the elaborate industrial plant needed to develop the desired technology and to provide the resources with which to do our research, including, of course, our medical research.[4]

It requires for us an effort to notice that this question of the size of the community appropriate for the nurture of the best in man has been foreclosed by the "progress" of recent centuries. Indeed, we no longer have communities but rather more or less common enterprises. If I may suggest in images what has happened—perhaps irreversibly happened because of modern technology, including that which is applied (as I have just noted) to medical research—I should say that we no longer have in our political community a *ship of state*, with the solidity and the assurance and the majesty a well-built craft can have, even in turbulent waters, but rather we have the *jet airliner*, with both the obvious attractiveness of that aircraft for serving certain desires and its vulnerability. Consider why the jet airliner can be so easily hijacked—and imagine one man pulling a knife and trying to hijack an ocean liner. Is not modern life, in our massive communities, essentially like the very attractive and yet fragile jet airliner I have just described?

Without proper communities, we cannot produce good men as a matter of course. One might be produced here or there by chance, from time to time. But without proper communities, we can be expected eventually to forget what good men are, for we make it difficult to attain a common understanding of such things and to encourage their development.[5] The freedom I have already referred to, if it can be called that, means there should be in principle no such common understanding, certainly no common understanding authoritatively provided us.

V

Our remaining neglected question—"What is a good man?"—is related to the question of what the best kind of community is. These two concerns may sometimes conflict with one another, but they usually go hand in hand.

This remaining question must now be confronted directly. An answer to it has, of course, been implied in much of what I have already said. How have we *dealt* up to now with this question about the good man? We have, in effect, subverted it by denying that there *is* a peak toward which man should move. Consider the implications of our idea of progress and of our antipathy toward the idea of preserving any status quo, even should we arrive some day at what we at this moment consider "the best." We stress the "self" and "individuality"—which come down (do they not?) to private will, to random private desires. We are suspicious of superior men—and even resent the notion that there may be "superiors" and "inferiors." We insist that there are no "better" or "worse" men but only those whom we might call better or worse for certain (essentially arbitrary?) purposes. Indeed, we would prefer to call them merely "different" from one another, with each man entitled "to do his own thing."

We insist in our medical research about men (to bring the question back to the interests of this audience) that both the body and what was once called the soul (not by the Christians but by the Greeks) are ultimately subject to material analysis. You should also consider—as men and women dedicated to medical research—the implications of modern psychiatry. One often encounters in psychiatry today (as in much of Christian opinion before it) a curious blend of sentimentality and irresponsibility, with a disposition (against which Machiavelli, for one, rebelled) to sacrifice the strong to the welfare (if not the whims) of the weak. This is one practical effect of an egalitarianism devoted to the satisfaction of desires, with all desires in principle equal.

Consider, further, the implications of modern research concerned with the brain. It seems to be accepted that the most significant human activities are rooted in matter. Thus, for example, is not the use of electrodes in the brains of cats and monkeys, to say nothing of the brains of men, based upon the assumption that the mind is ultimately susceptible to mechanistic analysis? It is the human, it is believed, that is being explored in this way. That which might have once been thought of as the distinctively, even sacredly, human is reduced to nonhuman terms. Does not this make it more difficult, in an irreverent age, to preserve respect for the human?

But, someone might object, this is where the search for truth leads us; this is how we learn to treat the sick. Consider, first, the cause of truth. Should not a distinction be made, for the sake of the good life, between resolutely seeking the truth and indiscreetly (if not even childishly) exposing to public view everything one learns? Can mutual self-respect, or communal piety (and hence social self-restraint), be preserved when the brain is generally advertised to be subject to such exploration and manipulation?[6]

One can see in what I have said about both psychiatry and brain research how the good of the community, and the development of the best, may be subverted to the service of individual desires and fears. One can also see here that if decisions about such matters are left to private persons—that is to say, researchers, patients or doctors—the tendency will "naturally" be toward more and more activity on behalf of the afflicted.

We must take care, in short, lest the community be transformed into a hospital ward.

vi

What should be done? What *can* be done?

All analysis and discussion of this character—of the three questions I suggest have been neglected—depend on what the human soul (to use the Greek term) is like, what its nature is, that is to say, what it is in its highest state. The highest state of the soul, we were told some 2,500 years ago, is the knowing soul, not the doing soul, not even the helping or healing soul. Is this so? Should not this ancient teaching be reconsidered? Such reconsideration could help us examine, if not reestablish, the proper hierarchy among the activities of men.

The sensible remedy in our circumstances might be to call a general moratorium on the radical research we have had described for us today so long as there continues the present confusion about the most important questions. Such self-restraint would testify to a recognition on our part that there is something in man and in communities superior to the service both of the body and of the preservation of life—something else worthy of perpetuation across the generations. In addition, such a moratorium would find the resulting pressure of unsatisfied desires inducing us to think seriously again about the matters with respect to which the present confusion exists.

A moratorium of this kind is, of course, as impossible politically as would be the abolition of television.[7] But what about the occasional unilateral moratorium, the moratorium by the thoughtful man—the man who *is* quite familiar with work in the research fields we have had described for us today? Would it not be generally useful for a few such men to recapture the freedom they have surrendered and to turn the full force of their informed attention toward the old questions about the nature and nurture of the truly human? Such constructive liberation would include, of course, a serious study of the greatest students of the human soul, a study sadly neglected for decades, at least in scientific circles.

Perhaps I can put in a much more practical form than I have thus far my challenge of the usefulness of much of contemporary research into how our minds work. Are we, indeed, on the way to learning the truth about the workings of the mind? I gather that it seems to be generally believed among the acknowledged specialists that we have today, as someone observed this morning, "a better understanding than ever before of how our minds work." My impression is, however, that this "better understanding" (if it be so) is accompanied today by less competence in the *use* of the mind than has been evident heretofore. For one thing, we are less likely than have been our more thoughtful predecessors to recognize the truly important questions (both theoretical and practical) and to direct our minds to such questions. This is despite the fact that these questions have long been discussed on the highest levels. That is, we no longer recognize the best working of the human mind; we no longer regard such working with respect; we are no longer moved to emulate it.

This lowering in the level of intellectual competence suggests to me that we do not appreciate and hence cannot readily investigate how our minds do work. We see minds working less well than they need be, less well than they have heretofore, and we do not seem to notice that this is so.

vii

The most thoughtful examinations over the centuries both of the soul and of ethical questions are by and large neglected among us, with preference routinely given instead to crude contemporary experiments in "philosophy," which are neither novel nor interesting but rather uninformed and even presumptuous.

Perhaps it is inevitable, because of the goals and methods of our science, not only that we should fail to recognize the highest working—that is, the *true* working—of the human mind but even that we should, in effect, make such working virtually impossible hereafter, if only because we divert the best minds from the most serious pursuits.

All this is related, in turn, to the far from salutary transformation among us of the most heroic and noble deeds into a sophisticated pursuit of something we have even heard labeled as no more than "reinforcers" (that is to say, bodily pleasures). Here, too, we observe a marked failure to understand and to respect the best.

Thus, we find ourselves unequipped to observe, to understand, or to emulate the best either in the thought or in the deeds of those who have gone before us. We are thereby crippled in what we ourselves may think or do.

This does seem to me a sad state of affairs for a generation that aspires to "the social control of human behavior."

VIII. Pollution, Ancient and Modern

> And this we [of Salomon's House] do also: we have consultations, which of the inventions and experiences which we have discovered shall be published, and which not: and take all an oath of secrecy, for the concealing of those which we think fit to keep secret: though some of those we do reveal sometimes to the state, and some not.
>
> Francis Bacon, *New Atlantis*

i

We are concerned about "the pollution of our environment." What can that mean? It can mean mere change from what we are accustomed to or from what we expect. Change from either the accustomed or the expected concerns us. It concerns us because the customary is something we are comfortable with. But we suspect we can be comfortable with a number of other customary arrangements (as is seen in the strikingly different cuisines of the peoples of the world).

On the other hand, change may concern us because both the customary and the expected are grounded upon some notion, however imprecise, of what is good for man. When we speak of "what is good for man," what do we mean by *man* and what do we mean by *good?*

The determination of what man is may be complicated in our time by the argument that what man or any other animal is depends essentially on his environment. That is, man has been shaped by responses to challenging and threatening external stimuli to become what he now is. He remains thus adaptable. However polluted the atmosphere may become, we can believe, it is highly unlikely that there will not survive descendants of what we now know as man.

One may even be tempted to argue that there are not likely to be any environmental changes which will really be bad for man nor—perhaps, strictly speaking—good for man either. We see, that is, that

This talk was prepared for a symposium, "The Legal and Economic Aspects of Pollution," The University of Chicago, Chicago, Illinois, April 13, 1970. The proceedings of the symposium were published in 1970 (with the same title) by the Center for Policy Study, The University of Chicago.

The symposium panel included R. Stephen Berry, Ronald H. Coase, Harold Demsetz, Milton Friedman, Theodore J. Lowi, and Thomas W. Vitullo.

just as *man* is infinitely malleable, physically as well as socially, the .good which we have alluded to is reducible in modern terms to *self-preservation*. Our current concern merely reflects, when considered this way, the throes every species must go through while evolving—that is, while adapting itself to suddenly changed circumstances.

Are not we as moderns obliged to argue that there is no standard by which changes in man or in the life of man can be evaluated? And yet our concern about the pollution of our environment is likely to persist. That may be because we are simply reluctant or unequipped to grasp arguments which may seem to us uncomfortable—that is to say, arguments to which we are not accustomed. Such reluctance or inability would be a problem for the psychologist—with opinions about pollution being like any other opinions shown to be obviously mistaken but which one nevertheless refuses to surrender.

ii

But there is another, a more interesting, alternative to consider with respect to our concern today regarding the pollution of our environment. That is, our general concern may reflect an awareness of what we are and what is good for us, an awareness men of common sense have, and have recourse to, despite the orthodox opinions of modernity about such matters as evolution and what the good is or whether it can be known. This commonsense awareness may be made more explicit if we consider further the two terms that are so fashionable in current discussions—*pollution* and *environment*.

Is not a judgment implied in the word *pollution?* We moderns should, perhaps, be using such words as *change* or *transformation* or *alteration*, or even more "technical" terms such as *deoxidation* or *petrolification* or *automobilification*. Indeed, we could even say *modernization of our environment*—that is, the .environment as subjected to the effects of modern developments.

Despite our enlightened emancipation from the ways of our forefathers, we do speak of *pollution*, using a word that goes back to a Latin term for defilement. To pollute is, we are told by *Webster's Second International*, "to make or render something impure or unclean, ceremonially, physically, or morally; to impair or destroy the purity or sanctity of; to defile; desecrate; profane; corrupt; befoul." One is at once reminded of sacred things—an altar or sacrificial offerings, things that can be polluted. It is a sense of uneasiness about the defilement of the sacred, drawing upon memories of former awe buried in our language—it is this sense of uneasiness that we moderns invoke when we mobilize ourselves to do battle against pollution of our environment.

But just as the term *pollution* permits us to unearth and invoke that which we had thought long buried—and buried none too soon, some would say—the term *environment* permits us to conceal from view what it is we are out to protect from defilement. Just as *pollution* is a term that reaches into our distant and more pious past, *environment* is a term distinctively modern in the way we use it. *Environment*, which goes back etymologically to a notion of that which surrounds us, is a word which has a scientific ring to it. It seems to be free of "value judgments."

What is significant here is what we may really mean when we refer to our environment. I suggest that when we talk about environment we are really talking about nature—that nature once thought to provide not only the wherewithal man needs in order to live but, even more important, the standards according to which man should live. I suggest that what is suppressed by the use of such terms as *environment* (as well as by *ecology*, which was coined, I believe, in the nineteenth century) is the idea of nature. It is the suppression of nature—the centuries-old project for the conquest of nature that we have inherited—which may be at the root of our troubles—not only because of what we thereby do with and to our environment but even more because of what the determination to conquer nature already has done to our ability to reflect upon what man is and what is good for him. This has had consequences far more serious than any pollution thus far of our environment.

iii

Pollution of our environment is an affliction we are likely to be able to deal with effectively in and for the immediate future. After all, the national concern has been mobilized, considerable expertise is being recruited for this effort, and it is unlikely that legal barriers will be permitted to stand in our way. The recruitment of expertise in various disciplines is testified to by the interest in this subject of my colleagues on this panel. That is to say, the immediate practical problem is, I believe, well on its way to resolution when widespread interest, especially the interest of intelligent men, is aroused. There is no question but that the attention of the community has been engaged. I cannot know, of course, considering how volatile public opinion can be, how long community attention will in fact be engaged. But there are enough ecological "horror stories" that will surface from time to time to reengage faltering attention again and again, if the stories are not overdone or if the remedies advanced are not themselves so questionable as to put people off.

The present concern can be reinforced and sustained by legislation, especially by that legislation which makes certain measures economically attractive, thereby enlisting the voluntary efforts of ingenious men in the pursuit of gain. (I suppose I should add my opinion that not only is pollution itself a sign of industrial civilization but also that the human race probably has never been in better shape physically than it is today.) My own immediately practical suggestion for helping control pollution, aside from that which is implicit in what I have just said about realizing the significance of the current engagement of public concern, is that we never ride when we can reasonably use our legs—whether horizontally or vertically. That is to say, a kind of communal temperance is called for, to be encouraged and guided in appropriate cases by political decisions.

My use of the term *temperance* reminds us again, as should *pollution*, of old-fashioned ways of thinking. Undermining any dedication to temperance, however, is our implicit faith in the idea of progress. This conflict between temperance and progress is similar to that between our concern about pollution and our pursuit of the conquest of nature. The tension seen here is expressed in practical terms by the realization that there is, as we have again and again been reminded, always a price to be paid for whatever improvements we seek. We should be aware of this and be prepared to deal with it politically and humanely.

The idea of progress, if it is to mean something other than mere change (and here I am returning to the beginning of my remarks), must have, like the notions of pollution and environment, something solid and unchanging to which it has reference. My remarks on this occasion may be understood, therefore, as addressed primarily to those among you who are open to the truly serious and enduring questions to which a genuine community of inquiry should address itself. The concern with the current problem of pollution can best be justified, for us in the university community, if it should move us to reconsider the truly vital questions for man, question that may have prematurely been considered settled.

The threats of serious environmental pollution—"the good news of damnation"— have prompted us to make explicit the awareness we may always have had of the nature of man and of nature itself. That is to say, unadorned common sense may be, here as elsewhere, coming back into its own, shining through the scientific terminology and facile presuppositions of modernity. (One's immediate awareness of things does not require, and may even suffer from, scholarly documentation.)

We are thus given the opportunity once again to inquire—an activity which should appeal to that in us which makes man essentially what he is—to inquire into the nature of nature and into what guidance, if any, there is for man in nature. Only thus may we be able to discover what the enduring human questions really are—to say nothing about how we may begin to answer them.

Whether one is truly open to such questions may depend upon, among other things, the kind of man one is—that is, upon the character one has, which in turn is somewhat related to what one happens to know.

Rites of
Passage

IX. What's Really Wrong With George Anastaplo?

On April 24, 1961, the Supreme Court of the United States, by a vote of five to four, affirmed the action of the Illinois Supreme Court which, by a vote of four to three, had upheld the decision of the Committee on Character and Fitness of the Illinois bar which, by a vote of eleven to six, had decided that George Anastaplo was unfit for admission to the Illinois bar. This was not Anastaplo's only such experience with power structures. In 1960 he was expelled from Soviet Russia for protesting harassment of another American, and in 1970 from the Greece of the Colonels. As W. C. Fields might have said, any man who is kicked out of Russia, Greece and the Illinois bar can't be all bad.

> C. Herman Pritchett, 60 *California Law Review* 1476 (1972)

i

L ast night, I attempted to show, elsewhere on this campus, what is *right* about permitting men such as the National Commander of the American Nazi Party to speak on college campuses.[1] This morning, as if to do justice by redressing the balance, there has been assigned to me the topic "What's Wrong with George Anastaplo?" That there is something wrong is suggested by the bar admission controversy that began in this state thirteen years ago with my defence of the Declaration of Independence and in the course of which I have been repudiated by

---

This talk was delivered at The College of Law, The University of Illinois, Champaign-Urbana, Illinois, May 14, 1963. It was published, in installments, in The Carterville [Illinois] *Herald*, November 19, 1964, p. 1; December 3, 1964, p. 2; December 10, 1964, p. 2.

The bar admission case discussed in this talk is *In re George Anastaplo*, 3 Ill.2d 471, 121 N.E.2d 826 (1954), 348 U.S. 446, 349 U.S. 908 (1955) (Justices Black and Douglas, dissenting), 18 Ill.2d 182, 163 N.E.2d 429 (1959) (Justices Bristow, Shaefer and Davis, dissenting), 366 U.S. 82 (Justices Black, Douglas and Brennan and Warren, C.J., dissenting), rehearing denied, 368 U.S. 869 (1961).

The 1961 majority opinion in the Supreme Court of the United States has been described as follows: "To what extent, consistently within the protection afforded by [the First Amendment], and without forfeiture of the privilege sought, applicants for admission to the bar may withhold information concerning their political affiliations and beliefs has presented another problem which the [Supreme Court of the

the Committee on Character and Fitness sitting in Chicago, by the Supreme Court of Illinois, and by the Supreme Court of the United States.[2]

I suppose the answer to the question of precisely what is wrong with me would depend on whom you talked to since my case began in November 1950. The most radical, and in some ways the most revealing, criticism I have run across concludes an impassioned 1951 letter from a bar examiner to his colleagues on the character committee (of which he was, ex officio, a member):

> [T]he whole pattern of the applicant's behavior seems to border on the psychopathic and if he were approved on other grounds by the Committee I would seriously recommend that the Committee obtain the report of a competent psychiatrist, as has been done in other cases. The applicant's demeanor and conduct were even more impressive along these lines than they were in relation to questions of anarchism and communism—his supreme egotism and his persecution complex, for example.
>
> If I were to judge the applicant upon his own appearance and presentation, I would say that his impact upon society will be so slight that whatever we do will be of little importance, but because of his influence upon some of the strong-minded members of this Committee I am led to predict that his admission will be cause for serious regret.

This letter, I should note, came to me by chance, many years after it was written. Its troubled author was one of the few members of the committee who never said a word in my presence during my nine appearances before the seventeen-member committee. In fact, the only thing he did openly was to glower at and to vote against me every opportunity he had.[3]

United States] has not resolved uniformly. . . . [In the *Anastaplo Case*,] where there was an absence of independent evidence that the petitioner ever had been a member of the Communist Party, or of any organization which might cast doubt on his loyalty, Illinois authorities were upheld as having been warranted in admonishing petitioner that, according to their established rules, a refusal to answer, albeit on First Amendment grounds, questions pertaining to such membership, would be deemed obstruction of their function of cross-examining him with a view to ascertaining his fitness to practice law, and the basis for denial of his application for admission. These officials acknowledged that they drew no inference of disloyalty or subversion from the applicant's refusal, but maintained that public interest in the character of an attorney overrides the applicant's desire to keep his views and associations to himself." *The Constitution of the United States of America: Analysis and Interpretation* (Washington: Government Printing Office, 1964), pp. 908-909.

The criticism I like best is that found in the generous dissenting opinion of Justice Black:

> [T]he entire course of his life, as disclosed by the record, has been one of devotion and service to his country—first, in his willingness to defend its security at the risk of his own life in time of war and, later, in his willingness to defend its freedoms at the risk of his professional career in time of peace. The one and only time in which he has come into conflict with the Government is when he refused to answer the questions put to him by the Committee about his beliefs and associations. And I think the record clearly shows that conflict resulted, not from any fear on Anastaplo's part to divulge his own political activities, but from a sincere, and in my judgment correct, conviction that the preservation of this country's freedom depends upon adherence to our Bill of Rights. The very most that can fairly be said against Anastaplo's position in this entire matter is that he took too much of the responsibility of preserving that freedom upon himself.[4]

My response in the Petition for Rehearing on that occasion may be taken by some to reflect that "supreme egotism" detected by our deservedly anonymous Bar Examiner:[5]

> Perhaps it is true that petitioner "took too much of the responsibility of preserving [his country's] freedom upon himself." 81 S. Ct. at 995. But he was young enough to hope that Americans who would not heed old precepts might yet learn from new examples.

I suppose, in any event, that most of those who have opinions about my matter would agree on one thing, that what is wrong with me has been that way a long time. Perhaps, indeed, I am incorrigible, a three-time loser, even a hopeless case.

At least I hope so.

ii

I was moved to reminisce when I recalled, upon receiving your challenging invitation, that it has been twenty years since I won our county scholarship competition and entered your university as a freshman in the Engineering School at the height of the Second World War. A number of incidents came to mind, incidents of days so long past as to permit me to speak publicly of them at this time. It is almost as if I contemplate another person, just as the title assigned me for this talk encourages an attitude of naive impersonality. On the other hand, if I seem to make too much of these recollections, you will appreciate that they *are* my own. For better or worse, you have licensed me to talk at length about myself, perhaps even to celebrate myself as I was once privileged to be.

Champaign-Urbana was a long way from home, in more ways than distance. I recall that it took me a while to realize that it was not good form for strangers to greet each other on the street up here, as they did down in Carterville, the Southern Illinois town of 2,800 people from which I had come. I recall that I was introduced to military life through the campus R.O.T.C., about which I remember almost nothing aside from striking up an acquaintance with a Negro freshman from a village near my home town, someone whom I still run into on the "El" in Chicago. I also recall that the University of Illinois was known, even in those days, for its generous attitude toward Negro students. I worked on the *Daily Illini* and, aside from a math course under a benevolent white-haired professor, got very little from my classes. In fact, but for a couple of episodes I will presently recount in an effort to help you better to understand my case, I recall surprisingly little about my first and only semester at college here.

My mind was really elsewhere: the lovely high school senior whom I happened to meet just a few weeks before leaving for college and, of course, the attractive war thousands of miles away.

iii

The war I felt obliged to do something about. At times I was afraid it would be over before I could get there. A good deal of my time that semester was spent fighting The Battle of Chanute Field, trying to get into the Air Force (it was the Army Air Corps then), as an aviation cadet. But I was underweight, and besides I had a heart murmur and high blood pressure. The heart trouble, I kept telling the doctors, was due to excitement; as for the weight I did try to remedy that by eating much more than I wanted. Bananas and milk temporarily took care of the weight problem and a sympathetic flight surgeon finally let me get by on the physical. It was not until after I got my wings and commission that my heart began to behave itself.

I realize it is no longer fashionable to make such an effort to serve one's country. Indeed, even then, some of my more knowledgeable campus associates advised that it would be foolish to try to undo what nature had done for me. But I was young—only seventeen—and did not know better. It was, I grant you, a young man's game. I must grant also that the game seems to have lost much of its attractiveness with the introduction of the incredibly destructive nuclear weapons. But, to get back to the simpler days of 1943, I never regretted my successful efforts to enlist. In fact, I remain dubious to this day about anyone of sound body who, not being a pacifist, deliberately evades military service in a not-unjust war.

It is one of the minor ironies of my bar admission case that I continued to hold a reserve commission in the Air Force at the very time when the Supreme Court of Illinois, in a remarkably uninformed opinion, unanimously affirmed the unanimous decision of a hostile character committee that I had not removed "doubts as to [my] ability to take the oath of lawyer in good conscience."[6] I must confess that I never dreamed, while flying all over the world with the Air Force, that in only a few years I would be so belligerently excluded from the practice of law, on a question of loyalty to the Constitution, by a tribunal made up almost entirely of men who were never privileged to wear their country's uniform.[7]

No serious effort to establish my loyalty—at least, none that made any impression on me—had been made when I volunteered during the war for what was considered dangerous duty. I was surprised and, it must be admitted, disappointed to find that memories could be so short and ingratitude so pronounced. But the experience was not wasted. I at least learned what fear and pettiness can do to men. The comrades I had flown with in the Air Corps—most of them were little more than boys —had been neither petty nor fearful.

iv

The second episode I alluded to involved another battle fought in Champaign, The Battle of East Green Street—and the issue, a more enduring and important one, anti-Semitism.

My Green Street housemates were, for the most part, older than I; they nad been around more—and they had picked up decided opinions about Jews that could be summed up, most delicately, in the suggestion that they should all be sent "back" to what was then known as Palestine. I enjoyed the distinction of being the lone dissenter, at least the only one who spoke up. We fought many a skirmish. They were not malicious, only ignorant.

I must confess my ignorance as well—for to the best of my knowledge, I had never seen a Jew before I went to college. None that I knew of lived in my home town. Nor did I really know much about what was going on in Germany at that time. It was, I like to believe, that I simply thought the attacks unjust to the victims and demeaning to the attackers, something someone of spirit naturally could not permit to pass unchallenged in his presence.

Indeed, as I look back now, I believe the most effective single lesson I ever received on this subject came during an assembly in our high school gymnasium a couple of years before, just after the war started. A newsreel showed the Japanese diplomats in Washington at the time of the attack on Pearl Harbor; some of the youngsters in our audience booed—and the principal, a physically powerful man with a firm sense of decorum, immediately stopped the film and shamed his students with the reminder that "we don't behave like that." War, he gave us to understand, did not justify the suspension of the rules of behavior he always insisted upon in *his* school.

This reflects, I suspect, the decisive condemnation of anti-Semitism as well as of any other bullying or exploitation of some men by others. Decent men just don't behave like that.[8]

▼

It must have been almost a decade later—I believe I had already been excluded from the bar—that I received a remarkable letter from one of the boys with whom I had argued through those long nights in Champaign. He wrote to thank me for my efforts on behalf of the Jews. He had stayed on at Illinois—and my arguments or at least my attitude had somehow stayed with him. Within a year or two, he wrote, he was a leader in interfaith activities of Christians and Jews on the campus. Indeed, the spirit of his letter was such that I never read Charles Dickens' memorable story to my children on Christmas Eve without thinking of the Scrooge-like conversion of my fellow student.

Please do not misunderstand me. This lad was intelligent—and perhaps it was only inevitable that he should find his way. But I was nevertheless struck by the realization—and that realization, I believe, is appropriate for the prospective young lawyer to take to heart—that one seldom knows the extent of one's influence.

vi

I turn now to a few general observations suggested in part by what I have related of my experiences.

The best things you will ever do, and in which you will take the greatest pride, are likely to seem much harder to others than to you. No one will make you do them. In fact, your most distinctive contributions as a lawyer will come when others will want to *stop* you from behaving yourself. You must not expect popular support even when you do what is really expected of you.[9]

If you are a competent lawyer, and manage to establish yourself as conscientious, the *most* you can hope for from most of your fellow citizens in time of crisis will be silent disapproval: they, at least, may not attack you publicly. Sustained public support is likely to be rare, unless organizations find it in their interest to mobilize it.

Only two men of the older generation in my home town, for instance, have (so far as I know) ever declared publicly that I may have been right in my bar admission controversy or, at least, that I was as well-qualified as the next applicant for admission to the bar. The editor of the local weekly newspaper was one; the other was, as one might have expected, the high school principal I have already referred to. These two men were bitter political opponents while I was growing up. This is the only issue on which I have ever known them to agree. Those of my own generation in my home town, to say nothing of most of my teachers there and elsewhere, have retained a discreet, if not disinterested, silence. They might even want the world to believe that it sees in my character a philosophical miracle, an effect without a cause. I, on the other hand, appreciate what I truly owe to men who do not yet care to claim their reward.

What is the significance of the silence I speak of, a silence broken by such honorable and gratifyingly articulate exceptions as Irving Dilliard's, a trustee of this university? Timely intervention by a few more men who knew better, especially teachers of law, would have deterred the committee from that shabby bullying of helpless young applicants which is so unworthy of a learned profession. You can read and evaluate the record and opinions for yourselves—and decide whether I am correct in my remarks about the nature and extent of the support you can expect for the occasional vital cause you may be privileged to champion.[10]

Perhaps you will also find some basis in the record, as well as in what I say today, for the almost irrational resentment reflected in the bar examiner's letter from which I have quoted. Certainly, there is something valid in the remark recently made by a leading member of my character committee, which was to the effect that his colleagues and he were really moved to deny my application because "Anastaplo always conducted himself before our committee as if he was better than us." There may be something to that.[11]

vii

Of course, I should be the last to say that I am better. But I *will* say I have a better memory. That is, I recalled, when others did not, the lessons taught to us all, even as children, about how one should behave—lessons that most men are so unfortunate as to tend to forget in time of crisis. It would be a hopeless task for any leader in troubled times if there were not among his people this reservoir of instruction upon which to draw.

Thus, you have probably known for years the most important things you need to know for the practise of law. You happen to have been raised in decent communities. There still remains general agreement among us—one has only to watch television Westerns to appreciate this—about the most common and, *for your purposes as lawyers,* the most important virtues. What you are likely to learn in law school is, for the most part, the necessary but subordinate technical elaboration of what you already know.

It is your duty, as the leaders you will be at the bar, to lead even when you do not think there are followers. Your influence cannot be measured by simply counting heads. If you insist upon and develop the elementary standards of decency long accepted by our community, your fellow citizens will come around in the long run. They have no place else they really want to go.

You have been shown, as have I, what those standards are. You need to be alert, however, against the sometimes sophisticated, the sometimes ignorant, smothering of the almost instinctive awareness of right and wrong that our way of life has habituated you to. Fortunately, the old-fashioned virtues, such as courage and justice, are still too deeply ingrained to be easily worn away even in these troubled times.

One ignores these virtues only at the risk of sinking into an ignoble life emptied of meaning and joy.

viii

You may suspect that what I have been talking about is not the stuff that lawyers and law are made of. The court decisions in my case may feed your suspicion. But, even before I retired from the practice of law, those decisions had been narrowed down from unanimous denunciations to one-vote margins, with the dissents clearly having the better of the argument.

Besides, I can "pull my rank" on you with the reminder of a fact mentioned by your chairman: I did do very well academically in one of the best law schools in the country. And this I was easily able to do, even though much of my time during those years was devoted to courses in other parts of the University of Chicago, because of a discovery I made early in my law school days: the law relies for the most part on simple notions of what is right and wrong.

This discovery is central to much of what I have said and done over the years. Thus, all the sensitive student needs to do, in order to "get on top" of a field of substantive law, is to learn the terms employed in that particular field and become familiar with the few peculiar exceptions for which history (that is, chance) is responsible.[12]

Thus, also, the first question you should ask, *once you get the "facts" of a case straight*, is, "What is the just way of settling this issue?" And in most cases, that will be the principal question you will need to answer.

As a practicing lawyer, you will need also the fortitude as well as the good sense to act upon your answer.

ix

Do I exaggerate? If I do, it is in a good cause—and perhaps exaggeration is inevitable in any popular discussion of the moral virtues. But lest you think I have no authority other than my experience and observations to support what I say about the foundations of the law, permit me to close in a lawyer-like manner by submitting for your consideration a venerable precedent. It is *Langbridge's Case*, Common Bench, 1345— you must at least admit that this is authority of long standing—relating to a suit to recover land. The party defendant (called the tenant) made default; whereupon Langbridge prayed that he might be admitted to defend, because the tenant had only a life estate, and the remainder was in himself. It is the exchange between the lawyers and the justices that interests us here, an exchange that went something like this:

Huse (for the petitioner) produced a deed showing the gift.

R. Thorpe (for the demandant): You see plainly that his right is not proved by record or by fine, and we cannot have any answer to this deed nor is it an issue to say that he has nothing in remainder; and since we cannot have an answer to his statement, we pray seisin.

Sharshulle, J.: One has heard speak of that which Bereford and Herle [former judges] did in such a case, that is to say, when a remainder was limited in fee simple by fine they admitted the person in remainder to defend, and it was said by them that it would be otherwise if the limitations were by deed *in pais*; but nevertheless, no precedent is of such force as that which is right.

Hillary, J.: Demandant, will you say anything to oust him from being admitted?

R. Thorpe: If it so seems to you, we are ready to say what is sufficient; and I think you will do as others have done in the same case, or else we do not know what the law is.

Hillary, J.: It [the law] is the will of the Justices.

Stonore, C. J.: No; law is that which is right.[13]

It is on this note that I close the reminiscences of a quarter century which you have elicited: "Law is that which is right." Perhaps it is his deliberate (however naïve) belief in that proposition that exposes best of all what is really wrong with George Anastaplo.

"The Practice
of Politics"

X. Obscenity and Common Sense

PROLOGUE

"How like a man who's reluctant to speak you are,"
[Glaucon] said. "You'll think my reluctance quite appropriate, too," [Socrates] said, "when I do speak."
"Speak," [Glaucon] said, "and don't be afraid." . . .

Plato, *Republic* 414c

Is a volatile decadence inevitable in our community because of what our prosperity and our numbers both permit and reflect?

To speak of prosperity today (for a people spared as ours has been war's devastation and instructive austerity) is to speak of a successful pursuit of material happiness by countless millions, the repeated satisfaction of the multitude of desires that flesh is heir to. To speak of community is to imply restraints upon self-expression—to imply discipline and limitation upon what one might want to do or to say. But the very prosperity the community cherishes has been made possible among us by the energy and ingenuity that have come with the unleashing of private desire.

A respectable everyday image of the secure self-indulgence we have earned may be seen in the air-conditioned automobile, in which rides a family or a couple or even a lone potentate sealed off from nature and the rest of mankind, as it cruises the highways maintained and policed by the community. Contact among men is fragmentary. Each is legitimately on his own.

And since each man *is* on his own, what can he do but explore the potentialities of his psyche? The requirements of the community can be kept to a minimum (one even hears of the government as merely an "umpire"), and private adventures are called for. Only the timid or the crippled refrain from experiments in the arts, in narcotics (both physical and spiritual), in "experience."

This article was published (with the title, "Obscenity and Common Sense: Toward a Definition of 'Community' and 'Individuality' ") in *Toothing Stones: Rethinking the Political*, Robert E. Meagher, editor (Chicago: Swallow Press, 1972) and, with additions, in 16 *St. Louis University Law Journal* 527 (Summer 1972). It incorporated a talk given at Shimer College in 1965.

But when each is thus on his own, it is the rare man who can escape the futility and ultimately the despair that await the self-indulgent. And even the rare man—as witnessed in Martin Heidegger's political experiment of the 1930s—can go basely wrong in discerning an escape route for himself and for the anxiety-ridden community he would redeem. That is, even the rare man can forget what every decent man is aware of, that there are cures worse than mortal afflictions. (See Aristotle, *Nicomachean Ethics*, III, ix. Cf. the beginning of Plutarch's *Pelopidas*.) At what seems to be the other end of the contemporary political spectrum, we have the observation by Joseph Stalin's daughter, "For twenty-seven years I was witness to the spiritual deterioration of my own father, watching day after day how everything human in him left him and how gradually he turned into a grim monument to himself." (See the discussions of tyranny in Averroes, *Commentary on Plato's Republic* 85.7-86.21, 94.29-102.15.)

The thoughtful man realizes that there is necessarily a tension, in a healthy community, between the demands of the public and the charms of the private. To sacrifice either one to the other is to deprive mankind of something essential to the full flowering of the human being or to the competent dedication of citizens. (See Homer, *Odyssey*, XII, 41-54, 153-200. Cf. Plutarch's *Antony*.) Yet to balance properly the contending claims of the public and the private is, indeed, difficult: men who are not restrained and guided by institutions and traditions tend to vacillate between rigidity and abandon, between anarchical selflessness and tyrannical selfishness.

The thoughtful man also realizes that communities, like the men who make them up, are mortal: contending forces cannot be held in balance forever. He realizes, that is, that there is nothing to wonder at in the discovery that the community in which he happens to find himself is in process of disintegration. Such disintegration, which may even have its interesting facets, can come after impressive successes in realizing some of the goals that have been long aspired to by mankind. (Indeed, it is no mean achievement to have so harnessed the resources of nature that men are now able, for the first time in the history of the race, both to walk on distant planets and to destroy overnight almost all of their own kind.)

Citizens, as such, care about the community. They not only take it seriously, but *they* regard it as potentially immortal—and hence they can always be expected to "keep on trying." Citizens may resent, therefore, the detached (even amused) curiosity of the thoughtful man: they cannot help but make an effort (even when things seem desperate) to purge their community of its grossness and decay and thereby to attempt to restore it to a healthier condition. Of course, they are likely to mistake symptoms for underlying causes and thus to leave the causes untouched, but that *is* the way of citizens: appearances are for them quite important. Citizens are not wise men; they may, in the best of times, be informed men. They do not go to the root of things—*that* is left to founders and to the teacher of founders.

Consider, as an example of what dedication to the community can mean, how concerned citizens may speak about the contemporary problem of obscenity. The subject is in some respects rather pedestrian, but it nevertheless raises in a practical manner enduring questions about the relation of community interests and individual self-expression. The allure of the prurient can thus be put to good use: for when one talks intelligently about obscenity one is obliged to talk (or at least to think) about the role of the community in shaping and preserving the character of citizens and hence of the regime itself. (In this way, citizens and citizenship can contribute to the full development of the human being.)

The *logos* of citizens who have been influenced (in the Periclean tradition) by both poetry and philosophy—a speech that may be aware of but cannot be expected to repudiate the presuppositions of their community, including the attraction for the community of the economic fruits of relatively unencumbered individuality—may, it seems to me, go something like this:

LOGOS

"But," [Socrates] said, "I once heard something which I trust. Leontius, the son of Aglaion, was going up from the Piraeus under the outside of the North Wall when he noticed corpses lying by the public executioner. He desired to look, but at the same time he was disgusted and made himself turn away; and for a while he struggled and covered his face. But finally overpowered by the desire, he opened his eyes wide, ran toward the corpses and said: 'Look, you damned wretches, take your fill of the fair sight'."

Plato, *Republic* 439e

i

There is so much uncertainty in the accounts our more articulate fellow citizens have left us as to the significance of obscenity today that scarcely anything is asserted by one of them which is not called into question or contradicted by the rest. Still another account[1] is justified only if it can escape from the present confusion by going back to old and, in some instances, perhaps even first principles.

Politics, Aristotle reminds us, is the master art: something must recognize what is highest in the community and must order the activities of the community in accordance with that which is highest.[2] Even a political order which, in the name of liberty, refuses so to arrange matters is itself based on an opinion of what is highest: that is, the invocation of liberty (with its tendency to cherish privacy) reflects an opinion of how the best may be secured.[3]

We are obliged to ask what the end of government is. A Supreme Court justice provided, in 1890, an old-fashioned American answer to this question:

> The protection of the safety, the health, the morals, the good order and the general welfare of the people is the chief end of government. *Salus populi supreme lex.* The police power is inherent in the States, reserved to them by the Constitution, and necessary to their existence as organized governments. The Constitution of the United States and the laws made in pursuance thereof being the supreme law of the land, all statutes of a State must, of course, give way, so far as they are repugnant to the national Constitution and laws. But an intention is not lightly to be imputed to the framers of the Constitution, or to the Congress of the United States, to subordinate the protection of the safety, health and morals of the people to the promotion of trade and commerce.[4]

A century earlier, James Wilson, one of the principal draftsmen of the American Constitution, had observed in the Constitutional Convention:

> [I cannot] agree that [the protection of] property [is] the sole or the primary object of Government and society. The cultivation and improvement of the human mind [is] the most noble object.[5]

We observe in turn that it may be imprudent to talk of any important activity of man as strictly or altogether "private": much of what is cherished as private depends upon, and at least indirectly affects, civilization, which is "publicly" established and maintained.

ii

Thus we are obliged to confront the question: what makes men as they are? This question presupposes that there is no effect without a cause, a proposition which seems as valid here as in the other affairs of men, as well as in nature generally. What then can obscenity (whatever it is) be expected to do to the shaping of men's character and conduct?

The evidence, we are told again and again, is inconclusive. But this conclusion is pronounced from the perspective of modern social science, which often seems determined to disregard what common sense tells us. Is not longstanding and virtually universal community opinion as to what makes people behave, and misbehave, worth something? There are, in any event, many matters about which social science is at least equally inconclusive—as, for instance, about the effects of various economic measures, of diplomatic and military measures, of desegregation measures, and of welfare measures—and yet we appreciate that lawmakers should be permitted if not obliged to regulate conduct with respect to these matters, even to the extent of life-and-death decisions. If, that is, the same degree of certainty were generally required that is demanded with respect to obscenity, there would be (for better or for worse) far less legislation than we now deem necessary.

Furthermore, if it cannot be shown that there are no bad effects from obscenity, it cannot be shown either that there are good effects. In fact, it would seem to follow that there can be little harm in attempting to suppress something so inconsequential in the life of the community. Certainly, the community may (because of its "prejudices") find obscenity highly offensive, whatever the causes of or justification for such an attitude. Why not permit the community, then, to control or discourage that which happens to be so offensive to it? Why should not the community's "taste" be permitted to prevail over that of individual producers and consumers of what the community considers "obscenity"? Thus, one can see that the argument from lack of knowledge about the effects of obscenity—which would, by the way, seem to suggest that good literature has no determinable effects worth encouraging either!—can be employed to support suppression as well as permissiveness.

But is the case as inconclusive as it is said to be? What *do* we think education does for men?[6] Must we not grant that there is a place for restraint and even for a sense of reverence in a community, that without these the noblest life, perhaps even a simple decent life, is unlikely if not impossible? Plutarch tells of Thales, the poet,

> whom Lycurgus, by importunities and assurances of friendship, persuaded to go over to Sparta; where, though by his outward ap-

earance and his own profession he seemed to be no other than a lyric poet, in reality he performed the part of one of the ablest lawgivers in the world. The very songs which he composed were exhortations to obedience and control, and the very measure and cadence of the verse, conveying impressions of order and tranquility, had so great an influence on the minds of the listeners, that they were insensibly softened and civilized, insomuch that they renounced their private feuds and animosities, and were reunited in a common admiration of virtue. So that it may truly be said that Thales prepared the way for the discipline introduced by Lycurgus.[7]

There are ages, that is, when the artist is taken seriously.

iii

We return to a consideration of the possible effects of public obscenity. One legal scholar has collected from the literature "four possible evils" against which obscenity legislation is directed:

(1) the incitement of antisocial conduct;
(2) a psychological excitement resulting from sexual imagery;
(3) the arousing of feelings of disgust and revulsion; and
(4) the advocacy of improper sexual values.[8]

He adds in a footnote at this point:

It is possible to assert a fifth evil: the impact of obscenity on character and hence, slowly and remotely, on conduct.

He then appraises the possible evils in this manner:

It is hard to see why the advocacy of improper sexual values [No. 4] shall fare differently, as a constitutional matter, from any other exposition in the realm of ideas. Arousing disgust and revulsion in a voluntary audience [No. 3] seems an impossibly trivial base for making speech a crime. The incitement of antisocial conduct [No. 1] . . . evaporates in light of the absence of any evidence to show a connection between the written word and overt sexual behavior. There remains the evil of arousing sexual thoughts short of action [No. 2]. What puzzled Judge Bok and amused Judge Frank was the idea that the law could be so solemnly concerned with the sexual fantasies of the adult population.[9]

Is the first possibility ("the incitement of antisocial conduct") to be dismissed as easily as is here assumed? We should recall our comments on the degree of certainty and on the kind of evidence usually required for legislative purposes. Are we so materialistic as to believe that the striking changes in behavior we have witnessed in recent decades have not been preceded by *any* changes in ideas? It should be noticed that the third possibility ("the arousing of feelings of disgust and revulsion") has had added to it in this appraisal the fact that the disgust and revulsion are created among a voluntary audience. Even so, do we as a community want, or want to permit, activities in a voluntary audience (made up of strangers, not of relatives and intimate friends) that *are* likely to arouse disgust and revulsion?

The answer to this question depends, in part, on how seriously we should regard the fifth possible evil, the one that most sophisticated intellectuals today would tend to overlook (or, at least, relegate to a footnote): "the impact of obscenity on character and hence, slowly and remotely, on conduct." Suppose the worst obscene materials became generally available and, for some (perhaps accidental) cause, even generally attractive or at least generally tolerated. Should we not expect in such circumstances a vitally different spirit in the community? Would there not be here an "educational" influence that schools and families and churches would be expected to make desperate efforts to counteract? Would it matter to the community which of the contending opinions prevailed? If it would matter, what could legitimately be done by the community to support decisively the opinion it favored? Is it not naïve to assume that obscenity can never prevail in the marketplace if the community acts merely as "umpire"?

Still another, related, evil has been staring us in the face all along. One does not have to read much of ordinary obscene writing to realize that the people who develop and distribute this stuff are, for the most part, corrupt or, at least, very low if not sick people. And they, in effect, attempt to make others like themselves, evidently succeeding in some cases. That is, one does not need to determine whether bad *actions* result from such materials: for even worse than bad actions is that one should think or talk like the authors of these books and magazines. There is no problem about "cause and effect" *here*. Is not this an evil that a self-respecting community has a right to be concerned about? We recall James Wilson's insistence in 1787 that "the cultivation and improvement of the human mind [is] the most noble object" of government. And we are reminded as well of Aristotle's observation (in the concluding pages of the *Nicomachean Ethics*) that sensible political effort is necessary for the general realization of human goodness in a community.[10]

We venture to suggest a seventh (also related) evil about which the community may legitimately be concerned, and that is the evil of ugliness and of things that make for ugliness. Do we not have the right and perhaps even the duty to establish and preserve what we consider beautiful? Certainly, it will be granted, when the concern is directed to keeping billboards off our highways or to protecting our forests, our waterways, and our cities from depredations. Why not when we deal with the moral beauty (that is, the character) of our people as well?

All this presupposes, of course, that we *do* have some idea of what a good man looks like and that we also have some idea of how to make and keep him that way. Perhaps even more important for our immediate purposes, all this presupposes that it matters very much, in defining and reinforcing a community, that it be shown to one and all that there are things which will be ardently (even, to some degree, blindly) defended. Do not both the morality and the morale of a community depend on such dedication?

iv

And yet there is the cause of liberty and of intellectual curiosity, even the cause of truth itself.[11] For this is the elevated ground on which the better champions of obscenity stand, not in the low swamps of tne unprincipled, self-serving purveyor.

We are obliged to look even more closely at the obscene. Is there not here essentially the perennial question of the attitude men should take toward intimate things, toward peculiarly private things? The consumer of obscenities tries to eat his cake and have it too: he takes pleasure in looking at private things, but in such a way that they are not treated by the voyeur as private. If he should succeed completely in exposing everything to public view, then his special pleasure would disappear. What would he "have" to try next?

But, one might ask, why preserve what some regard as merely a conventional distinction between the private and the public? Because, it can be answered, of the nature of things. We are reminded of Sophocles's *Antigone*, with its deadly recognition of an ultimate irreconcilable conflict (as well as intimate tie) between the public and the private, between the city and the family. We are reminded also of the reticence exhibited by Plato in his account, in the *Phaedo*, of Socrates' last day. We are given much of the conversation between Socrates and his companions that day. We are shown something of the death of Socrates late that afternoon. But we are not given the final exchanges between Socrates and his wife and children. Nor are we shown Socrates' final bath in preparation for death: he retires into another room to wash himself. An old friend covers Socrates' face as he dies. Not everything is open to public display.

And yet, it might be asked, does not such reticence keep us from the truth? This depends on how much one needs to see in order to understand certain things. Delicate matters have to be handled delicately, if they are to be properly understood. Indeed, mere exposure may impede understanding, if only because it manhandles what is delicately made. One learns more of human nature, and of the nuances of human character, in the novels of Jane Austen than in the plays of an Edward Albee: in the former, the subject is ministered to by the artist; in the latter, the personality and hence the deficiencies of the author who insists on saying everything intrude and block the view.[12]

v

The "quarrel between the ancients and the moderns," it has been noticed, "concerns eventually, and perhaps even from the beginning, the status of 'individuality.' "[13] It is in its excessive effort to serve the cult of "individuality" that we see a critical deficiency of obscene writing, insofar as such writing may present a public problem for us today.

Such writing (whether or not adapted to the stage or to film) must, if it is to continue to titillate the consumer, deal in novelties.[14] But there is something self-defeating about this: practices of a more and more bizarre character must be conjured up. Where this sort of thing is the dominant concern of an author (or of his public), the off-color songs, stories, and jokes that satisfied earlier generations are replaced by a series of fantastic inventions. One need only look through a few contemporary works of this character to detect an intrinsic despair, a despair reflecting the groping of people broken loose from their moorings.

These moorings, which law attempts to discern so as to reinforce, are the dictates of nature. They are perversely acknowledged by the pathetic efforts of the professional obscenity producer to present the antics of his characters as the truly *natural* way. They must assure themselves and their customers that they practice what nature preaches, an assurance which would be more persuasive if the practices described remained somewhat more constant than they do. This instinctive concern to show themselves in conformity with nature should move us to wonder what *is* truly natural. But to investigate this properly, one needs a seriousness of purpose and a self-restraint that cannot coexist with the restlessness of the seeker after mere sensual pleasure.

Ultimately, the obscene must be rejected because it is neither true nor useful.[15]

vi

Let us now make explicit a definition of the obscene that has been assumed in what we have been saying.

The obscene is, as a concerned man has written, "that which should be enacted off-stage because it is unfit for public exhibition."[16] A decent community senses that there are things which, although perfectly proper behind closed doors,[17] it is better not to probe publicly without very good reason, and then only with tact and great care. This "off-stage" formulation, which does draw to some extent upon contemporary standards and practices, is useful for understanding the phenomena with which we have been dealing. Although it may not be immediately useful for legal purposes, it should underlie, inform, and guide the community's approach (legal and otherwise) to these problems.

The courts often have recourse today to a definition that, although somewhat circular, gives a fair indication both of the community's concern and (to put that concern in practical legal terms) of what a jury can be expected to find. That is, it is said that obscene productions are those which "appeal to the prurient interests," and hence minister to "shameful or morbid interest" in bodily functions, particularly the sexual —functions customarily kept private. The emphasis of the community *is* on the sexual, but this emphasis need not be seen as a depreciation or resentment of the sexual life of man. Rather, it may be seen as an effort to protect human sexuality and the joyfulness of love and of lovemaking from the demeaning exploitation of them by the purveyor of obscenities.

When the community thus acknowledges the importance of the sexual, it may not reveal its own obsessions but only its instinctive appreciation of the facts of life and of love. For it is essentially acknowledging the virtue of temperance as fundamental (at least in time of peace) to the other moral virtues that citizens should develop. And when we consider the virtue of temperance—the proper attitude toward bodily pleasure—it is to be expected that our primary concern should be with that most intense (and hence most diverting) of bodily pleasures, especially since it is critical as well to the proper ordering of the family and to the procreation and nurture of children.

We all know, or know of, people who are warped in their attitude toward sexual activities, either their own or those of others. Some of these people "express themselves" as producers and consumers of obscenities. Others of them "express themselves" in efforts to police what everyone says about sexuality. But it is only fair to recognize that those seeking to police others do deal with matters in which the community has some legitimate interest. It is against the *exploitation* of sexual activity, then, that obscenity sanctions may be said to be primarily directed. Such exploitation includes the building up of expectations that cannot help but be thwarted, to the detriment both of the defrauded consumer who is frustrated and of the community that must minister to his frustration.

There is an 1868 legal formulation by Lord Cockburn which (although somewhat eclipsed in this country in recent years) seems to have merit:

> I think the test of obscenity is this, whether the tendency of the matter charged as obscenity is to deprave and corrupt those whose minds are open to such immoral influences, and into whose hands a publication of this sort may fall.[18]

This formulation could, when used as a basis for prosecutions, be modified in one respect, by providing explicitly for what may have been implied, "into whose hands a publication of this sort *is intended* to fall." This permits, in the interest of an efficient fairness, a common-sense distinction between material written for and distributed among adults and materials destined for children. This test of "deprave and corrupt," which may be limited to materials dealing with specified bodily functions or perhaps even extended to certain portrayals of violence, is one that draws upon contemporary standards. It has as one advantage that it takes character for granted as a vital concern of the community.

Can it be honestly maintained that the normal writer or bookseller does not really know what his community desires in a particular case? Is it not significant that purveyors of obscenities almost invariably know what is being referred to when customers make requests of them? This suggests that the problem of definition for legal purposes may not be, in the ordinary case, as serious as it is sometimes made out to be. Con-

sider how adept the typical politician is, even when most impassioned
during heated election campaigns, in shying clear of public obscenity.

We all have, and have had from childhood, a fairly good idea of
what the community expects in public—as good an idea as we have of
what is expected in the way of due care on the highway, in the way
of due care on the part of the physician, in the way of due care on
the part of the cook or of the innkeeper in serving his guests, to say
nothing of the standard of good faith in commercial transactions. And
when the self-confidence and authority of a community are stable, what
it expects in public it is very likely to get. In such circumstances the
law, which serves primarily to ratify explicitly what the community
does expect, has to be invoked but rarely. That is, there may be something seriously wrong when, as among us today, frequent recourse to
obscenity prosecutions has been thought necessary by the community.
(Perhaps such recourse is a crude way of reassuring ourselves that there
is a community.)

There are, of course, borderline cases in any attempt by the community to establish what it means by obscenity. That should always
be expected when the law draws lines. But we should not, in the name
of realism, be unrealistic about what we understand each other to mean.
Few reasonable men, and for good reasons as well as because of long
established opinion, would permanently condemn such works as the
Bible or Shakespeare or even the delightfully bawdy Chaucer—and it
simply avoids the problem we confront to pretend otherwise by singling
out (as is sometimes done in debate and in litigation) certain passages
in such books. There is no reason why a healthy community, aware of
what it is doing, cannot treat borderline cases sensibly.

Certainly, it is not sensible for a community to allow itself to be persuaded that it does not or that it should not care deeply about its sensibilities. The following exchange from the trial transcript of the prosecution of a Los Angeles dealer for selling what, from every indication
(in both the state's and the defendant's briefs), is a miserable piece of
trash exploiting (and thus promoting?) a variety of sexual fantasies, is
illuminating:[19]

> *The Court:* . . . Would you read it?
> *Defense Counsel:* I have read it as part of my job, your Honor.
> *The Court:* Thank you, sir, for saying as part of your job. I read
> it because it was my duty.
> *Defense Counsel:* And I say to your Honor with as much

honesty as I can, and I think your Honor knows I have always tried to be at least as straight as I can—

The Court: There is no question about it.

Defense Counsel: I do not believe that book is obscene. I do not believe that book has a substantial tendency to corrupt or deprave persons by arousing lustful thoughts or lascivious desires. Now, I think there is much that can be said about the book that it is not good. I think that as a literary work it has much to go before it qualifies. But, your Honor, that book should be killed by the Saturday Review or the New York Times Book Section, not by law. And this is the point I would like to make, your Honor: That there is a lot of merchandise put out every day, a lot of books, which form the same classification that your Honor would place this in terms of not by good standards, by good judgment, reaching out and saying that this has sufficient value to warrant our time and reading. But that doesn't make it criminal, your Honor.

The Court: If you have read the book, sir, you discovered the young woman in that case was a perfectly normal woman and after the experience [described in the book] became a perfectly abnormal woman. Now, if that isn't acting upon a normal mind, that kind of a plot, I don't know anything that is. And we do know, sir, we unfortunately have had many years of contact from time to time with this and we do know that a perfectly normal person, that on certain occasions, being subjected to certain things, becomes changed and altered. Now, I have heard this story—I have heard it so many times when I have been in a position as a Public Defender and I have represented them and I asked "How did you get that way?" and had the same story repeated time after time, being subjected to it. It is like intoxicating liquor. It affects some that are otherwise perfectly normal until the experience. And that book there, I thought, was a perfect illustration of a normal person, one whose thoughts were entirely different, had never entered upon that field, upon being subjected to it forcibly became an entirely altered person. The book, I thought, carried its own proof. And I cannot contemplate you or anyone else or myself reading beyond a certain portion of it if we didn't have to do it because of some duty to perform.

Defense Counsel: But I would say this, your Honor, I would say this, that having read this, and I really don't consider myself to be different than the average, normal person, that I could sit on the jury here too, that after having read that book I don't believe that I was either a better or a worse person. I don't think I was corrupted. I don't think I was depraved, and this is the point, your Honor, that I want to hammer home.

The Court: I was depressed, sir. I was depressed, very depressed.

Defense Counsel: Your Honor, I thought I was wasting my time.

The Court: I know your point. You think I would reject it so quickly—I would. But remember, sir, I am not a young man.

Defense Counsel: I am not talking about you, your Honor. I am talking about myself. I am a young man and I am saying I wasn't corrupted. I wasn't depraved. And I don't believe [the prosecuting attorney] was corrupted or that he was depraved or that any other normal person would become corrupted or depraved.

The Court: Yes, but we are in the position of physicians. Physicians are not expected to catch the disease in order to treat it.

Defense Counsel: I think in this area, your Honor, we are all subject to the same whims of fate. We are not special people, your Honor.

The Court: We try to keep ourselves from getting affected, don't we?

Defense counsel (a specialist in obscenity cases) made essentially the arguments of the sophisticated intellectual in the service of the arts; the judge, on the other hand, expressed the sometimes confused opinions of the concerned community. The exchange recorded here warrants careful examination. Is the judge (shaped by the conventions of the community) so clearly wrong that his experience and impressions should be disregarded? "I was depressed, very depressed" is the lament of one who believes he sees his fellow man led astray. To rely, on the other hand, upon the denunciations of the *New York Times Book Review* or of the *Saturday Review* to "kill" such books as this is rather unrealistic: the clients of this particular bookseller would no more be influenced by what those august journals said than those journals would even notice the existence of such books as these.[20]

It may be true that we cannot be certain about the effects of such books. But, to return to what we have already said, is not a healthy community one in which it is known that both citizens and their government *care* about influences that may (in the considered opinion of men of common sense) deprave and corrupt, care enough to *try* to do something about them?[21]

vii

When we look again at "deprave and corrupt," we may see something that is basic to contemporary opinion. There can be little doubt that the position taken here is not one which would recommend itself to most intellectuals today. May not the underlying difficulty be that they are skeptical of anything being truly "depravity" or "corruption"? That is, does not the intellectual who, although ahead of his time, does have his effect in time—does not the intellectual see such judgments as mere matters of taste?

To be able to speak objectively of depravity and corruption, there must be some reliable opinion among us of what a decent man, a good man, and perhaps even a good community look like. Again, we are obliged to turn to the guides nature provides us and to take seriously any inquiry about them we may come upon.

It is well to notice also that we have been speaking about the more obvious cases of obscenity; the less obvious, and in some ways more pervasive and perhaps even more critical, cases are obviously much more difficult to police. Consider, for instance, the photographs in respectable journals and on television portraying the intense grief of men and women who have just lost a loved one. Or consider the stories reporters have pried out of a family that has just suffered great misfortune. Such things as this, to say nothing of much of the advertising and the exploitation of violence even in the magazines and newspapers most self-righteous about obscenity, cannot but contribute to the corruption of the moral spirit of the community.[22] If we keep in mind what the obscene really means—that which should be enacted off-stage—we are better able to judge and influence what is done all around us. This is clearly an aspect of the problem about which legislation can do little and an enlightened, confident public opinion can do much.

The potential gravity of the situation today is suggested by what has happened to, and because of, influential intellectuals: they, with their denial of the reality of goodness as anything other than mere taste, do affect the spirit of the community. It is evident that lawyers prosecuting obscenity cases are remarkably defensive about what they are doing. They are, at heart, converted to the cause of their opponents who proclaim themselves in the service of truth and liberty. We have attempted to show what the truth may be in such matters. We question whether men subjected to the intellectuals' prejudices in these matters are truly free.

We return to the question: What is a good man? We should not forget that we do have an answer, if only a tentative answer, in the light of which we have shaped and continually revise our educational and political institutions. We should, in short, not insist on ignoring what we do know.

viii

Nor should we ignore what we know to be on the other side of the coin. Certain public and private actions can, despite the best. of intentions, only make matters worse. In fact, it is possible that much of the distrust today of the official challenge to obscenity has been caused by serious abuses by censors of their power in recent centuries. Of course, the possibility of abuse of a power is no argument against its use. But, one must wonder, is crippling abuse inevitable in the exercise of this particular power?

Have the legions of decency learned how to restrain themselves in their crusade? There is no doubt a tendency among them to want to go beyond what is strictly necessary or even defensible, despite the fact that one best teaches restraint by exercising it oneself and explaining how and why one *is* exercising it. But, as we have noticed, the censorious often do have (with all their faults) what the typical purveyor of obscenities rarely has: the interest of the community at heart. In addition, they usually work out in the open and are thus subject to public scrutiny and control—at least, much more so than the self-serving purveyor. Is not puritanism (with all its disagreeableness) less destructive of virtue and beauty than licentiousness (with all its attractions)?

It should be acknowledged that any serious effort to police obscenity will, almost inevitably, sweep out (at least temporarily) some serious books as well. We cannot expect juries to be as perceptive in this respect as trained book reviewers and students of literature. We can expect here what is true of all legislation, that a few good things may be caught up with the massive bad. But, on the other hand, may not certain good books seem to the undiscerning public so much like bad books as to make it difficult to distinguish them? If certain good books are permitted to circulate freely, will the trash that crudely resembles them follow in their trail? Is this what has happened since the Second World War?

The proper training of lawyers, especially those who prosecute and who sit as judges, should provide a substantial safeguard against indiscriminate indictments. But there are no foolproof programs. Each of the alternative courses of action available to us today has undesirable effects. Presumably, the serious book will have more to be said for it, even before a jury, and can probably be depended upon to win a place for itself in time. In any event, we should take care lest our insistence upon always having only the best leads to the subversion among us of simple goodness.

Once we see the problem for what it is—once we again recognize that there are good books and bad, virtue and depravity, wholesome influences and pernicious—, we can do something about the problem in the ways that only an alert, self-confident public can. That is, we can try to do even more than we do with our educational institutions, not only by providing the proper medical and moral training for our children but also by reviving an informed dedication to liberal education.[23] And we can make even more use than we do of intelligent private action. Perhaps most important, we can let it be known that we regard as contemptible—and in this there may occasionally have to be some hypocrisy—those who traffic in such materials which even a child can recognize to be obscene.

But, unfortunately, a reformed public opinion may not suffice. The problem has become what it is today—and, indeed, has become a problem at all—partly because of technological developments that, with respect to production and distribution of printed matter and film, permit businessmen to have their effects in communities far removed from those in which they live (where, presumably, the opinions of their neighbors would be more apt to shame or intimidate and hence restrain them). And, it should be recognized, some men simply do not care what others think of them, especially if callousness serves either financial gain or simple rebelliousness or an illness of the psyche. That is, the law may be of some use in such matters, even if not rigorously enforced. Indeed, it may suffice, in making clear the opinion of the community and in setting the tone of public discourse, to compel the distribution of obscene wares to return to its former tolerated "under the counter" status.

The principal cause of excessive—even obscenely excessive—and hence self-defeating suppression is indignation that runs away with would-be ministers of justice. Still, the just man—the man who cares primarily for the welfare of the community—must nevertheless be prepared to say (*or to tolerate*, if not to support, *those who say*), as did Lear after his betrayal by Goneril and Regan, "Touch me with noble anger." But he should never do so without keeping in mind Shakespeare's *Measure for*

Measure as well as the opening scene of *King Lear* and the closing scene of *Othello*.

ix

But what of the Constitution? That is not a critical concern for us on this occasion. One is not induced to examine seriously the relevant constitutional principles if one does not believe there is good reason, political or moral, for the community to concern itself about the production and consumption of obscenity. It is that concern, illuminated by what common sense has always had to say about such things, to which we have addressed ourselves. A preliminary survey of constitutional considerations should suffice at this time.

The principal constitutional safeguard here is that of "due process of law" (in the traditional procedural sense)—and, indeed, that in itself places formidable obstacles in the way of any government which would enforce rigorous obscenity statutes. *Due process guarantees would require*, for instance, *that the determination of what is to be used* in the classroom and of what is to be available in public libraries *should be left primarily to the informed judgment of the bodies entrusted by the community with that duty*, that is, the responsible faculties and librarians of those institutions. Due process also requires that the accused, in the ordinary criminal case, be punished only for what he did, having been put on notice about what he should not do, and having had an opportunity to meet the case submitted against him.[24]

"Freedom of speech and of the press," on the other hand, need have very little bearing on this problem, at least as these guarantees are found in the First Amendment and applied to the States by the Fourteenth Amendment. These guarantees are designed primarily to assure that our people will be able to discuss freely the matters that concern us as a self-governing body politic. Most literature is not directed *immediately* to such concerns. Here, too, there is the problem of drawing lines—but again, it seems obvious that most of the material we have been talking about has little or nothing to do with examinations of political issues or with the decisions which we as citizens have to make and which we are entitled to discuss freely.

What we *are* entitled to discuss freely is whether obscenity should be restricted by law and how rigorously, and whether any particular course of action taken by our governments is proper and desirable. We are entitled to discuss, for instance, whether recourse to legal action is, considering the temper of the times, much more likely to hurt than to help matters. Certainly, the prudent community will not want to allow its justifiable distaste for obscenity to mislead it as to what is feasible.[25] Thus, freedom of political discussion must be retained unabridged if citizens are to remain sensibly sovereign: the degree and means of community discouragement of obscenity should be examined from time to time, as circumstances change. This is the way of free men.[26]

Citizens who truly respect freedom should take care lest its good name and good works be repudiated by the confusion of responsible liberty with either insatiable self-indulgence or mere exhibitionism, to say nothing of the restlessness of a fashionable but thoughtless modernity.

EPILOGUE

> ... "It wasn't for nothing," [Glaucon] said, "that you were for so long reluctant to tell your story."
>
> Plato, *Republic* 414e

This citizens' speech, then, can be said to be a speech by and to citizens in defense of common decency and perhaps the common good. It is, although not without its difficulties, a salutary speech for licentious circumstances, one that stands for (even as it exhibits) restraint and hence civilization. No doubt, another speech would be appropriate for a repressive age. Among the contemporary circumstances to which this speech is tailored is that which finds the country so large and so poorly instructed as to make it hard for anything but the most banal to become truly common, thereby smothering (or at least concealing) what is at the heart of American aspirations.

It is also a speech that, as I anticipated, takes for granted certain fundamental presuppositions of the community, perhaps the very presuppositions that may be at the root of recurring troubles of the nature addressed here. That is, ours *is* (has it always been?) a community in which it is respectable to believe that everyone is licensed and even counted upon to do as he pleases with his own. The primary purpose of the community is seen by many as permitting self-pleasing (which they may be pleased [or is it that they are troubled enough by?] to call self-expression and even self-fulfillment [but without acknowledging a standard of wholeness that the self should measure up to]). Thus, it is often taken for granted among Americans (and in most Western countries today?) that parents may do with their children pretty much as they please, that lovers may (in the fashion of the Cyclops?) do with each other as they please, and (perhaps this doctrine inspired the modern faith in the importance of privacy) that a man may do with his soul pretty much as he pleases.

Nor do citizens, as citizens, really question their dedication to the particular community in which they happen to find themselves. They, as citizens, are sworn to preserve and defend, not to examine and transform (and, if need be, repudiate), their given way of life. Indeed, they are easily led to believe that they are obliged to be steadfast, even unscrupulous, in its defense. Citizens (of whom there are, strictly speaking, fewer and fewer in modernity) are made to feel they would be nothing without the community: their lives would have no meaning; scrupulousness would become empty, and even a mockery. The most they may do by way of radical reform is to call for a return to the principles of the regime that has made them and their forebears, not to what would truly be "first principles." Thus, citizens as such are essentially conservatives.

Conservatives tend to be aware of the limits that the community is entitled to place on the desire for self-expression, especially when such expression takes the form, say, of public obscenity. But they do not like to dwell upon the fact that the question of obscenity is intimately related to the question of property, to the question of what one may legitimately do with one's own, and indeed to the question of what *is* really one's own. One may sometimes wonder, as one considers contemporary passions, whether Americans as a people still have anything in common but a devotion to the principle of unlimited acquisition and to the principle of unimpaired enjoyment of whatever happens to be acquired. One may also wonder what all this means: Are private property and genuine citizenship ultimately irreconcilable? What should be done when some want to acquire (and to "share," once acquired) what others insist should be kept private? Does not the community have to determine what should constitute "acquisition" and "enjoyment"? What is for these purposes the authoritative community? What standards should it use in making the required determinations? Does the trafficker in obscenities emerge as the true capitalist? Or is he really a prophet of comprehensive socialism?

Thus, the problem of obscenity may have at its core unsettling questions about the deference of private property to private desires. Still another, and perhaps, the most critical, challenge ignored by citizens is that which questions the fundamental presupposition that it *is* legitimate for a community to regulate, on the basis of what seems reasonable, a variety of attempts to intensify and enjoy the motions of the soul. Do we not find concealed here the enduring question which underlies any serious debate about the regulation of obscenity? Political men claim the right to judge what the artist may say and how he may say it. The artist, on the other hand—and this includes the greatest—insists that only he is equipped to determine what he should say and how, even whether obscenity should be employed by him (especially in comedies) to achieve the effect sought for.

Citizens, although their principal arguments usually do not recognize this fully, need not limit themselves to the regulation of obscene publications: their fundamental concern really is with *any* literature (whether or not obscene, whether trash or a classic) that may have a harmful effect in the circumstances in which the community happens to find itself. That is, one challenge to citizenship is, in its most elevated form, whether the philosopher-king (that peak on which human reason and political power meet) is equipped and entitled to judge the social utility of art. One has indeed risen from the "low swamps" of obscenity when one addresses oneself to this question and its corollaries:

Socrates speaks of an ancient quarrel between philosophy and poetry, between reason and art. How is this ancient quarrel to be understood inasmuch as both parties to it sincerely pursue the good? Both poetry and philosophy are touched by *eros:* one sees truth in beauty, the other beauty in truth. Both recognize the role of chance in human affairs, but in different ways: it may be a matter of chance whether philosophy emerges in the community, but its course thereafter is, in principle, prescribed; poetry, on the other hand, can be said to be always in language and with mankind, but the courses it follows depend on chance.

Thus, all philosophers may be considered, in their essentials, identical (just as there is, for beings with our natures, one best city that reason can discover): to be right-thinking is to arrive, upon serious inquiry, at the conclusions of others like oneself—at the conclusions others have come to or would come to in like circumstances. (Cf. *Hamlet*, I, v, 164-167.) Discrepancies in conclusions require investigation, reconsideration, and correction on one or both sides.

The poet, however, may not care whether he contradicts another poet. (Cf. *Republic* 349b-350d.) He seems to cherish—or, at least, is often cherished for—individuality: he strives to create, to make something *his* way, thereby making manifest something that may never have been evident before about man, about the poet himself, or about the world.

The philosopher, in order to associate himself with timeless thought, abstracts from material things; poets, in making the most of and out of themselves, delve into—sometimes even revel in—the material, at least into how the material happens to appear to them at the moment. The diversity among poets is related to the flux in that matter by which they must take their bearings: the ebb and flow of their inspiration may reflect the shifting stimuli emanating from constantly changing matter.

The poetic activity regarded by poets as creative is discerned by the philosopher to be essentially imitative. The philosophic activity regarded by the philosopher as discovery is dismissed by poets as sterile. Poets see the philosopher as fettered, but nevertheless tyrannical. The philosopher cautions the poetical against willfulness, if not even anarchy. One seems to stand for liberty (spiritual as well as social), the other for virtue (intellectual as well as moral): poets are, in inclination, moderns, whereas the philosopher is, if anywhere, an ancient.

The thoughtful observer may be moved to conclude that there can be no bridge across the timeless gulf that divides poetry and philosophy —but then he remembers Plato and Shakespeare and is obliged to reexamine his conclusions.

XI. Canada and Quebec Separatism

> O wad some Power the giftie gie us
> To see oursels as ithers see us!
> It wad frae monie a blunder free us,
> An' foolish notion:
> What airs in dress an' gait wad lea'e us,
> An' ev'n devotion!
>
> Robert Burns, *To A Louse*

i

I am concerned in this report to discuss the extent and effect of self-deception on the part of English-speaking and French-speaking Canadians alike in the current French-Canadian separatist crisis. Americans can learn from such inquiries as this not only what the problems of their Canadian neighbors are but, perhaps even more important, something about themselves as well and about how governmental power should be exercised in the pursuit of domestic tranquility and the good life.

My discussion on this occasion draws upon three visits to Canada since the separatist crisis became acute in October 1970 as well as upon recent events and examples in the United States and abroad.[1]

ii

Spring has come to the Province of Quebec—and with it the sense that a nightmare is over, that it is time for awakening, for renewal. It now seems ages—not a mere seven months—since the October 1970 kidnappings of two men (one a foreign diplomat, the other a provincial minister) that rocked Quebec and, indeed, much of Canada. The federal government of Pierre Trudeau invoked on October 16 (for the first time in peacetime) the War Measures Act, thereby giving the government of Canada virtually unlimited powers to deal with what was declared to be an "apprehended insurrection" (that is to say, an anticipated attempt at insurrection).[2]

This report (with the title, "Canada and Quebec Separatism: The Self-Deception of Decent Men") was prepared in May 1971 for the Chicago *Sun-Times*. It followed the author's annual course at Rosary College in Comparative Government (which used to include a mid-semester field trip by the class to Quebec).

Parliament endorsed in October 1970 the invocation of this act and then enacted, on December 3, legislation to replace it. This replacement, the Public Order (Temporary Measures) Act, authorized the police to arrest without warrant and to hold without bail or trial anyone suspected of having engaged in terrorist activity in Quebec Province. This act was by its own terms scheduled to lapse on April 30, 1971, unless extended by Parliament. No action was taken by the federal government to extend the act at the end of April, despite the request of the Quebec provincial government that it do so. Quebec Province has now reverted to the protection of the ordinary criminal code. It seems to be assumed by the federal government that the moment for emergency measures has passed. It is this return to normality that helps make it seem a nightmare is over.

The Public Order (Temporary Measures) Act of 1970 was considered, in the federal parliament and out, a distinct improvement over the War Measures Act originally enacted in 1914, even though the police continued to do under the Public Order Act essentially what they had done under the War Measures Act and its regulations. But "War Measures" is an ominous, sobering banner under which to exercise governmental powers—something like the suspension among us of the writ of habeas corpus. "Public Order" and "Temporary Measures" sound far less menacing than "War Measures," even if substantially the same powers are exercised by the police. In political matters, the *sound* of things can be vital, a fact reflected both in the importance for politics and politicians of rhetoric and in the irresponsibility of demagoguery and demagogues.

The sensible politician appreciates the role and limits of rhetoric. He realizes, that is, that the facts may eventually catch up with even the most astute rhetorician, especially in modern democracies with their lively press and their volatile publics. There are in Canada, and especially in Quebec Province, certain facts that have become evident since the October crisis. There has been, for instance, an erosion of support for the proposition that the invocation of the War Measures Act had been necessary. Public opinion may have been virtually unanimous behind Prime Minister Trudeau in October when he invoked the Act: the public sentiment in his support was much like that which greeted General MacArthur in 1951 when he returned to the United States from Japan after having been relieved of command by President Truman or much like that which was unleashed in Lt. Calley's defense when he was convicted for his part in the My Lai massacre. But the MacArthur sentiment faded as the American people began to realize that it is good for neither the country nor the military to have generals take away from their civilian superiors the conduct of military policy and foreign affairs. And the Calley sentiment has already begun to fade away as the American people have come to realize that no army can remain healthy, self-respecting, and hence effective if it does not purge sadists and murderers from its ranks. It was to President Truman's credit in 1951 that he did not panic in the face of the outburst of sentiment for General MacArthur.

There was in the invocation of the War Measures Act by Mr. Trudeau's government in October 1970 something traumatic—much as there was in the use of the police by Mayor Daley in Chicago during convention week of August 1968. In both cases, the immediate, almost instinctive, public support of the exercise of authority was based on the proposition that the government "must know what it is doing," that it must have had information which called for the vigorous, dramatic, even harsh, measures resorted to. And, in both cases, has not responsible public opinion come to see that the government had overstated its case? Of course, every government must take precautions: the worst must be prepared for *in some fashion*. But to prepare oneself for the worst is one thing; to misinterpret the evidence, and to allow either indignation or panic to govern, is quite another. Thus, just as it became evident during the "Chicago Conspiracy Trial" of late 1969 that Mr. Daley simply had not had any substantial cause for alarm in August 1968, so it has already become evident in Canada that Mr. Trudeau did not have any substantial cause for his alarm of October 1970.

It is the duty of responsible leaders not to lose control of themselves, especially when their conduct can lead upon exposure to a loss of confidence in either the good faith or the good sense of government. Mr. Trudeau's response in October 1970 to the two kidnappings (one of which led, shortly after his invocation of the War Measures Act, to the death of the provincial minister) appealed to those who believe that harshness is decisive in dealing *among us* with the breakdown of "law and order." This harshness, in the face of what was regarded by many Canadians as an unprecedented threat, did win him immediate public support. But, as one critic pointed out, he had used a sledgehammer to smash a peanut. One problem with such misuse of tools is that the government is tempted, lest it should look foolish in retrospect, to employ something more than even a "sledgehammer" "next time." A foolish use of power by government may be, in the long run, more dangerous for its credibility and effectiveness than even a callous abuse of power.

. An even more serious problem in maintaining law and order may be that if a sledgehammer is inappropriately used, the peanut seems, and hence becomes, far more important than it might otherwise have been. The peanut, on this occasion, turned out to be two small independent "cells" of the Front for the Liberation of Quebec (F.L.Q.). We now know that the October kidnappings were carried out by two handfuls of amateurs. In fact, the second kidnapping seems to have been a spontaneous response to publicity about the first. What was needed in Montreal in October 1970 was calm, efficient police work, not the premature proclamation of a national emergency.

But, it has been said in defense of Mr. Trudeau and his colleagues, the government could not have known at the time how extensive the plot was, how pervasive the threat to the country was. To say this, however, is merely to say in a different way that what *was* needed in Montreal in October 1970 was calm, efficient police work. Similarly, in Chicago in August 1968, it would have made all the difference in the world if the local government had been publicly encouraged by President Johnson and Vice-President Humphrey to keep the city police calm, to suspend enforcement of the curfew regulations in the parks during the week of the Democratic Convention, and even to set up soup kitchens and entertainment in Lincoln Park. Instead, there was an "escalation" of "confrontations" that culminated in the disastrous televised assault by the police on unarmed demonstrators at Michigan and Balboa, an assault made even worse by the subsequent government decision to insist upon the disgraceful masquerade known as the "Chicago Conspiracy Trial."[3]

The actions of the Canadian governments (both provincial and federal) have made the F.L.Q. far more notorious than it need have been. Indeed, one might even wonder whether the government and the F.L.Q. need one another: each exaggerates the sins and powers of the other; each can thereby justify its own activities and magnify its own accomplishments; each can thereby also ignore its own limitations and problems. But, it should at once be added, the Canadian government has been more moderate in its deeds than in its language, even though its powers under the War Measures Act were virtually unlimited. It should also be added that the F.L.Q. is important not in itself but rather as a symptom of the centuries-old problems of Quebec Province.

iii

It should be evident to anyone who has ever visited countries where serious oppression does exist—such as, for example, Greece and Czechoslovakia—that Canada has been a free country throughout the 1970-1971 crisis. This is not to deny that several hundred Quebec citizens were picked up on suspicion in October and November and held days and even weeks without charge, without counsel, and even without interrogation—but it takes far more than this to affect the fundamental character of a community, especially when (as in this case) it was clear that the emergency measures were temporary and that the officials entrusted with extraordinary powers were decent men (however mistaken they may have been about the facts of this particular crisis).

One need only compare what has happened recently in Canada with the situation in Greece today. It is clear that the usurpers who seized power in Athens four years ago (in 1967) have never had any intention of willingly surrendering power to a legitimate government. It is also clear that the Greek usurpers are anything but decent men: indeed, they were misfits in the army officer corps, which they have exploited and dishonored by their deliberate deceptions and systematic tortures. Thus, it is much easier to understand and assess what is going on in Greece today or what went on in Czechoslovakia in 1968 (after the Russians moved back in) than it is to assess what has been going on in Canada. It is virtually impossible for informed men not to see the Greek government and the Czech government for the tyrannical regimes that they have been, whereas informed men can honestly differ about what is happening and (even more important) about what should happen in Canada.[4]

Little has been done by the Canadian government, I have said, to impose serious constraints upon the people of Quebec. But then, little has *had* to be done. This, too, reflects how limited the immediate threat was. (What makes Canada interesting for the sympathetic foreign observer is that the government may have at the same time both panicked and restrained itself, a curious combination.) On the other hand, there is much that needs to be done to deal, not with outbreaks of terrorism but with the serious, enduring problems of the Canadian federation. But there may be, considering the state of the deepest French-Canadian opinion (which the F.L.Q. merely exaggerates), relatively little that any national government can do. Indeed, to place the emphasis upon either terrorism or the F.L.Q. and upon the measures thought necessary to combat them is to deceive oneself as to what the serious threat to Canadian unity is.

iv

To speak of "Canadian unity" is to speak of something that has perhaps never existed: it is to treat *two* countries, one English-speaking, the other French-speaking, as one—two countries that have been either separate *or separable* for two hundred years. The English-speaking majority of Canada has never had either the sense of purpose or the ruthlessness that would have permitted it to force the French-speaking minority to abandon its way of life. And, with the sober warning of Algeria and Vietnam all too fresh, the English-speaking majority today is not likely to insist upon having its way at all costs.

There *is* evident in Canada a vital difference between two ways of life, a difference that the decisive linguistic disparity reflects and reinforces. Each way of life—one that stresses community, the other individual enterprise—has something to be said for it: each has something in it both attractive and unattractive; each has something in it that both appeals to and threatens the other.[5] Indeed, the self-restraint and sobriety of Canadians—the fundamental decency of the national community that the alert foreign visitor cannot help but notice—may be in large part due to the realization among them that quite divergent ways of life have had to accommodate themselves to one another. In the United States, on the other hand, we have had the advantages (as well as the callousness) of the "melting pot." (It is when the majority does not choose to admit a minority into the melting pot that troubles develop among us.)

The differences in ways of life in Canada have led to, among other things, differences in standards of living between the English-speaking and the French-speaking, and differences in standards of living have in turn reinforced fundamental political differences. But, it should at once be said, an equalization of the standard of living throughout Canada is not likely to eliminate the deepest French-Canadian passion for independence. For it is precisely in that part of Quebec Province best off economically—the Montreal metropolitan area—that the most serious agitation against the federal power may be found today. It is there that most of the educated of the Province may be found. It is from Montreal that there come the teachers who are shaping the French-speaking youngsters of the Province. A majority of the present generation of French-speaking law school students in Quebec Province seems to favor an independent Quebec—and lawyers have long been very influential in Quebec life (as they were in France during the French Revolution). If the trend of the past ten years is a reliable guide, the generation that will be in law school ten years from now is likely to be, unless it should become bored and apathetic, virtually unanimous for independence.

The present generation of law students remains enough like its elders to want to assure itself that independence can be achieved without the sacrifice of the standard of living which French Canadians *do* have, a standard of living which (although lower than that of much of the rest of Canada) ranks high among the peoples of the world today. The next generation of law students, however, may well regard independence as so vital to its happiness that it will dismiss as irrelevant its possible adverse effect on the standard of living. Thus, it can turn out that although economic disparities have fed the fires of separatist discontent heretofore, the very success of the federal and provincial governments in improving economic conditions and employment opportunities in Quebec Province may contribute to the intensification of independence sentiment among the next generation: the greater such success, the higher the level of education that should follow for French Canadians; the higher the level of education (considering what passes for education today), the less concern may there be among the younger French Canadians for the economic consequences of their political enterprises and aspirations. Indeed, if things continue as they have the past decade, it will be only when prosperity and hence leisure and education come to more and more French Canadians that more and more of them will come to dwell upon their distinctive "national" character and to insist upon their emancipation from domination (political as well as economic) by the English-speaking majority.

Thus, it seems to me self-deceptive for the English-speaking (and their many allies among the French-speaking) to assume that separatist sentiment will diminish significantly among the shapers of opinion as the standard of living rises in French Canada. But this assumption seems to be at the heart of the policy of the Trudeau government. It seems to me also self-deceptive, in the short run, for the authorities (whether they be French- or English-speaking) to believe (if they do believe) that the emergency measures they have resorted to heretofore have addressed themselves to the serious threats to "Canadian unity." However that may be, the only question in Montreal during my most recent visit a few weeks ago (in March 1971) was *when* violent separatist sentiment will again begin to manifest itself and in what form, not *whether* it will do so. (I suspect that kidnapping has been exposed as unduly risky, partly because of its cumbersomeness: the victim must be cared for and concealed. The recourse by government to emergency measures temporarily smothered certain recourses to violence, but it has also exposed the government's fundamental vulnerability, at least as long as the government responds as it did in October.)

The battle for the unity of Canada is not likely to be won either in the criminal courts or on the economic balance sheets of the Province of Quebec. The battle for the preservation of Canadian unity faces first of all the need to *establish* a unity to be preserved. One needs only to drive the few hours it takes to move on the highway from Montreal to Ottawa to realize how French is Quebec and how English is most of the rest of Canada. It must be difficult for the French Canadian to regard the federal capital city of Ottawa as in any significant way *his*. The English-speaking Canadian may well regard Ottawa as the capital of his country; the French-speaking Canadian can hardly regard himself in Ottawa as much more than a tourist in a foreign country. One is tempted to wonder what would happen if the federal parliament should be moved to Montreal or even to the outskirts of Quebec City.

v

I have examined thus far primarily the self-deception of the forces working for "Canadian unity," that self-deception which culminates in the frequently repeated reassurance that the government has only a small minority of troublemakers to contend with in French Canada. (It has been convenient, but unrealistic, for government apologists to dismiss such troublemakers either as foreign agitators or as native-born psychotics.) The self-deception on the part of the separatists—the law-abiding as well as the more militant—should also be noticed to round out this report.

There is first of all the failure of the separatists to face up to the economic consequences of "going it alone" upon the severance of Quebec from Canada. Even though the principled French-speaking separatist may not be ultimately concerned about the economic consequences of independence, his elders (including the majority of the French Canadians who work the farms and man the shops of the Province) *are* concerned about such consequences. *Their* concern can be relied upon by the federal government and by others opposing separation. Separatists are obliged, therefore, to speak to the mundane question of the economic consequences of the separation they seek.

Some separatists go so far as to insist not only that independence would not lower the standard of living for French Canada but that it would (after an initial period of readjustment) even raise it. That is, separatists can be heard to argue that an independent Quebec would no longer be exploited by the rest of Canada. They may even go so far as to argue that a sovereign Quebec would also be better able than Quebec Province is now to protect itself from American economic exploitation. It is difficult to see, however, that this argument makes economic sense. The American exploitation of Canada that is complained about (and not only in Quebec Province) is related to the presence of large-scale American investment in Canada—but without that investment, Canada's standard of living would inevitably fall (unless such capital can be secured from other countries—and there is no reason to believe capital could be secured from those countries on better terms than from the United States). In any event, it is difficult to see how an independent Quebec could "protect" itself from "exploitation" when Canada (which is four times larger and somewhat more prosperous than Quebec) cannot do so.

The serious problem upon separation would not be that of policing American investment in Quebec but that of persuading American investment that is already there to stay and of encouraging new investment to come. All other things being equal, Americans will probably prefer to invest in the English-speaking part of Canada rather than in a French-speaking Quebec that is completely on its own, especially if its separation from Canada should be preceded by considerable agitation and violence. In addition, Quebec would be deprived, upon separation, of the government services and financial aid now available to it from the rest of Canada—services and aid extensive enough to make some of the other provinces believe that Quebec is really exploiting *them*. One need not insist that separation will lead to severe economic dislocations in Quebec; one need only see that, at best, it is difficult to be sure that it will *not* do so, and such uncertainty can itself have serious economic effects even before separation.

It is difficult, in any event, to expect that an independent Quebec will be better able than Canada is now to withstand the economic influence of the United States upon its life. The dilemma faced by all of Canada in this respect is reflected in recent comments by Mr. Trudeau. He was questioned on his attitude about American investment in Canada. "We feel," he said, "that Canadians would rather have a job, even if it's American capital, rather than no job." The Prime Minister repeated on that occasion his opposition to the suggestion, which some have made, that Canadians attempt to buy back ownership of companies owned by nonresidents. He called this "a waste of money and a waste of opportunity," warning that if Canadians spend their money to buy back companies that are already foreign-owned, they would not have money to build hospitals and schools, clean up pollution or develop new industries. "We have the choice to stop our development now by halting foreign investment," Mr. Trudeau said. "It would mean we would reduce our standard of living."

What makes the nationalist choice more difficult in Canada than it is in countries such as China or even Cuba is that the American alternative is always immediately available to Canadians. They are constantly aware of, and hence attracted by, the American standard of living. This is true of French Canada as well. The most dedicated French-Canadian separatists may despise such attraction as "decadent," especially when it depends on large-scale American investment—but the attractiveness of an American-style standard of living remains a political fact with which serious separatists must somehow come to terms.

vi

The economic self-deception I have referred to is dramatized politically by the attitude of the French-Canadian separatist toward the future status in Quebec of the European immigrant. The typical immigrant in Quebec Province—there must be at least one-fifth of the present population of the Greater Montreal region who have come from Europe since the Second World War—learns English upon coming to Canada, even if he should live in Quebec. He elects to send his children to schools where the principal instruction is in English. *That*, one is told by dedicated French separatists, will cease upon independence: the immigrant may continue to learn English, if he chooses, but he (and, even more important, his children) will have to learn French first of all, especially in school. Since it is unusual for an immigrant to learn well more than one foreign language, the separatists' requirement means that English would be sacrificed by the typical immigrant settling in Quebec. The establishment of French as the primary language for families of immigrants also means, however, that there would be both a large-scale exodus of immigrants now in Quebec and the refusal of most potential immigrants to settle there. This means, in turn, that the labor force in Quebec Province would come to be limited to the French-speaking people already there and to the relatively few French Canadians who would return from the rest of Canada to an independent Quebec. This means, finally, that the American-style standard of living most Quebecers want—a standard of living that depends in the immediate future upon an ever increasing labor pool from which an expanding industry may draw—would be highly unlikely.

The separatists who insist that immigrants will continue to settle in a Quebec that *is* officially and thoroughly French-speaking can only do so by not talking seriously with the immigrants already among them. That is, such separatists ignore and hence misunderstand and antagonize the immigrants in much the same way as English-speaking Canadians misunderstand and antagonize the French-speaking.

It should be obvious that few European immigrants will want to "lock" themselves (and, even more important, their children) into an economy of only five or six million, when they could become eligible for movement into the rest of English-speaking North America either by choosing to learn English (as they now do in Quebec) or by going directly to those parts of Canada where English would be available as the principal language of their schools. That is, the immigrant would have little reason to confine himself to Quebec (which is what learning primarily French is taken by him to mean). It is *partly* because French-Canadian workmen know only French that they are restricted to a small market and hence suffer more than do most Canadians from unemployment. Or so it is said. When confronted by these contentions, the French-Canadian separatist insists that things would somehow work out upon attainment of independence—but his more sober, even though less educated, elders somehow "know better."[6]

Perhaps his elders also know that the Canada in which the French and English find themselves *is* a decent society, that it is an open (or, at least, openable if not opening) society, but one in which old-fashioned virtues, aspirations, and even pieties still have meaning. Is it not self-deceptive on the part of separatists to believe that an independent Quebec is likely to be a better community than that in which they now find themselves? *Is it not self-deceptive to assume that decent communities are easy to come by or to preserve?* Is not this peculiarly modern delusion at least as serious a self-deception as that of the many English-speaking Canadians who smugly believe that their French-speaking fellow citizens have no legitimate grievances, that the troubles in Quebec Province are merely the work of an insignificant minority of troublemakers in need of discipline?

vii

It should be recognized on behalf of the Canadian federal government that it has *not* tried to "save face" at this time by deceiving itself or its constituents into continuing to believe that the emergency measures prematurely resorted to last year are still needed (even though very little has really changed since October). Perhaps, in fact, the federal government has learned that dramatic emergency measures are rarely a substitute for competent police work and serious political action and that they often play into the hands of the very extremists against whom they are directed. Indeed, the growing self-restraint of the Canadian government suggests, in a world accustomed to well-meaning but futile escalations of violence, one more argument for the worth of Canada as a political entity.

It should be recognized, on the other hand, that the self-deceptions of the French-Canadian separatists could culminate in one dismal blunder, the emergence of an independent Quebec so beset by economic and social turmoil that the repressive measures which would then "have" to be resorted to by a French-Canadian government against French Canadians could make the War Measures Act seem very tame indeed. Is it not the duty of both French-speaking and English-speaking intellectuals to forestall such a development? Is this not the time to substitute rigorous analysis and responsible rhetoric for thoughtless, even though "principled," self-deception?

Or is it, rather, romantic self-deception for an American to recognize that there is much that is attractive and worth preserving in the Canada now available to the French-speaking and the English-speaking alike? Should not such a recognition provide for Canadians of good will, who are aware of the alternatives abroad that are much more oppressive and far less enlightened than what they now have in Canada, a reasonable basis for enduring unity?[7]

XII. Vietnam and the Constitution

> Every art and every investigation, and likewise every
> practical pursuit or undertaking, seems to aim at some
> good: hence it has been well said that the good is that
> at which all things aim.
>
> Aristotle, *Nicomachean Ethics* 1094al

i

What do Dr. Daniel Ellsberg and Gen. John Lavelle have in common besides their evident willingness to engage in acts of "insubordination," the former by disregarding security regulations with respect to certain classified documents known as the "Pentagon Papers," the latter by disregarding orders with respect to the deployment of bombers in Vietnam? Is it not prudent to assume that both men are patriotic Americans?

How should these two kinds of patriotic insubordination—leakage of classified documents and disregard of bombing directives—be treated by us? The White House evidently takes one far more seriously than the other. That is, vigorous efforts were made in June 1971 to keep the press from publishing the Pentagon Papers. Attempts are now being made to imprison the men alleged to have distributed those papers to the press. On the other hand, the general who (upon exposure) admitted his deliberate and repeated disregard of bombing directives has been permitted to escape court-martial (but *not*, it is salutary to believe, the enduring censure of his fellow officers) and to retire with a generous pension.

ii

Are not the "priorities" of the White House misplaced? We are accustomed to, and even depend upon, the unauthorized disclosure of classified documents in order to help the press make the government

---

This article was published in the Chicago *Tribune*, June 25, 1972, sec. 1A, p. 1. It was reprinted with the title, "Vietnam, Insubordination and Self-Government," in 118 *Congressional Record* E8414 (October 5, 1972); also in 118 *Congressional Record* E8480 (October 10, 1972).

behave itself. But we cannot permit generals (and certainly not in a nuclear age) to conduct war as they choose. Thus, we cannot know what we (as a sovereign people) are doing if vital information is systematically kept from us; nor can we control what is done in our name if our public servants (whether military officers or their civilian superiors) may act as they believe best and thereafter attempt to conceal from public inspection and public discussion what they have done.

There are obviously circumstances in which information should be kept secret; there are also obviously circumstances in which a soldier should refuse to obey an order given to him. But should not the presumption be both in favor of full disclosure of information and in favor of compliance with orders (especially when the orders are of a restraining character)? However that may be, we simply cannot allow military men to determine how (or if) a war is to be fought; nor can we allow the Executive Branch of the government to dictate what (if anything) will be revealed about its policies and its conduct.

Both military insubordination and government secrecy usually subvert efforts by Americans to govern themselves.[1]

iii

American self-government depends not only on adequate information among the electorate and sufficient control *by* the electorate of what public servants do. It depends, as well, on the moral sobriety of our people. Indeed, no impassioned or corrupted people can truly govern themselves, for they are so crippled morally that they cannot be said either to know or to choose what they are doing. (In such circumstances, chance rather than rational public discourse determines events.) The most important revelation of the Pentagon Papers, therefore, may have been their confirmation of the moral obtuseness, if not even simple callousness, of the men who have tried to act on our behalf in Indochina.[2]

There is little to be found in the Pentagon Papers indicating any day-to-day awareness among our public servants of the serious moral problems posed by our willingness (and, at times, even eagerness) to sacrifice to our supposed long-term security interests the lives and property of the Vietnamese. We were willing to inflict considerable immediate damage upon a distant (and much weaker) people in order to spare ourselves *some* possible damage in the remote future. Let us hope that the American people went along with what was done there in their name primarily because the threat to "us" was exaggerated and the damage to "them" was played down.

It remains to be seen how critically we have damaged the American soul in the process.

iv

The physical damage we are visiting upon Vietnam, North and South, has again been intensified in recent months. The North Vietnamese government can be said to have brought much of this damage on its people by launching its current brutal offensive. But such an observation, comforting as it might be to some, still leaves open the fundamental question of whether *we* should be in Indochina at all. The most troublesome aspect of what we are now doing in Indochina is that the American public has again allowed itself to be lulled into acquiescence, partly because of spiritual fatigue and disillusionment, partly because of its traditional reluctance to question the judgment of its President in his conduct of foreign affairs (at least not before election day), and partly because of the virtual elimination of American casualties by the withdrawal from Vietnam of almost all our combat ground troops.

It is a pity that the North Vietnamese do not realize that it is in both their interest and ours that they release immediately and unconditionally, into the custody of a neutral country, all their American prisoners of war. It would then be difficult for the basically good-natured American public to continue to believe that we are entitled to inflict upon Vietnam the devastating aerial punishment we have unleashed. Even so, do we not already know enough, without waiting either for more revelations or for the parole of American prisoners, to be able to recognize our present conduct in Vietnam as bordering on the barbaric, however "successful" it may eventually be in promoting what is likely to be no more than a temporary cease-fire in Indochina?

v

We cannot survive as a vital body politic without the integrity that comes from a public respect for old-fashioned civility. It is that integrity which makes self-government possible among us and keeps public servants in their place even when we cannot watch them. We must take care, in any event, lest partisan success in one "confrontation" encourage everyone to become reckless elsewhere. (The theatrical

Cuban Missile Crisis of 1962 comes to mind.) We have the duty, that is, to study and to supervise what is happening and what is likely to happen in the conduct of our affairs abroad.

Is it not the duty of the press and of Congress to examine what is being done in our name and to do what they can to shield from government prosecution those who make patriotic efforts to expose to public inspection what the Executive Branch tries to keep concealed from the American people (especially when what is concealed from us, and even from Congress, is known to our antagonists)?

Is it not also the duty of Congress and of the press to insist that there be no compromise with the constitutional principle of civilian, and ultimate public (and hence rational?), control of our awesome military power?

vi

Self-government depends on both self-confidence and self-criticism. We should not forget that a war has been prosecuted by us for a decade without the constitutionally required declaration of war. Such radical insubordination by the President, in which Congress has improperly acquiesced, makes both the disclosure of classified documents and the disregard of bombing directives seem rather modest by comparison. Indeed, the wonder is that we have not, in our prosecution of this misconceived war, subverted even more than we have the political morals and the constitutional morale of the country.

What we *have* subverted profoundly is the necessary confidence in the institutions of this country on the part of both our more articulate youth and our more conscientious military officers. That confidence must now be reestablished, beginning with our willingness and ability to face up to the facts of the past decade—including the attractive but dangerous illusions of President Kennedy's Crusade.[3]

vii

Need it be added that to question the morality of what we have allowed to be done in our name in Indochina does not excuse what the North Vietnamese and their allies have been doing and may intend to do there and elsewhere?

In fact, it is still another argument against what we have have been doing in Indochina that we have become, in the prosecution of this war, too much like the enemy we have conjured up: devious, ruthless, and implicitly contemptuous of constitutional principles.

XIII. The Case for Supporting Israel

> And I will give unto thee, and to thy seed after thee,
> the land wherein thou art a stranger, all the land of
> Canaan, for an everlasting possession; and I will be
> their God.
>
> *Genesis* 17:8

i

It is difficult, in these perilous times for Israel, to speak responsibly
about what should be done by the United States to ensure that the
terms upon which the Middle East fighting ends are terms that do not
leave Israel crippled and vulnerable.[1]

That the United States will continue to do something on Israel's
behalf is highly likely. How much we will do, and in what spirit and
on what terms, depends in part on official assessments by us of American interests in the Middle East, assessments in which global strategic
considerations will necessarily play a part. But these assessments should
depend as well on something much deeper and finer than transient
strategic calculations. They should take account of our relation as a
free and humane people to a like-minded people in Israel. Indeed, such
a relation can even be decisive in defining our permanent national interest in the Middle East.

My long and intimate association with Jews in the American academic community has kept me somewhat more aware than I might
otherwise have been of the problems and aspirations (as well as the
sometimes aggressive, if understandable, self-righteousness) of Israel.
On the other hand, my opposition since the beginning to the misconceived American involvement in the Vietnam War helps make me
aware of the care and self-restraint with which the United States should
use its great power all over the world.

It is impossible at this time not to appreciate on campuses the dis-
tress of one's Jewish friends at the bleak prospects for Israel, whatever
the outcome of present hostilities. It sometimes seems that, unless the
Americans and Russians jointly insist upon and guarantee a just settle-

---

This article was published in the Chicago *Sun-Times*, October 21, 1973, sec. 1-A,
p. 1. It was reprinted in 119 *Congressional Record* E7040 (November 5, 1973).

ment in the Middle East, war will continue for generations—a war the Israelis can never win and the Arabs can never lose. The prospects of that can be, for both Israelis and Arabs, quite demoralizing—and for world peace quite dangerous. Sarajevo should remind the Great Powers of the limits of limited war.

ii

It has been noticed that American foreign policy is influenced, both in the Executive and in Congress, by the well-organized and articulate Jewish minority in this country. It is, of course, always somewhat a matter of chance who one's friends happen to be—if only because chance does affect what people one comes to know and thereupon to like or to dislike. But it should also be noticed that the reasons why Jews are here in a politically significant minority, and why they remain an identifiable and hence cohesive minority, have very much to do with why both they and all other Americans should be concerned about the appropriate relations between the United States and Israel.

The affinities between these two countries are neither accidental nor superficial. Both countries are among the few in the world that are made up almost entirely of immigrants or the descendants of fairly recent immigrants. That is, both countries have nobly served as havens for the persecuted and the dispossessed of the earth. Both countries are also among the few that embody and somehow represent an idea. One looks back to the Old Testament for its heritage, the other to the Declaration of Independence. For better and for worse, the two countries are very much alike. They, like us, are fundamentally Western in orientation, in standards and in ways of conducting political and social affairs.

But there are not only affinities to bring us together. There are debts as well, debts owed to the Jewish people and (considering the sentiments of most articulate and informed Jews I know) owed by extension to Israel as a convenient, if not even necessary, homeland of world Jewry. Our debts reach back to the contribution of Jews to our heritage, the contribution of that demanding message that came out of the desert to challenge a decadent European paganism. There is also the contribution made by the Jews of the West in the two World Wars, those wars that can be said to have made it possible for the Arab peoples to escape German imperialism and to begin to achieve a national consciousness. And there is as well the awful price paid by the Jews at the hands of the Nazi tyranny which threatened to engulf all of

Europe. One cannot help but wonder sometimes whether that price really had to be paid, whether the West did all it could and should have done to keep the Nazis from doing what they did. We cannot permit, for the good of our souls, another such awful miscalculation with respect to the fate of Jews.

Still another miscalculation we should guard against today is that of assuming we surely know better than the Israelis what is good, or safe, for them. Our attention is easily diverted from the Middle East; we have many other legitimate concerns all over the world as well as at home; and, all too often, we simply cannot know as well as involved people on the spot what is going on and what is likely to happen.

The Israelis are, it is safer to assume, probably better judges of their long-run interests than we here are likely to be. I do not suggest that we give the Israelis a blank check. But we should be aware of our limitations and of our preoccupations elsewhere. We should also be aware that the Israelis are a sophisticated and intelligent people who are more than likely to be aware, in turn, of what it is appropriate and prudent to try to secure from the United States. (However that may be, no one should want to see American soldiers fighting in the Middle East.)

The Israelis will no doubt make mistakes—or seem to make mistakes. For instance, they may even be tempted, should they drive the invading Egyptian forces back across the Suez Canal, to relieve themselves of their corrosive Palestinian refugee-camps problem by evacuating into the Port Said area the Arab inhabitants of the Gaza Strip. They may even consider themselves obliged and justified, in the event of a crushing victory won after the great sacrifices they are now making, to force a permanent demobilization of their neighbors, employing the promise of preventive strikes to ensure that their injunctions are obeyed. Such a *Pax Judaica*, which would have the added advantage of promising to ease a ruinously costly arms race in the area, may become particularly attractive to Israelis if they should consider themselves likely to be abandoned by the United States. That is, desperate circumstances may call for desperate measures, even more desperate measures than the two I have just mentioned.

iii

But, the fair-minded American must also wonder, is a policy of guaranteeing the continued existence of Israel truly just to the Arabs?

Western radicals do speak of "Israeli colonialism" and of "Arab liberation movements." This kind of talk strikes me as, at best, irresponsible sentimentality. What serious problems among one hundred million Arabs, aside from the unrest created by incessant anti-Israeli propaganda, will be solved by the subjugation of a country of three million Israelis? The Arabs, it is said, are a proud people who must "save face" after having been defeated repeatedly by the Israelis. Is such face-saving really more important than the preservation of the only sovereign Jewish community, in the world, a country of fewer than ten thousand square miles flanked by millions of square miles of Arab territory? One is reminded of the Nazi insistence upon the Sudetenland.

It is, it should be added, impossible to determine, without qualification, to whom Palestine "belonged" before Israel was established. Possession is put forward by Arab spokesmen as decisive for their claim, but that is not as decisive on their behalf as is sometimes believed. That is, a British mandate preceded the establishment of Israel and before that a long Turkish rule. But, it will be said, the resident Arab population had been kept from rightful possession by foreign occupiers. This, however, reminds one that Jews, too, have been kept from what they considered rightful possession, even longer and by even more foreign occupiers. Thus, the claims of the Jews are even older than those of the Arabs, their possession much more recent.

Of course, such considerations cannot be conclusive, but they do point up the difficulty of determining abstract property rights in such circumstances. It should also be added that one basis for a just allocation of the resources of the world is that they should be in the hands of those who will make the best use of them for mankind. Can it be denied by any detached observer that the level of civilization in Israel today, and in the foreseeable future, is markedly superior to that found in any of its belligerent neighbors?[2]

Should not all the Arab peoples of North Africa and the Middle East profit from having in their midst—as an example of what can be done with modern technology and social democracy—an imaginative and industrious people such as the Israelis? Are not adaptations of the Israeli experiment, financed by the vast oil wealth of the Arabs, the true source of liberation for the Arab peoples of the world?

It should be noticed, in passing, that Middle Eastern oil may not be as critical for us as is sometimes thought. We can, in the short run, adjust to politically inspired oil shortages by raising prices and thus consuming less. Our sacrifices, in the interest of a humane foreign policy, are more easily to be endured by us than the sacrifices that would tend, after awhile, to undermine the restraint-of-trade conspiracy among the oil-producing countries. Indeed, the Arabs should be made to understand that their refusal to supply Western markets can only mean, in the long run, more and hence cheaper fuel supplies than there would otherwise have been available. That is, the international economy can be expected to adjust to the deliberate withholding of Middle Eastern oil just as it did to the closing of the Suez Canal.

What should we do now? We should, of course, do what we can to stop the current hostilities on terms the Israelis can live with. One condition for being able to do so is to make it clear to the world that we will not be blackmailed by threats to our standard of living. I do not presume to argue for a particular policy in the Middle East. But I have suggested why we should be inclined to continue to support the Israelis, why our sympathies must remain with them. These sympathies, properly understood, are also with those Arab peoples who have been exploited by demagogues and by desperate, if not reckless, leaders.

Should not Arab honor be appealed to over the heads of their exploiters? Everyone should be reminded that the Arabs are capable of behaving better than they have been moved to do in recent years. Their illustrious past should not be forgotten, either by them or by us. Jews and Arabs, for centuries at a time, lived with one another in peace and harmony. There is no good reason why this should not happen again to their mutual advantage. Indeed, one of the richest periods of Jewish thought, to which the work of the late Leo Strauss is an eloquent tribute, was when Jews lived under Moslem rule in Spain and elsewhere.[3]

The Jews of the world should be permitted to repay what they have gotten from their Arab benefactors—but to do this properly they seem to need a justly defensible country of their own in the Holy Land.

XIV. Impeachment and Statesmanship

> It has been frequently remarked that it seems to have
> been reserved to the people of this country, by their
> conduct and example, to decide the important ques-
> tion, whether societies of men are really capable or not
> of establishing good government from reflection and
> choice, or whether they are forever destined to de-
> pend for their political constitutions on accident and
> force.
>
> *Federalist* No. 1

i

If one is to believe what one reads in the papers these days, the impeachment of the President by the House of Representatives seems
more likely than it did a few months ago. Those writers who are generally regarded as most informed about political matters seem to be of
that opinion.

Thus, the New York *Times* could begin its lead editorial of February
20, 1974 (entitled "Toward Impeachment") with this observation: "The
nation is moving inexorably toward an impeachment trial of President
Nixon. His conviction by two-thirds vote of the Senate is by no means
certain but his indictment by the House of Representatives sitting as
grand jury for the nation appears increasingly likely." It is evident that
the editors of the *Times*, as well as of some other respectable journals,
believe that Mr. Nixon's impeachment and subsequent trial are called for
in the present circumstances.

Two recent special elections, to fill vacancies in the House of Representatives of seats from Pennsylvania and Michigan, make a House vote
of impeachment seem even more likely to many political commentators.
That is, those elections have seen "safe" Republican seats fall to Democratic challengers, and in contests that suggest the standing of the President had affected the results. One of those seats, as you probably know,
had been vacated by Gerald Ford upon assuming the vice-presidency.

This talk was delivered at the University Church of the Disciples of Christ, Chicago, Illinois, February 24, 1974. It was published in its entirety in Chicago *rap*,
March 11, 1974, p. 1, and in an abridged form in the Chicago *Tribune*, April 20, 1974,
sec. 1, p. 16.

These losses, representing a switch of significant proportions in voter sentiment, have made Republican members of the House of Representatives even more nervous than they were already about the November elections in which all of them must secure reelection if they are to continue their Congressional careers. It is recognized among them that Mr. Nixon and his Administration are for them a serious liability. If still another safe seat falls in a special election—another election *is* scheduled in Ohio in early March—, panic may well set in among Republicans interested in political self-preservation. One can then expect serious efforts to be made by them to remove Mr. Nixon from office, preferably by resignation, but if necessary by impeachment in the House and conviction in the Senate. Some desperate Republicans can be expected to be among the leaders in such repudiation of the President, especially if damaging indictments (with fresh revelations) are handed up in the weeks ahead against various of his former associates.[1]

Thus, the issue is not being allowed to fade away: Democrats, some Republicans, and the press continue to regard it as an issue. The President is indeed on the run. I expressed last October my serious reservations with respect to what was going on then: this impeachment, I said at that time, was playing with fire.[2] I had occasion in January to restate some of my reservations in a letter to a thoughtful student who had dissented from my earlier public statement on the subject: "It now appears that the impeachment issue will be with us (or can well be with us) through 1974. That is, the House Judiciary Committee, it is said, may not have its report ready until June. Then how long will it take the House to act? If an impeachment is voted, will Mr. Nixon resign? If he does not resign, how long will that trial last? Will it run concurrently with the election campaign of 1974? If an impeachment is not voted, what will those who want an impeachment say and do? How much more of this continuing turmoil is good for the country? What *is* the mature way of handling something so disruptive as this? What *would* Mr. Nixon be able to do— what harm would he be able to inflict, what harm would he want to inflict—if the entire matter should be dropped right now?" These questions seem to me still timely, especially when one realizes that even if nothing else happens, Mr. Nixon and his successors will be much more cautious hereafter about how they allow the powers of the Presidency to be employed.

I suspect, by the way, that *one* reason impeachment remains a live issue is that a number of comfortable people are rather bored: they are open to a little constitutional drama, perhaps indeed, *in part*, because of the genuine (calming) accomplishments of certain of Mr. Nixon's policies.[3] The dramatic or theatrical has had more to do with what has happened thus far, with the development of this issue and with the shaping of public opinion, than may be proper. The "Watergate Hearings" conducted by the Ervin Committee are a case in point. But it should be recognized that there are people who, although favorable to the President (or at least unfavorable to his accusers), nevertheless believe that impeachment and trial would help clear the air.

However that may be, everyone should also recognize the risk, in any extended proceeding, of a partial paralysis of the country's government, and the risk, over the long run, of deep recrimination.

But it should further be recognized that a momentum has probably set in which *can* lead to impeachment and which counsels of moderation can do little to slow down, let alone stop. Even so, we can at least try to understand what is going on and thereby learn something about ourselves and our institutions.

ii

What *is* there to be learned? I believe I can suggest one of the important things to be learned, and thereby provide a basis for our discussion this morning, by developing here a provocative proposition about citizens such as you who, for lack of a better term, one can call "liberals." A candid examination of the current drive for impeachment—the standards employed, the passions aroused, the arguments used—permits liberals to see the "McCarthy period" from the other side of the pursuit. That is, all this permits sensitive liberals to realize what it feels like to be on the hunters' side of a witch-hunt for a change.

Far be it from me to suggest that liberals today (such as the American Civil Liberties Union, which is pushing impeachment) are really behaving like Senator Joseph McCarthy or like Representative Nixon in his heyday. Of course, there are differences: there is now, for example, more of a conscious effort to be fair than there was then. Still, there are disturbing resemblances, including the extent to which the unleashing of certain passions has led to a cavalier attitude with respect to evidence. That is, the parallels are remarkable, including the reliance in each of the pioneering cases of the two periods—the Hiss case in the 1940s and the Watergate case in the 1970s—upon bizarre recordings to dramatize the matter for the public. (I refer to the "pumpkin papers" microfilms and to the "Watergate tapes.") Perhaps liberals can, if they look into their own souls, come away from all this with a more sympathetic appreciation of what moved Senator McCarthy, his predecessors and his allies of a quarter century ago.

Liberals should remind themselves, for instance, that their counterparts of the 1940s saw the threat to the country to be at least as critical as that now seen to be represented by Mr. Nixon. After all, Joseph Stalin and those who supported him (in this country or abroad) were not angels: there was a good deal of evil, both in deeds and in intentions, let loose in the world at that time. Certainly, some of the Stalinists were worse than any of the crowd around Mr. Nixon.

Even so, what should have been done about Alger Hiss, who was (by the late 1940s) no more (if that) than an ex-Stalinist, an ex-Communist of a decade or so before?[4] Should not that case have been regarded as "ancient history" and had the books closed on it? Would not that have been the mature thing to do? Did not the good of the country require such a tacit amnesty, lest unhealthy passions be aroused and orderly self-government be threatened? May it not be obvious to us *now* that that is how that matter should have been handled *then?* But what about Mr. Nixon's misdeeds and those of his lieutenants? Could we not live with them? Has the turmoil stirred up by their investigation and prosecution been worth the satisfaction of exposure? Or, put another way, are not anti-Nixonites at least as unrealistic about seeing danger to the country at this time as anti-Communists were in seeing it back in the 1940s?

Or, to put my challenge still another way, is not John Dean the liberals' Whittaker Chambers? Mr. Dean is not as interesting (or as imaginative) as Mr. Chambers. But does he not serve the same function, that of the persuasive reformed co-conspirator who brings down the mighty? Is it politically healthy that those in exalted positions—whether Mr. Hiss or President Nixon—should depend, for their security, on the likes of Mr. Chambers and Mr. Dean? Should the standing of an administration—whether Mr. Truman's (or Mr. Roosevelt's), on the one hand, or Mr. Nixon's, on the other—depend on such patently self-serving, if not unreliable, witnesses?

I grant you that there would be a kind of poetic justice if Mr. Nixon, the unrelenting Congressional inquisitor, should be brought to bay by methods similar to those by which he rose to preeminence.[5] But we need not concern ourselves for the moment with what *he* "deserves" but rather with what the country needs. Furthermore, as I have said, liberals can learn what it means to be in hot pursuit "in a good cause": when pursuit is hot, the quality of evidence does not really matter; the sense of an ominous threat, and of the bad character of one's quarry, suffices. At the core of such pursuit is, I am afraid, a dominating self-righteousness. I am reminded of what Robert Bolt says in his review of the cast of characters for his play about Thomas More, *A Man for All Seasons*, when he describes William Roper as having "an all-consuming rectitude which is his cross, his solace, and his hobby."[6]

iii

I find it rather revealing of the temper of these times that it is for us so hard to say, as a people (or for liberals to say, as a faction), what it is believed that Mr. Nixon may be guilty of. That is, what *are* the offenses which warrant impeachment? I have this past week, in preparing this talk, asked a half-dozen informed people what they consider *the* critical count for purposes of impeachment. I got a half-dozen quite different responses. I find this suspicious—not conclusive, mind you, but suspicious. What unites all the would-be impeachers, it seems to me, is not really the evidence against Mr. Nixon but their animus against him, an animus that is (I grant) understandable. But is it constitutional?

Certainly, "loss of confidence" should not provide the basis for impeachment. Ours is not—and probably should not be turned into—a parliamentary system. Effective parliamentary government depends on pervasive social restraints on the authoritative public opinion, which restraints we simply do not have. We should take care not to turn "loss of confidence" (or even "a pattern of misconduct") into an impeachable offense. A President *should* sometimes be quite unpopular, even for a long period of time, if the common good is to be served. The purpose of Presidential impeachment, it should be remembered, is not to serve as a recount of the last election, or as a censure of elected officials or as a way of gratifying public opinion. Rather, it is to permit the Congress to remove from office a President whose conduct threatens grave injury to the common good— and not all conduct, at that, but conduct of a certain character which threatens such injury. (Thus, it was never seriously believed, so far as I know, that Herbert Hoover could have been constitutionally impeached during the Great Depression. He might well have resigned when his ineffectiveness had become evident?) Does not our form of government assume that the time to make the critical moral judgment of candidates is before an election? Our "options" are much more limited afterwards— and properly so, lest there be constant reconsideration with its consequent unsettling effects. Certainly, the essential information with respect to

Mr. Nixon's character, and with respect to his way of conducting his political business, was available to the electorate before his 1968 election to the Presidency. Is it not instructive that a people be obliged to live with this kind of mistake until the next election?

The kind of Presidential conduct which threatens grave (if not irreparable) injury to the common good includes, in addition to certain indictable crimes, the waging of undeclared war (certainly if waged against the known desire of Congress) and the repeated and deliberate refusal to enforce constitutional laws the Congress clearly intends to have enforced. (One option always retained by a President is that alluded to by President Lincoln when he said that if Congress should insist upon reenslaving any man who had been freed by virtue of his Emancipation Proclamation, someone other than he would have to serve as Congress's instrument.) Congress, it seems to me, should be able (and without any possible judicial review) to remove from office a President who insists upon exercising powers he does not constitutionally have or who refuses to exercise powers he may have a duty to exercise. Must Congress first go through the form of enacting legislation making such behavior "high Crimes and misdemeanors"? Has not such behavior always been, under our constitutional dispensation, implicitly an offense for impeachment purposes?

Of course, common sense is called for in considering what behavior Congress should take seriously. And, as I have suggested, one should be suspicious when so many counts are alleged, and all of a sudden, against an experienced politician. The fact is that with a bureaucracy as large as ours, and with the informal manner certain things have come to be done, it is not difficult in certain administrations to start things unravelling. I am reminded of Lincoln Steffens' account (in his *Autobiography*) of how "crime waves" can be generated by enterprising reporters—that is, by reporters who begin to publish stories about everything that routinely appears on the police blotter. I do not mean to suggest that Mr. Nixon and his subordinates have not misbehaved—but I do wonder whether their misbehavior is of a magnitude to warrant the extraordinary remedy we are now considering. Indeed, I have the impression that a good deal of the misconduct being discussed (especially with respect to the coverup) is something that was stumbled into, with no clearly wicked intention and with no overall awareness of the seriousness of what was being done. Let us consider some of the counts of impeachment that have been proposed.

A responsible, articulate, intelligent, and well-informed Democratic politician I know decided last month that Mr. Nixon should be impeached.[7] He had not supported impeachment before it was opined by experts that a critical 18½-minute segment of a "Watergate tape" had been deliberately erased while the tape was under the control of Mr. Nixon. This politician (a lawyer and former member of Congress from this district) explained that his decision to support impeachment, made with "great sadness and reluctance," was dictated by the seriousness of five charges "now pending against the administration and the President of the United States." He is reported by the press to have listed the charges as

1) "Improper handling of the President's personal financial affairs."

2) "Improvements on Mr. Nixon's properties at San Clemente, California and Key Biscayne, Florida at taxpayers' expense."

3) "Illegal solicitation and receipt of campaign contributions."

4) "The activities of the White House 'plumbers.' "

5) "The Watergate tapes and disclosures of erasures."

Are these serious charges? I must say that they strike me as rather trivial charges for impeachment purposes, whatever may be said about them as confirming what we have long known about Mr. Nixon's character and conduct. And yet, these seem to be all that so well-informed a lawyer (himself a former member of the House Judiciary Committee) sees on the record *as we now have it.* Let me consider each of the five charges briefly, in reverse order.

5) "The Watergate tapes and disclosures of erasures." Does not the seriousness of this charge depend, in large part, on the seriousness of the conduct the tapes supposedly deal with? Was not the Watergate burglary itself really quite trivial, however much leverage it has provided for an investigation into the Administration? Do we want to insist that comprehensive Administrative records (such as the extensive tape recordings in question here) should be made available to Congressional investigators or to grand juries? Is not any resulting "contempt" of court or of Congress essentially an ancillary charge, depending for its significance upon the original seriousness of the conduct for which a "cover-up" may have been intended and to which the tapes relate? Should it not be appreciated that if "everything" may be brought out, once a suspicion has been created, then all administrations are vulnerable to a remarkable extent? Is not to insist on public access to all tapes and documents to exhibit something of the political ruthlessness Mr. Nixon himself exhibited in his youth? At worst, is not a refusal to produce evidence against oneself no more than evidence of bad intention, something like evidence of "flight" in a criminal prosecution? That is, is such evidence significant only if

other, more substantial, evidence is also available? We should, in assessing Mr. Nixon's "suspicious" stubborness, reflect upon the prescription in *Federalist* No. 51, "The interest of the man must be connected with the constitutional rights of the place."

4) "The activities of the White House 'plumbers.' " Which activities, precisely? The burglary of the office of Daniel Ellsberg's psychiatrist is usually referred to. Such a burglary is clearly illegal, let us say. But how serious is it? Compare it with Mr. Ellsberg's unilateral decision to distribute to the press forty or so volumes of "Top Secret" documents relating to a war still in progress. If liberals can applaud (as many do) one decision, should they be so critical of the other? (I say this even though I believe the press was entitled to publish the Pentagon Papers.[8]) Consider what the so-called plumbers can be said to have been *somewhat* concerned about: espionage not only on behalf of foreign powers but also, and perhaps even more important in the circumstances, on behalf of one government agency against another. Were they concerned about efforts (say, in the Pentagon) to sabotage American foreign policy, perhaps for the sake of a tougher line? How seriously are such extralegal activities to be taken, especially when undertaken so amateurishly and so ineffectually in the plausibly sincere belief that national security required them? How much of such activities—whether burglaries or tape erasures—are to be assumed to have been immediately known to and directed by the President? What difference *do* such activities (or their punishment) make to the common good?

3) "Illegal solicitation and receipt of campaign contributions." Is this a count that Congress can take seriously? How many members of Congress have never sought or at least accepted improper donations? But, it will be said, a President can deliver much more for donations made to him. Are we to assume that the support of organized labor for virtually every Democratic Presidential candidate since 1932 was given without something expected (and routinely received) in return? Cannot the same be said about agricultural contributions and legislation? Illegal corporate contributors have been having fines levied against them of $5,000, the maximum penalty under the law. Does this suggest an offense serious enough to warrant impeachment proceedings? Is it not obvious that it will be difficult ever to establish a clear case of "bribery" in such circumstances? Is not exposure and recourse to the ballot box all one can rely upon here, unless fundamental changes are made (as they perhaps should be) in the law respecting contributions and other campaign practices?

2) "Improvements on Mr. Nixon's properties at San Clemente, Cali-

fornia, and Key Biscayne, Florida, at taxpayers' expense." This seems to call for a taxpayers' suit, not an impeachment proceeding, to recoup for the Treasury any funds mistakenly employed. And while we are at it, should not the tendency of members of Congress to provide themselves palatial offices and facilities be looked into? That is, is not a general tightening up by Congress of the national purse strings the response which is really called for?

1) "Improper handling of the President's personal affairs." Here there can be honest differences of opinion about complicated taxation issues that can best be resolved in the appropriate agencies and courts. Even so, it *can* and perhaps should be said of Mr. Nixon (as did the *Des Moines Register*, when his tax returns were revealed), "He stretched for every advantage he could get within the letter of the law."[9] But it is quite another thing to say that backdating of a deed of grant (if that was done) is clearly criminal and that Mr. Nixon realized what was being done on his behalf. Is not all this the sort of thing that bears upon the need for tax law reform and upon whether certain men (or certain kinds of men) should be elected to public office in the first place?

None of the five charges I have briefly dealt with seems to me to allege conduct that (even if true) has much to do with how effectively Mr. Nixon has performed or can be expected to perform his principal duties as President. Indeed, the crisis we have been undergoing is an "accidental" if not something of a "phony" crisis. That is, there is little about the way the country was being governed that called for it. Or, put another way, if none of the improper or illegal conduct we now know of had ever been discovered, it would not really have mattered much to the welfare of the country. This suggests the triviality of most of these matters—or the peculiarly personal character of them. In fact, have not most of the revelations been generated by the discovery of the Watergate burglary, itself an inconsequential activity that was discovered by chance?

But, it will be asked, is it not immoral to cover up illegal activities? Still, it should also be asked, is it not irresponsible (and hence immoral) *not* to cover up certain activities or at least to play them down in some circumstances? Consider, for example, the cover-up we are now witnessing in Congress with respect to some of Mr. Kissinger's wire-tapping and related activities. Responsible men in Congress seem to realize that it would not do the country any good to have Mr. Kissinger undermined at this time. Are we all not aware of *this* cover-up? And are we not condoning it? How do we conceive of *our* morality in thus acquiescing?[10]

Maturity is called for in considering such problems—and this means, in effect, maturity on the part of leaders in Congress, in the press and among the public. Impeachment of a President should not have to depend on the unravelling of a mystery ("Did the President know?" "Should he have known?" "Which witness is to be believed?"). Rather, impeachment should be directed to massive, palpable threats to the country, not merely to unseemly or ordinary criminal behavior.

In addition, it should be noticed, a double standard is being employed in considering Mr. Nixon's pettiness and shortcomings. (Use of such a double standard also brings to mind some features of the McCarthy period.) Far more serious as Presidential misconduct than anything alleged of Mr. Nixon, it seems to me, has been certain known conduct of his Democratic predecessors, conduct that did not then lead those who are now Mr. Nixon's principal critics to push for impeachment.[11] In fact, many of these critics look back with approval to those very same predecessors. Consider, for example, Mr. Kennedy's Bay of Pigs fiasco, his Cuban Missile Crisis gamble, his use of F.B.I. agents to intimidate newsmen in the middle of the night after the steel price rise, and his fatal escalation of our involvement in the Vietnam war. Does not all this disclose an improper "pattern" also, a far more threatening pattern than that seen in Mr. Nixon's conduct?

Similar "indictments" can be drawn up as well against Mr. Truman. Consider, for example, his establishment of a pervasive and extralegal loyalty review program for government employees—something with far more serious effects than all of Senator McCarthy's efforts. In fact, that program was one of the conditions for the Senator's depredations. Then there was Mr. Johnson. Consider, for example, his conduct in Vietnam after his pacific assurances to us during the 1964 campaign, as well as his accumulation, while in public office, of a fortune considerably larger than Mr. Nixon's. As for cover-up on a grand scale, and a cover-up that Congress must have been aware of at the time, there is the Bobby Baker case. A sense of proportion *is* called for in these matters.

I have noticed in recent months that many of Mr. Nixon's critics are obliged, in order to be able to push their case against him with a clear conscience, to deny his considerable foreign policy accomplishments. They deny to him what he has done (or dismiss them as Mr. Kissinger's accomplishments). At the same time, in domestic affairs they attribute harmful effects to him which simply are not realistic. Consider, for example, the vigorous efforts of the A.C.L.U. to have Mr. Nixon impeached. On what ground? Because of the threat by his administration to civil liberties. What *is* the A.C.L.U. talking about? His desires? But only his desires? That is, has not Mr. Nixon's administration been remarkably ineffective in suppressing civil liberties? Have not the critical civil liberties been in better shape since 1968 in this country than they have been at any time since just before the First World War? What condition will they be in if impeachment proceedings should be botched (whether or not Mr. Nixon is convicted), thereby letting loose recriminatory passions in this country for years to come?

I have already alluded to the ultimate responsibility that rests upon our "opinion leaders." They should realize how fragile political reputations really are and how vulnerable most politicians are to searching examination both of their careers and of their underlings. I should add, for the benefit of liberals who are considering what to do now, the recriminatory passions I have referred to are likely in the long run to benefit one politician, and one politician alone, a certain Southern governor, that nationally prominent politician who has been most discreet about the entire impeachment controversy.

iv

Discretion on *our* part, in turn, does compel us to notice some redeeming features of the current controversy, at least in its present stage.

The moral sense of the American people *is* being appealed to and thereby revived, a moral sense which prosperity and a dreadful war had blunted. But that moral sense needs guidance and restraint. There is a limit to the degree of public sophistication to be expected.

It can also be said that the "system" is somehow working. It is somewhat reassuring that considerable research and debate are going into the problem of what is an impeachable offense: the House Judiciary Committee seems determined not simply to vote its prejudices. In the course of the current debate we do see efforts to get back to first principles—this is evident in the many references in the press these days to the *Federalist Papers.* But first principles also include the virtue of prudence—and that should be made more of than it has been recently.

In addition, it should be acknowledged that we *are* seeing the Presidency being cut down somewhat closer to constitutional size. But we should also realize that Mr. Nixon is paying now for the sins of every Democratic President since Franklin Roosevelt. That is, just as Alger Hiss and others were the scapegoats for the Cold War (and perhaps somewhat for the Second World War), so Richard Nixon may be the scapegoat for the steady Presidential usurpation of Congressional power since the 1930s. A determined Congress, it should again be noted, can effect much of what may be legitimate in the drive toward impeachment simply by controlling more sensibly than it has the purse in its custody.[12]

Finally, in this catalogue of redeeming features of the current controversy, it is reassuring and instructive to see someone such as Mr. Nixon obliged to invoke constitutional privileges in order to defend himself: the limits of "law and order" are at last being appreciated by him and his partisans.

Let us assume that impeachment is on its way. What should we do now? Should not the President be encouraged to resign, on the eve of an impeachment vote? Some people disparage such a step: they would like to see a trial which would "bring everything out in the open." Is this a mature desire? Does it not fail to appreciate how much public opinion always rests upon the unexamined? Would not resignation be the simplest and safest way out for the country, with Mr. Ford then "cleaning up"?

But, it will be said by others, such a "cleaning up" would put Mr. Ford in too strong a position for reelection in 1976. To say this, however, is to imply that it is not Mr. Nixon alone who is irresponsibly selfish. Certainly, all this calls for considerable self-restraint by the press and Congress if we are not to become, on this occasion and in administrations to come, unduly dependent on chance exposures and hence chance developments—on "accident and force."

If there is to be an impeachment, what offenses should be used to get Mr. Nixon out of office? That is, what is the best that can be made now of the mess in Washington? What precedents do we want to establish? What standards do we want to endorse? There is, as I observed in my talk last October, a limit to how seriously such crimes as burglary should be taken, even when aggravated by an attempted obstruction of justice.

In any event, we should be aware of two dangers in how we conduct any impeachment we embark upon. We can so conduct it as to make impeachment all too frequent a threat in the years ahead. Or we can so conduct it as to lead to another century-long repudiation of the impeachment remedy, thereby depriving ourselves of this vital safeguard for the truly serious cases. Is not all this another way of saying that presidential impeachment is an awesome process, deliberately to be held in reserve?

A third danger should also be anticipated, that of breeding a general

cynicism by "letting Nixon get away with it." A deliberate withdrawal from further impeachment proceedings at this stage would
require a statesmanlike explanation on the part of Congress, followed
by ratification of such an explanation by the responsible press. Certainly it should be recognized that Mr. Nixon has already been ade-
quately "put in his place" and that he cannot really get away with anything, no matter what happens now.[13] Rather, it should be explained,
the country can be understood to be sensible enough to know when it
has learned and done enough to take care of itself in its present circumstances.

v

A recognition of the awesomeness of impeachment brings us back to
the beginning of our discussion on this occasion. Politics, I have in
effect argued, is not as simple a calling as ready recourse to impeachment would suggest. It is hard to believe that the conduct and issues
being discussed today as grounds for impeachment are so critical that
they should have dominated the public mind for the past year and that
they should continue to do so for the coming year.

It is also hard to believe that the country has been served well by a
controversy which has required, and still requires, its President to
devote so much of his time to such matters. Let us hope, not only for
our sake but even more for the sake of generations yet unborn, that he
has not significantly altered his policies at home or abroad merely out
of deference to his vulnerability to impeachment.[14]

Whatever happens—and perhaps it is the most imprudent feature of
all this, that it is impossible to say what the serious consequences *are*
likely to be of what we are doing to ourselves—whatever happens, a
few should be permitted and even encouraged to indicate their serious
reservations about the single-minded hounding of the President that all
too many are engaged in. Those few can help prepare us to deal with
the possible reaction to our present excesses, an unthinking reaction
which can be far more serious for constitutional government in the
United States than anything done either by Senator McCarthy a generation ago or by the men around President Nixon in recent years.

It would be most useful if liberals, at the height of the power at
which they now find themselves, would provide the country a model
of deliberate self-restraint and magnanimity which could help us all to
control our self-righteous saviors in the years to come. Magnanimity

and self-restraint would dictate, at the very least, an offer from Congress, on the eve of impeachment, of complete immunity for Mr. Nixon from any future prosecution for any past conduct in the event he should resign. Also salutary, it seems to me, would be an arrangement whereby everyone else involved in the offenses thus far alleged as abuses of Presidential power would be granted pardons. Indeed, I tend to believe it would be ungracious of Mr. Nixon to resign his post without pardoning prospectively (as I believe can be done) those of his associates who have misbehaved out of dedication to what they mistakenly took to be the Presidency and the common good. All this could be accompanied by a general amnesty for those who illegally opposed American participation in the Vietnam war.[15]

In short, American involvement in that war, of which "Watergate" and its ramifications are really a part, should be brought to a merciful end.

vi

I should like to begin to close by returning to Thomas More and William Roper, More's would-be son-in-law. A passage from Bolt's *A Man for All Seasons*—a passage that no doubt draws on the language of Thomas More himself—suggests in a dramatically useful form some of the things I have been trying to say this morning about law, evidence and precedent.

The passage exhibits Thomas More, the Lord Chancellor, prudently counseling constitutionalism and restraint to the self-righteous and the fearful. More had been urged to arrest a potential enemy, Richard Rich. "For what?" More asks. He is told that Rich is dangerous; that he's a political spy; and, finally, that he's bad. To which More replies that there is no law against being bad. Thereupon follows the passage I want to quote, especially those exchanges between Thomas More and William Roper which should caution us whenever we are tempted to pursue vendettas against men we do not (and perhaps should not) like:[16]

Margaret More: Father, that man's bad.
Thomas More: There is no law against that.
William Roper: There is! God's law!
More: Then God can arrest him.
Roper: Sophistication upon sophistication!

More: No, sheer simplicity. The law, Roper, the law. I know what's legal not what's right. And I'll stick to what's legal.

Roper: Then you set man's law above God's!

More: No, far below; but let *me* draw your attention to a fact —I'm *not* God. The currents and eddies of right and wrong, which you find such plain sailing, I can't navigate. I'm no voyager. But in the thickets of the law, oh, there I'm a forester. I doubt if there's a man alive who could follow me there, thank God . . .

Alice More (pointing after Rich): While you talk, he's gone!

More: And so he should, if he was the Devil himself, until he broke the law!

Roper: So now you'd give the Devil benefit of law!

More: Yes. What would you do? Cut a great road through the law to get after the Devil?

Roper: I'd cut down every law in England to do that!

More: Oh? And when the last law was down, and the Devil turned round on you—where would you hide, Roper, the laws all being flat? This country's planted thick with laws from coast to coast—man's laws, not God's—and if you cut them down—and you're just the man to do it—d'you really think you could stand upright in the winds that would blow then? Yes, I'd give the Devil the benefit of law, for my own safety's sake.

vii

Perhaps such conversations had the desired effect on William Roper. In any event, Roper did marry Thomas More's eldest daughter and, after More's death, wrote a useful life of his father-in-law. And in that *Life* there is recorded certain advice by More to his successor as Henry VIII's counsellor—advice that (it seems to me) is appropriate for everyone of us to consider (in the interest of prudence and constitutional government) in advising not only lionlike kings, presidents, and their would-be impeachers but also the sovereign public itself.

Thomas More's timely advice goes like this:[17]

> Maister Cromwell, you are nowe entred into the service of a most noble, wise and liberall prince; yf you will followe my poore advise, you shall, in your councell-givinge unto his grace, ever tell him what he oughte to doe, but never what he is able to doe. Soe shall you showe yourselfe a true faythfull subjecte, and a right wise worthy councellor. For yf the lyone knewe his **owne** strengthe, harde were it for any man to rule him.

XV. Race, Law, and Civilization

> The Negro race, like all races, is going to be saved by its exceptional men. The problem of education, then, among Negroes must first of all deal with the Talented Tenth; it is the problem of developing the Best of this race that they may guide the Mass away from the contamination and death of the Worst, in their own and other races. Now the training of men is a difficult and intricate task. Its technique is a matter for educational experts, but its object is for the vision of seers....
>
> W. E. B. Du Bois, *The Talented Tenth*

i

Permit me to open these remarks by repeating for you a passage from Cicero with which I like to open the University of Chicago classes I conduct from time to time on Euclid's geometry:[1]

> . . . the remark made by Plato, or perhaps by someone else, seems to be particularly apt. For when a storm at sea had driven him to an unknown land and stranded him on a deserted shore, and his companions were frightened on account of their ignorance of the country, he, according to the story, noticed certain geometrical figures traced in the sand, and immediately cried out, "Be of good courage; I see the tracks of men."

This quotation from Cicero should remind us of the perennial question: What does it mean to be a human being? Must not any answer to this question that is worth taking seriously recognize the true nobility of the human being which can be seen only in the full development of that reason which makes man human? Indeed, I submit to you, a proper understanding of the quotation from Cicero I have shared with you could well be decisive in any informed effort to speak to the questions raised for Americans both by the subject of this talk and by "the political writings by black Americans."

This talk was delivered at Middlebury College, Middlebury, Vermont, April 25, 1974.

The citations in the text are to Herbert J. Storing, editor, *What Country Have I? Political Writings by Black Americans* (New York: St. Martin's Press, 1970).

I will, in an attempt to guard against misunderstanding, develop in several different ways the things I propose to say on this occasion.

ii

What *does* it mean to be "human," to be truly civilized? Or, to put this question in a form that goes back to antiquity: What is philosophy —and what are the conditions for its emergence?

Philosophy seems to have depended, for the single sustained emergence of which we can be certain, upon a rare combination of conditions and circumstances, so rare indeed that they who happen to be the trustees of the philosophical enterprise at any particular time should guard it with great care. But proper guarding depends on some awareness of what philosophy is and what it depends upon.

I have referred to a single sustained emergence of philosophy of which we can be certain, an emergence that seems to have originated in ancient Greece (perhaps drawing together influences from Babylon, Egypt, and Persia) and which has come down to us as an integral part of what we call Western Civilization. Even Marxism, which serves as the carrier these days of Western thought to much of the world, has been decisively shaped in certain critical respects by the philosophical tradition it would replace or, at least, reform.

That which has emerged in other places in the world, independent of Western influence, may be quite thoughtful and most civilized—but it is not philosophy, that organized and deliberate inquiry which strives for knowledge of the whole by the aid of natural reason alone. Consider the principal "alternatives" to Western philosophy—to philosophy, strictly speaking: Confucian thought, Judaism, and the Indian tradition.

Confucian thought is characterized by its evident determination to confine itself to ethical concerns; again and again, the Western reader is struck by the unwillingness of Confucius to address himself directly and systematically to questions about the origins and the very nature of things. If there *is* a serious examination of such questions, it is well concealed, deliberately kept from view and certainly not intended for any but a very few. Why this should be so would require a long discussion.[2] The real question, however, may be *not* why Confucius did not take that one step more, behind the Veil, which Socrates and his forerunners did take, but rather what permitted the Greeks to do so. That is, we should recognize how rare the emergence of philosophy may really be.

Still another alternative to philosophy is the kind of "understanding" seen in pre-Christian Judaism. There may be seen *there* a direct and systematic account of the origins of things, but not of the very nature of things. In fact, I have been told, there is in Biblical Hebrew no word for "nature"—and this seems appropriate for a way of thought that is rooted in an opinion that has God as the cause of all the things we know—the cause of their origins (at least in their present form) and the cause of their continuation. Does not the notion of *nature* presuppose or assume there is for the universe an order and an ordering principle which are independent of any will, human or divine? Such an account of things as that of the ancient Hebrews rests ultimately (in its own terms) upon revelation, in a special time and place—upon revelation that is not generally accessible to unaided human reason. It is an account philosophy can make use of (and indeed it is woven by now into the fabric of Western Civilization), but it is not itself, strictly speaking, philosophical—however thoughtful it may be and however illuminating it may seem to less privileged peoples.[3]

The only other alternative to philosophy of which I know a little, and which can be taken seriously as a "contender," is that of the Hindus. We can see significant traces of it in so sophisticated a man as Mohandas K. Gandhi, a man who is a curious combination of the European Enlightenment and of traditional Hinduism. Indeed, Hinduism itself is rather curious in that it seems to cherish and to be saddled with (if not crippled by) a number of institutions whose original purpose has long since been lost sight of.[4] Both mathematics and astronomy do seem to have flourished among the Hindus, but evidently not in such a way as to provide the critical impetus for that leap into philosophy that culminates in inquiry for its own sake into all things.

Consider what the conditions were for the emergence of philosophy itself: a certain kind of political community seems to have been necessary, that which we know as the *polis*. This may be another way of saying that civilization and civilized leisure are needed for philosophy. This in turn presupposes a level of material development that is hardly primitive.[5] Nor can the language necessary for philosophy, or the writing to which such language can be reduced, be primitive. One suspects that some languages are more suited than others to serious consideration of serious questions. Indeed, some languages seem to have built into them profound observations about the very nature of things. And, I suspect, a certain kind of poetry is useful, if not even needed, before philosophy can emerge—a poetic tradition in which certain kinds of questioning, or at least a certain kind of thinking, are presupposed. Homer and Hesiod come to mind. Then, when all is right, the critical questions may emerge—and be developed by a people still fresh in their view of the world.[6]

Such, perhaps, were the conditions that permitted philosophy first to find its home in the West.

iii

But, one might well ask, what does all this have to do with an assessment of "the political writings by black Americans" you have been studying? It has both nothing to do with such an assessment and yet everything—nothing, in that the considerations I will be drawing to your attention usually are of scant interest to the writers you have been studying; everything, in that these considerations (or their absence from such writings) are fundamental to any truly serious understanding of what the West means and what should be done to "preserve and defend" it during the coming century, the century for which some of you will be training students to carry on in the great tradition.

Permit me, for the moment and perhaps for the rest of this day, to sound parochial. The great tradition I have just referred to depends on philosophy and is, as I have indicated, rooted in the West. It is in the West, and in the West alone, that we can be certain that philosophy has permitted men to realize fully their human potential—in the sense of being deliberately aware of what they are and of what they are doing, of being aware of themselves as thinking beings and as moral beings.

In speaking as I do, I do *not* refer to what is loosely called "philosophy," to what is found in such expressions as "my philosophy of life," or "the philosophy of the Germans" (or the Swiss or the Italians, to say nothing of the Turks or the Pygmies or the Arabs), or even "the philosophy of stamp collecting." "Philosophy" is carelessly used today in place of "opinion" or even "prejudice." But philosophy is, as I have already indicated, that organized and deliberate inquiry which strives for knowledge of the whole by the aid of natural reason alone. This means, among other things, that it requires and develops knowledge of the truly knowable things, those things (if any) that truly *are* and hence may be said to be eternal. It requires and develops knowledge of the nature of things and, indeed, of the nature of nature—that knowledge which is necessary if one is truly to know what and how things are. And it requires and develops knowledge of knowledge itself, of what it means to know and hence of what makes a thing truly knowable. All this, in turn, may lead one to the realization that one's knowledge is limited, that one may know all too often only that one does not know, but that in so knowing one at least senses what it is to know, that it is worth knowing that which is truly knowable, and that at least certain questions are always worth getting "to know better."

Philosophy, thus understood, offers itself both as an end in itself and as a guide to life. As an end in itself (something a practical people such as we Americans are can easily lose sight of), it permits us to be truly, perhaps even fully, human, providing and permitting us that self-conscious understanding of the most important things men and women always yearn for and seek through love and drink and poetry and politics. "Euclid alone," a poet tells us, "has looked on Beauty bare."[7] And, we might add, only philosophy permits one to understand what such looking really consists of, what "looking" means, and what the limits are of looking and indeed of "Beauty bare." Philosophy, thus understood, does not have to be either explained or justified: those who *sense* what it is need nothing more to be reminded of what reason means to mankind; those who have no inkling of what it is must settle for philosophy (for what they take to be philosopy) as a useful guide to life.[8] Of course, the philosopher does not "mind" being useful, as long as usefulness is kept in its proper place.

Philosophy as a guide to life can also take the form of political philosophy, that interest in political things which is decisively illuminated by philosophy. Political philosophy, Professor Leo Strauss has said, is "the attempt to understand the nature of political things." Even so, as Mr. Strauss has also said, "A political thinker who is not a philosopher is primarily interested in, or attached to, a specific order or policy; the political philosopher is primarily interested in, or attached to, the truth."[9] Thus, the political thinker, who is really a political man, is primarily interested in the good, as he understands it, for a particular people. "As he understands it"; "a particular people"—ay, there's the rub: for the good he longs for and attempts to advance is, ultimately, an unexamined good, just as the people whom he would serve is, ultimately for him, a matter of chance.

Political philosophy, as a guide to life, provides knowing critiques of political life. Such critiques eventuate in, if they do not implicitly depend upon, carefully considered opinions not only about the best way of life but also about the best possible regime for human beings.

That best possible regime, we can provisionally say, is one in which philosophy can find a welcome and secure home and in which philosophy can reciprocate by ruling if not the city at least the rulers of the city. Knowledge of the best possible regime, however rarely such a regime may be realized, does provide standards by which ordinary regimes may be assessed and according to which they can be improved now and then, here and there. Or, put still another way, political philosophy instructs us in the nature and uses of *prudence*, including the recognition and support of those political men who (although not political philosophers themselves) somehow divine what prudence is or calls for.

Philosophy and political philosophy have been, I have said, discovered only in the West. And—with what I am about to say we get closer to the subject of this afternoon—the American people find themselves, by a set of curious chances, the principal custodians for the coming century of the philosophical tradition. Most peoples of the world want some of the technological, material fruits of that tradition. We here—a people who can go to the moon *in large part out of a desire to know*—happen to be in a position to want, or at least to enjoy, *more* than the mundane fruits of that tradition. It seems likely that if we lose our way—and certainly if we "go under"—there may well descend upon mankind (so far as philosophy is concerned) a new "Dark Age," perhaps even an age of universal tyranny.[10]

America, then, with all her sins and shortcomings, remains "the world's best hope," the guardian for all mankind of the best of the West. The best can continue to be cherished, if not here, at least in a world somehow kept in a civilized condition in large part because of American power. I have observed that we have, with this recognition of the role of the United States as the guardian, or if you will, the step-guardian, of the philosophic tradition, gotten closer to our subject on this occasion. Indeed, one might go one step further and say that we have already dealt in the most important respect with that subject, the attempt to assess the "political writings by black Americans." That is, there is a sense in which everything else I say now should be anti-climactic: the decisive critique has already been made, if only implicitly, of those writings and of any political movements nurtured by them, especially insofar as those writings attempt to repudiate or to "rise above" the American political tradition by encouraging recourse to sources and standards outside the West.

Thus, I have said (have I not?) that it is highly unlikely that such writers as you have been studying have anything better to look to than what is to be found in their Western heritage. "Your heritage," some descendants of slaves might reply, "not ours!" But, I suggest, they are grievously mistaken, for this is indeed the heritage of all thinking men. Besides, the families of most such writers have been in this country far longer, and have been shaped far more, by the American tradition than the whites they criticize. Their sacrifices, sufferings, language, and thought make them Americans, whether they like it or not.[11] Whatever may be said of Africa and its heritage, these Afro-Americans have nowhere else to go. And, indeed, whatever may be said of American injustices and obstacles, they have no place better to go. They are, for better *and* for worse, heirs of a great tradition, a tradition that they have (as citizens) earned the right to enjoy and (as human beings) incurred the obligation to perpetuate.

I suspect I have already said more than enough to provide material for discussion not only this afternoon but well into the evening. But perhaps I should, before we move into a general discussion, say even more than I have, anticlimactic though it may be. That is, it might be useful to spell out some of the implications of what I have thus far said for race relations in the United States and for an understanding of the men and women who write about such things and around whom disciples and movements gather from time to time.

iv

Much of what I have to say on this occasion is addressed to students who should not need to be told of the injustices of racism in the United States or elsewhere. Rather, it is addressed to students who *do* need to hear not about the so-called Negro question but about the human question. What *does* it mean to be human and what should we aspire to?

Central to these inquiries is the requirement that we remain able *to* discuss serious issues fully (even if at times irresponsibly). To do this, we need a sense of restraint (on the part both of government and of vigilantes)[12] and an awareness of what the critical issues (and appropriate intellectual inhibitions) are. That is, we need freedom of speech and the disciplined temperament that makes the use of such freedom effective.

There are two principal intellectual difficulties that stand in the way of the instruction appropriate for a proper ordering of race relations, one difficulty that can be summed up as "cultural relativism" and another that can be described as the "bad conscience of the white man," especially the more sensitive and decent white intellectual.

First, let us look at cultural relativism, something that challenges what I have said about philosophy. It is assumed today by intellectuals that every people has a culture, that all cultures are equal. Thus, we are told that we are not entitled to say that one culture is superior to another. All we are permitted to say (we are told) is that cultures are quite different from one another and (we are further told) that such differences do not really matter.

In what sense *are* cultures equal? They are equal in *being* there. That is, there may be a certain, or limited, validity to them because they *are*, because they exist. They may even be equal in "satisfying" their respective peoples—if one means by that that they satisfy their peoples with respect to the tastes those peoples happen to have. That is, such peoples may not know differently or know better. And, one can say, all cultures are equal because each of them contributes to (or makes possible) the existence of a people. (I use "culture" on this occasion in the loose sense in which it is usually employed today.[13])

Perhaps some intellectuals would concede the "inferiority" of the culture of any people whose death rate is so high that it is dying out. Thus, survival would be a test. But, it must be countered, what does "survival" mean? Does it refer only to a people and its cities? Or does it include the memories of and heritage from a people? Certainly, peoples with both high and primitive cultures can survive for a very long time as well as suddenly face a challenge to their physical survival which they cannot successfully meet.

Does it make sense to refuse to distinguish "superior" and "inferior" on any basis but that of an ability to preserve oneself physically? (Besides, is it not highly likely that all peoples are mortal?) Does not the refusal to draw distinctions between higher and lower fail to recognize and to appreciate what every civilized man accepts when sophistries have not beguiled him, that there are indeed faculties which distinguish men from the animals and the development of which requires considerable effort and competence? Certainly, both the most distinguished academician and the quite illiterate peasant sense that when the mind of a man goes, *he* goes. It must be a rare man who would not sacrifice his bodily senses or sexual powers or physical mobility, to say nothing of a limb or an organ, if necessary to preserve his reason.

Thus, common sense tells us that the Abyssinians several thousand years ago (with their arts, sciences, and language) were not only different from but better than the men who roamed the British Isles with painted bodies, a bare subsistence, and a crude language. Is it not apparent that the Abyssinians were to be preferred to the Britons? Cannot we see—do not all sensible men see—that these two cultures were not merely "different"? Were they not markedly and significantly different? It is not necessary to consider one people superior in heredity or to condemn the other for its faults. It is possible and sufficient to observe the manifest cultural superiority of one people, no doubt in large part because of the circumstances in which it found itself.

Common sense tell us, that is, that one culture may .be superior to another in that one brings out more than the other the distinctively human, that which virtually all men sense to have a higher dignity and a greater worth. We need not decide whether ancient Abyssinia or eighteenth century America or fifth century Athens or Elizabethan England or Confucian China was the very highest. It suffices for our immediate purposes to recognize them all as higher than the cultures of innumerable long-lived primitive peoples.

Common sense takes us one step further. If it should be assumed that all cultures are equal, then what need is there to trouble oneself with improving either one's own culture or that of others, except perhaps to insure mere survival? For if a culture is improved more and more, it will someday have become something quite different from what it once was, so much so as to be essentially different, a different culture. Yet, would we not have to admit that the much "improved" culture was not really better than what it had been before "improvement" (or better than the original culture is wherever else it may happen to exist unaltered)?

Of course, the suspicion would be entertained here and there—and perhaps even among some of you—that the standards by which various alternative cultures might be judged are essentially "the white man's standards," not those appropriate for all men. But would not the best available standards be likely to present themselves as such (that is, as "the best") among the opinions of the people or culture that, shall we say, happened upon them? On the other hand, it may be necessary for a people to take, if only temporarily, the standards of its inferior culture seriously, if only to permit pride and the vitality of one's own to develop. But a caution is in order: if one is not careful, if one does not realize what one is doing, one may well settle for a second-class culture in the course of avoiding "the white man's culture." This would be, in effect, a voluntary slavery, a fatal, or at least crippling, freedom.

And one would thereby have surrendered to the descendants of one's oppressors the very best, that best which one's forbears had earned for one the right to participate in and which one's own talents may qualify one to enjoy.

Is it not apparent that both Frederick Douglass (whom W. E. B. Du Bois called, with some justice, "the greatest of American Negro leaders" [p. 96])—that both Douglass and Booker T. Washington would endorse much of what I have just said, at least to the extent of recognizing Western (and, indeed, even North American) culture as superior to that from which *their* forebears had been pirated out of Africa? Did not these men, with memories of the great deprivations of slavery still fresh behind them, have their eyes and souls open to the genuinely superior?

But consider, on the other hand, the inspired exhortation of Du Bois himself (another superior man):

> We cannot reverse history; we are subject to the same natural laws as other races, and if the Negro is ever to be a factor in the world's history—if among the gaily-covered banners that deck the broad ramparts of civilization is to hang one uncompromising black, then it must be placed there by black hands, fashioned by black heads and hallowed by the travail of 200,000,000 black hearts beating in one glad song of jubilee. [p. 81]

Even so, we should notice that he does see what the West offers as *thus far* superior—so much so, as we shall see in the passage immediately following this one, that the American Negro is called upon by him to lead his African brethren to the heights reserved for them among the stations of mankind. Thus, he goes on to say,

> For this reason, the advance guard of the Negro people—the 8,000,000 people of Negro blood in the United States of America —must soon come to realize that if they are to take their just place in the van of Pan-Negroism, then their destiny is *not* absorption by the white Americans. That if in America it is to be proven for the first time in the modern world that not only are Negroes capable of evolving individual men like Toussaint, the Saviour, but are a nation stored with wonderful possibilities of culture, then their destiny is not a servile imitation of Anglo-Saxon culture, but a stalwart originality which shall unswervingly follow Negro ideals. [p. 81]

We can see here—in this statement of 1897, which may have had, and may even continue to have, immediate political justification—we can see here several misconceptions that have plagued and perhaps even dominated to their detriment many of Du Bois' more gifted successors. What does "stalwart originality" mean? Indeed, is not the taste of Americans for originality, for constant change and hence novelty, something in need of constant restraint? Certainly, a thing is not good simply because it is either new or one's own. In fact, one should remain on guard against the lure both of the ever novel and of the overly familiar. What, precisely, are the "Negro ideals" that should be unswervingly followed? Circumstances may limit or even shape the ability of any particular people to realize the very best, but such limitations and adaptations are essentially temporary compromises rather than something to be permanently desired. Finally, what should be said about Du Bois' abhorrence of "a servile imitation of Anglo-Saxon culture"? Certainly, a *servile* imitation of anything is to be avoided, but not a disciplined dedication to the best which "Anglo-Saxon culture" offers, a dedication that includes a periodic insistence upon singling out and correcting whatever may be deficient or misdirected about that culture.

The best of Anglo-American culture, I should add, is reflected in its language, that language in which Shakespeare so revelled that our thought has been enriched ever since. But is it not evident that there has been, among us, since the time Du Bois emerged, a general deterioration in language and hence in thought? Thus, of the seven writers you are assigned to study in your anthology, the three rooted in the nineteenth century (Douglass, Washington, and Du Bois) seem to me clearly superior to our four contemporaries (Martin Luther King, Malcolm X, Stokeley Carmichael, Charles Hamilton)—superior in their use of language, superior in the solidity of their thought, superior in their general political sense. Indeed, our contemporaries—in this, too, they are distinctively American—tend to be sentimental and undisciplined.

This brings us to what I have called the "bad conscience of the white man."[14] This bad conscience—which dwells, for the most part, on barbaric acts of commission and omission performed decades, if not even centuries, ago by white men whom our contemporaries of bad conscience never knew (and with whom, for most of the troubled intellectuals, there is not even a distant blood tie)—this bad conscience hurts all races, all peoples, for it leads either to a general malaise and a loss of nerve or to dubious standards and reckless conduct. Among its results are a reluctance to make a proper use of the law to further the ends of civilization and a tendency to encourage the worst elements among whatever deprived people is being catered to, thereby making it even more difficult than it would otherwise be for the more sober and the more orderly among such people to control and to elevate their own communities.

For men of bad conscience, the spectacular tends to be more attractive, if only because it dramatizes the sins and shortcomings being repented of. Of course, the spectacular can be the saintly. But it is more apt to be the flashy and cheap, the blatantly rhetorical, the irresponsible and violent. Especially is this so when the voracious "mass media" cast about for dramatic material. Thus, naïve exhortations about bullets and revolutions and armed uprisings are given far more "exposure" than the sober cautions that are more likely to express the settled opinion of most responsible people, irrespective of color. Consider, for example, the 1964 remarks of Joseph H. Jackson, perhaps the most sober twentieth-century author in the anthology you are studying (so sober, indeed, that he can easily be passed by in any selections from this anthology):

> We cannot win our battle through force and unreasonable intimidation. As a minority group we cannot win outside of the protection and power of the just laws of this land. Read history with open eyes and attentive minds, and we will discover that no minority group has and can win in a struggle by the direct confrontation of the majority and by employing the same type of pressures and powers that the majority possess in abundance. The hope of the minority struggle is with the just laws of the land and the moral and constructive forces that are germane to this nation's life and character. [p. 139]

The sentimentalists among us—for men of bad conscience do tend, at least these days, to be sentimentalists—these adventurous intellectuals should be reminded that the United States is not Algeria, that an American civil war along racial lines would make the ravages of Reconstruction look like child's play. Thus, I had occasion to observe in a 1968 talk made a few days after the murder of Martin Luther King— at a time when rioting had broken out in some American cities: "Mr. King preached a doctrine of dedicated nonviolence—a doctrine supported in his speeches by arguments both principled and pragmatic. There is one further argument, however, which should also be noticed by anyone who cares for his Negro friends and for the soul of America, and that is the dreadful vulnerability of our Negro fellow citizens (an easily identifiable minority) if the confrontation in this country between black and white should really be taken to the streets."

Firmness is called for in the defense both of law and order and of civil rights and racial justice. But such firmness calls for self-confidence, rather than a bad conscience, on the part of those who shape the opinion of the public. The West, at its best, provides standards and guidance enough for good men everywhere. We should not allow either relativistic ("value-free") social science or a pervasive guilt to undermine knowledge of and respect for the good and for the very best.

v

Men as diverse as Frederick Douglass, Booker T. Washington, and W. E. B. Du Bois saw Africa as destined to be awakened by the efforts, example and influence of the ex-slaves of North America. The depressed level of African culture, they seem to have recognized, had something to do with the openness of African tribes to the cruel ravages of the slave-hunter. Similarily, for example, one can recognize that Byzantine decadence opened the way to the ascendency in the fifteenth century of a vital Turkish power and led thereafter to four hundred years of Greek subjection to Turkish tyranny.

Should one go so far as to argue that it was even good for Africans to be forcibly removed to the United States, whatever ill effects such callous greed might have had upon both the slaveholder and his country? Surely to go to the United States as slaves was not the best way to go—but there was no other way to go in large numbers and thereby to be ushered into the modern world. Was this too high a price to pay for Western civilization? In a sense, the price for such conversions has always been high, "too high"—as one can see by reflecting upon the *Iliad* and its aftermath.

What *should* have been done about slavery in the nineteenth century? Was not the gradualist policy of Abraham Lincoln the correct one, taking due account of both the circumstances of the slaves and the prejudices of the whites? To be justified in pursuing such a policy, however, one must know where one is, where one is going, and what one should want. This meant, in Lincoln's circumstances, that the preservation of the Union should have been recognized as good for the slave and nonslave alike. It meant, also, that the limitations of public opinion had to be respected, that the attractions as well as the folly of radical abolitionism in this country had to be recognized. It meant, in short, that the virtue of prudence had to be exercised.[15]

Prudence reminds one, among other things, that there is a limit to predictability in human affairs. Consider, for example, the effect of American independence on slavery. Thomas Jefferson had originally included in the Declaration of Independence a complaint that the British king had vetoed "every legislative attempt [on the part of the colonists] to prohibit or to restrain this execrable commerce," referring to the slave trade he had just described as "piratical warfare," a waging of "cruel war against human nature itself, violating its most sacred rights to life and liberty in the persons of a distant people . . ."[16] No doubt many informed men in the 1770s and 1780s thought that it was but a matter of time before the liberated Americans would in turn be able to liberate their slaves.

What happened afterwards in the United States is a long and tangled story. Not only slavery but also the slaves themselves prospered on this continent, with the result that the prospect of emancipation became at the same time more risky (financially, if not also socially) and even more of a moral necessity. Consider, on the other hand, what happened in the British Empire. Would not the Americans, as British subjects, have been affected by the movement within the Empire for compensated emancipation, a movement anticipated by *Somersett's Case* as far back as 1772 and culminating in the remarkable successes of British abolitionism in the 1830s?[17] Or, put another way, did not American Independence provide slaveholders, perhaps inadvertently, more concentrated power than they could have had within the Empire?[18] Still, on the other hand, perhaps Independence also provided the pirated African more of an opportunity, in the long run, to develop his natural talents as a human being, talents his native circumstances might have suppressed for another millennium.

It is hard to say "what might have happened" if different political arrangements *had* been made. Prudence, one *can* say, is aware of the limits of predictability. Indeed, is it not this very uncertainty that contributes to the philosopher's fundamental reservations about the ultimate value of political life? Moderation *is* encouraged in one by the awareness that it is difficult to know, to be sure, about what one is doing. Moral passion all too often attempts to substitute intention for understanding. Indignation permits us to believe that we know more than we can, that we have access to more certainty than the circumstances (and the very nature of human things) permit. It is indeed difficult to step back and to observe what is really going on.

What *is* happening among us today? How do race relations fare? I suggest that unless we can recognize the remarkable progress that has been made—a progress that it is unfashionable for impassioned militants to notice—if we cannot recognize progress when it is clearly there, we deny that any progress can ever be made, for we really deny that there are standards by which judgments can be made about such things. Consider what Frederick Douglass could say in 1848 and compare it with what we know today:

> We are not insensible to the various obstacles that throng the colored man's pathway to respectability. Embarrassments and perplexities, unknown to other men, are common to us. Though born on American soil, we have fewer privileges than aliens. The school-house, the work-shop, counting-house, attorney's office, and various professions, are opened to them, but closed to us. This, and much more, is true. A general and withering prejudice—a malignant and active hate, pursues us even in the best parts of this country. [p. 45]

But, he went on to say,

> The fact that we are limited and circumscribed, ought rather to incite us to a more vigorous and persevering use of the elevating means within our reach, than to dishearten us. The means of education, though not so free and open to us as to white persons, are nevertheless at our command to such an extent as to make education possible; and these, thank God, are increasing. [p. 46]

Was not Douglass correct in his prescription that serious application to education, to whatever education *was* made available, was the only sure way out of slavery? It was Douglass, I remind you, who had said in 1852 that nothing was "settled" which was not right. (p. 30) It was also Douglass who had warned, in 1849,

> Where "knowledge is power," that nation is the most powerful which has the largest population of intelligent men; for a nation to cramp, and circumscribe the mental faculties of a class of its inhabitants, is as unwise as it is cruel, since it, in the same proportion, sacrifices its power and happiness. [p. 40]

This warning (which you might want to remember in diagnosing what I call the "New York Yankees syndrome") found expression in the repeated emphases by Booker T. Washington upon the necessity for the North of rehabilitating the South and upon the necessity for the country of establishing on a firm economic footing more than four million freedmen. And he argued, again and again, "No race that has anything to contribute to the markets of the world is long in any degree ostracized." (p. 61) Reliance is placed by him, that is, on the workings of commerce, on the color-blindness of the desire to prosper.[19]

Still, it is prudent to keep in mind the caution of W. E. B. Du Bois, "[W]e black men seem the sole oasis of simple faith and reverence in a dusty desert of dollars and smartness." (pp. 91-92) Certainly, institutionalized greed is a power to be reckoned with and to be held in check. But, it is also prudent to keep in mind, a free-enterprise economy is more more apt, in our circumstances, to promote racial justice than any socialism which concentrates political and economic power, and hence the power of longstanding prejudice, in the servants of the majority. Indeed, a free-enterprise economy means that prejudice has to be paid for, that the prejudiced are quite likely to suffer personally and immediately for their misconceptions. Much the same can be said about "free-enterprise" politics as well—and points up the importance of the vote, that "currency" which provides the "purchasing power" of our civic life.

I have referred to what I call the "New York Yankees syndrome." I should explain. It is no accident that Hank Aaron, that descendant of slaves who recently broke Babe Ruth's record of total home runs, should be in the National League. It is an ironic accident, perhaps, that he should be a member of a Southern team and that Ruth's team should have been known as the Yankees, that Northern team which has paid the price of *its* prejudices. That is, the Yankees were one of the last major league baseball teams to integrate racially—and the once-perennial world champions have suffered considerably from their tardiness, as has the American League (which lagged behind the National League, which had pioneered with Jackie Robinson and the then Brooklyn Dodgers shortly after the Second World War). Any team, or league, that limits itself to white players deprives itself of access to the full range of choices available to others, and (considering that sports permit underprivileged men of considerable talent but of limited education to make something of themselves) deprives itself of access to perhaps as many as one-third of the best available athletes in this country today. Such a handicap is very hard to overcome—and the team or league that moves first, *if* it should be permitted to move at all, gains an advantage that can take decades for its competitors to overcome. And thus we have seen since the Second World War both the ascendancy of the National League and the subjugation of the Yankees.[20]

Notice my qualification, "*if* it should be permitted to move at all." That is, the law does play a role here, if only to prevent restraints of trade, if only to police combinations based on prejudice that would prevent some from offering effectively their goods and services in the market. But, it should also be noticed, the law can do even more than that *when the time is right*: that is, it can provide the critical "push" to consolidate and extend what economic and political forces have done. Thus, an experienced Chicago lawyer has recently observed, "When people learn that the law forbids discrimination, they will eventually learn not to discriminate at all. When the practice of discrimination disappears, the roots of prejudice of which it was an expression will eventually wither and die."[21]

Progress, it should at once be added, can never be as fast as one would like, because any political progress worthy of free men must take into account the lingering resistance of the ignorant as well as the insistent demands of the just. Even so, racial progress among us in recent decades *has* been remarkably steady—actually remarkable—and to refuse to recognize this is simply to disqualify oneself from being able to make a proper diagnosis of the serious ills which do still afflict us.

vi

A question remains: How then should the law be used now?

The answer: Carefully, but with determination.

One proper concern of the law, as of the community whose instrument the law is, must continue to be the education of the public. But no system of education can mean much if it is not guided by men who have some rough idea of what is good—of what would be an improvement, of what would be deterioration. This means, for example, that the delusive character of certain programs (such as most of those devoted to so-called black studies and those that make much of "black English") should be recognized, however necessary it may be for academic administrators to tolerate such programs from time to time in the interest of campus tranquillity. It should be recognized, that is, that most "black studies" programs constitute a betrayal of the students who devote to them the hard-earned resources of their parents and their community. Consider, in support of this assessment, an editorial (in

1971) in a publication of the N.A.A.C.P.—an editorial entitled "Black Nonsense":[22]

> The new cult of blackness has spawned many astounding vagaries, most of them intriguing and others merely amusing. One which has recently gained a measure of academic and foundation recognition is not only sheer nonsense but also a cruel hoax which, if allowed to go unchallenged, can cripple generations of black youngsters in their preparation to compete in the open market with their non-Negro peers.

> The New York Times and the Daily News report that New York City's Brooklyn College has enrolled some 50 Negro students in a course in "black" English taught as their native language by Miss Carol Reed, described by the News as "a young linguist who heads the language curriculum research project at Brooklyn College." The project is financed by a $65,000 Ford Foundation grant.

> It appears that Miss Reed (and she is not alone in this fantasy) is trying to transform a vernacular which is more regional than racial, i.e., more southern than Negro, into a full-fledged distinct language which the college offers as a course. This language is merely the English of the undereducated with provincial variances in accent and structure from locale to locale throughout the English-speaking world. One might as well call the cockney of the London East Enders or the speech patterns of the Appalachian whites separate languages. The so-called black English is basically the same slovenly English spoken by the South's under-educated poor white population.

> What our children need, and other disadvantaged American children as well—Indian, Spanish-speaking, Asian, Appalachian and immigrant Caucasians—is training in basic English which today is as near an international language as any in the world. To attempt to lock them into a provincial patois is to limit their opportunities in the world at large. Black children can master Oxonian English as well as any WASP child of the English Midlands. But each has to be taught the language. No one is born speaking "black" cockney, pidgin, standard, or "white" English. Children learn to speak what they hear and are taught. Let our children have the opportunity, and be encouraged, to learn the language which will best enable them to comprehend modern science and technology, equip them

to communicate intelligently with other English-speaking peoples of all races, and to share in the exercise of national power.

Black parents throughout this nation should rise up in unanimous condemnation of this insidious conspiracy to cripple their children permanently. It is time to repudiate this black nonsense and to take appropriate action against institutions which foster it in craven capitulation to the fantasies of the extreme black cultists and their pale and spineless sycophants.

Let the black voice of protest resound thunderously throughout the land.

To indulge oneself in the fantasies of most "black studies" programs, it should be added, is to be deprived of one's rightful share in the American heritage, that heritage earned by two hundred years of slavery in this country and thereafter by a hundred years of gradual emancipation, a heritage that resides in the English language and takes the sensitive human being back through Shakespeare to the very dawn of Western civilization and to philosophy itself.

We have thus returned to the beginning of my remarks this afternoon. Permit me to recapitulate by restating a few critical arguments. The contemporary fashionable approach—an approach, I should again emphasize, of supposedly liberated intellectuals, not of ordinary people who know what sacrifice means and who sense what they are entitled to get—the fashionable sophisticated approach may be seen in the contemporary authors assigned for your study. It is fashionable, that is, to hold that each group of people (as well as each man) need proceed only according to its taste, the taste which it happens to have. It is also fashionable to hold that there is no basis in nature for determining or refining standards. Indeed, it is said, one must somehow "make" one's standards. All this becomes, in practice, quite personalized and individualistic. It is, as I have already indicated, quite relativistic—and, I should now add, romantic and irresponsible. It is as well peculiarly *un*political.

The emphasis upon racial personality and upon racial ideals is, at bottom, a dependence upon, perhaps even a deification of, history and hence chance. W. E. B. Du Bois *can* add to such sentiments the aspiration of attaining "that perfection of human life for which we all long." (p. 80) But, he says elsewhere, "each soul and each race-soul needs its own peculiar curriculum." (p. 103) Does not this unwittingly imply that some races are intrinsically superior, some inferior? Or does it merely refuse to recognize that there is any truly superior curriculum?

However that may be—for one also sees in W. E. B. Du Bois, as in Booker T. Washington and Frederick Douglass before him, the recognition that the West provides a heritage which is (if only for the moment) superior to anything Africa can offer, even though Africans can contribute an ameliorating element—however that may be, some of Du Bois' more articulate (one might even say, spectacular) successors today do tend to reject their Western heritage. Thus, James Baldwin can conclude his article in your anthology, "The world is white no longer, and it will never be white again." (p. 225) But has not Europe (is not that what whiteness means for him?)—has not Europe already conquered (whether in the form of Marxism or in the form of modernity, to say nothing of our great intellectual tradition)? Has not the civilization of Europe, however diluted and even perverted it may sometimes appear, taken over the world to a surprising degree?

One of the underlying questions raised by all the readings you face is, as we have seen, whether the West offers, with all its defects, something essentially superior (for human beings) to non-Western life? Many in the East and in Africa seem to think so. That is, the superiority of the West does not lie for them only in guns, but rather (at least) in bread and medicine. But, it also seems, bread and medicine (to say nothing of guns) depend on European culture—that is, on its science, on its view of the world and of nature, and on the resulting technology. If superiority is denied—if the very idea of superiority is rejected—, then one must wonder why anyone should bother to change—or to complain. What, for example, are the Africans and Asians aiming at? Do not *they* want to move to what they take to be a superior condition?

The rejection of the Western heritage may be seen as well in the Carmichael and Hamilton passage, but there the rejection is put in terms borrowed from contemporary academic discourse. Thus, one sees there an emphasis upon "definition," upon the capture and exploitation of the "right to define." Mr. Carmichael and Mr. Hamilton can speak of "the right to create our own terms through which to define ourselves and our relationship to the society;" (p. 167) "those who have the right to define are the masters of the situation." (p. 168)[23] Emphasis is placing on "defin[ing] our own image." (p. 168) The insistence upon an image is, I believe, significant. Such insistence may see the problem of self- or race-development as essentially one of public relations. What this emphasis on defining means is the substitution of rhetoric for serious discourse, for political philosophy, and for jurisprudence. But even "rhetoric" is too old-fashioned a term: "propaganda" is better, especially since political life seems to be conceived of by them as essentially a state of war.

The emphasis throughout the Carmichael and Hamilton passage is on the changing and the new as good. Mr. Carmichael and Mr. Hamilton can speak of the "creation of new values." (p. 171) They can speak favorably as well of "expansion of humanity," of "an open society" and of "civiliz[ing] this country." (pp. 170-171) But these turn out to be, on examination, nebulous terms, or at least terms which are subordinated to their emphasis upon "defin[ing] their own goals." (p. 173) Thus, their emphasis is on definition as if *that* is the objective rather than merely the starting point of any serious endeavor.

Or, put another way, their emphasis is on the exercise of power rather than on dedication to an end.[24] Indeed, they themselves see American politics as "power-oriented"—and they want an "effective share in the total power of the society." (p. 175) But there is no serious concern with what such power is to be used for. That, presumably, remains to be "defined." It depends for them (does it not?) on chance and temperament. The direction, if there is any, seems to be *away from* whatever the white man stands for or cherishes. Does not this mean depriving oneself of the best of which we know, that best to which people of African descent (at least those in North America) have more than earned the right to make their very own? This is, indeed, a question that should be returned to again and again.

What this deprivation can mean may be seen in the passage in your anthology from Malcolm X. He is less coherent than any of his nineteenth century predecessors: such language as his, such a form of delivery and indeed of thought, would have been simply unthinkable for a Douglass or a Washington or a Du Bois. Is this a function of frustration? or of a radically expanded liberty which some do not know how to use? To what extent do personal ambition and the unthinking toleration of modern audiences contribute to such rhetorical excesses? Thus, at one point, Malcolm X can challenge his audience, "If you're afraid to use an expression like that. . . ." (p. 150) I should add that this man of considerable talent may have really been more restrained than he sometimes appeared, for he *can* be understood to advocate serious political effort. (See, e.g., p. 150.) But I should also add that his frequent *appearance* of lack of restraint may affect adversely many of the audience he continues to attract, people who need not only "an outlet" for their passions but also discipline and sobriety for effective lifelong endeavors.

Do audiences today prefer such disjointedness in thought? (This may be, by the way, one effect of television among us.) The pervasive incoherence and disjointedness in the sentiments of Malcolm X may be said to culminate in his outburst, "But when you drop that violence on me, then you've made me go insane, and I'm not responsible for what I do. And that's the way every Negro should get." (p. 155)

   "you've made me go insane"
   "I'm not responsible for what I do"
   "that's the way every Negro *should* get"
Is not such lack of discipline, such childish abandonment to one's passions and grievances, the new slavery? Surely there is not here the moral stature and intellectual rigor of Frederick Douglass, Booker T. Washington or W. E. B. Du Bois.

vii

A new slavery requires a new proclamation of emancipation. But what does it mean to "emancipate"? What does it mean to be free? Does it not mean not only that one is empowered to choose but also that one is *equipped* to choose, that one really knows what one is doing? And this means, ultimately, that the truly human in us is developed and sovereign: one must know what it is to think; one must know what is most worth thinking about; and one must know when one must settle, in particular circumstances, for less than the most rigorous thinking.

I return to what I have just said about "defining" and to what I said at the outset of these remarks about Euclid. By so returning to that North African geometrician I can perhaps suggest further, but only suggest, something about what it means to be a human being—what it means, that is, to think and to make sense of (or, should we not say, to discover the sense of?) the world around us.

Euclid sets forth, at the outset of his *Elements*, collections of definitions, postulates and common notions (or axioms). Where do the axioms "come from"? Do we not *somehow* generalize from experience, either in that we learn from experience or in that experience stimulates what is always "there" in the reasoning being? For instance, even a quite young student "knows," without being told or without being able to formulate it, that if equals are added to equals their sums will be equal.

Such axioms, however, need not be specifically geometrical. That is, they apply to other disciplines as well—and indeed may even be understood as a kind of justice. It is when we look at the *definitions* of Euclid that we can see the peculiarly geometrical material with which he works. Thus, we are told: "A point is that which has no part." "A line is breadthless length." "The extremities of a line are points." "A straight line is a line that lies evenly with the points on itself." And, skipping a few, "A circle is a plane figure contained by one line such that all the straight lines falling upon it from one point among those lying within the figure are equal to one another; and [that] point is called the centre of the circle."[25]

Where *do* such definitions come from? We have never really seen points, lines and circles—and yet we have somehow experienced them; we are somehow aware of them. Or is it, as we have seen that some believe today, that definition is essentially *creation*, an *act of will*, and nothing more than that? I do not believe that Euclid so believed. Rather, defining seemed for him a way of noticing and refining what men, as rational beings with bodies, already know (in some sense of "know"). That is, the things of which he speaks in the definitions are somehow perceived in or taken from nature, perhaps indeed taken from the very nature both of space and of rational perceptions of space—that space in which we move, that space "within" our minds through which we move things. The things we see with our eyes, for example, reflect roughly what points, lines, and circles are truly like.

The first and second definitions I have reproduced (about point and line) are intended to deal at the outset with materiality—with that grasp of things toward which people are "naturally" inclined, when they do not reflect on what they say about and do with the things of geometry. Thus, these two definitions eliminate (in points and lines, respectively) *partness* and *breadthness*. That which makes a point a point (position alone?) and that which makes a line a line (length alone?) are implied and accepted by these definitions. Do we not all "have" such things (whether innately or acquired) in our understanding already? Do we not sense what others refer to when they speak of such things? Is not he who defines both properly and usefully limited by what is ordained by nature—by the nature of things and by the nature of mind?

It is particularly important to correct the materiality of common opinion with respect to lines and points, because the visible representations that are so useful (if not even necessary) for human thinking about geometrical things, can mislead us. Such representations necessarily distort what they represent—unless we are alert to what they do stand for.

Do lines exist (what *does* "exist" mean here?)—do lines exist prior to, or independent of, our thinking about them? Are there not available, somehow, things such as lines and circles that we can discover (not create) when we look for them—and that the material world perceived by our senses incorporates to some degree, imperfectly but nevertheless revealingly? We have never with our eyes seen a circle—but we have seen representations of circles, which are useful for helping us understand circles. Such representations can be quite crude: they need only be "close enough" to give us an idea of the reality. Indeed, we speak of "getting the idea," of "seeing what you mean." Cannot we say that to think of points and lines and circles *is* to observe them: their very existence is attested to by our grasp of them?

The geometrician, I have suggested, abstracts (to use a modern term)—abstracts from bodies, from the material, to the ideas. The political thinker, on the other hand, should recognize that bodies (and the passions they generate) limit what can be done in practice with abstractions, with the ideas (say, the idea of justice). The political thinker *is* obliged to deal with men as he finds them, and as they are inevitably to be found, limited by their heritage, their mortality, and their resources. Indeed, he is obliged to recognize both that man *is* the defining animal—that corporeal being who formulates as premises the earliest things he becomes aware of—and that some men define better than others.

All too often the fact of a variety of ways of life leads men to proclaim that there simply is no basis for determining which (if any) of these ways is the best. But one should expect a diversity of ways, each with its claim to preeminence—and one should realize that only those who have at least a thoughtful sense of what each way of life is offering may be qualified to choose among them.

The inevitable disparity among men should not keep the thoughtful political man, or at least the teachers of such men, from recognizing that there *are* standards of excellence and that the highest calling of the human being may be to explore the nature of things with a view to understanding for its own sake. There may be found in the 26th Canto of Dante's *Inferno* an exhortation by the daring Ulysses to his comrades, an exhortation that can be said to have been anticipated in the "adventure story" Homer had told 2,500 years before. In Dante's story,

Ulysses urges his comrades to continue westward through what we know as the Straits of Gibraltar—an exhortation and an expedition that take them to their deaths: "O brothers! who through a hundred thousand dangers have reached the West, deny not, to this brief vigil of your senses which remains, experience of the unpeopled world behind the sun. Consider your origins: you were not formed to live like brutes, but to follow virtue and knowledge."[26]

We discern once again the tracks of men—and, as in the case of Plato's geometrician, they point West.

Epilogue

XVI. Citizen and Human Being

Thoreau, Socrates,
and Civil Disobedience

> That the *polis* is prior by nature to each one [of us] is
> clear. . . . He who is incapable of entering into com-
> munity, or on account of self-sufficiency has no need
> of anything, is no part of a *polis* and must therefore
> be either a beast or a god.
>
> Aristotle, *Politics* 1253a25

i

In an age of "conformity" principled self-assertion should be cherished even as it is distinguished from sentimental self-deception. Henry
Thoreau, who can be a delightful companion in the dark woods of
this world, is the recognized apostle of nonconformity. One even finds
this plea from *Walden* on behalf of the nonconformist enshrined in
placards confronting passengers in crowded subway trains:

> Why should we be in such desperate haste to succeed and in
> such desperate enterprises? If a man does not keep pace with his
> companions, perhaps it is because he hears a different drummer.
> Let him step to the music which he hears, however measured or
> far away.

This attitude is evident in the romantic extravagances of young men and
young nations of the modern world. (Indeed, the modern world can be
thought of as characterized by a radical romanticism which threatens
civilization and invites tyranny.)

Thoreau incites us to question the respectable. But what could be
more respectable than to be memorialized, as Thoreau now is, on an
American postage stamp? We dare, then, on the authority of Thoreau
himself, to question the dogmas he has promulgated, especially as they
are understood by crowds disposed to lawlessness.

This article was published in 54 *Southwest Review* 203 (Spring 1969). It incorpo-
rated talks given at the University of Chicago on Plato's *Crito* (in 1964, for the
Hillel Foundation Jewish Student Center) and on Henry Thoreau (in 1967, for the
Basic Program of Liberal Education for Adults).

The original title of this article was "On Civil Disobedience: Thoreau, Socrates,
and the Declaration of Independence."

Why should anyone follow one drummer rather than another? Is a drummer to be followed merely because he is distant? or because he is different from the one others are following? If a drummer even more distant than ours, or perhaps merely a different one, offers himself, should we then change our step? Must every man follow some drummer? or, at least, most men? If so, should not we attempt to assess the relative merits of the drummers who offer their music to us? If it does not matter what drummer we follow, why should we follow any drummer? Indeed, why should we conform to any music at all?[1]

May not something be said for having one drummer for the entire community to follow? Is this not, in fact, what "community" means, that body of men who follow the same drummer—and the better the drummer, the better the community? Whether the community's drummer should be respected depends partly on how much we value community itself. That is, what is man without the community? How much of what we know and cherish as human can exist independent of the community and its laws?

One's answer to these questions may depend on what one believes man in the state of nature to be. Thoreau's own belief is suggested by the opening sentences of his *Walden*:

> When I wrote the following pages, or rather the bulk of them, I lived alone, in the woods, a mile from any neighbor, in a house which I had built myself, on the shore of Walden Pond, in Concord, Massachusetts, and earned my living by the labor of my hands only. I lived there two years and two months. At present I am a sojourner in civilized life again.

He is, he seems to think, temporarily "in civilized life again." He believes, that is, he was not "in civilized life" when he was on "the shore of Walden Pond." We must wonder, however, how much "alone" anyone could be a mere mile "from any neighbor," "in Concord, Massachusetts," within walking distance of the Athens of North America. How much alone is a man when he knows that his native community is immediately available to him, when he knows that he can draw at will upon its resources and its people?

But one mile or one thousand may not be decisive: even more critical than the distance from civilization is what a man who steps in Thoreau's fashion "outside" civilized life takes with him. He certainly takes with him knowledge of how to build a house, as well as the tools for such an enterprise. Even more important, he takes with him knowledge of reading and writing, the tools of the language with which civilized life has invested him, that language which permits every man to reason and which equips the gifted man to rise above the community.

The pages Thoreau wrote "in the woods" were (he says) written primarily to explain himself to his townsmen. His body had gone down the road a piece, but not his soul. Indeed, it may be that a truly cilivized man can never leave civilized life, even if his physical departure should be permanent: he takes with him the marks and habits of civilization, shaping accordingly everything he thereafter sees and does.

It is because of his opinion of the ease of separating man from his community—an opinion reflected in his assumption that one could be a thinking, moralizing, writing human being independent of civilized life—that Thoreau can suggest in his antislavery essay on "Civil Disobedience" that one may secede from his immediate community as readily as the State of Massachusetts can secede from the American Union:

> . . . Some are petitioning the State to dissolve the Union, to disregard the requisitions of the President. Why do they not dissolve it themselves,—the union between themselves and the State,— and refuse to pay their quota into its treasury? Do not they stand in the same relation to the State, that the State does to the Union? . . .[2]

There were alive in Thoreau's day men who could recall when and how Massachusetts entered into the relation then existing between the States and the Union. But has there ever been a civilized man who recalled when and how men first came together into a community to escape the "desperate enterprises" of the state of nature? Indeed, to recall is itself the mark of civilized man, or the reasoning being, of the creature permanently educated and guided by long-established civilization.[3]

When Thoreau thought, while huckleberry picking, that "the State was nowhere to be seen," he was surely naïve. Perhaps, however, such a sentiment should be respected as calculated naïveté designed to influence civic-minded multitudes in the grip of what Tocqueville calls "virtuous materialism." Still, it is prudent today not to neglect the threats to community, and hence to the opportunity of man to rise above the community, which are implicit in Thoreau's essay on the duty of civil disobedience: it is this essay, not *Walden* (with its respect for nature, for simplicity and self-reliance, and for godlike excellence), that is now so influential among us.

The authoritative American alternative to Thoreau's sentimental dogmas about political life may be found in the Declaration of Independence. The Declaration recognizes our dependence upon the community, a dependence that both induces and entitles us to alter or to abolish our government when it becomes destructive of the ends for which governments are instituted among men, "and to institute new Government, laying its foundation on such principles and organizing its powers in such form, as to [us] shall seem most likely to effect [our] Safety and Happiness." Thus, the Declaration of Independence reminds us that there are standards outside and above the teachings of particular governments, standards superior even to what our own government might at any moment believe or choose. The right of revolution implies, that is, the supremacy of reason in human affairs.

Thoreau sometimes speaks as if the traditional right of revolution is much the same as what he means by the duty of civil disobedience. But the Declaration of Independence does what Thoreau could never discipline himself to do: it takes government seriously. The Declaration recognizes the practical necessity of civilized life for man and addresses itself in a responsible manner to the question of how that life can best be organized in the ever changing circumstances that men confront.[4]

ii

The best-known classical alternative to Thoreau is, of course, Plato's *Crito*, in which Socrates considers it salutary to permit himself (and hence philosophy) to be identified with simple law-abidingness. The Platonic Socrates, in his recognition of the practical necessity of civilized life for man, is closer to the Declaration of Independence than to Thoreau. This, in any event, is the intended appearance of the dialogue. What does this dialogue, the *Crito*, say? That is, what emerges from the conversation between Socrates and Crito?[5]

Socrates lies under sentence of death. His old friend Crito wants to use his money and influence, and the money of others (both Athenians and foreigners), to save his friend from the undeserved execution which is to come in a day or two. Everything has been arranged: only one thing further is required, and that is the willingness of Socrates to cooperate in the flight to the North. We are reminded of the Underground Railroad and the many deeds of heroism and self-sacrifice by which, through it, men were saved from harsh fates. But Socrates will not cooperate: he continues to acquiesce in, even to court, death in the manner we saw in his trial. That is, he exhibits in private the attitude which had been seen in public. Of course, he has reasons that the distraught Crito is unable to contradict. Thus, a tired old man is left to the fate he wants, having lived a full and, by and large, good life.

This, then, is something that the dialogue can be said to have said: and there are some among us who would see the story in just about these terms (however buttressed by psychological language), especially if they confronted someone whose reputation did not intimidate them.

iii

The dialogue and what it says can be seen as well primarily in terms of the reasons Crito is given to satisfy him that Socrates does right in not leaving.

The political community, without which few of the good things of human life would be possible, depends on laws. The laws are sometimes misapplied by mistaken men—but everyone would agree that most of the laws are salutary. If a man lives in a community—if he does not leave when he has the opportunity to do so—he consents to being bound by the application of those laws in his case.

If he insists upon passing judgment upon each law with which he is confronted, he is merely inviting anarchy. For it is difficult to deny the same privilege to others—and some will thus be induced to act against good laws they might otherwise have obeyed. Socrates must concede there are laws that are salutary, laws that are necessary for his city and for all cities. But there is a sense in which all laws are equal: for the subversion of one law leads to, permits, perhaps even encourages the subversion of others.

The citizen implicitly enters into an agreement in order to profit from the community. But what the community does may sometimes seem to injure him. This any reasonable man knows when he enters into or persists in an agreement of this kind. But he does persist, because he also knows that in human affairs, where ignorance and chance are unavoidable, mistakes will be made and things may not always work out as they should.

An old man especially knows this: Socrates is who he is—has become what he is—because Athens has been (and even now continues to be) what it is. He has always recognized the value of law—and to run away now would be to undermine the law, to discourage the law-abiding, even to make himself appear ridiculous, and all for a few years of life (or, as it is put, for a banquet in Thessaly). This would confirm the opinion of those who had brought him to trial as someone who had subverted the city.

Indeed, the dialogue has come down to us as the classic statement of the case for law-abidingness.

iv

But it is not the dialogue that makes this statement, we may happen to notice after another reading. The case for law-abidingness is made not by Socrates but by the laws. Socrates rarely speaks in his own name during the concluding part of the dialogue. That is, almost one-half of the dialogue reports the laws speaking through him, speaking to Crito and arguing for law-abidingness.

The laws say precisely what one would expect to hear from them. Every law expects to be obeyed: it states an imperative; it demands obedience; it knows no alternative. And all laws are in this respect, birds of a feather. They do not really care for argument: they will use it, preferably in preambles, but only to secure obedience.[6]

Socrates is asked whether he agrees that this or that law has been salutary—and from this limited agreement, the laws suggest that he agrees that all are salutary.[7] The laws are, in a sense, unscrupulous. But they do hold out to the citizen the alternative of going elsewhere if he does not like the regime. They do not point out, however, that wherever one goes, there will be laws—and laws that will make essentially the same argument. Where is one really to go? The alternatives held out by the laws are illusory: the laws a man *does* want to flee are those immediately confronting him in their unjust application.

The laws, we also notice, are many; and the many were dismissed by Socrates early in this conversation with Crito as unreliable, indeed as the authors of opinions that are not worth much. Socrates prefers the thought of one who may know to the opinions of the many. The many are loud and insistent and can wound or kill; the laws, too, confront Socrates with the prospect of what their brothers in Hades will eventually do to him if he should flaunt them here on earth. The laws are so noisy that, Socrates says at the end, he cannot hear any other argument. They would drown out the voice of reason. Yet Socrates had said at the beginning of this conversation with Crito that he was one who would not be moved but by reason.[8]

Indeed, the laws can even be said to be intent only on looking out for themselves.

v

We cannot, however, leave it at this. For it is Socrates who uses the narrow-minded laws. It is he who brings them on the stage to speak the piece that can be expected of them.

He cannot simply agree with what they say: they do not reason, they merely draw upon their traditional opinions. Socrates has been known to disregard, even to disobey, what seemed to be the law of Athens—and to counsel the self-righteous, as in Plato's *Euthyphro,* not to be overly zealous in enforcing the law.

But there is one special factor Socrates must take into account in framing his answer on this occasion: Crito, a decent man. We would not want Crito, feeling as he does, not to try to do something to help his friend. But does Crito understand what would be truly helpful? He is perhaps too much concerned about the opinions of the many, despite his long association with Socrates. That association—they are of like age and deme—may have been based on causes to some degree accidental. They may be somewhat like the boyhood chums who continue their affection and concern for one another long after they would have ceased to find each other attractive in the guise of strangers. The very considerations that Crito brings forward reveal the kind of considerations with which he must be countered: the opinions of the many must be countered by the opinions of another, perhaps more refined, "many."[9]

Crito is present on this occasion because of dubious arrangements he has made with Socrates' guard. And he is prepared to make similar arrangements for getting Socrates away. That is, he is disposed to use his wealth to get his own way. Both in his willingness to use his wealth and in his emphasis on the overriding value of self-preservation, he is bound to the body to a degree that Socrates cannot accept.[10]

There may be laws that should be broken, there may be occasions that call for flight. But someone such as Crito cannot be depended on to make the proper judgment. Rather, he is better off—as is the typical reader who comes from the dialogue with its evident lesson in law-abidingness—if he is persuaded he should act as is prescribed by law. For men are far more apt than not to break the law for the wrong reasons,—and such an attitude jeopardizes that stability of the community needed not only for civilization to develop and survive but also for the best to emerge.[11]

vi

The fact remains that Socrates does not flee. We confront, then, the question not of the reasons Crito and the typical reader are given, but of the reasons Socrates has for acting as he does.

One reason has been suggested: the political community is of inestimable value to man, and laws are essential to that community. In this Socrates agrees with the laws.[12] Another reason is suggested by the very fact of the dialogue's being presented to us: Socrates knew what the report would be that Crito (with the assistance of someone such as Plato) would convey to his fellows. Citizens who had condemned Socrates as a lawbreaker would see him as refusing to break the law, even in circumstances when they themselves would break it. For Crito had been concerned that he might be criticized, by the very people who had condemned Socrates, for not having used his wealth to help his friend escape.

Socrates, then, is not altogether unconcerned about his reputation. That is, he is concerned about reputation, not for its own sake but for the effect it will have. He is not concerned for the effect it will have on him, however, but for the effect it may have for philosophy and other philosophers—that is, for his true friends—in Athens and (as we now know) elsewhere.[13] The philosopher is made to appear law-abiding: the most private of men is displayed as most respectful of the public, as a just man. Nor is he oblivious to other appearances; he does not want to do the unseemly—that is, the ignoble, as distinguished from the unjust.

It is an old man who acts in this way. What would Socrates have done had he been much younger? What would he have done if he had thought he still had a more important contribution to make to philosophy or even to Athens than his death in these circumstances would make? We do not know. But we do remember that he had long before abandoned political life—had, in a sense, fled from the city—because not to have done so would have led to his destruction without doing any good either for himself or for others.[14]

vii

What then are the considerations Socrates would bring to bear in judging a particular situation? Before the laws are brought on the stage, there is (in the middle of the dialogue) this exchange (*Crito* 49d-50a):

> *Socrates:* . . . Consider very carefully whether or not you agree with me and share my opinion and let us begin our inquiry from the starting point that it is never right either to act unjustly, or to repay injustice with injustice, or to avenge ourselves on any man who harms us by harming him in return. Or do you disagree with me and dissent from my starting point? I myself have believed it for a long time, and I believe in it still, but if you differ in any way, explain to me how. If you still hold to our former opinion, listen to my next point.

> *Crito:* I do hold to it, and I agree with you: so go on.

> *Socrates:* My next point, then, or rather my next question, is this: Ought a man to carry out his just agreements, or may he evade them?

> *Crito:* He ought to carry them out.

> *Socrates:* Then consider this. If we go away without the city's consent, shall we be injuring those whom we ought least to injure or not? Shall we be abiding by our just agreements or not?

> *Crito:* I cannot, Socrates, answer your question, for I do not understand.

Since Crito cannot answer—since he cannot think through this particular problem—Socrates must handle him in another way: he must bring in the general arguments of the laws.[15]

The laws emphasize a covenant, not coercion alone, as the basis of their authority; and they speak of what preserves and of what undermines political communities. They speak, that is, of justice as they know it, identifying themselves with the city. Justice is ·for them obedience to the law— they acknowledge no bad law. Socrates, too, had been prepared to explore with Crito the demands of justice—but Crito was not equipped to cooperate. The arguments with respect to justice are there, that justice which should be employed in determining what laws should be enacted or repealed, in determining what laws should be covenanted with. But Socrates and Crito are in a place where it is not possible to know what it is like outside. They are, pursuant to law, in a confined, even unnatural, place; and even outside it is barely dawn. The more evident and unfettered inquiry into justice and the laws should be on other occasions and with other interlocutors.[16]

In any event, Plato's readers are left with the salutary suggestion that until they really know what they are doing, until they are equipped and disciplined enough to think through the reasons for appropriate disobedience in particular situations, they will do well to abide by the laws, to confine their activities to the means for redressing grievances that properly constituted laws provide. Otherwise, they become the prisoners of those who talk loudest.

viii

The laws, when they are permitted by Socrates to speak their piece, must make concessions they do not make everywhere. That is, they must be prepared to behave themselves.

Thus, the right of emigration has to be conceded by the laws: the dissatisfied citizen can leave with his property. The citizen must also be permitted, while he remains, to try to persuade the laws that they need amendment. Both of these rights, it can be argued, must be more than nominal if the laws are to be entitled to the moral stature with which Socrates invests them.

Still another condition is implied: there must be a trial according to law on an issue defined by law. That is, the laws, to justify themselves, must act like laws. The citizen can be legitimately addressed by the laws, as is Socrates in the *Crito*, only if the citizen's trial and conviction have been in accordance with properly constituted law.

The concessions the laws have to make, in order to win Socrates' implicit assent, raise them not only above the opinions of the many but above the typical laws as well. Thus, the *Crito* can be seen as, in part, an argument that Socrates and Plato make *to* the laws and to the political community on behalf of justice and even the life of the mind.[17]

ix

We are moved to wonder, by our invocation here on behalf of justice, whether we have in our preliminary assessment of Thoreau given him his due, however useful and even necessary it may be today for citizens to question certain of Thoreau's dogmas. He may be, after all, bigger and better than we are, especially in his wholehearted devotion to the life of the mind, to that life which challenges us as human beings to examine and to be prepared to discard the respectable opinions with which citizenship invests, comforts, and confines us. Indeed, we can imagine Socrates, an urbane human being of incredible daring, endorsing as salutary for the life of inquiry the declaration of independence with which Thoreau opens his essay on "Walking":

> I wish to speak a word for Nature, for absolute freedom and wildness, as contrasted with a freedom and culture merely civil —to regard man as an inhabitant, or a part and parcel of Nature, rather than a member of society. I wish to make an extreme statement, if so I may make an emphatic one, for there are enough champions of civilization: the minister and the school committee and every one of you will take care of that.

XVII. On Death
One by One, Yet All Together

> Cassius [to Brutus]: Of your philosophy you make no
> use, if you give place to accidental evils.
> Shakespeare, *Julius Caesar*, IV, iii

i

It is difficult today to strike the proper balance in talking about
death. To ignore it is to fail to appreciate something vital to human
life; but to make much of it is to fail to live.

It is unlikely that we have today anything really new to say about
death—anything really new and yet important—except to the extent that
certain modern notions (one might even say prejudices or illusions) about
it and about life generally have created new problems. It is unlikely, that
is, that we can notice about death anything truly important which others
have not known long before us.[1] Perhaps the best we can hope for is to
rediscover what has been noticed before—and to begin to reflect upon the
causes and consequences of our having forgotten what has long been
known.

A distinction should be drawn between what a thoughtful man may
know about death and dying and what is likely to be felt by most
people about dying and death. No serious discussion of anything human
is possible if one is not aware of such a distinction among men.

I believe it fair to say that the prospect of death is for the thoughtful
man *not* a matter for "anxiety" or "terror"—it may not even be for him,
upon contemplating his ówn death, a matter for awe. At most, it is
for him an occasion for curiosity. Indeed, considering the attitude of
most men through the ages toward the prospect of death, one might
even regard this dispassionate attitude toward death an indication, if
not the definition, of the thoughtful man. There may *seem* to most

---

This talk was prepared for a symposium, "Death and Dying," sponsored by the
Institute for Society, Ethics, and the Life Sciences, at the annual convention of the
American Association for the Advancement of Science, Chicago, Illinois, December
29, 1970.

The symposium panel included Leon R. Kass, Elisabeth Kubler-Ross and William
F. May.

The citations in the text are to William F. May, "The Sacral Power of Death in
Contemporary Experience," 39 *Social Research* 463 (Autumn 1972).

of us, it should at once be added, something austere and inhuman (perhaps, on occasion, something insensitive and even inhumane) about the opinion regarding death of the truly thoughtful man, however cheerful he may be on his own deathbed.[2]

To the extent, therefore, that the terms used by Professor William F. May, in his well-received paper, to describe death (whether the terms be his or those of others from whom he quotes)—"anxiety," "terror," "dreadful," "hideousness," "immensity," "trauma," "disturbing," "overwhelming," "tragedy" (a term much misused today)—to the extent that these terms strike a responsive chord in us, to that extent we are not thoughtful men but are rather bound up in the affairs of the flesh as men and women of the modern world.

The extent of the thoughtful man's abstraction from such affairs is indicated by his lack of concern about what becomes of his body after death: I will no longer be around, he will say; the body that remains has nothing to do with me; do with it as you please.[3] Dying is, for him, little more than a necessary inconvenience, an interruption (perhaps a permanent interruption) in the conduct by him of the life he should lead. If I "make an extreme statement," it is in order to be able to question—and even to suggest that we are entitled, if not obliged, to question—the current popular attitude about individuality and hence death, an attitude that contemporary artists and intellectuals have both ratified and encouraged.[4]

ii

I believe it useful to examine (on the basis of what one hears) how and why the thoughtful man regards death as he does. We should keep in mind as we do so the difficulty that even the thoughtful man might face in maintaining his equanimity in certain circumstances, the difficulty not so much of facing his own impending death but rather of accepting the death of someone close to him, particularly in circumstances in which death is premature and, therefore, in a sense, unnatural and thus awesome. We should also keep in mind the fact that one should speak about these matters at wakes and funerals in a manner different from that employed on other occasions.[5]

Only when we begin to sense how the thoughtful man understands such matters are we equipped to determine what the standard should be for most men, to determine what we can and should do to shape men generally with respect to dying and death, and to determine what we should do for men and women *as they now are* when they go, one by one, to their deaths. We should be concerned, if we are to have a healthy community, that there be felt toward death neither unseemly anxiety nor unnatural passivity.

What may the thoughtful man know, or at least think probable, about death and dying? When we consider what he knows, we might be in a better position to understand the attitude of most people, to advise them and to train the next generation. That is, to understand error, to see it for what it is—including the recognition of it *as* error, which is essential for dealing with it properly—one must of course have some notion of what the truth is.

In thinking about death the body comes first to view. There is no question that the body is useful to "us" and that "we" are attached to it: man, as animal, instinctively does many things to preserve himself.[6] The usefulness of the body depends partly on the fact that it is animated matter and hence can make contact and come to terms with the rest of the matter in the universe.[7] As matter, however, the body must be subject to change: its very effectiveness depends on this changeableness.

Change can mean, in varying circumstances, perception or suffering (including disintegration). Thus, we simply would not be what we are (for better or for worse) if we were not capable of such change (of which death is the most dramatic form). To wish away death or to try to conquer it may be to attack one vital condition of our humanity: indeed, one might even say there is something suicidal about such an attempt.

iii

How, then, is the body to be regarded and ministered to?

Mr. May has observed that the manifest function of our cadres of experts in "the helping professions *is* to provide the critically ill with better cure and care." (p. 468; italics added) But, he adds, "a latent social function of this specialization is the avoidance of an event [that is, death] with which we cannot cope." One must wonder if this is so to a significant degree. Are not many of the hospital abuses that have been noticed (for example, the demoralizing isolation, the "heroic" efforts to prolong "life," and the rigid administrative regulations) functions of the very effectiveness we *do* want in curing?

I suspect that many of the serious hospital abuses (aside from those due to bureaucracy itself) could be corrected only at the cost of reduced efficiency of the system of cure *and* care. Of course, the hospital and medical practices we have may make a certain kind of dying more likely: that is, these practices may provoke conduct not really required by the kind of lives we lead—and decent men with common sense should reform what they can of such practices. Still, the practical problem remains whether such practices (however they may be reformed) are not the result primarily of massive (and largely successful) efforts to cure disease, to eliminate pain, and to prolong life. If they are, are we prepared to sacrifice those efforts and their effects? Are we not usually willing to put up with most of the abuses (including the isolating and "dehumanizing" apparatus) if the "system" is generally likely to contribute to our relief? May it not even be callous to treat the "hopeless" cases in a radically different manner, so long as they are handled in hospitals?

Consider, for example, Mr. May's report of doctors who have observed that "in an Arabian village, a grandmother dies in the midst of her children and grandchildren, cows and donkeys. But our high level of technological development leads simply to dying a death appropriate to one's disease—in the heart ward or the cancer ward." (p. 483)[8] The villager will indeed die with her animals and grandchildren, *if* she should live so long. And in the process, all too often, will not her mode of living and dying make it less likely than among us that *her* grandchildren will live to be grandparents? I am suggesting, that is, that we should take care not to succumb to the all-too-human desire to try both to eat one's cake and to have it too.[9]

Consider, also, the significance of the current use of the term, "helping professions." This seems to me a vague and undisciplined designation, moving us away from the more rigorous language and purposes associated with specific arts (for example, the art of medicine). In fact, all professions can be said to be helping—including the teaching profession and the military profession (however misdirected both of these may be at times). To emphasize "helping" is to reinforce, perhaps even to endorse, an already pervasive sentimentality—sentimentality that comes, in large part, from our ability as moderns to minister to our bodies and to exaggerate and romanticize the pleasures (even as we dramatize the pains) of the flesh.

To lump together all the "helping professions" makes it easier to lump together as well our criticisms of them. Thus, the doctor's evasive replies to the dying patient and the undertaker's dressed-up language are seen by Mr. May as essentially the same. (p. 469) Yet are they not radically different? One is probably kind, certainly in intention: the other, may be sometimes selfish. One may be useful; the other, exploitive.

What *should* be said about the deception of the dying by the medical profession? The limitations of the patient and of his family and friends have to be taken into account, the limitations of the people they have (over many years) been allowed to become. For the good both of the community and of other patients, the limitations and needs of medical personnel have also to be taken into account: this is not for them *their* last terminal illness; they are entitled and perhaps even obliged to shield themselves from death to some degree. That is, ordinary doctors and nurses may also require some self-deception, particularly since it is likely that their effectiveness depends on the fact that they care deeply about healing: they have to contend with death constantly. Indeed, the thoughtful man, inasmuch as he is not moved as most men are by death, is not likely to be a good doctor.[10]

Mr. May's discussion of death and man's "identity with his flesh" seems to me the best part of his paper. (p. 480) But it does rest upon certain assumptions that should be examined. Consider, for example, the observation, "Part of the terror of death is that it threatens a man with a loss of identity with his flesh, an identity which is essential to him . . ." (p. 480) Does not this observation rest on the assumption that "a man" survives after death or exists apart from his body? What is the "his" referred to again and again in such discussions, the "his" that is independent of the body? It is observed that "Uncle John cannot be allowed to die and repose in solemn dignity." (p. 469) Is it not useful to realize that it may make no difference at all to "poor Uncle John"? It might matter, of course, to what was his family. It might help most men to respect the living if corpses *are* treated respectfully, even reverently. But here, as elsewhere, should not a distinction be observed between what may be true and what may be useful, between what a thoughtful man may know and what is likely to be felt by most people?[11]

Mr. May spoke in his paper of death as "the great individualizer." (p. 475) I suggest the following qualifications (which may be implicit in what he has said). Consider, as a sadly desperate effort to preserve individuality, the development among us of the undertaker's cosmetic "art."[12] Is not this development related to our faith in the prospect of unlimited "progress"? Thus, death threatens to undermine that faith in our boundless ability to *become*—that is, to be ourselves in an infinite number of variations. Death, if faced up to—if not concealed by euphemisms and cosmetics—should remind us of the natural terms of living things and hence of nature and of models for a good life, models that do not depend on one's individuation but rather on one's approximation to a standard guiding other men as well.[13]

Failing the concealment of death, we otherwise encourage individuation and discourage dedication to what we are tempted to dismiss as a "rigid" standard by insisting that each death is special. That is to say, undisciplined individuality easily deteriorates into the sentimentality I have already referred to. Sentimentality not only rests upon but also reinforces misapprehensions about the nature of life and death, thereby keeping us from understanding what we might otherwise understand about the most important things.[14]

iv

What *can* be known by the thoughtful man about death itself? We have returned—after preparing ourselves by considering the nature of the body, the roles of the "helping professions," and the "individualizing" effects of death—we have returned to the question with which we started.

Men *have* long known that "sleep is early practice in dying" (p. 483), that death and sleep resemble one another, that sleep is a counterfeit of death. Does not death seem to be like permanent sleeping? What, then, is so terrible about that, especially since death should not come as a surprise to the mature adult? For instance, one learns that when one is tired, certain things seem worse than they do when one is fresh. (Fatigue may, depending on the state of one's soul, even make things seem fearful and desperate.) I expect this demoralization can be even more prominent when one encounters unawares the massive "tiredness" of an impending natural death. But one does learn to recognize the depression that fatigue can bring on and to discount and compensate for such depression.

What of the fear of abandonment that the dying are said to have? (p. 483ff) Is it not salutary to believe that the only ones really being "abandoned" are the survivors? Are not they (the surviving community) the ones we should be (even as we go to our deaths) most concerned about, the community that can have its vitality sapped by an exaggerated fear of death and of dying (just as it may have its humanity stunted by an absence of all compassion in the face of death)?

Does not death threaten man with the loss of an illusion, a sometimes salutary illusion, about his ability to control his affairs? The prospect of death, properly considered, may help us see how much of an illusion this is, especially for mortals affected as much as we inevitably are (in our everyday lives) by "accidental evils." It may also help us see how relatively unimportant death should be, especially for anyone who understands what it is to be truly human.

And yet, it is fashionable today (unlike, say, among the ancient Greeks) to place the emphasis on the overwhelming importance of death. It seems to me a curiously distorted, even misanthropic, view of human life to insist that "an authentic relationship to death is the touchstone of authenticity toward all else." (p. 475) This insistence does seem to have the impressive authority of Martin Heidegger to support it—but we *as a community* should be cautious about taking lessons in dying from a man who has been so notoriously deficient in the conduct as a citizen of his own life.[15]

Does not this self-centered opinion about "an authentic relationship to death" depend on a notion of "self" that is independent not only of the body but of life itself?

v

The misanthropy to which I have referred may be partly the result of the bitter disappointment that can follow upon excessive expectations. That is, eternal life seems to many no longer to be possible—and yet man had come to believe it *was* possible, perhaps even virtually certain.

Earthly life is all too often judged by standards tinged by mankind's former expectations, expectations that remain in our literature, language, and traditions and hence shape us still. But earthly life is necessarily marked for most people by loneliness, afflictions, and uncertainties, by trials from which no reasonable man can ever hope to shield most human beings. Former expectations continue sufficiently attractive to make present woes, and particularly the woes of dying and death, more oppressive for the generality of men than they perhaps need be.

How one responds to death is (aside from the physiological changes, in a natural death, which may have psychological effects difficult to counter) probably the result of how one responds to other challenges. That is, it is primarily the result of the kind of human being one has been taught and habituated to become. That is one reason I prefer to see the emphasis put here upon life and the conduct of life as critical for serious examination.

vi

One is again obliged to wonder: what *is* the good life? how *should* a man conduct himself?

It is taken for granted in Professor May's discussion (as in most such discussions today) that all men are being talked about by him, when in fact *only* most men are. Thus, he observes, "Men evade death because they recognize in the event an immensity that towers above their resources for handling it." (p. 469)

What is, on the other hand, the effect of holding up a standard of how the best, of how *the* man, acts? Does not this provide a guide for *all* men, something to moderate their desires and to hold in check their fears? We should take care, in any event, not to legitimate cowardice.[16]

Thus, our concern should really be with the kind of human being we are and with the kind of life we lead, not with the death that awaits us all. To direct much attention to our response to death is to attempt to deal with merely the last fleeting manifestations ·of the kind of characters we have had formed.

Much is made today of what can be learned from the dying of most people. Is it not better to consider the death of those for whom it does not come as a surprise—of those few who are thoughtfully prepared for it?

Even better, is it not desirable to study seriously the *lives* of such people?

vii

Much of what one reads about how many, perhaps most, men die— how they have to be persuaded to "accept" the imminence of death— suggests that something is seriously wrong with the way most men live.

Our proper concern is, as I have said, with how men live. Life is really too short for the thoughtful man to devote to anything but the most important concerns, including the concern with how one should live—and particularly with how one should live so as to be able to begin to understand the universe in which men are so fortunate as to find themselves, even if only temporarily.[17]

Notes

I. Dissent in Athens: An Invocation of First Principles

1. The first five paragraphs of this note can serve as an introduction to all the notes in this book. (I turn to contemporary Greece in the sixth paragraph of this note and in the remaining six notes for this essay.)

The reader is urged, as with all the other essays in this collection, to begin by reading the text without reference to the notes. See, on how the notes are to be used and understood, Anastaplo, *The Constitutionalist: Notes on the First Amendment* (Dallas: Southern Methodist University Press, 1971), c. 2, nn. 1, 39, c. 8, n. 135; "American Constitutionalism and the Virtue of Prudence: Philadelphia, Paris, Washington, Gettysburg," 8 *Loyola of Los Angeles Law Review* 1 (Winter 1975), nn. 1, 48 (to be reprinted, with additions, in Leo Paul deAlvarez, editor, *Abraham Lincoln, The Gettysburg Address and American Constitutionalism* [Irving, Texas: University of Dallas Press, 1975]). See, also, Essay II, notes 1, 39, below.

A number of corrections for *The Constitutionalist,* a book which will be cited throughout this collection of essays, can be found in notes 3 and 4 of my "American Constitutionalism" article. Reviews of *The Constitutionalist* can be found, among other places, in *Dallas Morning News,* Nov. 28, 1971, p. 6H; *Panorama, Chicago Daily News,* Jan. 22-23, 1972, p. 7; 57 *Southwest Review* vi (Winter 1972); 8 *Criminal Law Bulletin* 350 (May 1972); *Showcase, Chicago Sun-Times,* June 18, 1972, p. 18; 60 *California Law Review* 1476 (Sept. 1972); *Nation,* Sept. 18, 1972, p. 218; *St. Louis Post-Dispatch,* Oct. 3, 1972, p. 3B; 21 *Newsletter on Intellectual Freedom* 165 (Nov. 1972); 404 *Annals of the American Academy* 291 (Nov. 1972); 1973 *Illinois Law Forum* 211 (1973); 17 *Modern Age* 93 (Winter 1973); 42 *American Scholar* 347 (Spring 1973); 3 *Publius* 2, 31 (Spring 1973); 20 *University of Chicago Law School Record* 3 (Spring 1973); 26 *Journal of Legal Education* 247 (1974); 68 *American Political Science Review* 774 (June 1974); *Academic Reviewer,* Spring-Summer 1974, p. 18; 61 *Journal of American History* 850 (December 1974); 4 *Political Science Reviewer* 169 (Fall 1974); 9 *Revue Juridique Thémis* 126 (1974). See, also, my "American Constitutionalism," n. 58.

Throughout this collection of essays, "cf." means "compare" and points to a qualification of or something different from what has just been said or cited. Unless otherwise indicated, all the references to notes are to notes in the particular essay in which such references are found. The notes in half the essays (I, VII, IX, XI, XII, XIII, XIV, XV, XVII) have been prepared or substantially modified for this collection. Changes have been made in the notes in all the other essays. Cf. Essay V, note 3, below.

See Essay VI, notes 19, 20, Essay XVII, note 17, below. See, also, Essay IX, note 7, Essay XII, note 2, Essay XVI, note 16, Essay XVII, note 4, below.

The "present Greek government" referred to in this talk had been established when a clique of colonels in key Army positions seized power in Athens in the early morning hours of April 21, 1967. A pall settled upon the country and remained until the military regime collapsed in July 1974.

The occasion for the 1967 usurpation was provided the colonels by prolonged constitutional turmoil to which virtually every prominent Greek leader contributed. On the other hand, it should be noticed, in assessing the military intervention of 1967, that during the two years of unduly publicized demonstrations and crisis prior to that coup, the gross national product of Greece continued to rise at a remarkably high rate (to the very eve of the coup), law and order were maintained throughout the country (only one Greek, a student, was killed as a result of these political agitations, and he accidentally by the police, during that 1965-1967 period), and elections (not a resort to organized violence) were obviously regarded by everyone as the only legitimate way to resolve the constitutional crisis brought on in July 1965 by the imprudent confrontation between a quite young King and his liberal Prime Minister.

The colonels, in order to consolidate the power they had seized, had recourse to deception, intimidation, torture and purges. In the process, they wrecked the economy of the country and turned a proud army into a despised police force. In short, a tyranny was established.

I had personally gotten a great deal from Greece before the colonels came. (In the five years preceding the coup, for example, I had conducted for my students annual archaelogical tours of the country from which my parents had emigrated to the United States a half century before.) It became evident, when the colonels came to power, that the people I knew in that country would not be able to speak openly. I therefore considered it my duty, for a variety of reasons, to learn what I could about what had happened there and why. I continued to visit Greece annually for this purpose, securing on each occasion accreditation as a foreign correspondent for American journals and newspapers. This accreditation was desirable both for the access it provided to government functions and functionaries and for the protection it offered to the unduly curious inquirer. The trips themselves continued to be financed by archaeological tours. I managed in this way to become something of an expert on contemporary Greek affairs, so much so that I was eventually asked (on the recommendation of Eleni Vlachou, publisher of *Kathimerini*) to prepare the article on contemporary Greece for the new edition of the *Encyclopaedia Britannica*.

2. What I had said theretofore in Washington is reflected in the first major article I published on contemporary Greek affairs, "Retreat from Politics: Greece, 1967," 9 *Massachusetts Review* 83 (Winter 1968) (*errata* noted in the Spring 1968 issue, at p. 208) (reprinted, with some corrections, in 115 *Congressional Record* E2632 [April 2, 1969]). See, also, Anastaplo, "Interview [of a Colonel] in Athens: A Reconstruction," *Chicago Sun-Times*, September 3, 1967, p. 28 (incorporated in the *Massachusetts Review* article).

I was from the outset identified with—and indeed, at times, was virtually the only American spokesman for—"the Karamanlis solution" in Greece, the suggestion that the most prudent immediate resolution of the continuing Greek crisis, a resolution to which the United States could contribute, was the return to power in Athens of Constantine Karamanlis (who had been in self-exile in Paris since 1963). Mr. Karamanlis, who served as Prime Minister from 1955 to 1963, was a conservative politician of proven effectiveness, a man who had shown he could exercise power vigorously without having to silence his critics. He was more apt than anyone else, it seemed to me, to secure the support of all factions in Greece, to be received by genuine public approval (not merely by the tolerant apathy or by the silent resentment found among many Greeks under the colonels' tyranny), and to be respected by his country's invaluable ally, the United States. He was remembered as a disciplined architect of the great task of reconstruction needed in Greece after the terrible destruction of both the Second World War and the even crueller Civil War which followed. Cf. Essay XIII, note 3, Essay XIV, note 10, below.

My last publication on Greek affairs before a rearranged set of colonels was swept from power in July 1974 was an article, "Bloodied Greece: No Way Out?", which argued in support of "the Karamanlis solution" (120 *Congressional Record* E2990 [May 13, 1974], H4116 [May 20, 1974]; printed earlier in an abridged version, *Baltimore Sun*, April 19, 1974). It included these observations:

The observer of Greek affairs gets an impression of helplessness, drift and malaise, with the new government going through the forms of moral regeneration and reform. But those forms have been made a mockery by revelations of the corruption around the recently deposed dictator who had also preached moral regeneration when he first came to power [in 1967]. It must be difficult for anyone in Greece to take seriously anything a military government says these days.

And yet, what way out is there? As economic conditions worsen, partly as a result of the shortsighted measures adopted by the colonels since 1967 in order to stay in power, acts of desperation (including exploitation of crises with Turkey) will be provoked on the part both of government officials and of their opponents. An explosion can be expected next fall or early winter, when students return to their universities from summer vacations.

The explosion came even earlier than I had anticipated, when a desperate government in Athens launched, or permitted the launching of, the coup against Archbishop Makarios in Cyprus. "Success" there (in the form of a union between Greece and Cyprus), it was no doubt hoped, would redeem the colonels at home.

3. The constitutional referendum discussed in my talk was conducted on Sunday, September 29, 1968. The announced result was a vote of 92.2% in favor of the constitution proposed by the colonels. The colonels implemented from time to time thereafter only so much of the constitution as suited their immediate purposes. See Essay IV, note 28, below.

I observed, by remaining all day in a polling station in Delphi, how the colonels managed to secure the vote they did. My report on this dubious balloting is included in my article, "Greece Today and the Limits of American Power," 54 *Southwest Review* 1 (Winter 1968) (reprinted, without section divisions, in 115 *Congressional Record* E1875 [March 11, 1969]). This article, along with the September 20, 1968 Athens talk in the text (which was reprinted in 115 *Congressional Record* E5156 [June 23, 1969]), no doubt contributed to the order prohibiting my entry into Greece which awaited me at Athens airport in September 1970. It was explained by an officer of the Greek Press and Information Service in Washington, when inquiries were made on my behalf the following year by a travel agent organizing an archaeological tour which I would have conducted:

I wish to stress particularly on what I told you about the existence in the U.S.A. of at least one hundred Greek-born or of Greek origin College and University Professors at the humanities, absolutely elligible and most competent for your purposes and who have not indulged in defaming Greece and distorting the truth concerning the country.

This explanation may be found in a letter of August 9, 1971. In the meantime I myself had been told by a Deputy Assistant Secretary of State, in a letter of August 5, 1971:

In the absence of Mr. Sisco, I am writing to inform you that the Ministry of Foreign Affairs in Athens has informed our Embassy that the Government of Greece has decided that your entrance to Greece will not be permitted. Reportedly, this decision was taken at a very high level in the Greek Government.

The State Department was probably correct in this report—one of the few times I knew it to be correct with respect to Greek affairs during those years which will prove so damaging to American-Greek relations for decades to come.

Lt. Gen. Orestes E. Vidales, who served nobly in the resistance to the colonels' tyranny, has said that I may have been the only native American to have been barred from Greece by the colonels. (He himself was deprived of his Greek citizenship about the same time.) Both of us devoted our principal efforts in these matters to correcting the policy of the American government toward Greece.

I note in passing that it does not seem fitting that any distinguished Greek (whether at home or abroad) who "prudently" remained silent during the colonels' usurpation should now be given a prominent post. That is, it is not good, either for the immediate morale of that country or for the long-term deterrence of opportunists, that trimmers should be rewarded. As for outright collaborationists: what *is* to be done to them? See *Genesis* 4:15. Torturers are, of course, another matter.

Citations to various articles by me on Greek affairs, as well as some discussion of that subject, can be found in Anastaplo, *The Constitutionalist*. Additional citations to articles on Greece can be found in Anastaplo, "American Constitutionalism and the Virtue of Prudence," n. 28. Citations to all my articles and other discussions on Greek affairs are included in my "Autobiographical Bibliography" (of January 1, 1975), which is available from me in mimeographed form.

4. My impressions of both Spain and Russia have been collected in a long talk, "Madrid and Moscow: On a Six-Month Camping Trip Across Europe in 1960," prepared for delivery at Otterbein College, Westerville, Ohio, April 1962.

My expulsion on July 28, 1960 from the Soviet Union is described in an account sent by me to Maurice F. X. Donohue, who was then my dean in University College, The University of Chicago. This account, sent from Helsinki on July 31, 1960, was published in the *Carterville [Illinois] Herald*, August 28, 1960:

Let me try, within the limits of this aerogram, to give you a more detailed account than I was able to include in my cable last night about my expulsion from the Soviet Union midway through our 15-day visit.

A group of three tourists, two Americans and an English girl, were said to have distributed the State Department exchange magazine, *Amerika*, on a Moscow street. I happened along, as did a West German teacher, after the alleged distribution had been made and a policeman had intervened. A crowd had collected. The German and I took pictures. I also called attention to myself, without intending to, by talking to the trio, advising them, first, to get out of the car and off the street into the Intourist hotel before which they were parked (and thereby reduce the attraction for the crowd that had gathered) and, second, not to try to drive out lest someone (particularly the policeman standing in front of the car) be injured.

The German and I were rounded up thereupon and added to the trio who were only then told they could not leave. All five of us were eventually removed to a police station. The Russians got the notion into their heads that we were all one party—whereas the German and I had never seen the other three before. [The German and I had been together for several hours. He was a *Gymnasium* teacher in West Germany.] Nobody could persuade them otherwise. Indeed, it was for them a conspiracy not only to distribute the magazine (which is supposed to be legal reading material) but to do it in such a way as to create an incident which could be photographed. (The precise offense was left as vague as I state it here. Furthermore, we were never given anything on paper.)

The "trial" was most interesting, at times even amusing. I think I learned a good deal about the Russian legal mentality. Before we knew it (literally), we were found guilty of subverting public order and required to leave the country as soon as we could drive out in our respective automobiles. (I will give more details about the proceedings on another occasion.)

I let the Russian officials know what I thought of their way of conducting themselves (towards both tourists and defendants). My impression was that the police major conducting the investigation, which turned out to be a "trial," was not accustomed to forthrightness on the part of accused persons. The proceedings opened with my refusal to hand over my camera for removal of the film until I had received from them a statement of their legal justification for such a request:

the major had the expression of one who was watching a strange creature from another world.

I took my photograph about noon; by suppertime we were packing to leave the country. (I should add that this is the only time during our visit that any question was raised about taking street photographs.) The original trio were leaving Russia in a couple of days anyway, so the order did not really affect their plans; furthermore, the expulsion order was revoked or suspended a couple hours after it was issued for the English girl as well as for the German teacher.

This experience of our final day in Moscow was well worth the loss of the subsequent week of our scheduled tour (which would have been spent in Leningrad, for the most part). The Russians, of course, were not moved by such benevolent considerations. Nor did they know that I had been trying for several days to visit a Moscow court room: the people of Intourist would not tell me the address of courts in the district, so that I might try on my own to look in on proceedings. (They were there, I was told, to help me see only things tourists are interested in, such as buildings, cultural monuments, etc.)

I shall try to provide you later my general impressions of the country, based, for the most part on my notes and reflections as I went along. Finally, I should add that the only magazine I distributed in Russia was a copy of the *Lawyers Guild Review* with my Closing Argument to the Committee on Character and Fitness in it, which I had given a few days earlier to a young man who had been telling me about the restrictions placed upon their life. I added a dedicatory inscription, "To a Russian: On how free men contend."

The Closing Argument referred to may be found at 19 *Lawyers Guild Review* 143 (Winter 1959). See Essay IX, below.

See, also, my argument for "increased contacts [with Russians] of the kind that only tourists can make", Letter to the Editor, London *Observer*, August 14, 1960 (reprinted, Anastaplo, *The Constitutionalist*, p. 565). Cf. *New York Times*, July 29, 1960, 2: 5; July 30, 1960, 5: 7; *New York Herald-Tribune* (Late City), July 29, 1960, 14: 6. It should be added that it was, partly because of the U-2 episode, a bad summer in Moscow for American tourists.

It should also be added that increased contacts by the Russians with the West (as well as other developments, of course) *have* had some salutary effects. Consider, for example, my argument, Letter to the Editor, *Chicago Daily News*, August 29, 1968, p. 14 (also, *Chicago's American*, September 7, 1968; *Christian Science Monitor*, September 9, 1968):

It is perhaps natural, in the face of the dramatic Russian occupation of its neighbor [Czechoslovakia], for Americans to proclaim that World Communism has not changed after all.

But such desperate appraisals do not appreciate how restrained the Russians have been obliged to be this time, compared with their [1956] Hungarian aggression, to say nothing of what they have ruthlessly done to each other from time to time. They have evidently felt the need to recruit for this adventure as many of their Warsaw Pact allies as they could induce to support them. Even so, they have not been able to force the support of Romania, although that Communist country is even more vulnerable to attack from Russia than was Czechoslovakia.

They had to acknowledge that they must negotiate further with the very men they have conquered, men who are themselves Communists and who dared challenge too effectively the Russian prescription of what Communism should mean in practice. It is important to notice that we find ourselves talking these days (almost unconsciously) about "the death of freedom" in Czechoslovakia, which means that Americans have been prepared to believe that some freedom is possible under Communism. It is also important to notice, in support of this belief, that not only did the gallant Czechs "lose," perhaps only temporarily, but also that they almost "won."

Our failure to recognize such facts as these—and these are merely illustrative— could lead us, in our curiously comforting insistence that World Communism has not changed, to become inflexible ourselves in the face of complex circumstances dramatically different from those on which too much of our foreign policy (including our folly in Vietnam) is based. Indeed, a hawkish revival in American foreign policy would probably undermine the cause of many of our Communist friends, in Russia and out, who have dared to argue (and who want to continue to argue) that the world is no longer as threatening as some of Stalin's fearful successors foolishly believe it to be.

We should stop to reflect upon not only what has happened but, even more important, upon what has *not* happened in Eastern Europe this week. Certainly, there is no need to match Russian blunders by blunders of our own, especially since we should know that we will remain for a long time to come the strongest power on this earth.

Here, as elsewhere, I use the version of my letter as it read prior to editorial revision. See, on Russia and the Russians, *The Constitutionalist*, e.g., c. 5, n. 131, c. 5, n. 138, c. 6, n. 1, c. 7, nn. 46, 66, 75, c. 8, nn. 58, 147. I saw in my 1960 visit to Russia only the tip of the massive iceberg described by Aleksandr Solzhenitsyn in *The Gulag Archipelago,* but it was enough to generate a profound sense of relief upon crossing over into Finland. See Essay IV, note 44, below.

5. King Constantine fled from Greece, in December 1967, after his unsuccessful effort to overthrow the colonels. His hostility toward the colonels was evident to me, on the occasions I visited him in Rome during the summers of 1968, 1969 and 1970. I continue to believe he and his country would have benefitted if he had followed my advice on more than one occasion that he return to Greece, even if without informing the colonels in advance (for example, by landing somewhere in the Peloponnesus by yacht), to provide moral support to those in opposition to the colonels. I also had occasion to say to both him and his "enemy" Andreas Papandreou (whom I have talked with only once, in Chicago) that they had far more in common than either of them had with the colonels.

My recommendations, from the outset, of "the Karamanlis solution" did not keep me from remaining on quite good terms with all the anti-colonels factions with which I came into contact in Greece and abroad. Indeed, I venture to believe that it was generally recognized that the solution I proposed did try to take into account the legitimate interests and understandable concerns of the various Greek factions. However that may be, I have found quite likable as human beings King Constantine, Mr. Papandreou, Mrs. Vlachou and Mr. Karamanlis (whom I visited several times in Paris). On the other hand, the colonels and their cohorts I met were (with the exception of Stylianos Pattakos) rather disagreeable people. Most influential Greek-Americans, in the manner of Hamlet's mother, preferred the crude upstarts to the more refined "Establishment"—and indeed lent their considerable influence to the tacit support by the American government of what the colonels were doing (and, through mock referenda, were pretending to do). See Shakespeare, *Hamlet,* III, iv, 49-109. Thus, one of the legacies of the colonels and their Greek-American supporters has been the "permanent" loss to Turkey of the choicest part of Cyprus. Had the Greek-American community directed against our collaborationist policy in Greece between 1967 and 1974 the efforts they have directed the past year against American policy toward Turkish aid, the colonels could not have survived six months—and Cyprus would continue to be united and independent. (It should also be added that if the Greek community on Cyprus had behaved better than they did toward the Turkish minority there since 1960, the Turks would have been far less inclined to exploit the pretext for invasion provided them by the colonels. Of course, even worse atrocities against Greeks on the mainland of Turkey help explain the Greek Cypriot attitude—but truly political men appreciate that revenge is not a luxury statesmanship can afford.)

I discuss the irresponsibility of American policy toward the Greece of the colonels in an August 1971 letter to the editor which appeared in several newspapers (in various forms; see, e.g., *Chicago Sun-Times*, August 28, 1971, p. 18):

It is often said by apologists for the Greek tyranny that it is no responsibility of the United States who rules in Athens today, that we Americans should not meddle in the internal affairs of Greece. That is plausible enough on the surface, especially since there are tyrannies (Communist and anti-Communist alike) all over the world.

But what if the United States should be in part responsible for the presence of the Greek colonels in power? Would not that too be unjustified meddling? Virtually every Greek leader who was of prominence prior to the colonels' seizure of power four years ago—whether he is royalist or anti-royalist, whether he is conservative or liberal, whether he is in Greece or abroad—had said that the United States does bear a heavy responsibility for the ability of the colonels to maintain themselves in power.

I challenge apologists for the Greek regime to name any politically important Greek leaders, known to the Greek public before 1967 and still alive today, who have not said what I have just reported them to have said. Whether the Greek leaders I describe are correct in what they have said about the United States is, of course, another question: but their deep resentment of what the United States has done and has permitted to be done in Greece the last four years exists as an ominous political fact that we Americans will have to reckon with in the coming decade.

Apologists for the colonels, in our government and out, emphasize the importance of the military bases and cooperation available to the United States in Greece today. But it should be remembered that such cooperation and bases were acquired by the United States long before the colonels seized power. Do the colonels' apologists have some other country in mind as an alternative ally for the United States in the Eastern Mediterranean when the Greek people finally manage to rid themselves of the tyrannical colonels and their collaborators?

6. The colonels' regime deteriorated markedly in 1972 and 1973, so much so that even previously enthusiastic Greek-Americans began to return to this country with reservations. An explosion came in November 1973 which culminated in the shooting in Athens of a number of students, a massacre in which the Greek government acknowledged a dozen dead and in which unofficial sources counted dozens if not even hundreds of dead.

The student demonstrations which were suppressed so bloodily on that occasion had been prompted by the general deterioration of the colonels' rule, a deterioration reflected both in a runaway inflation and in a general fatigue. The bitter discontent which the students expressed was obviously shared by much of the Greek nation as well.

One result of the massacre was a military coup on November 25, 1973 which removed from office the demoralized dictator who had been in charge since April 21, 1967. Another member of the original conspiracy of colonels organized this coup and attempted to establish himself in power. My understanding of how things stood then was reflected in a December 1973 letter which appeared in varying forms in a number of journals (e.g., *New York Times,* December 7, 1973, p. 40; 119 *Congressional Record* E7852 [December 7, 1973], H11566 [December 17, 1973], E8282 [December 26, 1973]) :'

The crisis which has toppled the bloody Papadopoulos dictatorship in Athens cannot be resolved, or even smothered, by recourse to still another military strongman, especially one with so much recent experience in torture of his fellow citizens. This crisis is rooted in the incompetence and arrogance of colonels who cannot be expected to handle intelligently the complex social and economic problems of Greece. Such usurpers cannot enlist the necessary services and good will of the better professionals, politicians and military officers of that country for the great work of reconciliation and austerity which Greece so desperately needs.

The shortsighted role played by our government since the colonels first took over in 1967 has already (and perhaps even permanently) compromised, in the eyes of the resentful Greek people, our legitimate interests in that country and hence in the Middle East. Among our mistakes of the past six years has been that of publicly backing the wrong men in Greece. I have found in my visits at the State Department and the Pentagon during this period, that our policy-makers have been remarkably unequipped to consider seriously the long-range consequences of the policies they were pursuing.

We should, before still another dictator becomes consolidated in Athens, try to redeem somewhat our good name by using our remaining influence in Greece and NATO to help the Greek people recover control of their own affairs. This can best be done, it seems to me, by vigorously encouraging the colonels to step aside for Constantine Karamanlis, the man whose prestige as a former conservative prime minister still recommends him to the Greek people as the best way to avoid the even bloodier crises which now threaten their country.

Greece may be the only country in the world today where the genuine popular alternative to domestic tyranny is so moderate and so experienced a politician as Mr. Karamanlis. What more can the Greeks or the United States hope for? Dare we or they risk further deterioration in Greece and in American-Greek relations? Everyone should realize by now that phony constitutions and fake elections cannot work in Greece today.

But the deterioration, as well as American bungling, continued—and the Cyprus debacle of July 1974 followed.

7. Constantine Karamanlis was sworn in as Prime Minister of Greece in the early morning hours of July 24, 1974. His return from Paris was greeted that night by the kind of spontaneous exultation which, if reports are to be believed, will never be forgotten by the multitudes who filled the streets of Athens.

The occasion for Mr. Karamanlis' installation was provided by the Cyprus crisis which threatened to embroil Greece in a general war with Turkey. It had long been evident that a general war was something the colonels could least afford: not only did they not have the country behind them but such a war would require full-scale mobilization and that would mean that the colonels would have to restore to positions of command the quite competent officers they had purged because of "disloyalty." The deteriorating position of the colonels in Greece had driven them to, or permitted, desperate adventures; their typical incompetence (evident, for example, in the state of the economy) led them to miscalculate what Turkey would do when Archbishop Makarios was overthrown as President of Cyprus. The colonels gambled, stumbled and lost. See Essay XVI, note 2, below.

And so the long nightmare ended—and politics could return to Greece, which meant that the Greek people could again make their own mistakes for a change. With a return of the Greeks to normal political life, things in that country **have** become too complex for an outsider to presume to understand, especially from a distance. (Tyranny does simplify "the facts." I have, by the way, no plans to return to Greece in the immediate future. Certainly, the Greeks no longer have any need for my "services.") The American observer *can* know enough, however, to counsel his own government to expect the consequences of our shortsighted policy since 1967. It is inevitable that the considerable American influence in Greece since the Second World War will be curtailed by any government which is obliged to defer to public opinion, and that includes a government with the remarkable popular support evidently enjoyed by Mr. Karamanlis today. A mature response on the part of the United States is to be hoped for as we now begin to pay the price of our folly—that folly which made much more, and may continue to make much more, of the Papandreou faction in Greece than the facts called for. (Mr. Karamanlis recognizes the corrosive effect of the Cyprus problem on Greek politics: "I have the responsibility without having control [over Cyprus]. In the end, I will have to pay." He has described himself as "the last pro-American Greek in Greece." *International Herald Tribune*, March 24, 1975, p. 8.)

Almost literally overnight, much of what I knew about Greece—and I did know a great deal, often much more than our "experts" in the State Department and the Pentagon—much of what I knew became superfluous. Does not this point up the circumstantial, even fortuitous, character of political life and hence its ultimate dubiousness? On the other hand, of course, there is a certain excitement to be derived from mixing in momentous affairs: floods of phone calls from across the country and abroad when a crisis breaks, conferences in Washington and elsewhere, even the challenge of physical threats and the need to take precautions to protect both one's informants and one's self from the attentions òf brutal, lawless men. There is as well—and this is what keeps such excitement from being mere adventurism—the awareness that one has, because of one's peculiar circumstances and talents, an opportunity and perhaps even a duty to do whatever one can to help relieve a friendly people of a tyranny for which one's own country may be in part responsible. But, it should be added, one should be prepared in such matters to settle for the satisfaction of a job well done: political men do not have the leisure to discourse with people who are no longer of use to them. (When asked what tangible "reward" I want for my services as a Phihellene, I have replied that I would settle for having a street in central Athens named after me. A small street would do, especially if it is one which my children's children can conveniently find.)

The duties and excitements of citizens do have their place—and they can be quite instructive if not indulged in to excess. That is, such activities should not be permitted to subvert the serious and sustained effort at understanding of which the human being is truly capable. (See Essay II, note 20, below.) Perhaps it should be a part of the education of the human being to follow closely the rise and fall of one tyranny during his lifetime. (If he is fortunate, that tyranny will not be in his own country.) But one cannot follow such things—one cannot really understand them— if one is not moved to pass judgment upon them. Thus, I knew too much about what was really going on in Greece, behind the facade which tourists were shown, to be able to visit that country in recent years with the interests, pleasures and diversions of former years.

What Greece *can* mean when times are normal is suggested by the descriptions of the country with which I open and close the unedited version of the article on contemporary Greece which I prepared a few years ago for the Fifteenth Edition of the *Encyclopedia Britannica*:

There is about Greece a vitality, all too often undisciplined, which makes many another European country seem tame and even dull by comparison. This is evident as soon as one sails into a Greek port or crosses a border: sounds, smells, movements, colors—the very tempo of things—conspire to heighten sensibilities and intensify expectations. But alongside all this is the serene coolness, even aloofness, of what remains in Greece from classical antiquity, the visible monuments which constantly stand as a challenge to (if not even a rebuke of) contemporary endeavours.

The vitality of Greece and Greeks can be said to stem from the heady mixture over centuries of many peoples and ways of life. That land, now the home of almost nine million people, has long been "at the crossroads"—at that place in the Balkans where "three roads meet," where Europe, Africa and the East converge, at that point in time where the ancient, the medieval and the modern coexist and conflict. The Greek is familiar with the Middle East: his language and food, to say nothing of his religion and history, are marked by exotic and even oppressive elements from Turkey, the Holy Land, Egypt and beyond. But he is familiar as well with the West, with the Europe to which the young go for training and for work, with the Americas to which so many have gone for a new home. Greeks, like the Jews whom they resemble in so many ways, have long been able to. adjust themselves as merchants in many climes and to many ways of life. But, also like the Jews, they have preserved in their heart of hearts a vital memory of the homeland to which they yearn to return.

This homeland is as much a state of mind as it is a place to be found on maps. The yearning to "return", then, is almost as strong among those who have never left Greek soil as among those who find themselves abroad. Perhaps it is a yearning to attain that which has never been but which has always been aspired to. It is a yearning evident in the melancholy of Greek music, the nostalgia which can be heard even in the lively tunes and ballads sung on festive occasions. It is a yearning which can be heard as well in interminable conversations, especially those with which Greeks refresh and recreate themselves through the long cool nights which follow blistering summer days. And it is a yearning which can be seen in the faces and deeds of the Greeks, a yearning which makes it impossible for them "to leave well enough alone." A perpetual restlessness, much like that which was said to characterize the political life of ancient Athens, is evident, a restlessness which can continue subterraneously despite surface conformity to the tyranny of the moment.

And, indeed, there have been many tyrannies in Greece, tyrannies which are as much a part of the much-discussed "Greek experience" as (if not even the most frequent result of) their volatile democracies. Perhaps, one might even say, memories of intermittent tyrannies remind Greeks of the unpredictability of human things, of the disaster which can follow upon prosperity, of the trials which even the most successful encounter from time to time. Life can be expected to be as hard, as unyielding and as toughening as the soil and the sea from which Greeks have for centuries wrested their livelihood. But it can also be as enriching and even as exciting as the landscape and light for which Greece has always been celebrated and which can be seen, if not at the moment or place where one is, then surely in a little while or down the road a few kilometers. . . .

. . . The future of the Greek monarchy remains a serious question, no matter what the eventual fate of the colonels; but the longer the colonels stay, the more vulnerable the monarchy is likely to become. The future of the country also remains a serious question: the fundamental alternatives facing the Greeks may be, in the decades ahead, the exciting dangers of Balkan politics or the complacent prosperity of closer association with the European community. Forces may already be at work among the Greeks over which neither the colonels nor their opponents have any control, including those forces which compel Greece toward

further urbanization and industrialization and toward greater exposure to the
homogenizing "culture" of the international mass media.

Continuity with the past, a very long past, remains Greece's burden as well
as her glory. The past and its significance are often obscure but always present.
Their very language constantly reminds Greeks both of what they have been
and of what they have aspired to. The ramifications of old influences go deep
and are unpredictable; they seem to make permanent solutions impossible, so
long as Greece retains its identity. Perhaps it is true for all peoples that there are
no "permanent solutions" and that most of what can be done in the present
depends intimately on what has happened in centuries past. But these limitations
upon political action and self-determination are much more evident in Greece
than in most other countries. After all, the light of Greece has long been known
to make many things clearer there than they are likely to be elsewhere.

I conclude this account of contemporary Greece by reprinting here a letter to
the editor I prepared in September 1971 (see, e.g., *St. Louis Post-Dispatch*, October 3, 1971; *Washington Post*, October 5, 1971):

The death in Athens September 20th of Greece's Nobel Laureate poet and
former diplomat, George Seferis, brings to mind what developed into a ritual
between us in recent years, a long visit by me to his home on the eve of my
departure each summer from Greece.

We discussed on those occasions his and his country's poetry. But we discussed as well, and this is what originally brought us together, the military
tyranny under which the finer spirits in his country have labored since 1967.
American apologists for the colonels' dictatorship should pause occasionally to
wonder why so patriotic and distinguished a poet and citizen as Mr. Seferis
detested as thoroughly as he did the barbarians in khaki who dare advertise themselves as the saviours of Greece.

George Seferis was indeed a man who loved, and loved deeply, his country
and who represented the best it has to offer today. It was because of this love
that he could write many years ago, "Wherever I travel Greece wounds me."

II. Human Being and Citizen: A Beginning to the Study of Plato's "Apology of Socrates"

1. The reader's familiarity with Plato's *Apology of Socrates* is presupposed. (Section
viii of this essay can serve as a reminder of Socrates' argument.) None of the
other works of Plato is referred to, but neither are they forgotten. See *The Constitutionalist* (Essay I, note 1, above), e.g., c. 9, sec. 4, c. 2, nn. 1, 39, c. 6, n. 54,
c. 7, nn. 30, 34, c. 8, nn. 70, 74, 135, 140, c. 9, nn. 7, 21, 23, 28, 30, 38, 39. See, also,
Essays VI, XV, XVI, below.

Many of the notes to this essay submit to the reader's consideration frankly
speculative and, it is hoped, moderately provocative commentaries upon a number of
passages in the dialogue which have suffered from having been either long ignored
or long settled by scholars. Cross-references are liberally employed to make the
notes less disconnected and hence more useful than they would otherwise be.
Many of the notes include a series of comments on a series of points in the related
text.

2. Cf. Plato, *Apology* 17c.

The god is careful in using Socrates' name; but men are careless in naming one
another (e.g., Meletus: "care-taker"). (23b, 25c) Not to know the names of others
(such as one's accusers) seems to be a handicap; in fact, it is "unreasonable."

(18c-d) See notes 30, 41, below. (Unless otherwise indicated, the citations in parentheses in these notes, as in the text, are to Plato's *Apology of Socrates*.)

Plato, we know, used Socrates' name many times in dialogues, but only once in the title of a dialogue. Is that single dialogue more about Socrates or about his way of life in the city than the others?

3. There may have been some who voted for conviction and against the death sentence (as well as vice versa). See notes 16, 50, below. Are those who sit in judgment in Hades the only true judges? (41a) See note 46, below.

4. We derive "category" from the Greek word for "accusation."

5. What is the status of the old in the *Apology?* The old accusers are the worst. (18b) Socrates says he had no old defenders. (18c) Cf. Plato, *Apology* 34d and Homer, *Odyssey*, XIX, 163. See notes 9, 22, 25, 40, below.

6. Socrates does not quote the official indictment precisely, but rather "about like this." (24b) Xenophon reports this as the official indictment: "Socrates is guilty of not acknowledging the gods the city acknowledges, and of bringing in other new daemonic things; he is also guilty of corrupting the youth." *Memorabilia*, I, 1. Diogenes Laertius (II, 40) reports, evidently from Athenian archives, a version which is virtually the same as that in Xenophon. See notes 9, 13, below.

Socrates attributes to Meletus an enigmatic version of the official indictment: "Socrates is guilty of not acknowledging the gods, but he does acknowledge the gods." (27a) See notes 9, 12, 13, below. Thus, the sequence of accusations by the city or the many is: (1) the old accusations (18b), (2) the old accusations in the form of an indictment (19c), (3) "the things which are at hand to say against all philosophers" (23d), (4) the official indictment (24b), (5) the enigmatic version of the official indictment attributed to Meletus (27a).

"Acknowledge" is used throughout this essay as perhaps more appropriate in the legal context than either "believe in" or "recognize." That which is rendered as "god" (as distinguished from "gods") might sometimes be better understood as "the divine." See note 49, below.

7. The role of prejudice directed primarily against Socrates is suggested by the fact that there *is* a stranger in Athens safely teaching for money at the very time of Socrates' prosecution. (20a-c)

Is not an account of the genesis or growth of something essentially an account of its nature? See notes 17, 21, 48, below.

8. Socrates' defense here may seem merely sophistical. But when he speaks of not teaching for money, he is making a popularly understandable distinction between himself and the sophists (whom he had described earlier as teaching for money). (20a) He does not attempt to make here the more important distinctions, such as between his and the sophists' opinions about the possibility of knowledge. This would require a greater understanding of the sophists, and even of philosophy, than his listeners are likely to have. See note 46, below.

This is not to suggest, however, that the matter of payment is irrelevant. The man who teaches for money is more likely to be directed by what the student, rather than what the teacher, thinks should be taught. (Of course, Socrates insists that he does not teach—but he does influence others, he does have imitators.) See Essay IV, note 50, below.

If Socrates had accepted exile and wandered about, he would have been even harder to distinguish from the sophists. His death, which can be said to show his respect for the laws of the city, assures the city that he is an Athenian. Deeds mean much more than words to his fellow-citizens. See notes 26, 33, below. See, also, Essay XVI, below.

9. The impression is given that corruption of the youth derives from Socrates' attitude

toward the gods of the city. The sequence of counts in the official indictment, as it is known from other sources, would have made such a derivation more difficult to suggest. Does not Socrates expect that the thoughtful student of his speech will remember the original sequence of counts and that he will notice and reflect upon Socrates' rearrangement? See note 6, above, note 13, below.

There is implied in the discussion of the horse-training example a fundamental question as to what makes men good, the city (with its laws and customs) or teaching and exhortation. See note 5, above, note 22, below.

10. Socrates' argument here presupposes the existence of cities: one is not 'free to move about altogether at will; or, at least, there are good reasons for preferring to stay in one place. The indictment also presupposes the existence of cities: it is the corruption of the youth of *this* city which is criminal. Exile would have meant that the Athenians were willing to let Socrates corrupt youth elsewhere.

The "weaker" can refer not only to the less just but also to the more vulnerable. The vulnerable (that is, unpopular) truth can be made stronger by so stating it that careful reading is required to perceive it. Socrates insisted that he taught the same to all, that he had no private teaching. (19d, 30b, 33b) This is not to say, however, that everyone understood him the same. We detect even in this dialogue both a surface meaning and a more guarded one. See notes 13, 39, below.

11. But he does consider his condemners and accusers blameworthy for having intended to injure him. (41d-e) He twice speaks in this context of condemnation and accusation in that order, suggesting even as he closes the observation with which he started, that he had been convicted long before the indictment was filed. (18b)

Does he not virtually charge the city, or at least his old accusers, of having corrupted the youth? (18c, 24c, 25a-c) All do seem agreed that the young *have* been corrupted? Or would the city (or the many) say that if the young have not been corrupted by Socrates, then they have not really been corrupted? See note 7, above.

12. Implicit in each of Socrates' transformations of charges seems to be the suggestion that his version in each case is the only one the city should be concerned about. Thus, the public avowal of atheism, of which Socrates is not guilty, may be a legitimate concern of the city. See note 49, below. That is, even if he should not acknowledge the gods of the city, he does not consider himself to have done anything calling for rebuke or punishment. (38a) Do his evident moral character and wisdom induce the reader to accept this self-appraisal?

Socrates mentions another charge, not by the city but by the sophisticated: "Are you then not ashamed, Socrates, of having followed such a pursuit, that you are now in danger of being put to death as a result?" (28b) He meets this reproach with an account of his life. The heroic cast of that account is designed to shame such critics. (28c) Cf. Essay XVI, note 9, below.

13. The rearrangement by Socrates of the counts of the indictment (see notes 6, 9, above) makes central the count respecting the gods of the city and thereby makes it easier for him to play the ends off against the middle. Thus, the first count is virtually reduced to the second; and the second is said to be contradicted by the third. See note 10, above. (This comment, like many others in this essay [e.g., note 40, below], presupposes that Plato devoted at least as much care and imagination to the arrangement of details in his dialogue as we can devote to their interpretation. See notes 39, 41, 45, below. See, also, Essay VI, notes 19, 20, 52, below.)

Whatever the daemonic thing is, it seems to be regarded by the authors of the indictment as the Socratic alternative to the recognized religious opinions of the city. Socrates himself calls it "divine and daemonic." (31d) See note 51, below.

14. Does this suggest that faulty reasoning underlies the accusations against philosophers? That is, the city cannot understand what Socrates is doing. Does, then, the weaker argument prevail in this trial? See note 10, above.

15. Socrates mentions later that they had heard him speak of this daemonic thing many times and that he had had it since childhood. (31c-d) See note 51, below.

   Why had the accusers added the charge about the daemonic thing? The failure to acknowledge the gods of the city could be overlooked as an instance of not uncommon neglect of civic duties, whereas the deliberate introduction of new divinities suggests treason or revolution. (At the very least, this charge reflects Socrates' intellectual discoveries.)

16. "And so the man proposes the penalty of death." (36b) Socrates had indicated during his first speech, partly in order to make clear to those who might vote for conviction what was implied by such a vote, that Anytus (the politician) was advocating the death penalty. (29c, 30b, 31a) See note 3, above, note 50, below. Thus, the poet adopts the manner of the politician.

   It does not seem that the laughter-provoking Aristophanes, although a great patriotic poet, had either called for Socrates' death or suggested he was an atheist. (18d, 19b-c)

17. Meletus had evidently described himself as "good and patriotic." (24b) See note 16, above. One danger of untutored patriotism is that it will be, as Socrates says of Meletus, "violent and unrestrained." (26e) This may come from caring too much about the wrong things. Does not Socrates suggest that it is likely that bad-natured men will rise to power both in an unrestrained oligarchy and in an unrestrained democracy? (See, on nature, note 7, above, note 21, below.)

18. The third speech does mention Triptolemus (of Eleusis) and Ajax (of Salamis), both of which places were under Athenian rule during Socrates' lifetime. But is it indicated by this dialogue, in spite of the imperialistic claims by patriotic Athenians, that neither Eleusis nor Salamis was yet subject to Athens during the lives of the two men mentioned? Cf. Homer, *Iliad*, II, 557-558 (an Athenian interpolation?); Sophocles, *Ajax* 202-203, 860-861, 1211-1221; Aristotle, *Rhetoric* 1375b29; Ovid, *Metamorphoses*, V, 645 sq., VII, 469 sq.; Plutarch, *Theseus, Aristides, Alcibiades*. However that might have been, Leon of Salamis, who is mentioned in the first speech, would have been considered an Athenian subject. (41a-b, 32c)

   It is appropriate that the second speech—the Athenian or familiar speech—should be the only one of the three in which no new names are introduced. It is also appropriate that Socrates should be the only Athenian mentioned in the third speech: he had just been condemned to death (cast out?) by the city. See notes 25, 37, below.

19. About one-third of those referred to by name in the first speech are strangers. But many fewer than one-third of the references there are to strangers. This *is* the defense of a philosopher who was an Athenian.

   Socrates' attachment to Athens is proverbial. His interpretation of the god's mandate (that he should seek out and examine all men reputed to be wise) evidently did not place him under the compulsion to travel. Perhaps he had heard enough of other places, which could have been confirmed by his military service abroad, and seen enough in cosmopolitan Athens of citizens of other cities, to regard his city as providing sufficient scope for his inquiries. In any event, Socrates regarded banishment or imprisonment, but neither death nor a fine, as a certain evil. (37c-d) No doubt his age affected his appraisal of both banishment and death. See note 39, below. Cf. Essay XVI, note 14, below.

20. The city, especially under a democratic regime, is virtually the many. The many are pictured as inferior to the few with respect to knowing how to do everything except create disturbances (which disturbances impede discussion and, hence, understanding). See notes 23, 34, below.

   The "human being" referred to here is that being who is fully human, for whom the life of philosophy is vital. The perfect citizen, on the other hand, is the gentleman, the political man who is responsive to the guidance of philosophy. See notes 26, 39, 52, below. Is the human being linked by Socrates with horses and the citizen with cattle, each with his distinctive virtue? (20a-b)

21. Does a philosopher prefer not to meddle with particular laws when he cannot refashion the constitution? Cf. note 12, above, note 39, below.

See J. Duncan M. Derrett, "The Trial of Sir Thomas More," 79 *English Historical Review* (July 1964), pp. 449, 467-474 (the section, "Verdict, Motion in Arrest, and Sentence").

A comprehensive reform would presuppose a greater respect for nature than a democratic people is likely to have. There is, I believe, only one reference to "nature" in the dialogue, and this is when the poetic art is accounted for. (22c) See note 30, below. Perhaps the role that nature plays in the lives of men and of cities is suggested in this dialogue (and especially for a democratic audience) by the use of the divine. See notes 46, 48, 49, below. See, also, Essay VI, section vii, below.

22. See note 28, below. Socrates' position on that occasion (when *six* generals were tried in a body and condemned to death) was ostensibly grounded upon his insistence on the law, rather than upon what was otherwise right or just. (32b) He seems to have thought that the people should not be encouraged to question the principle of law-abidingness. They cannot be expected, in ordinary circumstances, to respect any other form of justice (although Socrates, when he restates his reasons, adds "justice" to "law" [32c]). See notes 27, 46, below. See, also, Essay XVI, section vii, below.

Is not reliance simply on the law likely to be reliance on the old? See notes 5, 9, above.

It can be argued that Socrates, too, was judged as one of "a body," rather than on his own merits: he is identified with many others, past and present, who inquired about the things in the air and beneath the earth. (18c, 23c-d)

23. There is implied here a serious reservation about the principle of majority rule. See note 20, above, note 34, below. Among the things Socrates does know is that it is evil and shameful to disobey one's better, whether he be god or human being. (29b)

Is one reason for overnight consideration of a capital case that the people can be talked to privately and quietly, as human beings rather than as citizens, one by one rather than in a body? "The morrow brought repentance with it, and reflexion on the horrid cruelty of a decree [by the Athenians] which condemned a whole city [Mitylene] to the fate merited only by the guilty." Thucydides, *Peloponnesian War*, III, 36.

24. The chronological sequence of the battles was Potidaea, Delium and Amphipolis. We suspect that something is being indicated by this rearrangement, perhaps about the battle of Amphipolis which is placed in the central position. See note 13, above, note 41, below.

It is thought by scholars that Socrates participated in more than three battles. We wonder why he chose to mention these particular three. See note 27, below. We notice that Delium and Amphipolis were Athenian defeats and Potidaea a costly victory. See note 39, below. We also notice that the Athenian commander at the battle of Potidaea was Callias; at Delium, Hippocrates; at Amphipolis, Cleon. See Thucydides, *ibid.*, I, 63; IV, 101; V, 10.

The city, with which the family seems to be allied in this trial, has made Socrates' "body" what it is and can call upon it for the use of the city. Thus, Socrates the citizen serves in war as a soldier, in peace as a member of the assembly (evidently when chosen by lot); he also produces sons and thereby contributes to the perpetuation of the city. (To what extent are his services on behalf of the city for the benefit of philosophy as well?) See notes 34, 40, below.

The intimate relation between the city and its gods may be indicated in the fact that both the gods and the city are likened to horses. (27d-e, 25b) One or a few trainers of a horse are said to be better than many. (25b) See note 23, above, notes 44, 48, 49, below. But to win a horse race is of little value. (36d)

25. See, on Socrates' hubristic self-esteem, *Apology* 20c, 30a, 36d, 38a. See, also, note 26, below.

If a Pericles had continued to rule in Athens, or even an Alcibiades, the result of the prosecution (if there had been one) would likely have been different. Socrates mentions that the democratic partisans had recently returned to the city after the exile imposed by the Thirty Tyrants. (21a) Democratic Athens had been shaken to its foundations.

Socrates says he is surprised by the closeness of the vote. (36a) Socrates' surprise suggests that he underestimated the power of his words, underestimated the good will or the good sense of the ordinary citizen, or overestimated the prejudice excited by the old accusers. Perhaps there had been old defenders as well, after all— that is, the wisdom and strength for which imperial Athens was widely celebrated. (29d) See note 5, above. Athens is likened to "a horse, which, though large and well-bred, is sluggish on account of his size." (30e) There are reasons, that is, why this "gift of god" should have happened to appear in Athens. (31a-b)

Socrates' second speech is so Athenian in its character as to be the only one in which there are no oaths invoking the names of gods. See note 18, above. Socrates does refer there to "the god" whom he will not disobey. (37e) But this god is neither Athenian nor non-Athenian, but rather essentially "human" in that he is characterized by that perfection which would be found in the perfectly wise man. Indeed, insofar as philosophy finds its home in Athens, the Socratic god *is* the god of that city. In any event, the legally acknowledged gods of the city are strangers to Athens—and their ascendancy there is understandably precarious. See notes 29, 49, below. But, on the other hand, cities do control "their" gods somewhat—whereas Socrates' god imposes tasks which he must prefer to the city's command and to his own interests. (29d)

26. See, e.g., 30 *University of Chicago L. Rev.* 704, 717-719 (1963); 2 *Loyola Law Times* 8 (1962); 54 *Cornell L. Rev.* 920 (1969); 60 *California L. Rev.* 1476 (1972); 20 *University of Chicago Law School Record* 3 (1973). See, on the citizen-gentleman, 19 *Lawyers Guild Rev.* 143, 145, 159-160 (1959). Consider notes 39, 46, 52, below; also Essay IX, below.

By showing men how to conduct themselves in adversity, Socrates provides for Athenians a lesson particularly apt in a democracy, thereby moderating the influences which make for sentimentality, shamelessness and sensuality. (Cf. 39b1.) Although the adversity was not as dreadful as his fellow citizens conceived it to be, it was not as slight as his serenity leads some scholars to believe. See note 51, below.

There is something sobering about a judicial repudiation by one's fellow citizens, by the very men of all the world whom one has been taught to care most about and for whom one has even gone to war. (30a) The circumstances of a judicial encounter move a man to be as persuasive as possible consistent with duty and self-respect. (38d, 39a) A genuine effort to persuade, as is seen in Socrates' first speech, is demanded, not only to lend significance to the failure which may result but perhaps even more as a guarantee that one has not carelessly permitted fellow citizens to perpetrate an injustice. (19a, 30d) Such an effort, surviving as a continual exhortation, provides the basis for eventual vindication and reconciliation. (39c-d, 41e-42a) It can be an effort which one is free to design for the most enduring effect, however, only if one is not primarily governed by a desire for immediate success. See note 33, below.

27. Democracy and oligarchy are considered in this essay to be the two principal contenders among the regimes which are likely to prevail in a city. See note 33,

below. In this, as in the practical distinction between wisdom and virtue, we follow the greatest of Platonists, Aristotle. See notes 39, 46, below. See, also, Essay IV, note 14, below.

Socrates makes more of his civil courage, and hence justice, than of his bravery on the battlefield. The trial marks the third instance of resistance to the city, and more is made by him of such resistance than of his service in three battles on behalf of the city. See note 24, above. This emphasis recognizes that a city is not an armed camp, primarily organized for war: it is more concerned with justice than with bravery. (Justice is referred to many more times than bravery in the dialogue.) See note 42, below.

The three instances of resistance to the city suggest that Socrates denied that the just and the legal are identical. See note 22, above.

28. The verb used by Socrates (32a) has, in this form and context, the meaning of "take up for burial." But even if the word is rendered to include the rescue of living survivors, reference to the trial would remind of the intense religious passion which had led to the summary trial and execution of the victorious generals. See note 32, below.

Many of the Athenians present must have been familiar as well with the role played by the religious opinions, both of the people and of Nicias, in the disastrous Sicilian expedition a dozen or so years before. See note 37, below. Much could then have been salvaged for Athens even in defeat had Nicias accepted the doctrines of Anaxagoras alluded to earlier about the sun and the moon. (26c-d) Meletus is induced by Socrates to introduce these doctrines to any Athenian unfamiliar with them. See Thucydides, *Peloponnesian War*, VII, 50. See, also, Essay X, note 7, below.

29. The Athenians are requested by Socrates to rebuke his sons, just as he had rebuked the Athenians. (41e) That is, they are to do on the basis of his request what he said he had done on the basis of an oracle. Thus, Socrates is to be for the Athenians what the god had been for him. See notes 36, 47, below. Perhaps Socrates saw a need for something to replace the gods whom natural philosophy and sophistry were undermining. See note 24, above, notes 36, 40, 49, below. (Had this need grown more acute because money and moneymaking had become more important for Athenians during his lifetime, thereby undermining even more the good old way?)

Socrates does not say he believes the sun and moon to be other than stone and earth.

30. That is, they seek a name for themselves. See notes 34, 38, below.

Still another means of securing immortality is through one's children. But Socrates' neglect of his family, as a result of his way of life, implies a disparagement of the very ties that many men take most seriously. Thus, unlike Odysseus, Socrates does not anticipate meeting his parents in Hades. See note 37, below. Cf. note 40, below. His first reference to his three sons does concede something to the sensibilities of the members of the court. (34d-e) But the final reference to his children indicates that they require what the people generally require, that there is nothing special about them. (41d-e) He is more concerned about his true sons, the young men who are most like him. See note 21, above.

If, on the other hand, one accepts the more commonplace view of the end of political life as that of securing pleasure, one must consider the significance of the reference to "the great king [of Persia]." This most exalted of public men is said rarely to enjoy any finer pleasure than the dreamless sleep which is available as well to the private man. (40d-e) Earlier Socrates had observed, "The unexamined life is not livable for a human being." (38a)

31. Does he anticipate, however, that the name he will win can benefit the causes he

serves? Plato, we should notice, is mentioned as present and is even set off from the other three sureties. (34a, 38b) It is Plato who presents the life and even the thought of Socrates in a dramatic form, in a form which is most likely to attract popular sympathy. See Plutarch, *Nicias* 538-539 (XXIII, 1-6). See, also, note 46, below. Socrates, on the other hand, is too old to make up speeches like a youngster. (17c)

32. It is out of the opposition between these two men, with one championing constituted authority and the other personal merit, that the story of the *Iliad* develops. Socrates takes the second man as his model, at least in his attitude toward the prospect of death. (28c-d)

Three other members of the largely anonymous army which conquered Troy are mentioned by name: two of them, Palamedes and Ajax, are destroyed during the campaign; the third, Odysseus, is much more than a warrior (he even has occasion, in the *Odyssey*, to be nameless [IX, 366, 408; cf. IX, 504]). Socrates mentions the defeated Hector three times by name within a few sentences. (28c) The most illustrious heroic demigod is barely hinted at by a reference to his many labors. (22a) A great naval victory is recalled not by name but by reference to its shameful aftermath. (32b) See notes 28, 31, above, note 49, below.

33. In a sense, there are "old accusers" everywhere (for they are the many [19d]). No doubt the conviction in Athens would arouse suspicions against Socrates in many cities. See note 8, above. Thus, he seems to expect trouble from relatives of youths in all cities, even in those cities hostile to Athens and its institutions. (Do these relatives tend to be oligarchic in sympathy, since they are likely to be wealthy? [23c])

Nor is it decisive that no relative testified against Socrates in court: one may be as reluctant to admit publicly the corruption of a son or brother as of oneself. (33d) (Was Anytus a parent who overcame such reluctance?) Why, on the other hand, did not Socrates call any of these relatives to testify for him? Not only does he consider himself essentially self-sufficient, but a reliance primarily upon himself (except with respect to money [38b]) helps him to shape the proceedings into what he wants to make of them. See note 26, above.

Socrates refers to seven young associates whose relatives are present at the trial, relatives who are (he says) all ready to aid him, "the man who corrupts and injures their relatives." (34a) But with the exception of Crito, who had been singled out as of the same age and deme as Socrates, no relative of the young man volunteers to stand surety for the proposed thirty minas fine. (38b, 33e) Three of the four young men mentioned as present do volunteer. The omission of Aeschines from the list of volunteers, although he was present, invites an explanation. Perhaps he had no money. See note 41, below. Thus, of the seven families of Socratic associates, only three volunteered to contribute to the fine. The same proportion of the court voted for acquittal. There are more of the "many" than one suspects. (When death threatens upon disobedience to the oligarchy, Socrates stands entirely alone: five men had been ordered to fetch Leon from Salamis. [32c-d])

34. Socrates mentions only inquiries made of classes of men represented among the accusers. (Each of the accusers is angry with him on behalf of his class, not on behalf of the city as a whole. [23e] That is, each of them confuses the city's interest with his own.) Socrates' coupling of politicians and craftsmen in the person of Anytus (himself a tanner as well as a politician) reflects the democratic character of the regime.

We are told about both the poets and the craftsmen that they make many fine things, but that they mistakenly think themselves wise in other matters as well. The poets, in addition, are unable to explain the meanings of the things they make. (22b-e) But we are not told of anything made by the politicians; nor are we told what form their pretensions to wisdom took. We suspect that the politicians **were** exposed as essentially dependent on mere rhetoric, that they did not possess any art or science of their own. This conjecture is induced by the fact that the presence of the rhetoricians among Socrates' accusers is obviously not accounted for by him. We can imagine the terms of an attack upon rhetoric which would explain why rhetoricians were among the accusers of Socrates. (Hints of Socrates' opinion about them are given in his opening comments about clever speakers. [17a-18a])

Can the celebrated city of Athens be considered "the fine things" made, or at least preserved, by the politicians? Thus, the politicians, despite their limitations, are useful—and this Socrates implicitly recognizes by not making public the precise nature of their deficiencies. See note 24, above. These deficiencies had been recently brought home to the Athenian people as a result of military disaster, civil strife and exile. A critique of the politicians implies a critique of the people as well: we recall that the greater the reputation a man had for wisdom, the more deluded Socrates found him to be. (22a) Only in the course of the examination of the politicians is hatred said to have been provoked among both the men questioned and the by-standers. (21d) This suggests the intimate relation between the politicians and public opinion, providing still another reason why Socrates should not make more explicit here the peculiar deficiencies of the politicians.

35. Priests and oracles are likened to poets. The criticism levelled against the poets could be directed against oracles and priests as well. (22c) Socrates' daemonic thing can also be regarded as a kind of divination—but it is something he is moved to reflect upon and thus to explain the meaning of. See note 51, below.

36. Socrates counsels the people not to destroy this gift of god: "another such is not likely to come to you." (31a) We notice that the list of seven young associates which Socrates submits has Theodotus ("gift of god") as the central name: it is observed of Theodotus, alone of the seven, that he is dead. (33e) See note 33, above, note 41, below.

Socrates is so much a gift of the god that he neglects his own affairs. This neglect, he observes, is not human. (31b) Is it not divine? See note 29, above.

See, for the shift in emphasis from wisdom to virtue, note 27, above, note 46, below.

37. The four just men are "truly judges;" they "are said to sit in judgment" in Hades. (41a) Nothing is said of any punishments they impose. The attractions, not the terrors, of life beyond the grave are emphasized by Socrates here: he is more in-clined to comfort his friends (to whom he addresses his remarks) than to confound his enemies. (39a-40e) These friends are concerned about what is to happen to Socrates very soon. The opponents, on the other hand, are told (by means of a prophecy) of retribution which will be visited upon *them* very soon. (39c-d) Justice delayed is justice denied, especially when dealing with men whose hopes and fears look to the immediate.

Socrates' account of his excursion through Hades (which reminds of the earlier account of his adventures in Athens) is truly poetic. He adds to the traditional set of just men established by the poets a man claimed by Attica—Triptolemus of Eleusis. See note 18, above. He is, in this respect, a subtly patriotic Athenian: per-haps this addition should be regarded as a tribute to, and reflection of, those members of the court who voted for him.

The inclusion of Triptolemus could also be regarded as an affirmation of the institution of the Eleusinian mysteries, so critical to the life of Athens, which Alcibiades (a former associate of Socrates) was thought by many to have profaned. See note 42, below, note 28, above. See, on Socrates' disreputable "students," *Apology* 33a-b.

Another poetic account of an excursion through Hades is the one which Homer has Odysseus describe. *Odyssey*, XI. Odysseus, too, could be said to have encountered four groups and to have conversed with five persons in Hades. There are mentioned in the Homeric account, if one includes Odysseus and Homer himself, six of the thirteen men whom Socrates mentions in Hades. Odysseus mentions about twice as many people by name as does Socrates, half of them women (some of whom tell him their stories, and one, his mother, with whom he converses). (His father is still alive.) See note 30, above, note 42, below. The impression of Hades which Odysseus conveys is not the serene one indicated by Socrates' account, and not merely because he includes descriptions of the punishments exacted of Tantalus and Sisyphus. See note 39, below. A thorough study of the *Apology* would require a detailed comparison of Socrates' account of Hades with the accounts of the poets, at least of the poets mentioned by Socrates. See note 41, below.

38. Only the poets are referred to entirely by name (that is, without reference to unnamed "others" as well). This suggests that one can speak of a fixed, known number of poets of this calibre. Thus, the poets, not the "countless others" (41c), are most likely to have the glory or fame of which men speak.

Nothing is said about talking with the poets: the poets have already had their say. (Part of "their say" is about the men with whom Socrates does want to talk.) Nor is anything said about talking with the just men: they are characterized by their actions, not by their words.

39. Conspicuously absent from the names in Hades is that of the son of Thetis, the warrior king whose noble disregard of death Socrates had made so much of. (28c-d) See note 40, below. Odysseus, of whom Socrates reminds us both in this and in other respects (see note 37, above), had brought back from Hades a report which could be said to be a repudiation of the noble sentiments Thetis had heard from her son on earth. See *Iliad*, XVIII, 96-104. For the proud son of Thetis, who had while living (according to Socrates) made "light of death or danger" (28c, 28d), voiced a lament to Odysseus which it does not serve Socrates' immediate purpose to encounter in Hades: "Nay, seek not to speak soothingly to me of death, glorious Odysseus. I should choose, so that I might live on earth, to serve as the hireling of another, of some portionless man whose livelihood was but small, rather than to be lord over all the dead who have perished." *Odyssey*, XI, 488-491.

Only the careful reader (the kind of reader who, for example, works his way through intricate footnotes) is expected to remember and to reflect upon the second thoughts about death reported elsewhere of Socrates' noble model. The practical distinction we suggest (e.g., note 27, above, note 46, below) between virtue and wisdom may be reflected here in the distinction between what the usual reader will see and what the careful reader will discern. Socrates contributes to the moral betterment of one and to the political instruction of the other. See notes 10, 13, above. He urges citizens (note 26, above) to be more humane (that is, more responsive to the guidance of philosophy); he urges the human being (that is, the seeker for wisdom) (note 52, below) to be more civic-minded. See note 20, above, on gentlemen and philosophers.

We return to our illustration. The decisive quotation by Socrates from the son of Thetis (who explains to his mother why he must kill Hector) had been, "Straightway may I die, after exacting justice of the wrongdoer, that I may not stay here, a laughing-stock beside the curved ships, a burden upon the earth." (28d) Two of the changes made by Socrates in the Homeric text (*Iliad*, XVIII, 96-104) should be noted: "a laughing-stock" is added and "useless" (before "burden") is omitted. Each of these changes suggests questions. To what extent is the son of Thetis (or anyone else who is moved by glory) considered by Socrates to be unduly influenced by the opinion of the many? Would a younger Socrates, able to be of extended use by living either in Athens or in another city, have pursued another course in defending himself? See Essay XVI, below.

In addition, the Homeric version emphasizes the terrible thing which had come to Patroclus (that is, death). Socrates mutes this feature of that version even as he has his model in nobility emphasize that Hector is to have justice exacted of him. These changes suggest that Socrates cannot endorse this hero simply as Homer presents him. We are further induced to wonder what Socrates thought of the justice of Athens in the three battles in which his own participation is recalled. Did not Athens lose more than it gained in those battles, thereby making less critical for him the problem of justice? See note 24, above.

See, on death, Essay XVII, below.

40. Although Socrates observes that all who have died are said to be in Hades, he does not anticipate meeting any philosophers there. (40e) Had he had sufficient contact with them in Athens? The inhabitants of Hades are from olden times, whereas philosophy seems to be recent. Athens, then, is superior to Hades in this respect. The poets who had peopled Hades in ancient times seem no longer to have the power to do so. Perhaps we see even in this change the challenge posed to the poets by the philosophers and the sophists. See note 5, above.

Socrates is silent as well about oracles. Odysseus, on the other hand, talked with Teiresias, the man whom Circe described as the only one in Hades having understanding. *Odyssey*, X, 493-495. Is an oracle useful only to living men? (See note 51, below, on Socrates' daemonic thing.) Had Socrates moved beyond any reliance on oracles? Or does the disregard of Teiresias in Hades suggest that Socrates never really relied upon oracles?

Nor are any warriors to be sought out in Hades, except as they are either men unjustly treated or men reputed to be wise. Warriors, as warriors, are obsolete: they know nothing any longer of use, since men cannot be killed in Hades. (41c) See note 39, above. Are craftsmen equally useless in Hades? (Do not both warriors and craftsmen "minister" primarily to the body, that body in which mortality resides?)

41. We must reserve for another occasion our speculations about the other names in the *Apology*, as well as about a number of other problems which we can only touch upon here. See, e.g., note 37, above, note 51, below. Some patterns in the use of names may be impossible to work out satisfactorily today, even if one had perfect command of the Greek language, if only because several of the men mentioned are no longer well enough known. See note 33, above.

We suggest for the reader's consideration that appropriately central among the characters named in the first speech seem to be the son of Thetis, Thetis herself, Hector and Patroclus; in the second speech, "the god;" in the third speech, Musaeus and Hesiod. See note 13, above. (Is the decisive "combat" of the day in the first speech? In a sense, the central character of the central speech can be considered the central one for the three speeches.)

42. It is unlikely that we can improve at this time upon Aristophanes' characterization of the distinctive contribution to mankind of each of the four poets, except to add that the agriculturally-minded Hesiod was also known for his account of the origin of the world and of the gods. This would reinforce Socrates' interest in him.

Triptolemus, Socrates' nominee to the panel of judges, was revered as the founder of agriculture (and hence of civilization?). (The Eleusinian mysteries are thought to have been connected with this founding.) Socrates seems to share the civilized tendencies of both Hesiod and Triptolemus, to be more drawn to the human being than to the citizen. (The extreme version of the human being is the philosopher praised by Socrates; of the citizen, the warrior celebrated by Homer.) The political tendency of Socrates' thought and character is moderate and pacific with respect to matters both of peace and of war. See notes 26, 27, 40, above.

The less belligerent half of mankind is represented in this dialogue by three women (mortal and immortal) who speak truly: the Pythia at Delphi, Thetis, and Penelope. (21a, 28c-d, 34d; cf. 35b) Socrates says he will speak to both men and women in Hades, although only men are named. (41c) See note 37, above, note 48, below.

43. Palamedes was opposed by Odysseus and perhaps also by the leader of the army against Troy; Ajax considered both Odysseus and that leader his enemies after the arms of the son of Thetis had been awarded to Odysseus rather than to himself.

Each of the four groups encountered by Socrates in Hades, aside from the just men (who are the judges there), include a man who had returned to earth after having been in Hades: Orpheus, Palamedes and Odysseus.

44. One of the more prolonged uproars during the course of the trial comes when Socrates likens the gods and his daemonic thing to horses and a mule. (27a-e) He is obliged, at this point, to caution his listeners twice against interrupting him. (27b) See note 24, above, note 47, below.

Mules, it should be noticed, cannot reproduce themselves; Socrates' daemonic thing cannot be reproduced in others—it can only be replaced by something else. See note 51, below. (In any event, it should not be confused with what we now cater to as the conscience. See Essay VI, note 39, below.)

45. Is there not implied in the Socratic use of questions the assumption that an understanding of the whole is both necessary and virtually impossible for men to secure? That is, is it not true of all inquiries that the status of the answer one has depends on where one rests? Must we say that no matter what a man discovers, or how certain his conclusions appear, the next inquiry (so long as he does not know "all") may undermine or radically affect those conclusions? Is this why Socrates insists he does not know anything? What he does seem to know is the elusive quality of the truth as well as the superiority of wisdom to folly. (22e) The elusiveness is conveyed to the reader who attempts an interpretation of a Platonic dialogue. (See notes 1, 13, above. See, also, Essay XVI, below.) But does Socrates agree with the statement he attributes to the god, that human wisdom is of little or no value? (23a) See note 25, above. (Consider Democritus, Fr. 169: "Do not try to understand everything, lest you thereby become ignorant of everything.")

Socrates approaches each problem as if it were entirely new, as if it had never been considered before (as in the exchange with Callias [20a]). Socrates always asks questions—this indicates that he does not know; he is very good at asking questions—this indicates what he does know. See the text at note 6, Essay XV, below. See, also, Essay IV, note 13, Essay VI, note 42, below.

We should notice that the traditional accounts of the reasons for Sisyphus' punishment (having to roll uphill a huge stone which, just as soon as it reaches the top, always rolls down again) include his betrayal of the designs of the gods and his revelation to a father that Zeus had carried off his daughter. We are reminded of the charges against Socrates. (We should also notice that Sisyphus is considered in some accounts the father of Odysseus. Some say his punishment followed his apprehension after having practiced a deception which permitted him to escape from Hades. Would Socrates need to talk to anyone else in Hades once he has talked with Sisyphus? See notes 37, 43, above.)

46. This is Socrates' only conversation (recorded by Plato) with the Athenian people, a dialogue in which the interlocutor responds with disturbances and votes. See notes 22, 44, above.

The democratic attitudes of his audience no doubt influenced Socrates to make as much as he does on this occasion both of Chaerephon and of the oracle. See notes 20, 21, above. Chaerephon is the ground on which Socrates and the democracy can meet. (21a) See note 26, above, note 52, below. Had Chaerephon, despite his impulsiveness, by the very fact of friendship, served to protect Socrates against the harsher democrats? But Chaerephon is dead. (See, for an oligarchic "prosecution," Xenophon, *Memorabilia*, I, ii, 31-38. See, also, Essay XVI, note 9, below.)

The occasion may also explain why Socrates stresses his exhortations about virtue (insofar as these can be distinguished from inquiries about wisdom). He thereby displays himself as useful in terms the city can appreciate (for the city prefers deeds to words [32a]). How much time Socrates spent in the market place, or as a gadfly, remains a problem. His concern for virtue is reflected in both his conversations (exhortations) and his actions (resistance to the city's demands). But we recall that he *happened* to meet Callias (20a) and to be a member of the Prytaneum at the time of the trial of the generals (32b). (And one's native city, too, is the result of chance.) On the other hand, Socrates seeks out, in order to examine them, those reputed to be wise, both contemporary and ancient. (We assume here a practical distinction between wisdom and virtue, even though ultimately the truly virtuous must be wise: that is, he must know what he is doing, which means that he must know what is. See notes 27, 39, above.)

47. The Hades referred to is a place, not the god. But since Minos, Rhadamanthus and Aeacus are sons of Zeus, the existence of gods is implied (just as are the parents of mules [27b-e])? See note 44, above.

Had the priests of Delphi somehow divined that Socrates was the most restrained of the "philosophers" arising in their world? (Cf. 23a-b.) The refusal of the people of Athens to credit the oracle of Delphi with respect to Socrates suggests one difficulty in preserving the gods of the city. Did the ancient poets remain the only reliable authority about these gods? See note 29, above.

48. "Earth" (Ge, Gaea) comes first only in the coupling with "heaven" (Ouranos). (19c; cf. 18b, 23d.) This can be taken to suggest that Mother Earth is older than Ouranos, perhaps even that men and their cities may be older than all the gods except Gaea. See note 7, above. But would not the male element take precedence in the later Zeus-Hera coupling? (And is not maleness more evident in the life of the city and in war, in the citizen rather than in the human being?) Hera is invoked in a context where "helpers" abound. (25a) See note 42, above.

There is no mention of Poseidon, Athena or Hephaestus, the gods most intimately associated with Athens. (Cf. 28c: Thetis.) The invocation of "the dog" (21e) — of an animal which is both intelligent and man-loving—suggests a principle of authority, perhaps even of divinity, beyond the sometimes aloof, and even harsh, "gods of the city." (This invocation is resorted to when Socrates ventures to report the unpopular fact that the greater the reputation a man had in the city for wisdom, the more deluded Socrates found him to be.)

Almost all of Socrates' oaths piously invoke the accredited gods of the city. (26b) But he allows himself to be carried away into invoking as well the dog-faced god of Egypt, a god evidently not prescribed by his city. That is, Socrates is incorrigible.

49. Should the concluding passage be read with a skeptical "unless" rather than an assertive "except"? "But now the time has come to go away, I to die and you to live; which of us goes to the better lot is known to none except [unless?] to the god."

In any event, the god which emerges in Socrates' account, the unnamed god, does not depend on the poets. Socrates abstracts this god from what he knows of the world. A named god, on the other hand, brings with him his peculiar history, a history which may even include lying and harming of good men (and amorous adventures [27d]). Thus, the reason for not naming this figure may be different from the reason for not naming the two great political figures. See note 32, above.

Are the gods of the city "many," with the shortcomings of the many? But it may be impossible, except among the most favored people shaped by unusual circumstances, for the poets to make any other gods, and particularly a single god, steadily attractive to the many. Thus, these gods, as gods of the city, may be irreplaceable, whatever names they are given from time to time. Any people who dispense with "the gods of the city" may be driven to deify some other image of themselves—rulers or forefathers or the laws of nature or even "the laws of history." See notes 6, 21, 25, 29, above. See, also, Essay IV, note 47, Essay VI, note 51, below.

50. The city, if it could have risen above its prejudices, would have shown there was no need for Socrates' sacrifice. Perhaps it would not have been unjust to find him guilty of not acknowledging the gods of the city and then to fine him thirty minas. Since most men are fond of money, including (presumably) those who teach for money, this punishment would have restrained many of those whom one might want to restrain without in any way harming Socrates. Those who voted for conviction could have done so consistently with some such respectable opinion of their civic duty; but to vote for the death sentence in these circumstances reveals inhumanity or ignobility. See notes 3, 16, 39, above. See, also, Essay IV, note 47, below.

Are we not, on the other hand, the beneficiaries of this injustice, an injustice which led to the decisive dramatic formulation of the proper relation between philosophy and the city? See note 31, above.

51. One feature of the negative character of the daemonic thing is that Socrates may, at any time and unknown to him, be left alone in a great crisis. That is, he cannot be certain from moment to moment that his monitor is still active. Is this one reason why he must examine and·explain what it does and does not do?

The daemonic thing is referred to as a voice (or cry), not as speech. It does not give reasons: it seems to concern itself not with justice (which implies reasons) but with the unforeseeable effects of what Socrates is about to do or to say. It is more like the muse than like reason. Perhaps this, or an equivalent, is necessary for someone such as Socrates, who has no great instinctive "love of life." (37c) See note 40, above. See, also, note 44, above. Had others before Socrates, similar to him in all respects but this endowment, been destroyed early in their careers, either in trying to right injustices beyond their power to affect or in pursuing the truth in a manner which was dangerous?

The difficulty scholars have had in explaining Socrates' daemonic thing may confirm that it is something unique to him: others have no experience of it. In any event, Socrates' uniqueness is testified to even by his enemies: only he, of all the Athenians, "corrupts the youth." (25a)

52. Leo Strauss, "How to Begin to Study The Guide of the Perplexed," Introductory Essay, in Moses Maimonides, The Guide of the Perplexed, tr. S. Pines (Chicago: University of Chicago Press, 1963), p. lvi.

See, also, Strauss, (1) On Tyranny, An Interpretation of Xenophon's "Hiero" (New York: Political Science Classics, 1948; reissued, Glencoe: The Free Press, 1950); (2) Persecution and the Art of Writing (Glencoe: The Free Press, 1972), pp. 16-17, 24-25, 36-37, 105-107; (3) "Plato," in Leo Strauss and Joseph Cropsey, eds., History of Political Philosophy (Chicago: Rand McNally, 1963), pp. 7, 17, 22, 29, 30-31, 33, 37, 39-40, 60-61; (4) Socrates and Aristophanes (New York: Basic Books, 1966); (5) "The Liberalism of Classical Political Philosophy," The Review of Metaphysics (March 1959), pp. 393, 401-406, 425-426; (6) What Is Political Philosophy? (Glencoe: The Free Press, 1959), pp. 38-40, 91-94, 112-113, 119-122, 126-133; (7) The City and Man (Chicago: Rand McNally, 1964), pp. 37-38, 50-62, 77-78. See, also, Anastaplo, "On Leo Strauss: A Yahrzeit Remembrance," 67 University of Chicago Magazine 30 (Winter 1974). Cf. 17 Modern Age 93 (Winter 1973). But see 16 Revue Francaise de Science Politique 115 (Feb. 1966); 61 American Political Science Review 683 (Sept. 1967).

III. The American Heritage: Words and Deeds

1. There have been recorded as well many items which should suggest to the careful reader the flaws in Mr. Levy's interpretation. If, for example, the Blackstonian definition dominated American political thought, it is difficult to understand Alexander Hamilton's 1788 observation (in *Federalist* No. 84) that freedom of the press defied precise definition. See Leonard W. Levy, *Legacy of Suppression—Freedom of Speech in Early American History* (Cambridge: The Belknap Press, 1960), pp. 201-202.

   The passage from Blackstone may be found in his *Commentaries*, IV, 151-152.

   Various of the points discussed in this essay, as well as Mr. Levy's argument, are also discussed in *The Constitutionalist* (Essay I, note 1, above): e.g., pp. 102-104, 128-129, c. 2, nn. 7, 8, 9, 10, 11, 16, c. 4, n. 97, c. 5, nn. 1, 25, 65, 34, 36, 52, 143, 151-156, c. 6, nn. 29, 37, 38, 50, 71, c. 7, nn. 67, 77, c. 8, nn. 3, 18, 135, 181, c. 9, nn. 8, 9, 27, 28, 39.

   See, on "previous restraints," Anastaplo, "Preliminary Reflections on the Pentagon Papers," *University of Chicago Magazine*, Jan./Feb., March/April 1972 (reprinted 118 *Cong. Rec.* S11560 [July 24, 1972]) ; "Self-Government and the Mass Media," in *The Mass Media and Modern Democracy*, ed. Harry M. Clor (Chicago: Rand McNally, 1974). Cf. Herbert J. Storing, Book Review: Levy, *Legacy of Suppression*, 55 *American Political Science Review* 385 (1961).

2. Indeed, it can be said that there survived no Blackstonians in the United States by 1798. Even the Sedition Act changed Blackstone's formulation in certain decisive respects (e.g., by making truth a defense).

3. The role and significance of Virginia and some of her leading men (such as Madison in the U. S. House of Representatives) must be emphasized for a proper understanding both of the Bill of Rights and of freedom of speech and of the press in this country.

4. In the Virginia House of Delegates, December 13, 1798. *Resolutions of Virginia and Kentucky, Penned by Madison and Jefferson, in Relation to the Alien and Sedition Laws; and the Debates and Proceedings in the House of Delegates of Virginia, on the same, in December 1798* (Richmond: Robert I. Smith, 1835), p. 80 (cited hereafter as *Resolutions*).

5. February, 1799. *Ibid.*, pp. 9-10.

6. *Ibid.*, pp. 52-53.

7. It is of central significance that Jefferson tried to conceal the role he played in encouraging certain prosecutions. See, e.g., Levy, *Legacy of Suppression*, pp. 301-307. He stood by his words, not his deeds. Or, to put it otherwise, he (and the country?) "knew better" than he acted.

   The most casual historical research can inform us whether the particular case before us from time to time is nothing more than mere hypocrisy or sham. See, e.g., Essay I, above. Somewhat more difficult may be the determination of what is the effective law of the day. Thus, today, the effective law with respect to business transactions may be quite different from what businessmen might be told by their lawyers (about, for example, whether one may sell to a corporation of which one is a member of the board of directors). That is, businessmen are primarily interested in doing business (and making money), not in being wary of the odd case which lawyers must worry about. Indeed, lawyers are, by and large, a rather timid lot. See Essay IX, below.

8. One can, on the basis of the evidence Mr. Levy himself presents, support a contrary interpretation of the significance (for freedom of speech and of the press) of eighteenth century American experience. Thus, on the basis of Mr. Levy's materials alone, the title of his book could well have been, *The Generation In Which the Dam Finally Broke*, or even, *Legacy of Liberation*.

See, on "rhetoric," Levy, *Legacy of Suppression,* pp. 76, 80-81, 87, 105-106, 108-109, 116-117, 120-121, 135, 174-175, 177-178, 188, 215, 227. See, also, *ibid.,* pp. 44-45, 46-49, 63-64, 193-197.

9. Seditious libel was, at common law, a misdemeanor. *Ibid.,* p. 84. Thus, the penalty provided by the Sedition Act of 1798 was harsher than that at common law, and that provided by our twentieth century sedition act (the Smith Act) is harsher than that provided by the 1798 act. We can be sure, that is, that the punishment is "expanding."

10. See, e.g., *ibid.,* pp. 308-309. William W. Crosskey, in his *Politics and the Constitution* (Chicago: University of Chicago Press, 1953), has the salutary effect of making his student take the Constitution most seriously. Such respect for the Constitution may be seen as well in the work of Justice Hugo L. Black (whose recommendation, relayed to editors by Professor Edmond Cahn, led to the original publication of this book review in the *New York University Law Review* in 1964). See Essay IX, note 4, below.

I believe it can also be shown that the Bill of Rights is very carefully drafted, that it is not an instance of what it is now fashionable to call "studied imprecision."

11. *Resolutions,* p. 29. See, on the great statements which have come down to us, Anastaplo, "The Declaration of Independence," 9 *St. Louis U. L. J.* 390 (1965); "American Constitutionalism and The Virtue of Prudence" (Essay I, note 1, above).

12. See Essay XVI, below. We notice, for discussion on another occasion, Mr. Levy's dogmatic assumption that "freedom of speech" depends on the opinion that truth is "relative rather than absolute." *Legacy of Suppression,* p. 6. Cf. Anastaplo, Review of Hugh Thomas, *John Strachey, Showcase/Chicago Sun-Times,* Jan. 6, 1974, Sec. 3, p. 14. Cf., also, Essay IV, note 34, Essay VI, section iii, Essay XII, note 2, below.

13. *Resolutions,* p. 199. I observe of Mr. Levy's book, at pages 102-103 of *The Constitutionalist,* that it provides "a much more comprehensive account of [the suppression of Tory opinion during the Revolutionary period] than I can hope to set forth here, thereby relieving this discussion of the necessity of such a mournful account." See *ibid.,* c. 8, n. 98.

Mr. Levy wrote to me, in commenting on this review of his book, that he dealt more in history and I in poetry. In my response I drew on Aristotle, *Poetics* 1451b5: "Hence poetry is something more philosophical and of graver import than history, since its statements are of the nature of universals, whereas those of history are singulars."

IV. Natural Right and the American Lawyer

1. Lon L. Fuller, *The Law in Quest of Itself* (Chicago: The Foundation Press, 1940). This essay was originally prepared, pursuant to a commission from the *University of Chicago Law Review,* as a review of Lon L. Fuller, *The Morality of Law* (New Haven: Yale University Press, 1964). The author, who had been encouraged by the *Review* to "explore and develop [his] own ideas suggested by the work reviewed," refused to approve editorial changes which would have eliminated almost two-thirds of the manuscript he had submitted. (See the sentiment expressed in note 39, below.) The review was thereupon prepared by the author for use in Professor Malcolm P. Sharp's seminar in "Reasoning and the Law," University of Chicago Law School, March 1965, prior to publication in the *Wisconsin Law Review* (Spring 1965). See Essay VI, note 1, Essay IX, note 10, below.

See Peter P. Nicholson, "The Internal Morality of Law: Fuller and His Critics," 88 *Ethics* 307 (1974).

2. Fuller, *The Law in Quest of Itself,* pp. 5, 137. A useful development of these senti-

ments is found in Lon L. Fuller, *Reason and Fiat in Case Law* (New York: American Book-Stratford Press, 1943) (The Benjamin N. Cardozo Lecture, before The Association of the Bar of the City of New York, October 27, 1942). See note 48, below.

3. See Edward H. Levi, "The Natural Law, Precedent, and Thurman Arnold," 24 *Virginia Law Review* 587 (April 1938), for a useful introduction for lawyers to natural law (with special reference to Aristotle and Aquinas). The discussion is seriously marred, however, by the implications of the first footnote, "Whenever the word true appears in this article, the reader may put quotation marks about it." The influence of Thurman Arnold here and elsewhere in Mr. Levi's work seems decisive. See note 35, below.

On the scholarly self-restraint needed in the field of law and constitutional history, see Essay III, above.

4. The passage is from the article on "Natural Law," by Professor Leo Strauss, *International Encyclopedia of the Social Sciences* (New York: Crowell Collier and Macmillan, 1968), XI, 80.

The fact that law or convention was originally seen in contradistinction to nature suggests the legitimate impetus behind the positivist view of law. Does this suggest that natural right is, in this respect, superior to natural law? Natural right is the older formulation, one which is less influenced by theological developments. Natural law, on the other hand, seems to imply a lawgiver and is more apt to be related to revealed religion. (See notes 42, 43, below.) Natural law reminds of, and is perhaps influenced by, the concept of the natural laws of physics, chemistry, etc. But, for the most part, these two sets of terms are used interchangeably today. (The modern project of the conquest of nature may be intimately related to the depreciation in modernity of natural law and natural right. See Essay VIII, below.)

Mr. Strauss refers to "those simple experiences regarding right and wrong which are at the bottom of the natural right doctrines." *Natural Right and History* (Chicago: University of Chicago Press, 1953), p. 105. See, also, *ibid.*, pp. x, 31-32. He suggests as well that "The classic natural right doctrine in its original form, if fully developed, is identical with the doctrine of the best regime." *Ibid.*, p. 144. See, on the connection for Mr. Strauss between nature and human nature, Anastaplo, "On Leo Strauss: A Yahrzeit Remembrance," 67 *University of Chicago Magazine*, Winter 1974, pp. 30, 36.

5. Fuller, *The Morality of Law*, pp. 3-4.

6. *Ibid.*, p. 145. A related passage is reproduced in note 10, below.

7. Fuller, *The Law in Quest of Itself*, p. 128.

8. See, for the "marginal utility" language, Fuller, *The Morality of Law*, pp. 7, 15-19, 44, 181; for the "pointer," "scale," and "pressure of duty" language, *ibid.*, pp. 9-13, 27-30, 42, 170. See, also, Essay XII, note 2, below.

9. *Ibid.*, pp. 13-15, 30-32, 168-169.

10. *Ibid.*, pp. 95-96, 106-118, 147-148. Mr. Fuller's summary, *ibid.*, pp. 117-118, is instructive:

> . . . I have tried to see law as a purposive activity, typically attended by certain difficulties that it must surmount if it is to succeed in attaining its ends. In contrast, the theories I have rejected seem to me to play about the fringe of that activity without ever concerning themselves directly with the problems. Thus, law is defined as 'the existence of public order' without asking what kind of order is meant or how it is brought about. Again, the distinguishing mark of law is said to lie in a means, namely 'force,' that is typically employed to effectuate its aims. There is no recognition that, except as it makes the stakes higher, the use or nonuse of force leaves unchanged the essential problems of those who make and administer the laws. Finally, there are theories that concentrate on the hierarchic structure that is commonly thought to organize and direct the activity I have called

law, though again without recognizing that this structure is itself a product of
the activity it is thought to put in order.

An extended critique of the legal positivist doctrine could well begin with a
detailed analysis of Plato, *Republic*, I; Aristotle, *Nicomachaean Ethics*, V, vii.

11. Fuller, *The Morality of Law*, pp. 6, 12, 18, 117-118, 122-123, 145-151.

12. *Ibid.*, pp. 146-147.

13. Fuller, *ibid.*, p. 186. Mr. Fuller's concern lest he invoke the infinite may be sympto-
matic. *Ibid.*, p. 152. That is, he does not seem to appreciate why Plato and Aristotle,
even when they wrote about political and ethical matters, did so with some notion
of the whole (and hence the infinite?) in mind. Unless man does have some such
notion, he knows neither where (or who) he is, nor where he is going. One
alternative to a notion of the whole is nihilism; another (and related?), the deliberate self-delusion of existentialism. See note 47, below. See, also, Essay II, note 45,
above, Essay VI, note 42, below.

Consider, on the usefulness of a goal in view, Martin Gardner, ed., *The Annotated
Alice* (New York: World Publishing Co., Forum Books, 1963), pp. 64, 88-89,
104, 212, 314-315.

14. Fuller, *The Morality of Law*, pp. 10-15. Aristotle seems to be better regarded
(*ibid.*, pp. 19, 64, 94), but this may be due to a failure to recognize his similarity
to his teacher in this decisive respect (as well as in many other respects). See note 13,
above. See, also, Essay II, note 27, above.

15. *Ibid.*, pp. 5-6, 96. This observation applies primarily to the "morality of duty"—
but it is this which is particularly relevant to the law in Mr. Fuller's view.

Mr. Strauss (in the article on natural law cited in note 4, above) reports, "Modern natural law as originated by Hobbes did not start, as traditional natural law
did, from the hierarchic order of man's natural ends, but rather from the lowest of
those ends (self-preservation) that could be thought to be more effective than the
higher ends. (A civil society ultimately based on nothing but the right of self-
preservation would not be utopian.) Man is still asserted to be the rational animal,
but his natural sociability is denied. Man is not by nature ordered toward society,
but he orders himself toward it prompted by mere calculation. . . ." See Essay VII,
note 7, below.

Is there not in modern times a subtle shift in emphasis from the "rational" to the
"animal" in "rational animal"? It was not until the eighteenth century that man
was classified as *homo sapiens*. This designation, by Linnaeus, seems to have
ratified the tendency (even before Darwin) to place man among the animals, a
tendency which is indicated in the central place which had come to be given to
self-preservation among the aims of man. The animal, rather than the rational, is
reflected also in Mr. Fuller's reference to perception, feeling and desire. *The
Morality of Law*, p. 186. Cf. Aristotle, *Metaphysics* 980a21-982a2; *De Anima*
427a16-429a18; *Nicomachean Ethics* 1098a1-18. And, to anticipate the discussion
in Section vi of this essay, perception, feeling and desire do not depend as much as
the rational does on the preservation of civilization.

Consider, for the dependence of feeling upon the rational, Don Juan's observation (in George Bernard Shaw's *Man and Superman*), "Without a brain, Commander, you would enjoy yourself without knowing it, and so lose all the fun."
Consider, also, Anastaplo, *The Constitutionalist* (Essay I, note 1, above), c. 9, n. 38.
See note 34, below.

16. Fuller, *The Morality of Law*, pp. 3-4, 9-13, 132-133, 168-169.

17. Aristotle, *Nicomachean Ethics* 1179b31-1180a4. See, also, the remainder of this
concluding chapter of the work; Plato, *Republic*, II-III.

An appreciation of this ancient teaching reveals much that is uninformed in current discussions of subjects such as obscenity and capital punishment. See, e.g., Essay X, below.

18. The concluding article of the Northwest Ordinance of 1787 provided: "There shall be neither slavery nor involuntary servitude in the said territory, otherwise than in the punishment of crimes, whereof the party shall have been duly convicted . . ."

19. Abraham Lincoln, *Complete Works*, ed. John G. Nicolay and John Hay (New York: The Century Co., 1902), I, 570-571 (speech at Cincinnati, Ohio, September 17, 1895). See, also, *ibid.*, I, 204-205; 561-562 (on the raising of sugar cane in Ohio and Louisiana); 181-184 (on the effect of the Missouri Compromise); 622-624 (on slavery as clearly a moral question).

Lincoln knew that not everything could be done by law, and that care must be exercised in the laws which are employed. See, e.g., his Temperance Address, *ibid.*, I, 57-59. Our twentieth-century experiment with Prohibition is a case in point, even though Americans overestimate its significance. Compare the salutary effect in one decade of the Supreme Court decision in *Brown v. Board of Education*, 347 U.S. 438 (1954). Compare, also, Essay XV, below. But see Walter Berns, "Racial Discrimination and the Limits of Judicial Remedies," in *100 Years of Emancipation*, ed. Robert A. Goldwin (Chicago: Rand McNally, 1964); also, Essay V, note 6, below. See, as well, William Faulkner, *Intruder in the Dust* (New York: Vintage Books, 1972), pp. 203-204.

20. It may be true, however, that the very best men are not compelled by law. See Plato, *Republic* 619c. See, also, for a discussion of the "Cave" in the *Republic* as it bears on this question, Anastaplo, *The Constitutionalist*, chap. 9, sec. 4. See, on Lincoln's reshaping of the American heritage by means of his speeches, Anastaplo, "American Constitutionalism and The Virtue of Prudence" (Essay I, note 1, above), Part IV.

See, also, Plato, *Statesman* 259a-b, 261e, 308e-311c.

21. See, on the relation between the best and the traditional, Plato, *Republic* 376c: "Isn't it difficult to find a better [system of education] than that discovered over a great expanse of time?" See note 30, below.

Although Plato may not have set forth a natural law teaching, he is certainly a teacher of natural law teachers.

22. On justice and the morality of duty, see Fuller, *The Morality of Law*, p. 6, n. 4; on due process, see *ibid.*, pp. 39-44, 81, 96-106, 126. It is curious to see Mr. Fuller apparently dismiss as "purely formal" justice the requirement that "like cases be given like treatment." *Ibid.*, p. 4. Cf. Aristotle, *Nicomachean Ethics* 1131a10-1131b24.

23. Fuller, *The Morality of Law*, pp. 38-39. The extended examination is in *ibid.*, pp. 46-94. See, also, *ibid.*, pp. 96-102, 162-168, 184-186.

24. *Ibid.*, p. 39. *The ex post facto* prohibition would not be as critical as Mr. Fuller believes it to be if there should be natural right standards to guide the conscientious citizen in anticipation of adjustments in the positive law to take account of new circumstances. What may be said of the Nuremberg Trials in this respect? See Plato, *Statesman* 293c-297c. See, also, Anastaplo, "Due Process of Law—An Introduction," 42 *University of Detroit Law Journal* 195, 210, n. 30 (December 1964).

25. The first of these two quotations is from Fuller, *The Morality of Law*, p. 106; the second, *ibid.*, p. 146. Mr. Fuller adds, "Such a purpose scarcely lends itself to Hegelian excesses." *Ibid.*, p. 146. See note 13, above.

26. Aquinas, *Summa Theologica*, Pt. I-II, Ques. 90, A. 4 (*Treatise on Law*). This definition would apply to decisions of judges as well as to the enactments of legislatures.

27. Fuller, *The Morality of Law*, p. 154; also, *ibid.*, pp. 155-162.

28. Mr. Fuller's discussion of the South Africa example (*ibid.*, p. 160) makes one wonder

whether even more ruthless legislation could not take care of the "borderline cases" he depends upon to preserve his position against Mr. Hart's suggestion. Examples in opposition to Mr. Fuller's contention and in support of Mr. Hart's may be scarce, but this could well be because men who do not care about substantive justice will not restrain themselves with respect to the procedural decencies either. Should it become the practise, however, to judge regimes primarily by procedural standards, some peculiar situations would develop to illustrate Mr. Hart's contention (especially if American recognition and financial aid should be keyed to such considerations). (Did not this become evident, subsequent to the original publication of this essay, in the periodic recourse by the Greek colonels to essentially meaningless referenda to mask their tyrannical usurpation? See Essay I, above.)

Were not many of the scrupulous if very reluctant observances of laws supporting slavery, in both the North and the South of pre-Civil War America, instances of great iniquity consistent with rigorous adherence to the forms of the inner morality of law? No doubt, good men justified some of these observances (e.g., with respect to fugitive slaves) as necessary if even greater iniquities were to be avoided. See Anastaplo, "American Constitutionalism," Part III.

See, for another, although preliminary, study of due process, Anastaplo, "Due Process of Law—An Introduction"; also, Anastaplo, *The Constitutionalist*, p. 813; "Principle and Passion: The American Nazi Speaker on the University Campus," in Anastaplo, *Notes on the First Amendment to the Constitution of the United States* (University of Chicago Ph D. dissertation, 1964), p. 728. (Lists of depositaries for this dissertation may be found at 42 *University of Detroit Law Journal 55*, n. 3, 195, n. 1 [1964].) See, as well, note 23 of Anastaplo, "Freedom of Speech and the First Amendment," 42 *University of Detroit Law Journal 55* (October 1964), where there is discussed "Mr. Justice Harlan's unlawyerlike failure throughout his opinion [at 366 U.S. 82 (1961)] to respect the record made during the hearings before the character committee" in the course of the author's Illinois bar admission controversy. See Essay IX, below. See, also, note 52, below. Thus, we do recognize the importance of due process of law, but we also consider it important to keep it in its proper place.

See, for the Socratic endorsement of "due process," Plato, *Apology* 32b, 37a-b; Essay II, section iv, above. See, also, Plato, *Theaetetus* 172-173.

29. This was much more evident when the prospective lawyer read Blackstone. See the lecture, "Realism and the Practice of Law: A Lecture for Law Students" (delivered at the Northwestern University Law School), in Anastaplo, *Notes on the First Amendment*, p. 706; also, Essay IX, below, with its invocation of *Langbridge's Case*, Common Bench, 1345 (reported Year Book, 19 Edw. III, 375).

30. During the 1964 Presidential campaign, the candidates were obliged and sometimes able to rise to the occasion by joining the issue on a high plane. In doing this they drew on the best in the American heritage. Thus, President Johnson could speak of a great society in which "the least among us will find contentment, and the best among us will find greatness, and all of us will respect the dignity of the one and admire the achievements of the other." *Chicago Sun-Times*, September 4, 1964, p. 6. And Senator Goldwater could warn that the "great society" "is one in which there will be no failure, because in it there will be no reward for success. In it, there will be no individual responsibility and, therefore, no freedom." *Chicago Tribune*, September 19, 1964, p. 4.

Among contemporary professional men with immediate practical concerns, only lawyers and (to a lesser extent?) politicians are obliged in the ordinary course of their work to turn to authors of earlier centuries. Thus, the lawyer is continually reminded of and encouraged to respect the old and, indirectly, the good. See note 21, above. This recourse to earlier centuries also helps keep alive the natural right tradition among the bar. Consider, as well, Anastaplo, review of two books by Nikos Kazantzakis: *Chicago Sun-Times*, January 26, 1975, sec. 1-C, p. 6: "Also evident, of course, is that [Kazantzakis] is a modern intellectual as well. But what saved him from the alienated, curiously uninformed fate of most intellectuals today were his roots in the very old—his roots in both Classical and Byzantine Greek thought and art. Indeed, he could grasp the new more confidently and more responsibly because of his instinctive rootedness in the old. His inherited sense of humanity, as well as his artistic vitality, protected him from both the harshness and the purposelessness to which modern ideology is prone. . . ."

31. The place of nature in Shakespeare's thought is not easily overestimated. See *The Constitutionalist*, e.g., c. 9, n. 20.

As to the significance of language: when we speak of an "unjust law," what do we mean by it? For a legal positivist's discussion of this, see H. L. A. Hart, "Positivism and the Separation of Law and Morals," 71 *Harvard Law Review* 593 (February 1958). Consider, also, Cotton Mather, *Magnalia Christi Americana* (New York: Russell & Russell, 1967), II, 409 (emphasis added): "A man, finding it necessary to come into his house, he swore he would run a spit into his bowels; and he was *as bad as his word.*" Consider, on the "unnatural" diversity of languages among men, Mark Twain, *Huckleberry Finn*, chap. 14.

See Jacob Klein, "On the Nature of Nature," February 28, 1964. (Mimeographed copies of this lecture may be purchased from the St. John's College Bookstore, Annapolis, Maryland.) See, also, Anastaplo, "American Constitutionalism," n. 20.

32. The Preamble to the Constitution invokes standards which are not based simply on parochial opinion. More should be made as well of the Republican Form of Government guaranty in the Constitution. See *The Constitutionalist*, p. 820. Cf. Fuller, *The Morality of Law*, p. 178.

Much of what is being mined by the Supreme Court out of the Fourteenth Amendment is nearer the surface in the Republican Form of Government guaranty. For example, the critical issue in the reapportionment cases should not be simply that of equality but also whether effective republican government can continue under antiquated apportionment statutes in the States. The Court has cut itself off from reliance upon the guaranty—see *Baker* v. *Carr*, 396 U.S. 209, 218-232 (1962)—but its reasoning is not persuasive. Does not the Court assume (by looking primarily to the Fourteenth Amendment for support) that the framers of the original Constitution were not as concerned as they should have been or as the Court now is to assure properly elected State legislatures? See, on the Fourteenth Amendment, *The Constitutionalist*, p. 814. See, also, Essay V, note 8, below.

33. The craftsman must "appeal to" (that is, respect) nature if he is to do his job well. Thus, the positivist who writes well carries within him the seeds of his own destruction (as a positivist)? See, for example, the refutation of Thrasymachus in Plato, *Republic* I.

34. See Anastaplo, "The Declaration of Independence," 9 *St. Louis University Law Journal* 390 (Spring 1965). It is as a reminder of absolutes, and indeed of the nature of man, that the Declaration of Independence remains our founding instrument. See, also, Anastaplo, "American Constitutionalism," III, iv, vi. Cf., *ibid.*, IV, v; *ibid.*, Epilogue, ii.

The Declaration is important also in that it proclaims that there *are* "self-evident" truths derived from the nature of man. (What is fundamental to the nature of man is generally—one may even say, instinctively—recognized by most men and is reflected in the reassuring headline for a front-page newspaper report on a stroke suffered in December 1974 by Justice William O. Douglas: "Douglas left 'weak' on side; mind okay." *The State Journal-Register*, Springfield, Illinois, January 3, 1975, p. 1. See note 15, above.)

35. *The Spirit of Liberty—Papers and Addresses of Learned Hand*, ed. Irving Dilliard (2d ed.,; New York: Alfred A. Knopf, 1953), p. 81 (a talk delivered in 1930).

The attitude toward words as "empty vessels" raises serious problems. Consider the failing in this respect of Thurman Arnold, as discussed in Richard M. Weaver, *Ideas Have Consequences* (Chicago: University of Chicago Press, 1948), pp. 154-155:

> When we look more narrowly at the epistemological problem raised by the semanticists, we conclude that they wish to accept patterns only from external reality. With many of them the notion seems implicit that language is an illusion or a barrier between us and what we must cope with. "Somewhere bedrock beneath words must be reached," is a common theme. Some talk about achieving an infinite-valued orientation (this last would of course leave certitude and the idea of the good impossible). Mr. Thurman Arnold, who seems to have assimilated most of the superficial doctrines of the day, takes a stand in the *Folklore of Capitalism* even against definition. He argues that every writer on social institutions "should try to choose words and illustrations which will arouse the proper mental associations with his reader. If he doesn't succeed with them, he should try others. If he is ever led into an attempt at definition, he is lost."

This attitude toward language seems critical in works such as Edward H. Levi, *Introduction to Legal Reasoning* (Chicago: University of Chicago Press, 1949), an influential but curiously shallow book. See *The Consitutionalist*, p. 817; note 3, above.

Mr. Levi observed, after having been nominated Attorney General of the United States, "Law should not be regarded as just another pressure device, just another tactic or lever. I'm afraid that's the cynical view of it." *Chicago Tribune*, February 5, 1975, p. 1. But that is precisely the view of the law which a generation of law students got from Mr. Levi's essay on legal reasoning. Consider, in the light of the observation at the beginning of Section iv of this essay (about the academic positivist who is obliged to speak differently in the courtroom or on the public platform), Mr. Levi's remarks upon his installation as Attorney General: "We have lived in a time of change and corrosive skepticism and cynicism concerning the administration of justice. Nothing can more weaken the quality of life or more imperil the realization of the goals we all hold dear than our failures to make clear by word and deed that our law is not an instrument for partisan purposes and it is not an instrument to be used in ways which are careless of the higher values within all of us." 121 *Congressional Record* S1685 (February 7, 1975).

See, also, *University of Chicago Maroon*, May 9, 1952, p. 2; *ibid.*, June 24, 1966, p. 5; "On Leo Strauss," pp. 31, 32; Essay IX, note 10, below; note 50, below. See, as well, Essay XII, note 2, below.

36. Had this judge known Plato better, for instance, he would not have indulged himself in the observation, "For myself it would be most irksome to be ruled by a bevy of Platonic Guardians, even if I knew how to choose them, which I assuredly do not. If they were in charge, I should miss the stimulus of living in a society where I have, at least theoretically, some part in the direction of public affairs." Learned Hand, *The Bill of Rights* (Cambridge: Harvard University Press, 1958), p. 73. See note 20, above, note 39, below.

37. Fuller, *The Morality of Law*, pp. 10-11, 13; also, *ibid.*, pp. 32, 122.

38. *Ibid.*, p. 11; also, *ibid.*, pp. 9-13, 18-21. Cf. note 13, above.

Mr. Fuller can opine (*ibid.*, p. 18) that "It is characteristic of normal human beings that they pursue a plurality of ends; an obsessive concern for some single end can in fact be taken as a symptom of mental disease." An argument which he believes Socrates would not have made *(ibid.,* p. 15 [top]) seems to be the very one which Plato assigns him in the *Republic.* Nor does Mr. Fuller seem to recognize *(ibid.,* p. 20) that the attempt made in that dialogue *is* to ground an appeal to duty on something other than the principle of reciprocity.

These three curious interpretations by Mr. Fuller reveal a greater concern for establishing his position than for understanding the thought he confronts. Plato is not the only victim, however. It is not considered by Mr. Fuller a distortion of the Golden Rule if it should be qualified to read, "So soon as it becomes perfectly clear that you have no intention whatever of treating me as you yourself would wish to be treated, then I shall consider myself as relieved from the obligation to treat you as I would wish to be treated." *Ibid.,* p. 21. Is not his assessment of the morality of the Old Testament as predominantly "Thou shalt *not*" also a distortion? *Ibid.,* p. 6. Cf., e.g., *Micah* 6: 8.

39. Legal scholars and law review editors (who find it difficult to print an article as written) are not the only offenders. See, e.g., the lecture, "On the Use and Abuse of Old Books," in which Walter Lippmann's careless interpretation of Plato's *Phaedo* (in *The Public Philosophy*) is examined. This lecture is found in Anastaplo, *Notes on the First Amendment* (note 28, above), p. 473. See, also, Essay II, above, Essay XVI, below. See, as well, Anastaplo, "American Constitutionalism," n. 4; note 1, above.

40. The meat-eating prohibition is not considered a tenet of natural law and hence may be suspended in appropriate cases (e.g., for travellers) or even altogether abolished. Nor is any effort made to extend the prohibition, when it *is* in effect for Roman Catholics, to non-believers (e.g., by not permitting meat to be provided for in the Friday budgets of public aid recipients).

41. See Aristotle, *Politics* 1265a14, 1265a40, 1270a29-b6, 1326a5-b25, 1335b20-26. See, also, Plato, *Republic* 372b-c, 460-461; *Laws* 740, 930; St. Thomas More, *Utopia*, Bk. II (the section, "Their Care of the Sick and Euthanasia"). See, as well, Essay XVII, notes 5, 10, below.

On the other hand, the current permissiveness with respect to abortion is characterized by an insistent and sometimes even callous thoughtlessness.

42. Further development of these opinions (which bear on the effect of the absorption of natural law by theology) must be reserved for another occasion. It should be noticed that the Church does recognize certain means of "birth control," but even these seem to be grudgingly permitted. The assumptions and instructions regarding the "rhythm method" are too complicated, as well as even preposterous, to be natural. Would it not have seemed somewhat more in accordance with reason and nature for the Church simply to have insisted that there should be no attempt made at deliberate control of conception? Instead, this approved method has the effect of making much more of the role of sexual activity in the life of the observing couple than it deserves, even as it makes them more subject to chance than do other methods. It is difficult to regard the approved method as less contrived or less unnatural either in intent or in deed than some of the common and more effective methods employed by others. (Is not the "act" to which attention should be directed better understood as extending through months, if not even years?)

No doubt, many devout Roman Catholics have long agreed with this assessment. It has been said that a reconsideration of the rules is in progress and that an accommodation might even be made to the development of certain pills. It would be unfortunate, however, if a misreading of natural law should now require and permit recourse (in order to maintain the appearance of consistency) to the very method which may most seriously interfere with the natural processes of the human body. See note 43, below.

43. The tradition does not speak with one voice on all questions. For example, the difference between Aristotle and Aquinas, occasioned by the latter's explicit submission to Christianity, should be taken into account. See Harry V. Jaffa, *Thomism and Aristotelianism—A Study of the Commentary by Thomas Aquinas on the Nicomachean Ethics* (Chicago: University of Chicago Press, 1952). (Mr. Jaffa's Churchillian epigraph for his study bears on the questions touched upon in this essay: "It is baffling to reflect that what men call honour does not correspond always to Christian ethics.")

Perhaps critical to the Roman Catholic position on birth control is the remarkable status accorded to celibacy in its life. The "rhythm method" seems to be dignified as a kind of periodic celibacy.

See, on abortion, note 41, above.

44. Winston Churchill once warned, ". . . Beware acts of desperation by a cornered enemy. . . ." *Chicago Tribune*, Nov. 24, 1964, p. 8. And Nikita Khrushchev, in expressing doubt that an agreement banning the use of nuclear weapons in war could be completely effective, predicted, "The trouble is the losing side will always use nuclear weapons in the last resort to avoid defeat. If a man thinks he's going to die he'll take any steps." *Chicago Sun-Times*, August 16, 1964, p. 7. But *is* this true? Does not one's opinion about death very much affect how one lives and dies? However that may be, Sargent Shriver has recently expressed sentiments even more extreme than Mr. Khrushchev's: "The danger of nuclear war increases with relative weakness. If one side or the other believes that ultimate defeat is imminent, militarily, ideologically or economically, nuclear war will occur." *Ibid.*, March 28, 1975, p. 16. See Essay XVII, below.

Mr. Jaffa concludes *Thomism and Aristotelianism* with the observation (pp. 192-193):

This essay is devoted to what the author considers the fundamental problem of present-day social science. No one doubts that these problems are global in scope. The contest that is joined today will certainly be decided, in part at least, by the nature of the convictions that reasonable men, and men of good will, in all lands, can be brought to share. Obviously the view that any opinion as to what is good is equally good, the characteristic tenet of present-day positivism and relativism, cannot supply a frame of reference within which differences can be reasonably composed. But our social science, if it is to be of any use, must be addressed to Moslems and Jews as well as to Christians, to Buddhists and Hindus as well as to believers in the Bible; it must, finally, be addressed "not only to those who enjoy the blessings and consolation of revealed religion, but also to those who face the mysteries of human destiny alone."

(The final quotation is from Winston Churchill's address at the Mid-Century Convocation of the Massachusetts Institute of Technology, *New York Times*, April 1, 1949, p. 10.)

A place for the Communist must be explicitly recognized in this global conversation among "reasonable men" and "men of good will" (are there not many more of the latter than of the former?). See Essay I, note 4, above, Essay V, below. See, also, note 47, below.

45. *Chicago Tribune*, Nov. 11, 1964, sec. 1, p. 5. There appeared in the same issue (sec. 1B, p. 8) a report of the debate in the Vatican Council of the day before on whether nuclear weapons can be precise and limited enough in application ever to justify their use. See, also, *New Yorker*, Oct. 10, 1964, pp. 100-154; October 17, 1964, pp. 131-184.

"The shift in attitudes and techniques is reflected in the following figures: In World War I there were 9,800,000 killed, 5 per cent of whom were civilians; in World War II, of 52,000,000 dead, 48 per cent were civilians; the Korean conflict produced 9,200,000 dead, of whom 84 per cent were civilians." Tom Stonier, *Nuclear Disaster* (London: Penguin Books, 1964), p. 20. See, also, President Kennedy's speech on the test ban treaty, July 26, 1963. (This treaty, and its successors, may be seen as one salutary effect of the Cuban Missile Crisis.) .

Churchill recorded in 1930 as a lesson of the Boer War (*My Early Life—A Roving Commission* [New York: Charles Scribner's Sons; Scribner Library Edition, 1930], p. 232) (cf. "American Constitutionalism," n. 64):

> Never, never, never believe any war will be smooth and easy, or that anyone who embarks on the strange voyage can measure the tides and hurricanes he will encounter. The Statesman who yields to war fever must realize that once the signal is given, he is no longer the master of policy but the slave of unforeseeable and uncontrollable events. . . . Always remember, however sure you are that you can easily win, that there would not be a war if the other man did not think he also had a chance.

See, also, *ibid.*, pp. 65, 180-181, 320-321, 328-331. Perhaps the dedication to adventurous and spectacular competitions in space can be made to serve during the next half century as psychological, moral and political substitutes for war. (The epigraph drawn from Dante is relevant here: the greatest adventures in space await the man who seeks to know.)

46. The quotations are from "McNamara: A Power Who Banks on Power of Reason," *Chicago Sun-Times*, April 7, 1963, p. 48. Obviously, there are no simple or safe solutions: grave risks are run by any nation which pursues any of the courses ranging from unilateral pacifism to preventive war. What can be hoped for is that responsible leaders will so conduct themselves as not to be put in situations where they are confronted only by dreadful alternatives. (See Essays XI, XII, XIII, below.) And this means that serious negotiation must be pursued. (Thus, I could write at the time this essay was prepared a decade ago, in an effort to help keep things from getting out of control, the following paragraph:)

Lawyers who appreciate from their own experience the delicacy as well as the dangers of negotiation should be particularly eager to support publicly the President in any reasonable attempt he may see fit to make in order to come to terms with the Russians, Chinese and even the French. It is encouraging to notice that the President, in a press conference held amid "speculation that drastic innovations were imminent" in South Vietnam, met reporters on his ranch with the greeting, "I've been sitting here in this serene atmosphere of the Pedernales for the last few days reading about the wars you have involved us in and the additional undertakings that I have made decisions on." *Chicago Sun-Times*, Nov. 29, 1964, p. 1. It is also encouraging to notice that this President can be both tough and patient, a useful combination in certain difficult circumstances, especially when tempered by the compassion exhibited by him in the Jenkins Affair. It is discouraging, on the other hand, to learn of the combat use in South Vietnam of gas (even if non-lethal). One is reminded of the observation attributed to Tallyerand, "It is worse than a crime— it is a blunder." See Walter Lippmann's column of December 29, 1964, for a timely reassessment of America's "primary vital interest" in Southeast Asia. See, also, his columns of February 2, 9, 18 and 25, 1965.

It sometimes appears that sheer vanity on the part of political leaders is the critical obstacle which men have to deal with. See *The Constitutionalist*, c. 8, n. 150. Be that as it may, the arguments we are beginning to hear, from official sources, about the feasibility of limited nuclear war should be firmly dealt with. See e.g., *Chicago Sun-Times*, Jan. 25, 1975, p. 12, June 15, 1975, p. 12. ·

47. Mr. Fuller observes (*The Morality of Law*, pp. 181-182):

> So far in these pages a basic question has been passed over in silence. This is the question, Who are embraced in the moral community, the community within

which men owe duties to one another and can meaningfully share their aspirations? In plain straight-forward modern jargon the question is, Who shall count as a member of the in-group? That is a problem that has bothered all moral philosophers. Within a functioning community, held together by bonds of mutual interest, the task of drafting a moral code is not difficult. It is comparatively easy to discern in this situation certain rules of restraint and cooperation that are essential for satisfactory life within the community and for the success of the community as a whole. But this confidence in moral judgment is bought at a cost, for if there are no rational principles for determining who shall be included in the community, the internal code itself rests on what appears to be an essentially arbitrary premise.

See, also, *ibid.*, pp. 182-186.

Mr. Fuller touches here upon a problem of which there can be no completely satisfactory resolution. (One cannot even begin to understand the problem, however, if one makes too much of "plain straight-forward modern jargon.") Socrates was obliged to conceal the "essentially arbitrary premise" of even his best city behind a salutary myth. *Republic* 414d-e. Thus, he recognized that the truth can be deadly. *Ibid.*, 331-332. See the lecture, "Utopia or Tyranny: The Universal Declaration of Human Rights," in Anastaplo, *Notes on the First Amendment* (note 28, above). See, also, Essay III, above, Essay VII, below. (See, on the central importance of circumstances, Essay VI, notes 19, 20, below.)

The natural-right tradition has usually recognized the related and practically irreconcilable tension, if not conflict, between the life of philosophy and the life of the city. See Essay II, above, Essay XVI, below. Consider what Thomas More reports of the founder of Utopia:

> So he made the whole matter of religion an open question and left each one free to choose what he should believe. By way of exception, he conscientiously and strictly gave injunction that no one should fall so far below the dignity of human nature as to believe that souls likewise perish with the body or that the world is the mere sport of chance and not governed by any divine providence. After this life, accordingly, vices are ordained to be punished and virtue rewarded. Such is their belief, and if anyone thinks otherwise, they do not regard him even as a member of mankind, seeing that he has lowered the lofty nature of his soul to the level of a beast's miserable body—so far are they from classing him among their citizens whose laws and customs he would treat as worthless if it were not for fear. Who can doubt that he will strive either to evade by craft the public laws of his country or to break them by violence in order to serve his own private desires when he has nothing to fear but laws and no hope beyond the body?

Utopia (New Haven: Yale University Press, 1964), p. 134. Cf. Plato, *Republic* II.

48. Edward Gibbon, *The Decline and Fall of the Roman Empire* (beginning of Chapter 42). This is said of the blind general, Belisarius. See, also, Aristotle, *Nicomachean Ethics* 1905a25-26.

Serious consideration should be given to the revision and republication of Mr. Fuller's *Law in Quest of Itself* along with the Benjamin N. Cardozo Lecture (note 2, above). It should be made clear that the *ought* may have (in some respects) the objective character of the *is*. Thus, justice may exist as "choiceworthy for its own sake and therefore 'by nature.'" See the passage quoted in the text, at note 4, above.

49. See, on the contribution of the bar to republican government in America, "Closing Argument by George Anastaplo before the Committee on Character and Fitness," 19 *Lawyers Guild Review* 143 (Winter 1959), particularly the passages quoted by Justice Black in his dissenting opinion, *In re George Anastaplo*, 366 U.S. 82, 97 (1961). See, also, *The Constitutionalist*, Appendix F; Essay IX, below; note 46, above.

50. Fuller, *The Morality of Law,* pp. 43, 176. Consider, as well, the trusteeship invoked in Anastaplo, Letter to the Editor, *University of Chicago Maroon,* January 22, 1971, p. 6 ("A Modest Proposal"):

Our principal concern as teachers, in the current economic crisis, should be with the health of the universities, especially of those schools with the traditions, intellectual resources and aspirations of the University of Chicago. To permit a university such as ours to risk permanent damage from the lack of funds would be to betray both those who have gone before and those who will follow us.

Where may funds come from? Contributions and tuition readily come to mind. An already high tuition *is* going up even more. The administration is no doubt making all the efforts it can to secure funds from private donors. Perhaps more funds would become available from donors, as well as from the government, if military expenditures should be cut. But, however that may be, there does seem to be a critical immediate need—and the only remaining untapped source immediately available is obviously the faculty, the very faculty on whom much, if not most, of the University's funds is spent year in and year out.

Is it not more important that the University flourish than that its members should continue to be as comfortable as they have become accustomed to be? Does not money have to mean more to an institution than it need mean to the scholars who make up its membership? Are there not statutory means available by which this academic community can immediately legislate for the common good a reduction of the salaries of all teaching, administrative and research personnel by at least five percent for the 1971-1972 academic year? If means are not readily available for the faculty to act thus as a body, may not this be done by a serious campaign (conducted perhaps by the Council of the University Senate) to secure from each of us a pledge to permit his salary to be reduced seven percent for 1971-1972, contingent on similar pledges being secured from (say) seventy percent of this academic community? (This contingency arrangement would avoid the injustice and possible resulting bitterness of a minority having been induced to subsidize the continued prosperity of the majority of their colleagues.)

Such an enlightened communal effort would not only serve the University nobly but could also permit us to assure one another and the country at large that there *are* for us things far more important than money. Would not this be instruction, by both precept and example, worthy of our vocations as teachers? Only one member of the University community whose salary would have been affected by this proposal responded in any way to this letter—and he was a dying man. Much more popular among the faculty and administrators of the University was Anastaplo, Letter to the Editor, *University of Chicago Maroon,* February 16, 1973, p. 7 ("Epistle to the Barbarians"), in which the mindless misconduct of certain students was called into question. (That letter is reprinted in Anastaplo, "Self-Government and the Mass Media," n. 117; correction, "American Constitutionalism," n. 32.) See Essay II, note 8, above.

51. George F. Kennan, *American Diplomacy, 1900-1950* (New York: Mentor Book, 15th printing, 1964), p. 80. The men referred to by name are John Hay, Elihu Root, Charles Evans Hughes and Henry Stimson, all trained in the law.

52. This passage is taken from the opening pages of Anastaplo, *Petition for Rehearing,* Supreme Court of the United States, June 19, 1961, *In re George Anastaplo,* 366 U.S. 82 (1961). The entire petition may be found in *The Constitutionalist,* Appendix F. See notes 28, 49, above, Essay IX, below.

Various of the points discussed in this essay are also discussed in *The Constitutionalist* (Essay I, note 1, above): e.g., c. 2, n. 31, c. 3, n. 25, c. 4, nn. 32, 45, 94, 103, 107, c. 5, nn. 37, 43, 93, c. 7, nn. 35, 59, 77, c. 8, nn. 10, 28, 45, 56, 9?, 98, 135, 181, c. 9, nn. 3, 9, 20, 22, 39. Consider, as an effort to apply to the most immediate political affairs what one can learn from "the best models, both in word and in deed, for the conduct of oneself in public as well as in private affairs," Anastaplo, Letter to the Editor, *Crete, Illinois Record*, March 29, 1973, p. 16:

> Crete is to be congratulated in having attracted to public service so fine a citizen as Liese Ricketts. It would be hard to imagine any town in this state to be better served in its Township Supervisor than Crete would be if Mrs. Ricketts should be elected next week.
>
> Our country depends on thousands of dedicated citizens contributing many hours of imaginative effort to discussions of public issues during electoral campaigns. This is the way we inform and reassure one another about what is going on and about what we should want. When dedicated citizens do become available as candidates, it shows good sense on the part of a community to give them an opportunity to serve the common good by electing them to public office.
>
> Liese Ricketts is one of those civic-minded people who very much want to serve the common good. I have known her for some time through the courses in adult education she has taken ever since she graduated from the University of Chicago twenty years ago. I have found her, as I am sure those of her constituents who know her can testify as well, to be good-natured, intelligent, conscientious and, above all, energetic.
>
> Mrs. Ricketts is the kind of person to whom a sensible man would gladly entrust the handling of his affairs. As Township Supervisor she would enjoy doing, and doing well, what to others of less dedication would soon become tiresome drudgery. Not only would she enjoy performing her official duties, but the community should enjoy watching her work.
>
> One can depend on Liese Ricketts to be "on call" twenty-four hours a day as a public official. Indeed, one might even argue that she would work so hard at this job that it would do her, her family and friends a favor *not* to elect her as Township Supervisor. But in such matters, a community is well advised to consider primarily its own interest, not that of its candidates. In short, Mrs. Ricketts is one candidate who should not be allowed to get away.

Mrs. Ricketts *was* elected—and she has been deservedly busy ever since, instructively so. See Plato, *Republic* 345d-347e, 519c-521b.

V. Liberty and Equality

1. Various of the points discussed in this essay are also discussed in *The Constitutionalist* (Essay I, note 1, above): e.g., c. 4, n. 56, c. 5, n. 31, c. 7, nn. 30, 46, 81, 119, c. 8, n. 141; in Anastaplo, "American Constitutionalism and the Virtue of Prudence" (Essay I, note 1, above): e.g., nn. 33, 40, 64; "Freedom of Speech and the First Amendment," 42 *University of Detroit Law Journal* 55 (1964); Essays II and III, above; Essays XI-XV, below. See, also, *The Constitutionalist*, c. 7, n. 124 (p. 669).

2. See, on American politics, Jaffa, *Crisis of the House Divided—An Interpretation of the Issues in the Lincoln-Douglas Debates* (Garden City: Doubleday & Co., 1959); *The Conditions of Freedom* (Baltimore: John Hopkins University Press, 1975).

3. See Stephen C. Shadegg, *What Happened to Goldwater?* (New York: Holt, Rinehart & Winston, 1965), pp. 132, 155, 157, 213, 250. Cf. Jaffa, "The Case for a Stronger National Government," in Robert A. Goldwin, ed., *A Nation of States* (Chicago: Rand McNally, 1963).

   Mr. Jaffa originated (evidently for another purpose) the imprudent and hence impractical (even though theoretically defensible) "extremism" statement which others exploited in Senator Goldwater's Acceptance Speech at the Republican National Convention of 1964: "I would remind you that extremism in the defense of liberty is no vice. And let me remind you also that moderation in the pursuit of justice is no virtue." Shadegg, *What Happened?*, p. 165. See note 25, below.

It would be interesting to watch the Republican Party begin to regain its good old name as the party of freedom by taking the dramatic position that such legislation as the Smith Act is unconstitutional. See, for an interview with Mr. Jaffa, *New York Times*, Nov. 5, 1964, p. 20.

There is about this essay on Mr. Jaffa's book, more so than about any other in this collection, something of a period piece. Indeed, much of it was "dated" when it was first published in 1965. See Anastaplo, *Notes on the First Amendment* (Essay IV, note 28, above), pp. 699-705, 715-727. (Recent additions to this essay should be apparent.) Be that as it may, the immediate issues addressed and the way they were dealt with a generation ago should give the reader, and particularly the young reader, a useful sense of the problems and language of the Cold War. But the interest served here is not merely a historical one: underlying principles *are* touched upon; fundamental oppositions may be discerned; the next crisis can be anticipated, perhaps even moderated, if the last one (with both its aspirations and its folly) is seen for what it was. Even so, it *is* prudent to recognize that freedom of expression in *this* country today is probably more extensive than at any other time in the twentieth century. (See Essay I, notes 3, 4, above, on my expulsion from the Soviet Union in 1960 and from Greece in 1970. See, also, *The Constitutionalist*, Appendix B; Essay IX, note 2, below.)

See Essay XIV, below, on the instructive parallel between Whittaker Chambers and John Dean. See, also, Essay I, note 7, above, Essay VI, notes 19, 20, Essay XI, note 7, below; also, *The Constitutionalist*, chap. 6, n. 43.

See, on the United States as a bulwark against universal tyranny, the text in Essay XV, at note 10, below. Cf. Essay XII, below. The circumstances help determine where the responsible critic puts his emphasis from time to time. See Essay XI, note 7, below; also, *The Constitutionalist*, chap. 6, n. 43.

4. It is appropriate that Mr. Jaffa's collection of essays should be dedicated to Leo Strauss. See Anastaplo, "On Leo Strauss: A Yahrzeit Remembrance," 67 *University of Chicago Magazine* 30 (Winter 1974). See, also, footnote, p. 8, above.

Other publications by Mr. Jaffa include *Thomism and Aristotelianism—A Study of the Commentary by Thomas Aquinas on the Nicomachean Ethics* (Chicago: University of Chicago Press, 1952); "Aristotle," in Leo Strauss and Joseph Cropsey, eds., *History of Political Philosophy* (Chicago: Rand McNally, 1963); "The Limits of Politics: *King Lear*, Act I, Scene i," in Allan Bloom, *Shakespeare's Politics* (New York: Basic Books, 1964). (A critique of the *King Lear* article should begin with Mr. Jaffa's suggestion, in note 36 of that article, about the murder of Cordelia. Does not "theory" ruthlessly usurp the place of "practice" in that suggestion? See note 25, below.)

5. The priority indicated in his title is reinforced by his suggestion that liberty for Americans is grounded upon equality. See, e.g., Jaffa, *Equality & Liberty: Theory and Practice in American Politics* (New York: Oxford University Press, 1965), pp. 218, 167. See, also, Isocrates, *Areopagiticus* 20. Cf. "American Constitutionalism," n. 57.

6. Thus, an experienced attorney could say to me in 1960, while I was in Washington for the oral arguments in my unsuccessful Illinois bar admission case (and that of Raphael Konigsberg, who was seeking admission to the California bar), "If Konigsberg and you were Negroes, you would have been admitted long ago!" See *In re Anastaplo*, 366 U.S. 82 (1961); *The Constitutionalist*, Appendix F; Essay IX, below.

Compare a *Chicago Sun-Times* report (July 26, 1974, p. 2) upon a United States Supreme Court 5-4 ruling against busing in Detroit:

The ruling seemed to signal an end to an era in Supreme Court history. It was the first time since 1954, when the justices ordered dismantlement of "separate but equal" schools, that they voted against further racial integration in education.

The Court (within a day of this decision) announced its 8-0 decision on the Presidential privilege claimed by Mr. Nixon. See Essay IV, note 19, above, Essay XIV, below.

7. The approach to be adopted at any time should take into account what is then necessary for the nurture and preservation of good men as well as of the community. Mr. Jaffa has high praise for the American regime (*Equality & Liberty*, pp. 114-115):

Yet the American experience ranks in some ways, in my opinion, with the Athens of Pericles and Socrates, with the Rome of Brutus and Cicero, with the empire-church of Dante and Aquinas, with the England of Elizabeth and Shakespeare (as well as that of Macaulay and Churchill). The American form of government, in its failures as well as in its successes, reveals possibilities in the nature of man as a political animal as distinctive in their way as any revealed by any other regime in the great drama of Western history, possibilities that may have gone unrevealed but for their American apocalypse.

He reminds us (*ibid.*, p. 202), "Natural right is concerned, rather, with a means of evaluating the results of proposed courses of action." But what is one to make of the puzzling observation (*ibid.*, p. 193), that "in a world of the blind a single man with vision could not believe in the reality of the visible world"? Does this, too, reflect a preference for equality over liberty? Cf. *ibid.*, pp. 177-78; also, Plato, *Republic* 516c-517a. Could he not *see* that the others were blind?

8. Mr. Jaffa doubts that our institutions can be regarded as "designed" (*Equality & Liberty*, p. 4):

One can, I think, consider the American political system as essentially unplanned, if one considers that the party system is the central or prime feature of the whole. For the party system, or political parties as we now know them, were certainly no ingredient in the government envisaged by the founding fathers. But did not the original design or plan anticipate and permit adaptation to unforeseeable circumstances? The party system may be seen as serving in the role originally intended to be played by the States, by a class of educated men (including lawyers), and by what we know as the Electoral College.

Consider, as reflecting an opinion about the design of our federal system, my statement of June 21, 1970, "To the People of the State of Illinois" (which was published in several Illinois newspapers: e.g., *Chicago Tribune*, July 2, 1970, sec. 1, p. 20; *Chicago Daily News*, July 6, 1970, p. 14):

The Illinois Constitutional Convention sitting in Springfield has worked since last winter on a new constitution which threatens to be as cumbersome as the interest-ridden and suspicion-laden document (of some sixty pages) we have had since 1870. It should be possible for conscientious delegates of the experience ours have acquired in this convention to prepare in the remaining months scheduled for their proceedings a flexible State constitution stripped of all elaborations better left to legislation, executive decrees and judicial interpretations.

The familiarity and competence developed by our delegates with respect to State constitutional problems since the first of the year should now make it for them far more desirable and far easier than it would have been at the beginning of their deliberations to pare down our constitution so as to permit intelligent and efficient government in this State. Such a contribution to responsive and responsible government could help persuade American citizens to take our traditionally useful "State sovereignty" more seriously than many are now inclined to do.

The government of the State of Illinois could be defined (in a State constitution kept to bare essentials) as possessing all powers not delegated exclusively to the federal government by the Constitution of the United States and not prohibited therein to State governments, subject to such limitations (including, perhaps, with respect to taxation) as may be spelled out in a State bill of rights. Provision would also be made in such a State constitution for the selection, functions, privileges and regulation of the officers of the various branches of the State government, for the powers within the State of designated local governments, and for subsequent amendment of the new constitution.

All this could be best provided for in less than a dozen pages, with most details of implementation left for periodic adaptation to changing circumstances by the branches of the State government established pursuant to the constitution. By thus displaying self-discipline and self-confidence, Illinois would demonstrate to the country, at a time when more and more people are looking to the federal government to "get things done," that "States' rights" need not foster either prejudice or paralysis.

See *The Constitutionalist*, chapter 7; *ibid.*, p. 624 (on an "angel theory of constitutional law"). Cf. *ibid.*, p. 47. See, also, Anastaplo, "Federal Prosecutions and American Politics: A Note of Caution," *Chicago Tribune*, April 22, 1973, sec. 2, p. 3.

9. Student unrest in this country points up the problem. University administrators and faculty naturally regard themselves as superior to students. No doubt they are in many respects, which the students themselves recognize. The model for faculty behavior could well be that provided by Tocqueville, who instructs the true aristocrat how to deal fruitfully with a rising and vital democratic spirit which will not be denied.

Two critical problems have recently been brought, dramatically and effectively, to the attention of the academic community. We must devise means of adequate consultation with students on university matters affecting their lives. We must define publicly, before it is too late, the proper relation between a free university and our government. See Anastaplo, "The Daring of Moderation: Student Power and *The Melian Dialogue*," 78 *School Review* 451 (August 1970); Letter to the Editor, *University of Chicago Maroon*, June 24, 1966, p. 5.

10. Just as the issue of the proper treatment of the Negro tests American dedication to the cause of equality. See Essay XV, below.

11. He refers to "the evil teachings of National Socialism and of Communism" (*Equality & Liberty*, p. 15); he states that "the moral essence of Marxism and of Nazism is the same" (*ibid.*, p. 16); Nazism and Communism are identified as "foul doctrines hostile to human rights" (*ibid.*, p. 30).

Mr. Jaffa might even endorse the argument made by Senator Paul Douglas in the course of his 1966 reelection campaign, in which "he characterized Communism as being 'worse' than Nazism, because, while sharing the totalitarianism of Hitler's regime, Communism 'hypocritically' represents itself as standing for democratic ideals." *University of Chicago Maroon*, Feb. 18, 1965, p. 1. See note 16, below. But he surely would not go as far as did Richard M. Nixon in the quotation found in note 23, below. (I was told by Senator Douglas, several months before his unsuccessful reelection campaign began, that he did not believe the Vietnam War [which he supported and against which I had been speaking] would figure much in that election. He seemed to me, in this respect, out of touch with what was happening in the country, and I so indicated to him in that conversation. Even so, I prepared the following election-eve letter which was published in several Illinois newspapers in November, 1966: "Can we doubt that Paul Douglas will be remembered as one of the distinguished legislators of this century? Do we want to be remembered as the constituency that tired of its senator's intelligent and imaginative dedication to the common good?" See Essay IV, note 52, above.)

See Leo Strauss, *Liberalism, Ancient and Modern* (New York: Basic Books, 1968), pp. 230-231.

12. See S. L. Shneiderman, "A Visit with George Lukacs," *New York Times Book Review*, May 9, 1965, p. 30. See, also, on the self-contradictory nature of Nazism, Jaffa, *Equality & Liberty*, pp. 202-205.

The distinctions drawn by Karl Barth are significant and should moderate any disposition one may have to lump together the Nazis and the Communists. His 1958 "Letter to a Pastor in the German Democratic Republic" should be compared with his declarations against the Nazis in the 1930s. See, for instance, Karl Barth and Johannes Hamel, *How to Serve God in a Marxist Land* (New York: Association Press, 1959); Arthur Frey, *Cross and Swastika—The Ordeal of the German Church* (London: Student Christian Movement Press, 1938). The reader is advised to read the "Letter to a Pastor" with the care and compassion evident in its composition. See, also, "The secret letter from Alexander Dubcek," *Chicago Tribune*, April 13, 1975; "Czech Red invites Dubcek to leave," *ibid.*, April 17, 1975, p. 13. See, as well, note 22, below.

See, on "property," Essay X, Prologue, Epilogue, Essay XIII, note 2, below.

13. May not this conflict be subordinate to (if not even a product of) "the encounter between global technology and modern man," which Martin Heidegger regards as critical today? *An Introduction to Metaphysics* (New York: Anchor Books, Doubleday & Co., 1961), p. 166. Thus, Professor Heidegger evidently regards the Marxist interpretation of history as superior to all others today (except for his own?) because of what he considers its greater awareness of the alienation and homelessness of modern man. Indeed, he continues to see as "the inner truth and greatness" of the Nazi movement that it faced up to this "encounter." *Ibid.*, p. 166. See, on Martin Heidegger, Anastaplo, "On Leo Strauss," pp. 37-38; *The Constitutionalist*, p. 815.

14. Mr. Jaffa recognizes the danger of denying freedom to Communists, but evidently has no constitutional principle to fall back on with which to check abuses (*Equality & Liberty*, p. 181):

> Communists and Nazis, I maintain, have no right to the use of free speech in a free society. However, whether it is wise or expedient to deny them its use is another matter. I believe that the United States is a sufficiently civilized and a sufficiently stable community to bear the advocacy of almost anything, whether it be national socialism, Communism, or cannibalism."

See, also, *ibid.*, pp. 30, 44-45, 81-82, 86, 113, 179-180, 189; Essay VI, note 12 below. Cf. *ibid.*, pp. 16-17, 21-22, 186-187; also, the text at note 17, Essay VI, below. (Is the materialism criticized by Mr. Jaffa [*ibid.*, p. 187] as distinctively Marxist as he implies?)

> Mr. Jaffa does not consider it imprudent to argue, "To say that the Constitution protects the right to deny that all men are created equal is as much as to say that it protects the right to deny any obligations to obey its laws." *Ibid.*, p. 189. But have there not been good and law-abiding men who have doubted that all men are created equal (to say nothing of whether they have been "created")? See, e.g., *ibid.*, pp. 129-130, 137-138. Cf. Essay IV, note 47, above, Essay VI, n. 37, below.

15. See Jaffa, "Lincoln and the Cause of Freedom," 17 *National Review* 829 (Nov. 21, 1965).

16. See, for Lincoln's "model of charity," Jaffa, *Equality & Liberty*, pp. 166-168. Are circumstances in the United States today as serious as those Lincoln confronted?

Cf. *ibid.*, pp. 169-171. Have not our "security" measures weakened rather than strengthened us? See note 23, below. Certainly, the volatile, short-lived and perhaps even misconceived Weimar Republic is a dubious precedent or warning for republicans who go back to 1776. See *ibid.*, p. 183. Cf. Strauss, *Liberalism, Ancient and Modern*, pp. 224-225. See, also, Winston S. Churchill, "The Ex-Kaiser," *Great Contemporaries* (London: Odhams Press, 1937).

Mr. Jaffa's strictures on Communism—and, for that matter, on Nazism as well —need to be moderated by writings such as those of Milton Mayer: "Christ under Communism," in his *What Can A Man Do?* (Chicago: University of Chicago Press, 1964); *They Thought They Were Free* (Chicago: University of Chicago Press, 1955); "Ohne Mich," *Progressive*, March 1951, p. 12. Cf. *The Constitutionalist*, pp. 701-702. (Mr. Jaffa, Mr. Mayer and Senator Douglas share the unphilosophical, but engaging, distinction of being much more moderate and far less contentious in private conversation than in public, at least in conversations with me. See note 11, above.)

See, on Lincoln and the Civil War, Essay XV, note 15, below.

17. R. H. Tawney, *Religion and the Rise of Capitalism* (New York: Mentor Books, 1947), p. 39. (Mr. Jaffa, in his work on Thomas Aquinas, provides us a valuable study of the greatest of the Schoolmen. See note 4, above.) In a sense, Marxism may be understood as a way for certain deprived peoples to get where we are before we do! Are the "fair shares" insisted upon by Marxism dependent in large part upon a technology developed elsewhere? That is, is contemporary Communism essentially parasitic? Consider, for example, the implications of the description of medical services available in Shanghai, John Kenneth Galbraith, *A China Passage* (Boston: Houghton Mifflin Co., 1973), pp. 126-127. See Essay XIV, note 12, below. (Similarly, among us, does "medicine for the people" mean less research and hence a lower level of medical service for everyone?)

Marxism considers itself a science or, at least, a social teaching based upon science—but does it not regard as natural what is merely conventional and regard as conventional what may really be natural? Is it not, with its relatively unsophisticated notions about justice, essentially a distribution system rather than a production system—but a distribution system which, in effect, makes industrial production less efficient than it need be? Is not continual regimentation needed to keep most people from experimenting with private enterprise—at least at a time when material gratification itself is considered legitimate? Does not Marxism endorse the gratification of consumption at the expense of a selfish but nevertheless productive thrift?

It does not seem to be appreciated by ideological economists how much the entities (such as countries) to which economic "laws" are said to apply are themselves determined by political opinions and decisions. (Is there not in man an instinctive yearning for his own, upon which family feeling, the desire for property, and patriotism all draw?) Nor does it seem to be generally appreciated that the talented managers of large industrial corporations are really our servants: they are, by and large, underpaid, considering that they are (whatever their intentions or motives may be) devoting the only lives they have primarily to our comfort and gratification, to say nothing of the opportunity they provide to some to be assured of the sustained leisure necessary for a truly human life.

See, on Communism, *The Constitutionalist*, p. 812; Essay I, note 4, above; note 21, below.

See, also, John XXIII, *Pacem in Terris* (1963), pp. 158-159; the concluding paragraph of the United Nations speech of Paul VI (October 4, 1965); a poem by Secretary of the Interior Stewart L. Udall, "On Seeing a Photograph of Citizen Khrushchev at an Art Exhibition (1965)," *New York Times*, October 31, 1965, p. 45 (reprinted from the *Hudson Review*, Autumn 1965).

18. The influence of Christianity on Communism is evident, especially in the legitimation of radical equality and of the expectations thereupon nurtured. Thus J. M. Keynes could observe, in a valuable report, "Leninism is a combination of two things which Europeans have kept for some centuries in different compartments of the soul—religion and business." *A Short View of Russia* (London: L. & V. Woolf, 1926), p. 11.

See, on the secret desires of most men (which would be acted upon "as speedily as circumstances would permit"), Plato, *Republic* 359b-360e, 619c-d. (The words quoted are from the charge to the jury approved in *Dennis* v. *United States*, 341 U.S. 494 [1951].)

19. Our judicial institutions work best when limited to the consideration of everyday activities. That something is wrong with the Communist Party prosecutions is further revealed even by the fact that criminal trials should run through many, many months and that they should require many thousands of pages of testimony. It makes one doubt whether there has been *a* deed committed which citizens, including accused and accusers, can fairly easily ascertain to be criminal. (It is also hard to conceive of a "crime" on the part of the management of a corporation which takes months of detailed analysis and economic argument to establish in court.)

See Anastaplo, "Due Process of Law—An Introduction," 42 *University of Detroit Law Journal* 195 (1964); *The Constitutionalist*, Appendix D.

It should be acknowledged, despite the salutary argument in the text, that more may properly be done in defense of a just regime than of an unjust.

20. It was sad to observe recently [I could write in 1965] the public reaction to the sentimental request of Robert G. Thompson—a Second World War hero (Distinguished Service Cross) who was subsequently imprisoned under the Smith Act as a Communist Party leader—that he be buried in Arlington Military Cemetery. Much of our patriotism these days is characterized by a lack of grace and of generosity, to say nothing of gratitude. Cf. Dorothy Day, "On Pilgrimage," *The Catholic Worker*, March 1957, p. 3.

21. Mr. Jaffa's more temperate, and hence less harmful, case against Communism is implied in his chapter, "The Teaching Concerning Political Moderation," *Crisis of the House Divided* (see, e.g., p. 421, n. 29). See, also, Leo Strauss, *The City and Man* (Chicago: Rand McNally, 1964), pp. 3-6; Essay I, note 4, above.

The most sobering critique of Communism, however, may be found in such unintentional self-revelation as is seen in the description of the execution of Barambayev (a soldier) in Alexander Beck's novel, *On the Forward Fringe* (reprinted as "Judge Me," in Joshua Kunitz, ed., *Russian Literature Since the Revolution* [New York: Boni & Gaer, 1948], p. 811). See note 17, above, Essay XIV, section vii, below. See, also, Editorial, "Which Way Do the Refugees Flee?" *Wall Street Journal*, March 26, 1975; Essay VII, note 4, below. Cf. Aleksandr Solzhenitsyn, *The Gulag Archipelago* (New York: Harper & Row, 1973), p. 92, n. 42: "It has always been impossible to learn the truth about anything in our country—now, and always, and from the beginning." Consider, also, Karl Marx, *Capital* (New York: Modern Library, n.d.), p. 614: "this Russian soil, so fruitful of all infamies."

See, for a penetrating criticism of the racism at the core of Nazism, Montesquieu, *The Spirit of the Law*, book 15, chap. 5; and of the hedonism at the core of Communism, Nietzsche, *Thus Spake Zarathustra*, "Zarathustra's Prologue," sec. 5 (on "the last man"). See note 17, above.

One reassuring feature of the victory in 1975 of North Vietnam and the Viet Cong is that *spirit* (national, even more than ideological, spirit) prevailed over money and materiel. May not this even be an argument for American "idealism" against Communist "materialism"? It should also be noticed, however, that the more tyrannical regime prevailed in Vietnam over the less tyrannical. (Even so, is not Marxist tyranny permanently vulnerable in a way that a just, liberal regime need not be? See Essay XIV, note 12, below.)

22. See note 13, above. Professor Heidegger's disgrace arises from the provincial reliance he placed upon Nazism in confronting these problems. The distinction between Communism and Nazism is reflected in the fact that Georg Lukacs' lifelong association with Communism evidently has not raised among men of good will the moral problems engendered by Martin Heidegger's association of only a few years with Nazism. See note 12, above; Essay XVII, below.

23. Does not our Dominican Republic military intervention suggest that we have yet to learn how to make sophisticated identifications and distinctions respecting Communism? Cf. *National Review*, Feb. 8, 1966, pp. 107-114. The limits of American sophistication in this respect are suggested in the naïveté of a former Vice President who made his national reputation as an expert opponent of Communism in the United States:

The chairman of the national board of the Boys Club of America, Richard M. Nixon, has somberly announced that there have been some untoward consequences of Atty. Gen. Nicholas Katzenbach's recent listing of the DuBois Club (pronounced DooBOYS) as a communist front.

It seems that some Boys Club supporters, hearing the news on the air, have been wondering if they have been contributing to a subversive outfit. The Boys Club in Washington, D.C. got a bomb threat over the telephone from some character with more zeal than intelligence. Nixon thinks the confusion was deliberately invited by the DuBois Club's founders—"an almost classic example of communist deception and duplicity," he said.

Chicago Tribune, March 14, 1966, p. 16. See, also, *New Yorker*, March 19, 1966, p. 41.

The citizen can only hope that the sacrifices of Americans abroad are based on less ludicrous estimates than this of "Communist deception and duplicity." But one can detect here the state of mind ("more zeal than intelligence") that has virtually denied the existence of mainland China for almost two decades. The thoughtful citizen, concerned about how to address himself to Administration policy in Vietnam, can profit from Mr. Jaffa's discussion, in his chapter on patriotism and morality (*Equality & Liberty*, pp. 67-76), of Congressman Abraham Lincoln's attitude toward the American prosecution of the Mexican War. See Essay IV, section vi, above, Essay XII, below.

One can also detect here (it may now be added) the state of mind ("an almost classic example of communist deception and duplicity") which contributed to Mr. Nixon's Watergate entanglement. See Essay XIV, below.

24. See "Beliefs and Principles of the John Birch Society," 108 *Congressional Record* E4292 (June 12, 1962); Alpheus T. Mason, *Free Government in the Making* (New York: Oxford University Press, 1965), pp. 852-856.

25. We find in this concluding essay Mr. Jaffa's warning against the imprudence of substituting political theory for practical judgment. See note 4, above, Essay XV, section iii, below.

Certainly, experimentation (including experimentation in either liberation or repression) should be approached with caution. See, e.g., Anastaplo, "Politics versus Ideology: The Greek Case," *Journal of the Hellenic Diaspora*, Fall 1974, p. 28. Consider, as an application of longstanding principles and "prosaic common sense" to everyday circumstances, my letter to the editor about an airport in Lake Michigan (*Chicago Tribune*, Dec. 5, 1969; *Chicago Daily News*, Dec. 5, 1969; *Chicago Sun-Times*, Dec. 16, 1969):

Would it not be prudent, before we begin to sink a quarter of a billion dollars into a lake airport, to conduct at announced times repeated simulated landings and takeoffs to and from the spot in Lake Michigan where the proposed airport would be located? Such simulations could give us all a far better idea than we can now have of precisely what we would have to contend with, especially with respect to traffic patterns and noise, should the airport be put in the lake.

Consider as well the "take it easy" caution in the letter reprinted in Anastaplo, "American Constitutionalism" (Essay I, note 1, above), n. 33, Essay XIV, note 17, below. (An edited version of "Politics versus Ideology" has been reprinted in 121 *Congressional Record* E1746 [April 15, 1975].)

26. See Heidegger, *An Introduction to Metaphysics*, p. 13:

> . . . But what is great can only begin great. Its beginning is in fact the greatest thing of all. A small beginning belongs only to the small, whose dubious greatness it is to diminish all things; small are the beginnings of decay, though it may later become great in the sense of the enormity of total annihilation. The great begins great, maintains itself only through the free recurrence of greatness within it, and if it is great ends also in greatness. So it is with the philosophy of the Greeks. It ended in greatness with Aristotle. Only prosaic common sense and the little man imagine that the great must endure forever, and equate this duration with eternity.

Cf. Anastaplo, "On Leo Strauss," p. 33; notes 13, 22, below. See Dante, *Inferno*, XXVI, 112-120; Strauss, *What Is Political Philosophy?* (Glencoe: The Free Press, 1959), pp. 27, 35, 37-38, 54-55; Essay X, Epilogue, below.

VI. Law and Morality

1. W. S. Holdsworth, *Some Lessons from Our Legal History* (New York: Macmillan Co., 1928), p. 160. See, also, J. J. Rousseau, *Social Contract*, IV, vii. "Morality" is used in this essay, rather than "ethics," to conform to the usage of the first author discussed (Patrick Devlin).

The first half of this essay is developed from a talk, "Law and Morality: How to Write a Law School Exam," delivered March 31, 1966, before the Law Club, University of Michigan Law School. See Essay IX, section viii, below. The essay itself was originally prepared, pursuant to a commission from the *University of Pennsylvania Law Review*, but had to be submitted by me elsewhere. See Essay IV, note 1, above. I had occasion to observe at that time, in a letter to the editor of another legal journal, "I know from experience that it is almost impossible to get an American law review to take seriously the notion that something should be printed as submitted. Indeed, editors have told me that I am unusual in my concern about such matters. I mention this to let you know that I *am* considered unreasonable." The presumptuousness of editors today, and not just the student editors of law reviews, both reflects and contributes to the current difficulty of promoting careful reading and careful writing. Thus, the careful ordering of one's material is always vulnerable. See note 52, below.

2. See, as an introduction to this essay, Essay IV, above. Several of the points touched upon here are developed in *The Constitutionalist* (Essay I, note 1, above), appropriate citations to which may be found in Essay IV, note 52, above.

See, also, Eugene V. Rostow, *The Sovereign Prerogative* (New Haven: Yale University Press, 1962), p. 79: "Men often say that one cannot legislate morality. I should say that we legislate hardly anything else. All movements of law reform seek to carry out certain social judgments as to what is fair and just in the conduct of society." Consider, as well, Simonides' dictum (XIII, 95), "The city is the teacher of the man."

3. J. S. Mill, *On Liberty*, chap. 1. It will be convenient in this essay to refer to this position as "utilitarian." See note 23, below.
4. See the *Report of the Committee on Homosexual Offences and Prostitution* (generally known as the *Wolfenden Report*) (London, 1957), para. 13:
    We have therefore worked with our own formulation of the function of the criminal law so far as it concerns the subjects of this enquiry. In this field, its function, as we see it, is to preserve public order and decency, to protect the citizen from what is offensive or injurious, and to provide sufficient safeguards against exploitation and corruption of others, particularly those who are specially vulnerable because they are young, weak in body or mind, inexperienced, or in a state of special physical, official or economic dependence.
    See, also, F. A. Hayek, *Constitution of Liberty* (Chicago: University of Chicago Press, 1960), p. 451, n. 20.
5. *Wolfenden Report*, para. 61. The reservations recorded by James Adair, a member of the Wolfenden Committee, should be noticed. See, also, note 16, below.
6. See Anastaplo, "The Declaration of Independence," 9 *St. Louis University Law Journal* 390, 409-411 (1965) (as corrected in Anastaplo, "American Constitutionalism" [Essay I, note 1, above], n. 1). See, also, Essay V, above.
7. The Hobbes quotation is from Part IV, Chapter xlvi, of *Leviathan;* the Milton, from Book X of *Paradise Lost* (Adam thus addresses Eve; similar sentiments may be found in Milton's *Areopagitica*).
8. The first of these lectures, the 1959 Maccabaean Lecture in Jurisprudence read at the British Academy, spoke to the issues suggested by the passages from paragraphs 13 and 61 of the *Wolfenden Report* quoted above. The Lecture aroused considerable interest in legal journals.
    The collection of lectures (to which has been given the Maccabaean Lecture title, "The Enforcement of Morality," and which was published in London by the Oxford Press in 1965) will be cited hereafter as *E.M.*
9. *E.M.*, pp. ix-x. "So far," Lord Devlin adds, "the criticism has been destructive in character, offering an opening for some further positive thought on both these points." See the text at note 52, Essay II, above.
10. *E.M.*, pp. 24-25. See Bacon, *New Atlantis;* Hobbes, *Leviathan* (Oakeshott ed., 1955), III, xxxvi, pp. 284-285, xxxvii, pp. 290-291, xliii, pp. 387-388, 394-395; Rousseau, *Social Contract*, IV, viii; Essay II, above.
11. *E.M.*, pp. 9-10. See Essay III, above.
12. *E.M.*, p. 111. See Tacitus, *History*, III, 51, 72, IV, 1; Constantine Cavafy, "Waiting for the Barbarians." Consider, also, *E.M.*, p. 113:
    In the same way, while a few people getting drunk in private cause no problem at all, widespread drunkenness, whether in private or public, would create a public problem. The line between drunkenness that creates a social problem of sufficient magnitude to justify the intervention of the law and that which does not, cannot be drawn on the distinction between private indulgence and public sobriety. It is a practical one, based on an estimate of what can safely be tolerated whether in public or in private, and shifting from time to time as circumstances change. The licensing laws coupled with high taxation may be all that is needed. But if more be needed there is no doctrinal answer even to complete prohibition. It cannot be said that so much is the law's business but more is not.
    See Essay V, note 14, above. Cf. Essay IV, note 19, above.
13. *E.M.*, p. 110.
14. *E.M.*, p. 43.
15. Lord Devlin says that "only the criminal law can be used to enforce moral standards . . ." *E.M.*, p. 52. Is this distinction between the two instruments ("of teaching, which is doctrine, and of enforcement, which is the law"), quoted above

in the text at note 10, sound? Cf. *E.M*., pp. 82-83 and the passage quoted in note 12, above. See, also, note 24, below, with respect to various contradictions among Lord Devlin's statements.

See President Washington's First Inaugural Address.

16. The Wolfenden Committee observed that "it seems to us that the law itself probably makes little difference to the amount of homosexual behaviour which actually occurs; whatever the law may be there will always be strong social forces opposed to homosexual behaviour." *Wolfenden Report*, para. 58. See, also, *ibid.*, para. 226. But on what do such "strong social forces" depend? To what extent do they depend on the law and on private morality guided and shaped by the law? Does not much of the discussion of such matters by those taking the position of the Wolfenden Committee presuppose the continued operation of a desire for respectability "as a motive force on the individual"? *E.M.*, p. 74. What happens to the restraints of respectability when mobility and urban anonymity increase even as morality is designated a strictly private affair?

Did not the Wolfenden Committee find themselves, as a *public* body, *caring* (despite their stated principles) about the extent of what they as public citizens would consider private acts of immorality? When utilitarians acknowledge the legitimacy of the law's concern about the corruption of youth, what standard of morality is drawn upon? What if an alleged corrupter of a youth should advance the defense that he had carefully instructed the youth never to exhibit publicly his corruption? May the law legitimately be concerned about such corruption? Is not the separation of law from morality related to the distinction between state and society? "Social forces" are now expected, with aid from the family, to do without law what was once done by the *polis* (the city, which included what we know as state, church and society). See Essay II, above, Essay VII, below.

17. Harry V. Jaffa, *Equality & Liberty* (New York: Oxford University Press, 1965, p. 189 (Essay V, above). See Aristotle, *Nicomachean Ethics*, X, xi. Cf. Plato, *Republic* 619b-e; Aristotle, *N. Ethics*, VI, xii.

18. Consider Devlin, *Trial by Jury* (London: Stevens, 1956), p. 121:

> No one who has held [judicial office under the common law of England] can fail to be conscious of the power that flows, not from any quality of his own but from the position that has been made for him by the judges of England. This, far more than any personal talent that he may have, disposes a jury to listen with respect to the views of the judge on fact as well as on law.

Consider, also, Mr. Justice Devlin's humane yet competent charge to the jury in Sybille Bedford, *The Trial of Dr. Adams* (New York: Simon & Shuster, 1959), esp. pp. 236-237.

19. See, on the significance of the historical with respect to English law, Devlin, *Trial by Jury*, pp. 5, 41, 48, 57, 72, 88, 97, 109. "What matters," Lord Devlin concludes his *Samples of Law-Making* (New York: Oxford University Press, 1962), "is the law of England." See, also, notes 24, 46, below, Essay II, notes 22, 27, Essay III, above.

Democracy and the law of England may happen to be the best political institutions available today, but something more than history, a proprietary interest and familiarity is required to justify such an assessment. See notes 25, 26, 38, below. Consider, as well, with respect to all the practical problems I address in this collection of essays, my concluding remarks for an address of March 7, 1974 before a citywide conference of Chicago public school principals, "The Babylonian Captivity of the Chicago Public School System" (65 *Chicago Principals Reporter* 7, 17 [Spring 1975]):

> But difficult as present circumstances may be, they have been far worse. Things are looking up: there *are* signs of hope. Besides, it is well to remember—as we gather just a mile or so south of old Fort Dearborn—that difficult as things

are these days in Chicago, they were far worse here, in almost every way, a couple hundred years ago. They have probably been far worse as well, in those days and perhaps to this day, in those countries from which your forebears came to these shores. If it is any comfort to you, it can safely be predicted that things will no doubt be worse—in fact, far, far worse—in this place and in some distant time.

That is, after all, the way of human existence. Human happiness lies in making the best of whatever confronts us—and this requires a tolerable understanding of what has been known and done by those who have preceded us. It also requires that we not take ourselves too seriously, even as we embark upon challenging adventures.

. . . No doubt, generations after us will come to ignore issues by which we are consumed and will fervently devote themselves instead to problems which we have not bothered to notice. Things do manage to work their way out among a sensible people just as things do manage to get messed up from time to time, no matter how sensible a people may be. That is to say, chance *is* important in human affairs.

It is useful as well as instructive, if not even entertaining, to be able to step back now and then and to contemplate our troubles in a detached way. Is not creative detachment the privilege, the duty and the salvation of the humane individual? Should not such detachment contribute something precious to the productive, decent and interesting life to which you as educators have been so fortunate as to have dedicated yourselves?

Consider, on the dependence of property upon chance, Essay XII, section iii, below. See notes 39, 43, below. See, also, notes 20, 46, below.

See Essay I, note 1, above, Essay XVII, note 17, below.

20. *E.M.*, p. 118. The only restriction Lord Devlin recognizes upon the power of society seems to be that it judge "honestly." *E.M.*, p. 118. But should not competence be at least as important a criterion as honesty in such matters? Thus, one of Mr. Nixon's unrepentant White House lawyers recently asked, "Would you rather have a competent scoundrel or an honest boob in office?" *Chicago Sun-Times*, March 11, 1975, p. 10. Machiavelli comes to mind—and the recognition of necessities upon which he insisted, a recognition which (he believed) even makes it possible to conquer fortune much more often than had been formerly appreciated. See Essay XII, note 2, below; also, *The Constitutionalist*, chap. 6, n. 43.

Consider, on the relation of chance to necessity and how this may bear on the writing and reading of books, note 46, below. Consider, also, Malcolm P. Sharp, "Crosskey, Anastaplo, and Meiklejohn on the United States Constitution," 20 *University of Chicago Law School Record* 18, n. 51 (Spring 1973); *The Constitutionalist* (itself something of an experiment in disciplined elaboration), e.g., c. 2, nn. 1, 39, c. 6, n. 43, c. 7, nn. 23, 120, c. 9, nn. 12, 39; Essay II, note 13, above. Cf. the canny contrivances of Henry James' *The Turn of the Screw*.

Two lectures devoted by Lord Devlin to the advocacy of "popular morality" happen to be the only ones of the seven in his book delivered in the United States. They are clearly (necessarily so?) the weakest in the book.

21. See *E.M.*, pp. 93-94, for a disparagment of "the Superior Person" and of the "pursuit of absolute truth" coupled with a recognition of "the superior mind." Cf. *E.M.*, p. 100 ("the unending search for truth"). See notes 24, 37, below.

22. See Plato, *Crito* 44d. See, also, Jacob Klein, "History and the Liberal Arts," *Proceedings of the Colloquium on the Liberal Arts Curriculum* (Saint Mary's College, 1965).

23. The utilitarians are right in one respect: if nature and reason are not decisive in

the determination of moral values, then any morality should do. See Essay XV, section iv, below; notes 33, 35, below.

But is not the utilitarians' own use of reason essentially that seen in Hobbes' memorable lines, "For the Thoughts are to the Desires as Scouts and Spies, to range abroad and find the way to the Things desired . . ."? *Leviathan*, I, viii, p. 46. Cf., e.g., Aristotle, *N. Ethics*, I, vi-vii, V, vii, VII, xiii-xiv, IX, vi-viii.

24. *E.M.*, p. 17; also, pp. viii-ix. The subordinate place of reason in the affairs of man is evident in various of Lord Devlin's works: e.g., *E.M.*, pp. viii, x, 14-15, 17, 86, 126 (also, note 29, below); *Trial by Jury*, pp. 99-100, 102, 103, 121-124; *Samples of Law-Making*, pp. 19, 115.

This subordination of reason is reflected in the confusion found in his works with respect to many of his important points. Is this what comes of making so much of the "illogical compromises" of English law and of the belief that "in law-making logic will always be defeated by necessity"? *E.M.*, pp. vi, 83.

The opinions held by Lord Devlin as a sensible man of practical affairs are acknowledged in sections i and ii of this essay; his opinions as a modern "jurisprudent" (*E.M.*, p. 4) are examined in sections iii and iv of this essay.

25. This is not to deny that disgust and indignation may be usefully exploited by the legislator who knows what he is doing. But if he himself is moved by disgust and indignation, his judgment is likely to be impaired. Preferable is the attitude of the elders of Troy toward Helen and the attitude of the rulers of Socrates' best city toward the poets: they recognize the attractions and even the merits of that which they would expel from the city as a danger. Homer, *Iliad*, III, 156-160 (also, Aristotle, *N. Ethics* 1109b10); Plato, *Republic* 397e-398a. (Consider as well Odysseus and the Sirens: Homer, *Odyssey*, XII; *The Constitutionalist*, c. 8, n. 95.)

Thus, for example, one must remain on guard against Edmund Burke's indignation-laden rhetoric. Perhaps it is only natural that anyone (such as Burke) who sees the good primarily in terms of the ancestral should lay himself open to blinding passion on behalf of "one's own." The critical qualification in an argument is apt to be overlooked when "one's own" is at stake. A poetic, and hence more disciplined, version of Burke's conservative sentiments is reflected in W. B. Yeats' "Meditations in Time of Civil War."

26. *E.M.*, p. 9. See, also, *E.M.*, pp. 118-119. May not "society" be persuaded (as in 1776) that the rebels are right and the government wrong? The emphasis on the judgment of history may reflect an undue concern for mere survival.

Consider Ralph Waldo Emerson, *English Traits*, chap. 6:

The English power resides also in their dislike of change. They have difficulty in bringing their reason to act, and on all occasions use their memory first. As soon as they have rid themselves of some grievance and settled the better practice, they make haste to fix it as a finality, and never wish to hear of alteration more.

See *The Constitutionalist*, c. 5, nn. 25, 27. See, also, notes 43, 49, below.

27. See Anastaplo, "The Declaration of Independence," pp. 398-403, 411-413. Cf. *The Constitutionalist*, c. 9, n. 32.

28. A useful study on this subject is Jaffa, *Thomism and Aristotelianism* (Chicago: University of Chicago Press, 1952), with its suggestive epigraph from Winston Churchill: "It is baffling to reflect that what men call honour does not correspond always to Christian ethics." See Essay IV, note 43, Essay V, note 4, above. Cf. note 35, below.

29. Christianity must be taken, for Lord Devlin's purposes, as incorporating Judaism. *E.M.*, p. 19. If he had restricted himself to the proposition that religion may be useful and often necessary for general morality, there would be no need to chal-

lenge him. He occasionally suggests this, but elsewhere goes far beyond such a prudential proposition. See *E.M.*, pp. 4-5, 7, 17, 23, 24-25, 27, 43, 61-63, 83-84, 86-87, 92-93, 115, 122-123. See, also, note 24, above, note 51, below.

"Real crimes are sins with legal definitions." *E.M.*, *p.* 27. But even Thomas Aquinas would have preferred to use "vices" rather than "sins." See *Summa Theologica*, Pt. I-II, Ques. 96, A. 2 (*Treatise on Law*).

30. *E.M.*, p. 84.
31. *E.M.*, p. 9. Cf. *E.M.*, p. 62: ". . . the free-thinker in western civilization would, I believe, accept monogamy as good in itself." There seems to be difficulty distinguishing in Lord Devlin's lectures between the ultimate justification for morality and the historical conditions for the development of that morality in a particular country. See Essay II, note 49, above.
32. Consider *E.M.*, p. 86:
> When a state recognizes freedom of worship and of conscience, it sets a problem for jurists which they have not yet succeeded in solving. Now, when the law divides right from wrong, it cannot appeal to any absolute authority outside itself as justifying the division. All the questions which before were settled by divine law as pronounced by the churches are thrown open to debate when the decision is taken to admit freedom of conscience.

We are reminded of the passage from Hobbes quoted in the text at note 7, above.
33. Consider Leo Strauss, *Spinoza's Critique of Religion* (New York: Schocken, 1965), p. 30:
> The victory of orthodoxy through the self-destruction of rational philosophy was not an unmitigated blessing, for it was a victory not of Jewish orthodoxy but of any orthodoxy, and Jewish orthodoxy based its claim to superiority to other religions from the beginning on its superior rationality (*Deut.* 4: 6).

See Leo Strauss, "The Law of Reason in the *Kuzari*," *Persecution and the Art of Writing* (Glencoe: The Free Press, 1952). See, also, Anastaplo, "On Leo Strauss: A Yahrzeit Remembrance," 67 *University of Chicago Magazine* 32, 37-38 (Winter 1975); "American Constitutionalism," nn. 20, 61.

The unbeliever, on the other hand, is free to examine the ordinances attributed to God to determine the extent to which they are derivative from reason. See note 40, below.

The supremacy of reason does not mean, however, that the final end of human action is chosen. Aristotle, *Nicomachean Ethics* 1094a19-23. This end, dictated by nature, is perceived and desired by man. See note 23, above, Essay VII, note 3, below.
34. Milton, *Paradise Lost*, VI, 174-181.
35. "Moreover, virtue exists in man and god alike, but in no other creature besides; virtue, however, is nothing else than nature perfected and developed to its peak; therefore there is a likeness between man and god." Cicero, *Laws*, I, viii, 25. Cf. *ibid.*, I, x, 30.

A journal entry by Emerson suggests the inevitable ambiguity of any attempt to apply reason to the foundations of morality:
> At Sea, September 17, 1833. Yesterday I was asked what I mean by morals. I reply that I cannot define, and care not to define. It is man's business to observe, and the definition of moral nature must be the slow result of years, of lives, of states, perhaps of being. Yet in the morning watch on my berth I thought that morals is the science of the laws of human action as respects right and wrong. Then I shall be asked, And what is Right? Right is a conformity to the laws of nature as far as they are known to the human mind. . . .

Selections from Ralph Waldo Emerson, S. E. Whicher, ed. (Boston: Houghton

Mifflin, Riverside Editions, 1960), p. 14. Emerson's observation of human nature produced this entry a year later (*ibid.*, p. 99):

> . . . The whole power of Christianity resides in this fact, that it is more agreeable to the constitution of man than any other teaching. But from the constitution of man may be got better teaching still.

Lord Devlin seems to be drawing on what he has learned of human nature when he records such observations as "the fact that a woman does not usually commit adultery unless she intends the new association to be permanent, while a man is more casual." *E.M.*, p. 70. (See *The Constitutionalist*, pp. 547-548.) Is this true only of truly "feminine" women, not of anyone who happens to be a spiritual descendant of Sophocles' Antigone, whose "masculinity" was recognized by Creon as a serious threat? (See *ibid.*, c. 9, n. 32.) And what of the man who regards love as does the Socrates, or at least the Aristophanes, of Plato's *Symposium?* Such gratifying exceptions remind us that the law should not be expected to cope with the admirably extraordinary.

See Judah Halevi, *The Kuzari*, Part I, Sections 69-76.

36. *E.M.*, p. 89. See, with respect to the "conscience" referred to here and in note 32, above, note 39, below.

37. *E.M.*, p. 89. An acknowledgment of "the Platonic ideal" is evident, however, in Lord Devlin's declaration, "The unending search for truth goes on and so does the struggle towards the perfect society." *E.M.*, p. 100. But he immediately adds, "It is our common creed that no society can be perfect unless it is a free society . . . This is not the creed of all mankind." Is the creed that "no society can be perfect unless it is a free society" itself exempt from serious examination in the "unending search for truth"? Cf. Anastaplo, "The Declaration of Independence," pp. 403-404; Essay V, note 14, above.

38. *E.M.*, p. 89 (citing *Minersville School District* v. *Gobitis*, 310 U.S. 586, 596 [1940]). Such judicial behavior may well rest on the questionable theory that

> the lawmaker is not required to make any judgment about what is good and what is bad. The morals which he enforces are those ideas about right and wrong which are already accepted by the society for which he is legislating and which are necessary to preserve its integrity. . . . Naturally he will assume that the morals of his society are good and true; if he does not, he should not be playing an active part in government. But he has not to vouch for their goodness and truth. His mandate is to preserve the essentials of his society, not to reconstruct them according to his own ideas.

E.M., pp. 89-90.

Should not the lawmaker always assume "that the morals of his society are good and true" if, as Lord Devlin sometimes argues, the only basis for determining the morality of any society (or, at least, of a democratic society) is popular opinion?

The problem remains, of course, how any society develops its morals in the first place or reforms them thereafter. May not the great lawmakers, with their "judgment about what is good and what is bad," be decisive in this respect? Chance may play a critical part in providing them an opportunity to do their founding. See note 19, above.

Be that as it may, the general opinion of the community may be more responsive to morality than particular men whose self-interest is engaged. Thus, Nathaniel Hawthorne can speak (*Scarlet Letter*, c. 21) of "the general sentiment which gives law its vitality." Thus, also, the Governor's Commission on Individual Liberty and Personal Privacy (State of Illinois) could observe, in a 1975 memorandum accompanying the release of a proposed Fair Consumer Credit Reporting Act:

> The availability to the investigated individual of his [credit rating] file makes

it far more likely than heretofore that only information which is morally justified and legally permitted will find its way into that file.

See Essay IX, note 7, below.

39. Consider *E.M.*, p. 119:

> There may be times in the future, as there have been in the past, when a man has to set himself up against society. But if he does so, he must expect to find the law on the side of society. If in his struggle he is armed with a good conscience, he must put his trust, firstly, in the rightness of his conviction, secondly, in the knowledge that nothing that law-makers and lawyers can do can fetter the mind of man, only his body; and last but not least, in the certainty that law can be made effective only through human agents and that a law that is truly tyrannical will not for long command the services of free men.

Cf. *E.M.*, p. 121.

But can that truly be called "law" which is on the side of tyranny and against a good man? On what does Lord Devlin base "a good conscience" and "the rightness of . . . conviction" when his sovereign has already declared himself? May not tyranny be longstanding, turning free men into slaves? What does it mean to "enforce morality," to establish or to reinforce it by law, if the minds of men really cannot be fettered? See Plato, *Republic* 415d, 619b-e. See, also, note 17, above.

Is it not dangerous sentimentality to assume that only the body, and not the mind of man, can be fettered? Does not such sentimentality all too often take the form of loose talk about "conscience"? It is, of course, virtually impossible for us today *not* to use the word "conscience," even when we mean by it something old-fashioned (that is, pre-Christian). The contrast between conscience and a sense of shame is instructive: conscience is more private in its implications; shame, more community-minded. If one is not careful, the independence legitimated by conscience can degenerate into a disregard not only for what others think but also for thinking itself. That is to say, an emphasis upon steadfastness in one's conscience both depends upon and reinforces an emphasis upon individual will and upon the sincerity of that will. To make a virtue of sincerity is to mean, eventually, that there are no standards to be invoked, no public discourse to which one is responsible and in which one must participate. Among other developments which follow from the opinions generated by an emphasis upon private will and conscience are a legitimation of self-expression for its own sake and (in order that we might understand and perhaps shape, if only for the sake of therapy, the self which is being expressed) a concern for the unconscious, that chance constellation of psychic forces which determine *who* we are and *what* we will.

There can be, of course, something admirable in steadfastness itself, unless the cause in which one is steadfast is simply odious. But is not steadfastness something like courage, that virtue which Aristotle recognized to have so many dubious forms? Steadfastness may be something like justice as well—but that virtue too, has some dubious forms, as can be seen, for example, when it is regarded as essentially law-abidingness. Parmenides' goddess observed, "The heart left to itself misses the road." Fr. 7. Do not what is truly courageous and what is truly just depend upon wisdom? Do not they depend, that is, upon an awareness of the commands one has been given (the laws of one's city), upon the circumstances in which one finds oneself, and upon an understanding of what the simply best would consist of? See notes 19, 20, above, Essay VII, note 6, below. See, also, Essay II, note 44, above, Essay X, notes 13, 14, Essay XV, note 14, Essay XVI, note 4, below.

These observations can serve as an anticipation of the discussion, in the latter part of this essay, of Plato's *Meno*. See Essay II, note 44, above.

40. Consider, for instance, this passage from Fred Hoyle, *The Nature of the Universe*

(New York: Signet Science Library, New American Library, 1960), p. 121:
> And now I should like to give some consideration to contemporary religious beliefs. There is a good deal of cosmology in the Bible. My impression of it is that it is a remarkable conception, considering the time when it was written. But I think it can hardly be denied that the cosmology of the ancient Hebrews is only the merest daub compared with the sweeping grandeur of the picture revealed by modern science. This leads me to ask the question: is it in any way reasonable to suppose that it was given to the Hebrews to understand mysteries far deeper than anything we can comprehend, when it is quite clear that they were completely ignorant of many matters that may seem commonplace to us? No, it seems to me that religion is but a desperate attempt to find an escape from the truly dreadful situation in which we find ourselves.

Compare, on the other hand, a passage from Werner Heisenberg, *Philosophic Problems of Nuclear Science* (Greenwich: Fawcett Publications, 1952), pp. 43-44:
> Thus I return to the question posed at the outset: can science claim to lead to an understanding of nature? I have attempted to show how physics and chemistry—driven, we hardly know by what force—have continuously developed in the direction of a mathematical analysis of nature under the guiding principle of unification. The claims of our science to an understanding of nature, in the original sense of the word, have at the same time decreased. The attempt to prove impossible a perception-theoretical understanding of the latter kind, and to prove mathematical analysis the only possible way, appears to me as unwise as the opposite assertion, that an understanding of nature can be achieved in a philosophical way without a knowledge of its formal laws. . . .

See Aristotle, *Physics*, I, i-iii, II, vii. See, also, Heidegger, *An Introduction to Metaphysics* (New York: Anchor Books, Doubleday & Co., 1961), p. 13 (Essay V, note 26, above): "But what is great can only begin great. Its beginning is in fact the greatest thing of all." See, as well, Anastaplo, "On Leo Strauss," pp. 31 (where I posit an "ultron"), 36 (on the study of nature); *The Constitutionalist*, c. 9, nn. 38, 39; Malcolm P. Sharp, "Crosskey, Anastaplo and Meiklejohn on the United States Constitution," 20 *University of Chicago Law School Record* 3, n. 52 (1973).

41. Jacob Klein, *A Commentary on Plato's Meno* (Chapel Hill: North Carolina Press, 1965). Mr. Klein acknowledges (p. i) that "the final version of this book," which had been contemplated "some thirty years," "owes a great deal to the care of Eva Brann [a colleague at St. John's College]." An even better but considerably more difficult book, one is given to understand by those who know, is Mr. Klein's *Greek Mathematical Thought and the Origin of Algebra* (Cambridge: M.I.T. Press, 1968).

See, also, Klein, "Aristotle, An Introduction," in *Ancients and Moderns: Essays on the Tradition of Political Philosophy in Honor of Leo Strauss*, J. Cropsey, editor (New York: Basic Books, 1964). Citations to the *Meno* will usually be made here by reference to appropriate passages in Mr. Klein's book (which are, in turn, keyed to the dialogue).

An exceptionally accurate rendering into English of the *Meno* is available in a translation prepared by Mr. John Gormly for the introductory close textual reading tutorial of the Basic Program of Liberal Education for Adults, The University of Chicago.

Mimeographed copies may be secured from me of two lectures I have given on the *Meno* at the University (1959, 1963). See, also, *The Constitutionalist*, e.g., c. 5, nn. 94, 147, c. 9, n. 22.

42. Klein, *Commentary*, pp. 43, 60, 91-92, 183-184, 200-202, 209, 212, 214, 216-219,

221-222, 235. Cf. *ibid.*, pp. 84-85. Must one know all to know anything? *Ibid.*, pp. 86-87, 92, 216-217. Consider, in the opening lines of Parmenides, the words of the goddess:

> . . . Thou shalt inquire into everything: both the motionless heart of well-rounded truth, and also the opinions of mortals, in which there is no true reliability. But nevertheless thou shalt learn these things [opinions] also—how one should go through all the things-that-seem, without exception, and test them.

Does one know enough whereby to judge "all" when one knows "the motionless heart of well-rounded truth"? And has that heart been grasped by some? Cf. Heraclitus, Frs. 35, 40. See Essay II, note 45, Essay IV, note 13, above.

43. Does the boy recollect, however, or is Socrates merely putting words in his mouth? Klein, *Commentary*, pp. 102, 103, 105-106, 175-177. Perhaps it should be said that Socrates puts before the boy the alternatives which the boy would encounter if he should seek alone for the answer to the problem set before him. The boy would, if he looked long enough, happen upon both the two incorrect answers he gives as well as upon the visual arrangements of the figures which undermine those answers. He might even happen upon the arrangement which exposes to eye and mind the answer with which Socrates finally confronts the boy (and for which the boy had been prepared). True, these things did not "happen" to the boy; but Socrates did happen to him—and, in a sense, *that* can be taken as a summation of the experience and reflections the boy could have had proceeding alone, reflections and experience comparable to those which could well have happened to the first man who discovered what the boy is prompted by Socrates to discover. See note 19, above, Essay XV, below.

Mr. Laurence Berns (of St. John's College) has called to my attention the analysis in Section 119 of Kant's *Logic*, of "questions being directed either to the understanding or merely to the memory." Consider, also, the following passage in Willa Cather, *The Professor's House*, c. 10: "Latin, he owned, had been hard for him. But in mathematics, he didn't have to work, he had merely to give his attention."

44. I address myself in the text on this occasion to some points in Mr. Klein's *Commentary* bearing on the relation of law to morality. I merely mention in this note other points which a careful review of Mr. Klein's book should consider:

(1) The use of "excellence" (and "human excellence"), instead of "virtue," for *arete* is troublesome. It seems designed to induce the reader to look freshly at the term, but it disregards the tradition and later usage (such as that in Machiavelli), which are for other reasons instructive to keep in mind. Cf. end of Essay IV, above.

(2) Is there, in the elicitation by Socrates of an *arreton* (an "unspeakable") in the slave-boy example (Klein, *Commentary*, p. 185), a pun on *arete*? And is virtue also "unspeakable," something which (in this context, and like the diagonal) can only be pointed at, not precisely described?

(3) Also troublesome is the use of "shaped surface," instead of "figure" (or "shape") for *schema*. "Figure" *is* used when reference is made to the Euclidian *schema. Ibid.*, p. 65. See, also, *ibid.*, pp. 55, 62. The use of "shaped surface" is more cumbersome than colloquial, and deprives the text of the tension between the colloquial and the technical which is seen in the dialogue.

(4) Mr. Klein translates the first definition of *schema* as if "shaped surface" and "color" should be taken as convertible. *Ibid.*, pp. 59, 61. But the Greek does not seem to require this. Nor is convertibility necessary for an understanding of "figure": although color is always accompanied by figure, figure need not always be accompanied by color (unless one arbitrarily restricts oneself to figures which

can be seen). (See Essay XV, section vii, below.) Similarly, although virtue is always accompanied by (i.e., is dependent upon) knowledge, knowledge need not always be accompanied by (i.e., be dependent upon or concerned with) virtue. (See, on the relation of color to the definition of triangle, Rousseau, *The First and Second Discourses*, R. D. Masters, ed. [New York: St. Martin's Press, 1964], p. 125.)

(5) The definition of *schema* which presents it as that which always accompanies color is evidently regarded by Socrates as preferable to that which presents it as "the limits of solid." Klein, *Commentary*, pp. 58-59, 65, 70. Does this hint that Homer is wrong in regarding the divinely-endowed Tieresias as the only one "in his senses" among the dead in Hades, since Tieresias' blindness would keep him from grasping the preferred definition of *schema* (and, by analogy, of *arete* as well?)? *Ibid.*, pp. 255-256. (Or are we supposed to recall that Tieresias was not always blind?) Does this further suggest that that which comes by divine allotment (or by inspiration?) to man is not the best, and is indeed inferior to that which man seeks and discovers (or recollects) for himself? The preferred views of virtue and of figure see them more in terms of knowledge (and require more dependence on the reason) than do the alternatives advanced; the alternatives see them in terms of the limits of things of substance (statesmen-models and solids, respectively). See *ibid.*, p. 192. (Consider, on the relation of thinking to seeing: "Eyes and ears are bad witnesses to men having barbarian souls." Heraclitus, Fr. 13. "You can't depend on your eyes when your imagination is out of focus." Mark Twain, *A Connecticut Yankee in King Arthur's Court* [Scranton: Chandler Publishing Co., 1963], p. 560. Consider, also, Heraclitus, Fr. 101a: "Eyes are more accurate witnesses than ears.")

(6) Mr. Klein alludes to Socrates' "gentle hoax" with respect to the geometrical illustration of "hypothesis." *Commentary*, pp. 207, 211. Is this why no visual illustration is provided by Mr. Klein for this difficult example, whereas several are provided with respect to the much easier example used in the slave-boy incident? *Ibid.*, pp. 100-102. Is the problem posed here by Socrates genuine? If it is, is it not significant that Meno seems to grasp a very difficult illustration easily? (Or is he bluffing? He had theretofore objected whenever confronted with something which he had not understood or, at least, was not familiar with.) Has the capacity, as well as the training, of Meno been underestimated? Something more needs to be done, in any event, with the geometrical examples if one is to appreciate what each says about virtue, about the problems and stages of learning (or recollection) and about what may be called the "natural history of error."

(7) Mr. Klein, at *ibid.*, pp. 92-93, considers Socrates to have paused for an "inward" gaze. But should we not consider the possibility that what happened instead was that Meno, upon hearing a reference to "expert knowledge of the highest things," eagerly interrupted Socrates to urge him on? Did Socrates strike something deep in Meno, even an appetite for the mystical, which is related to the concluding sermon on divine allotment?

I have been told by Miss Brann, since the original publication of this essay in the *Wisconsin Law Review*, that something like Point 2 (of this note) has been made by J. G. Libes in *Iyyun, A Hebrew Philosophical Quarterly*, The Philosophical Society of Jerusalem, vol. 16, n. 3 (November 1966). Consider, in this connection, the Greek delight in the similarities of sounds and the play on these: Plato, *Cratylus;* W. B. Stanford, *The Sound of Greek* (Berkeley: University of California Press, 1967), pp. 11-12.

More could be said, than I have been able to say on this occasion, about such things as Mr. Klein's contribution through his *Commentary* to the understanding of cognition and his discussion therein of counting. (Is it not generally more prudent for an author today to use numbers for purposes of confirmation rather than as a means of making an argument? That is, he can confirm thereby that his work is carefully crafted. Even so, one can wonder what various numbers have in common: e.g., 1, 3, 4, 9, 7, 10, 13, 17, 26. Consider the Pythagorean understanding of numbers, e.g., Aristotle, *Metaphysics* 986a18. Consider, also, the "three dimensional" self-sufficiency that Chapter I of *The Constitutionalist* and Essay VIII of this volume have in common.)

45. Book Notice, 19 *Review of Metaphysics* 155 (September 1965).

46. A dialogue which does happen to come down to us may be much as its author wrote it. But the biographical and historical material which scholars regard as relevant to a dialogue depends on what survives, and that is usually a matter of chance. Plato knew Homer was read centuries after he wrote; he probably knew that Thucydides had intended his study of the Peloponnesian War as a "possession everlasting." Is it not likely, therefore, that Plato provides us with what is needed, in any particular work (or at least among his works), for its understanding? Should we not, that is, insist upon seeing the character of Meno not necessarily as an "archvillain" (despite the "mingled and mangled" memories of him which scholars would burden us with) but rather as it is portrayed in this dialogue? See Klein, *Commentary*, p. 240; also, *ibid.*, pp. 35-37, 67, 72, 79, 189, 199-200; note 49, below.

Something more should be told the reader, on the other hand, about the once well-known Athenian politicians mentioned at *ibid.*, p. 230. It should be noticed that Socrates examines and calls into question politicians of both the democratic and the aristocratic party in his conversation with Anytus. (It should be noticed, as well, that the Thucydides referred to there is not the historian but the politician.)

Central to the development of both the human being and the citizen, and of the relation of one to the other, may be the productive tension among us between chance and necessity. See, e.g., Plato, *Republic* 329e-330a; notes 19, 20, above.

47. Something of that third reading is indicated in two digressions. The digressions are Chapters V and VII of the *Commentary*. (The first is so labelled by Mr. Klein.) They can be taken as parallel to the geometrical "digressions" from the discussion of virtue found in the *Meno* (at Klein, *Commentary*, pp. 99-102, 206-207). In both the *Meno* and the *Commentary*, the first digression comprises the central section of the work (with the second coming, in each case, shortly thereafter). (See *ibid.*, p. 30, on a "digression" which is central to another Platonic dialogue.) Mr. Klein acknowledges, *ibid.*, pp. 108-109, that his explicit digression into "what is said, and not said, in [other] dialogues about recollecting, learning, and forgetting" may isolate "these themes from the dramatic context in which they appear." See *ibid.*, p. 27, for an argument for reading various dialogues together.

For the student of the *Meno*, as distinguishable from the student of Plato, Chapters V and VII of the *Commentary* are indeed digressions and could well be reserved for the end.

48. Mr. Klein makes nothing of the "Greekness" which both Gorgias and Socrates presuppose in those with whom they deal. Socrates assures himself that the slave-boy is Greek and speaks the Greek language. *Ibid.*, p. 98. A similar condition had been suggested by Socrates in his description of Gorgias: for Gorgias "makes himself available to any Greek wishing to ask him, and there is no one to whom he does not give an answer." *Meno* 70b. Cf. Klein, *Commentary*, pp. 40-41. What is the significance of Greekness? Is it simply that it is common to both parties to the transaction? Or does it imply Greek life, a life which permits and nourishes a Socrates or a Gorgias? The linking of Socrates and Gorgias in this manner (as well as elsewhere in the dialogue) suggests that there may be something essentially

the same in the two men, in what they are trying to do or, at least, in what they esteem. See Essay II, section vii, above.

49. *Ibid.*, pp. 238-239. The next quotation in the text is from *ibid.*, p. 240.

   Meno is burdened with memories. Indeed, he seems to be the archetype not of villainy but of those who, in Emerson's words, "have difficulty in bringing their reason to act, and on all occasions use their memory first." Note 26, above. (But what if virtue depends upon knowledge, and knowledge upon reason?) It is in Socratic "recollection" that human reason manifests itself. (C. S. Lewis quotes Samuel Johnson as having said, "People more frequently require to be reminded than instructed.") See, for a sober discussion of the relation of virtue to knowledge, Aristotle, *Nicomachean Ethics*, VII, ii-iii; also, *ibid.*, I, vi-vii. (See, for the Johnson quotation, *Letters of C. S. Lewis*, W. H. Lewis, editor [London: Geoffrey Bles, 1966], p. 281.)

50. Anytus, the democrat, swears "by Heracles": he relies on him whom he believes to have been strongest among men? Plato, *Meno* 91c. It is curious that Mr. Klein not only overlooks this oath and its implications (would not Anytus, considering the many "the strongest," invoke them against the subversive sophists?) but even mistranslates it as "O no, Socrates"! *Commentary*, p. 227. Indeed, his "tackling" of the oaths in the dialogue leaves something to be desired. *Ibid.*, p. 77. Perhaps Mr. Klein is determined to have us figure out enough of the dialogue to make it truly our own.

   Is one purpose of the teaching about the divine allotment of virtue that of prudently inducing equality-minded democrats to acknowledge the political effects of natural distinctions among men? See Plato, *Republic* 558b. See, for the democrat's view of the relation of training to nature, Twain, *Connecticut Yankee*, p. 217. See, also, *The Constitutionalist*, c. 8, n. 115.

51. Even the "best city" must provide itself oracles as aids for maintaining among men generally what reason has prescribed. Plato, *Republic* 414c-d, 427b-c. See, also, Xenophon, *The Cavalry Commander*, I, 1-2; III, 1; IX, 7-9; Twain, *Connecticut Yankee*, chapters 41-44. Richard Hooker argued (*Of the Laws of Ecclesiastical Polity*, I, viii): "The general and perpetual voice of men is as the sentence of God himself. For that which all men have at all times learned, Nature herself must needs have taught; and God being the author of Nature, her voice is but his instrument. By her, from him, we receive whatsoever in such sort we learn."

   Consider, as well, Strauss, "The Law of Reason in the *Kuzari*," p. 130:

   > To deny that religion is essential to society, is difficult . . . for anyone who puts any trust in the accumulated experience of the human race. To assert it, would amount to ascribing some value even to the most abominable idolatrous religion; for the proverbial gang of robbers, or the lowest and smallest community, cannot be supposed to adhere to the one true religion or to any of its imitations.

   "Let us not forget," Mr. Klein would have us remember, "he is talking to Meno." *Commentary*, p. 255. A similar caution is appropriate in reading every Platonic dialogue. The *Crito*, for instance, is usually misunderstood on this account. See Essay XVI, below. See, also, Essay II, above.

   Should one speak, as at Klein, *Commentary*, p. 18, of "quot[ing] Plato himself"? But see Aristotle, *N. Ethics*, e.g., 1172b29.

52. Klein, *Commentary*, p. 18. It is fitting and proper that Mr. Klein's closing citation should be to Leo Strauss, *On Tyranny: An Interpretation of Xenophon's "Hiero"* (New York: Political Science Classics, 1948), another contemporary effort to help us recollect the lost art of reading. See Essay XV, note 8, below.

Mr. Strauss, at pages 24-25 (of the 1963 edition of *On Tyranny*, published by the Free Press), reports,

. . . I have tried to understand Xenophon's thought as exactly as I could. I have not tried to relate his thought to his "historical situation" because this is not the natural way of reading the work of a wise man; and, in addition, Xenophon never indicated that he wanted to be understood that way. I assumed that Xenophon, being an able writer, gave us to the best of his powers the information required for understanding his work. I have relied therefore as much as possible on what he himself says, directly or indirectly, and as little as possible on extraneous information, to say nothing of modern hypotheses. . . . It goes without saying that I never believed that my mind was moving in a larger "circle of ideas" than Xenophon's mind.

He expresses the hope, at page 27, "that the time will come when Xenophon's art will be understood by a generation which, properly trained in their youth, will no longer need cumbersome introductions like the present study." See note 1, above.

VII. In Search of the Soulless "Self"

1. Consider, for instance, Hobbes' suggestion that "the Thoughts are to the Desires as Scouts and Spies, to range abroad and find the way to the Things desired." *Leviathan*, I, viii. See Essay VI, note 23, above.

   What do we believe to be the source of the desires we happen to have? And what is the legitimate role of the community in shaping those desires? See Essays IV, VI, above. "From the monarch, as from a never-failing spring, flows a stream of all that is good or evil over the whole nation." Thomas More, *Utopia* (New Haven: Yale University Press, 1964), p. 17.

   Consider the implications of the deliberate appeal to and even the intensification of the lowest desires seen in the blatant promotion in Illinois the past year of a State Lottery. See Editorial, "Why Isn't the Church Fighting Lotteries?" 91 *Christian Century* 1163 (Dec. 11, 1974); Adam Smith, *Wealth of Nations* (index: "Lotteries"). Cf. Andrew Greeley, "The Search for Common Good," *Chicago Tribune*, sec. 2, p. 4.

   See, on modern science, Essay VI, note 40, above; Anastaplo, "American Constitutionalism and the Virtue of Prudence" (Essay I, note 1, above), n. 43.

2. See, for an extended argument in favor of the abolition of television in this country, Anastaplo, "Self-Government and the Mass Media: A Practical Man's Guide," in *The Mass Media and Modern Democracy*, Harry M. Clor, ed. (Chicago: Rand McNally, 1974). The first part of that article makes the case for "no previous restraint" of the press, a case which recognizes the right and duty of a self-governing people to discuss fully the public business; the second part considers the character needed in a people if it is to be able to govern itself—and the effect of television on that character is diagnosed. See Essay X, below.

   See, also, *The Constitutionalist* (Essay I, note 1, above), c. 5, nn. 136-138.

3. See, on death, Essay XVII, below. Has not our modern concern with the "self" intensified (or, rather, distorted) our concern with death? Descartes' radical explorations (for the sake of absolutely certain truth) into the self may have undermined what had once been grasped (instinctively? naturally?), both that one *does* exist for awhile and that life is, by and large, good. What a self-centered Descartes exaggerated (man's uncertainty about what had been previously taken as given), no one since has been able to restore to its proper proportions—and we eventually come upon such things as Nietzsche's "abyss." See G. R. T. Ross, ed., *The Philosophical Works of Descartes* (New York: Dover Publications, 1955), p. 322. See Essay VI, note 33, above.

See, on the self, *The Constitutionalist,* e.g., c. 5, n. 90, c. 6, n. 75, c. 7, nn. 124, 77, c. 8, nn. 3, 45, 193. See, also, Essay X, notes 13, 14, Epilogue, Essay XVII, notes 2, 4, 5, below.

4. I should hasten to add that I am not addressing myself here to "the population explosion" problem, See Essay IV, notes 41, 42, above.

See, on the *polis, The Constitutionalist,* c. 7, nn. 35, 59, 67, 77, 111, 113, c. 8, n. 1. See, also, "American Constitutionalism," nn. 1, 6, 22; Essay X, Prologue, below. Cf. *Construction Industry Assn.* v. *City of Petaluma,* 375 F.Supp. 574 (1974).

See, for what an excessive regard for the *polis* does to serious education, Howard R. Swearer, "Higher Education in Contemporary China," *The Key Reporter,* Winter 1974-1975, p. 2.

5. See Essays IV, VI, above, Essays VIII, X, below. See, also, *The Constitutionalist,* c. 9, sec. 4. Cf. C. S. Lewis, *That Hideous Strength* (New York: Macmillan Paperbacks, 1965), p. 71, where a character says:

> I happen to believe that you can't study men; you can only get to know them, which is quite a different thing. Because you study them, you want to make the lower orders govern the country and listen to classical music, which is balderdash. You also want to take away from them everything which makes life worth living and not only from them but from everyone except a parcel of prigs and professors.

Does "knowing" without "studying" presuppose something innate which can be relied upon? See, on the conscience, Essay VI, note 39, above.

6. This is aside from the question of whether the particular patient is indeed helped. This is also aside from the question of whether one would (should?) want such help in the care of one's own, or in case one falls prey oneself to a disease which medical science is able to deal with. See Aristotle, *N. Ethics* 1145a7-11; Essay XVII, note 5, below.

See, on obscenity, *The Constitutionalist,* e.g., c. 5, n. 126; Essay X, below. See, for the relation between the contemporary invocation of privacy and the old-fashioned respect for piety, Henry James, *The Aspern Papers; The Constitutionalist,* c. 8, n. 133. See, also, Essay IX, note 7, below, Essay VI, notes 38, 39, above. See, for a thoughtful introduction to the problems of privacy, Howard P. White, "The Right to Privacy," 18 *Social Research* 171 (1951). See, also, Essay X, note 17, below.

7. We again see, however, that the proposal of an impractical remedy may nevertheless be useful for understanding and assessing what we *are* doing. Plato's *Republic* comes to mind.

My exchange with one of the Bethesda panel bears upon the argument of this essay (I am the first speaker in the following excerpt):

A.: . . . You used, on at least two occasions [in comparing us moderns with the ancients], the notion of progress, that "we" are better than "they." I find that heartening because any serious notion of progress has someplace, if only dimly, an awareness of what *the best* is. Are you prepared to say there *is* a best?

B.: I thought I was addressing that question in my talk this afternoon. There are ways in which we act to make things as we call them, "better," and we do say that this is good and that is not good, and so on, and I suppose that if you have good and better, you have a best, but the notion of the evolution of a species or of a culture never gives you the opportunity of foreseeing the final state. If it's a question of eschatology, I pass.

A.: May I comment on that? Look, you can't talk about the better or the good without a notion of the best. I think you do have a notion of the best.

I think you have a notion of the best by which you guide your life and on which your own comments just now are based. Your notion of the best, I think, whether you recognize it or not, is a full development of the human reason, primarily with a view to understanding man and the world around him. I think that's your secret best. If that is so, then we can begin to talk seriously about which societies, which cultures, are more apt to contribute to that, and which ones are less apt to contribute to that. We don't talk about survival as [the basis for] judgment. For instance, you observed that survival is the only value by which we will be judged. That simply is not true. That is not a fact. We know—we look back over ancient "cultures" (as we call them) and we see some that we judge and judge very highly, and by any ordinary notion of survival, they have failed, compared to the trivial or bestial, barbaric culture which overwhelmed them. And yet I think *you* would say that they were better than the ones that conquered them. If you don't say it, I think that you would have serious problems talking about progress. If you *do* say it, then, as I say, we can begin talking seriously about what makes for the best man, what the proper questions are and how one goes about discovering what [the answers to] those questions are.

B.: I take survival to be a value only in a survival framework, and if you like to call that begging the question, you can. . . . You can't judge a culture simply by choosing those particular features that you admire, and say that Greek culture was great because of its law and its sculpture and so on. It was extremely weak in many respects and it happened to be weak because it overlooked the fact that it made itself extraordinarily attractive to barbarians, and that was a weakness. . . . in the long run, I think the culture which abandons its interest in surviving is not going to survive and in that sense it is a weak culture, and not a good culture.

See Essay IV, note 15, above.

See, on the idea of progress, *The Constitutionalist*, e.g., c. 7, nn. 41, 107, 122; on evolution, *ibid.*, c. 9, n. 38. See, also, Essay XV, below.

VIII. Pollution, Ancient and Modern
(There are no notes for this essay.)

IX. What's Really Wrong With George Anastaplo?

1. " Principle and Passion: The American Nazi Speaker on the University Campus." This talk, as well as "Realism and the Practice of Law" (given to a class on professional responsibility at the Northwestern University Law School) may be found in *Notes on the First Amendment* (Essay IV, note 28, above). See, also, *The Constitutionalist* (Essay I, note 1, above), c. 5, n. 69. See, as well, Essay XII, note 2, below.

   See, on the expulsions from Russia and Greece referred to in the epigraph, Essay I, notes 3, 4, above.

2. See, for extensive citations and various materials relating to my bar admission case, *The Constitutionalist*, Appendix F. A chronology of the case (which began in 1950 and ended in 1961) may be found at *ibid.*, pp. 334-335. I was born in St. Louis in 1925. My troubles with the Illinois bar began in November 1950. The first recorded votes against me in the character committee and in the state supreme court (1954) were unanimous. The committee had, on June 5, 1951, announced to me its decision in the following one-paragraph letter (which is now framed on my study wall):

The Committee on Character and Fitness of applicants for admission to the
bar for the First Appellate Court District of Illinois has carefully considered the
proofs submitted by you and the evidence before the Committee in connection
with your application for admission to the bar of Illinois. I am directed by the
Committee to advise you that you have failed to prove that you possess such
qualifications as to character and general fitness as in the opinion of the Committee would justify your admission to the bar of Illinois.

The committee said nothing more until compelled to do so by the Supreme Court
of Illinois three years later. (In the Spring of 1975 the Illinois Board of Law Examiners reverted to the bad old days by requiring each bar applicant to state, "I understand that I will not receive and am not entitled to a copy of the [character
committee] report or its contents. . . ." This kind of silliness suggests the bar
examiners are in need of a refresher course in the elements of constitutional law.)

The best official statement of the case against me may be found in *The Constitutionalist*, p. 348ff; the syllabus of the 1961 opinion of the Supreme Court of the
United States, at *ibid.*, p. 366. The most entertaining and perhaps even instructive
statement of the case against me may be found at *ibid.*, pp. 338-340. See, also, *ibid.*,
p. xi, c. 2, nn. 1, 7, c. 3, n. 20, c. 4, nn. 32, 107, c. 7, nn. 72, 89, c. 8, nn. 36, 88,
96, c. 9, nn. 13, 38. See, as well, Essay V, note 6, above.

I served throughout this litigation as my own attorney. See Essay II, note 33,
above. The decade-long setting for all this is suggested by an episode described by
me in a March 1, 1959 letter to Alexander Meiklejohn: "I met a State Department
official at a friend's home last Sunday. The official was a little put out when my
friend told him about my bar admission matter. When we parted half an hour
later, the State Department chap said to me, 'I'm glad to have met you. Of course,
I won't mention this to anyone when I get back to Washington. But then things
are getting better: five years ago I wouldn't have stayed in the same room with
you.'" Our recovery from Cold War follies was then in progress—but not far
enough along to head off the sacrifices in Vietnam.

3. I have even heard it said that this committee member has become a federal judge.
That is hard to believe. See Shakespeare, *Hamlet*, I, i, 56-58.

I gather that a number of committee members have had second thoughts about
what they did in ruling against my various petitions during the 1950s. Some even
wonder what "possessed" them. Even so, none of those who voted against me have
publicly repudiated their position, despite what is often said to be a general admiration and even pride among the bar today for the position I took then. Of course,
these men were never either imaginative or enterprising. Be that as it may, it now
seems likely that one of my distressingly respectable children will be admitted to
the Illinois bar a quarter century after I first aroused the self-righteous fears of a
woefully uninformed and really rather shameless character committee. See *In re
Anastaplo*, 366 U.S. 82, *Transcript of Record* (U.S. Supreme Court, 1960), pp. 18-20,
111-112, 123-124, 316.

See Anastaplo, "On Leo Strauss," 67 *University of Chicago Magazine* 32, n. 1
(Winter 1974); also, Essay VI, note 39, above; note 13, below. See also, Plato,
Republic 549c-550b; *Fables of Aesop* (London: Penguin Books, 1964), p. 205.

See, on paranoia, Anastaplo, "American Constitutionalism and the Virtue of
Prudence" (Essay I, note 1, above), n. 33.

4. *In re Anastaplo*, 366 U.S. 82, 114 (1961). Justice Black's entire opinion is reproduced
in *The Constitutionalist*, p. 367. See *ibid.*, p. 337. Elmer Gertz observes that excerpts
from this opinion were "read, by his choice, at Black's funeral service." *Showcase/
Chicago Sun-Times*, sec. 3, p. 16. See, also, Norman Redlich, "Justice Black at
Eighty: The Common Sense of Freedom," *Nation*, March 21, 1966, pp. 322, 325-
326; "Proceedings in the Supreme Court of the United States in Memory of Mr.

Justice Black," April 18, 1972, 405 U.S. v, xxiv; Malcolm P. Sharp, "Crosskey, Anastaplo and Meiklejohn on the United States Constitution," 20 *University of Chicago Law School Record* 12, 18, n. 45 (Spring 1973); Essay III, note 10, above.

The character committee declared itself to be more concerned with the un- answered questions about my "beliefs and associations" relating to possible member- ship in the Communist Party and in "Communist Front" organizations than about the similarly unanswered questions asked both about my possible membership in organi- zations such as the Ku Klux Klan (as well as the Republican and Democratic Parties) and about my religious beliefs. Perhaps most disturbing of all for them, although their candor with respect to this in their final report left much to be desired, were my opinions about the Declaration of Independence and its authori- tative teaching about the right of revolution. See Anastaplo, "Malcolm P. Sharp and the Spirit of '76," *The Law Alumni Journal* (The University of Chicago Law School), Spring 1975.

See, on the Declaration of Independence and the right of revolution, pp. 54, 80, above.

5. My complete final petition is reproduced in *The Constitutionalist*, p. 381. See, on Justice Harlan (who wrote the opinion for the Court, an unlawyerlike opinion in that the evidence in the record was not respected), *ibid.*, p. 824. See Essay IV, note 28, above.

6. *In re Anastaplo*, 3 Ill.2d. 471, 475 (1954). By 1959, the author of the earlier unani- mous opinion (*The Constitutionalist*, pp. 338-340) could muster only a bare majority in support of a *per curiam* opinion which concluded with the observation (18 Ill.2d. 182, 201):

> By failing to respond to the higher public interest, Anastaplo obstructed the proper functions of the Committee on Character and Fitness. By virtue of his own recalcitrance he failed to demonstrate the good moral character and general fitness to practise law necessary for admission to the bar of this State.

7. I learned several years later that one member of the 1954 Illinois Supreme Court had had experiences similar to mine in his successful attempt to enlist for service in the *First* World War. *Paris, Illinois Beacon-News*, November 13, 1961, p. 1 (obituary of Chief Justice George W. Bristow). This judge repudiated the 1954 opinion (to which he had subscribed) with a remarkable dissenting opinion in 1959. 18 Ill.2d 182, 201. A tribute to him may be found in *Notes on the First Amendment*, pp. 699-705. See, on the problem of civic gratitude, Essay II, note 26, Essay V, note 20, above.

The present status of my bar admission application is indicated in a letter of mine to the President of the Illinois State Bar Association, January 15, 1969, in response to what seems to have been a law student's prank:

> A local attorney was kind enough to inform me last night that I seem to be listed in the just-published issue (January 1969) of the *Illinois Bar Journal* as having applied for membership in the Illinois State Bar Association. . . . I should like to point out, in case this entry does refer to me, that . . . I was *not* admitted to the bar in 1963 [the date given in the listing]. Indeed, so far as I know, I am not now nor have I ever been a member of the Illinois bar (see 366 U.S. 82 [1961]). . . . I have never applied for admission to the Illinois State Bar Associa- tion, nor have I ever authorized anyone else to do so on my behalf. I have always assumed one must be a member of the bar to qualify as a member of the Associa- tion. (In fact, I have not, since I "retired" from the "practice of law" in 1961, attempted to secure admission to any bar or to any legal professional association.)
>
> . . . I observe that you make the following request in publishing your list of applicants: "Member are urged to examine the following list and advise the Committee on Admissions, in a signed letter, as to the fitness or unfitness of any

applicant." I imagine that a few of your members who recall my bar admission adventures (which began in 1950) will feel obliged to remind you of my professional status and my consequent ineligibility for admission to your Association.

I would appreciate it, therefore, if you would indicate in the next issue of the *Journal* that I have never applied for admission to the Association and that I myself promptly called the published misstatements to your attention. It does not look proper for me to be·recorded as seeking something to which I am not legally entitled and to make false representations about myself in the process. . . .

If you should learn who [the lawyer listed as my sponsor] is and what he is up to, I would like to be informed. One could say on his behalf, if one is inclined to be charitable, that he really knows a lawyer when he "sees" him, the official records to the contrary notwithstanding. But, I am afraid, two decades of sustained error on the part of the Illinois Bar and of the Supreme Court of Illinois cannot be so easily corrected: it does seem to be generally agreed that I am not a lawyer, and perhaps we should leave it at that.

See 57 *Illinois Bar Journal* 606 (March 1969); *The Constitutionalist*, p. 408.

I myself consider my exclusion from the Illinois bar permanent and perhaps even appropriate. I have indicated to the Illinois Supreme Court that I would accept a license if offered to me but that I did not intend to institute proceedings on my own (except in the most technical sense, if the court or the bar should otherwise make the arrangements for my admission). See *ibid.*, pp. 406-407. A further application by me for direct admission to the bar of the United States Supreme Court, if only for pedagogical purposes, is not however foreclosed. I *have* attempted this before but the Court has yet to address itself to the merits of my petition. See *ibid.*, pp. 408-417.

This bar admission controversy has been central to my professional (including my consequently constricted academic) career. That controversy exhibits an instructive combination of chance and necessity, something which is central to the life of both the human being and the citizen. See Essay VI, notes 19, 20, 46, above. The good which came from the controversy, which was considerable, was in spite of my "judges"; the personal damage which came from it, which was also considerable, is now beyond their power really to repair.

I have, of course, made abundant use of my legal training. The most recent use (1974-1975) has been as Advisor and Research Director for the Governor's Commission on Individual Liberty and Personal Privacy (in association with Bernard Weisberg and Ellen M. Flaum, who have been serving, in an impressively competent and most conscientious manner, as Chairman and Executive Director,· respectively, of this Illinois Commission). See Essay VI, note 38, Essay VII, note 6, above.

8. What I have since learned about Jews is suggested by Anastaplo, "On Leo Strauss," pp. 34-35, 37-38; *The Constitutionalist*, p. 816; *Notes on the First Amendment*, pp. 600-602, 790-802; Essay XIII, below.

9. Instructive on this point is Harper Lee's sensitive novel, *To Kill a Mockingbird* (Philadelphia: J. P. Lippincott Co., 1960). See, on the significance of one's oath, Thomas More, *Selected Letters* (New Haven: Yale University Press, 1961), pp. 217-221.

10. See, on Mr. Dilliard, *The Constitutionalist*, p. 813. The high school principal referred to was Elbert Fulkerson; the newspaper publisher, Frank Ledbetter.

How unnaturally passive even the young were in the 1950s—at least as bad in their way as their impassioned successors today—is suggested by the fact that the student editors of the *University of Chicago Law Review* could be compelled in late 1951 by their law school dean (who went on to become President of the University of Chicago and thereafter Attorney General of the United States) to return to me an article about my exclusion from the bar which they had commissioned me to write and which they had been prepared to publish. See *Constitutionalist*, p. 380, p. 401 (item 32), c. 8, n. 28, c. 9, n. 13; Essay IV, note 35, above; *The University of Chicago Maroon*, May 9, 1952, p. 2. This enterprising law school dean is recorded as having stated in response to questions, before a United States Senate committee in 1955 (studying eavesdropping on juries), "Now, Mr. Counsel, the Anastaplo case involved a great many questions. I am not an authority on the Anastaplo case. I am afraid that if—I am afraid that if I—I do not want to make a misstatement about this. I was not particularly involved in the Anastaplo case." *Ibid.*, January 10, 1975, p. 5. (I, on the other hand, found him too much "involved" in the case.)

"I am afraid that if—I am afraid that if I—" can serve as a fitting epitaph for a generation of talented, ambitious but unbecomingly timid lawyers. See "Disappointment in Justice," *Newsweek*, April 14, 1975, p. 15. See, also, 65 *Columbia Law Review* 1184, 1193 (1965). Timid men in power *can* be counted upon to advance (or, at least, not to resist) reforms if the time should be obviously ripe for them. But see Bob Wiedrich, "Political addicts wreck a career," *Chicago Tribune*, June 2, 1975, sec. 2, p. 4 (on "the oldest dodge among practitioners of self-preservation—the sacrifice of the handiest sucker on the altar of expediency").

11. See Aristotle, *Nicomachean Ethics* 1167a28-1169b1; *The Constitutionalist*, pp. 361-362. I also believe I "conducted [myself] before the Committee" as a lawyer should. Thus, on February 5, 1960, I wrote the character committee the following letter, a copy of which was sent to the Supreme Court of Illinois:

No doubt the Committee is aware of the final disposition of my matter by the Illinois Supreme Court. Because of the limited period during which one may appeal, I must now proceed with steps to prepare the case for consideration by the United States Supreme Court.

I should like, nevertheless—especially since I have never regarded my matter simply as a "test case" but primarily as a serious effort to gain admission to the bar—, to make every effort to settle this controversy in a manner consistent with the principles and sensibilities of all parties. I wonder, therefore, whether, in the light of the Record and of the various opinions filed by the members of the Supreme Court of this State, the Committee is willing, upon my bringing the standard applicant's questionnaire up-to-date since my last hearing (and assuming there is nothing improper indicated therein respecting my activities since the most recently executed application), to certify me for admission to the bar at this time.

I am sure that, if an understanding should be reached beforehand, the matter could be formally brought before the Committee—for example, by a rehearing, to which an applicant is entitled six months after rejection—so as to return jurisdiction of the matter to the Committee.

The Illinois Court has, by a 4-3 vote, confirmed the power of the Committee to insist on certain questions. But, as I read the three opinions, the Court does not advise the Committee that it must insist on such questions. Thus, my inquiry is, in effect, whether the Committee, having been upheld by its Court in its claim of power, now wishes to exercise that power to the legal limit in this particular situation. I am moved to make this effort partly because three members of the Court have explicitly endorsed, without challenge from their colleagues, my qualifications for the practise of law.

I write as I assume an attorney would on behalf of his client—as an attorney trying to learn whether a long-standing controversy can be settled in such a way as to avoid the unnecesary expense, effort or risk that an appeal might require of all parties. And, to be perfectly frank, I do not look forward, either as attorney or as client, to the many months of litigation that lie ahead, especially if they can be reasonably and honorably avoided by a settlement out of court.

I hope the Committee is able to give my suggestions due consideration.

The Committee secretary responded on February 17, 1960, in a terse letter which reflects the gracelessness and the lack of magnanimity (cf. Essay XIV, section v, above) which were always exhibited by this seventeen-member committee of influential lawyers:

Referring to your letter of February 5, 1960, I have been instructed by the Committee on Character and Fitness to advise you that the Committee is of the view that there is nothing before it upon which it can act.

In any further proceeding, the Committee will be bound by the action of the Illinois Supreme Court and of the Supreme Court of the United States if that Court takes the case.

And so the case went to Washington—where the committee got the majority of the Supreme Court and I got a magnificent dissenting opinion from Justice Black. It was, I believe, a fair trade—that is, each got what was wanted: the committee got more lawyers like themselves telling them they could do what they pleased; I got a memorable vindication by a real judge. See Essay II, section i, above, Essay XIV, note 15, below.

12. Cf. Xenophon, *Memorabilia*, IV, viii. See Essay II, above, Essay XVI, below.
13. "*Naynl; ley est resoun.*" *Langbridge's Case*, Common Bench, 1345 (reported Year Book, 19 Edw. III, 375). Cf. Essay IV, note 35, above; also, note 10, above.

A prominent lawyer who once served as chairman of my character committee was heard wistfully to recall in the Fall of 1974, at a time when one Nixon Administration lawyer after another had been "exposed," that I had confided to the committee in 1951 that the American bar needed me more than I needed the American bar. This committee member, too, has had second thoughts (or, rather, feelings) about what he once did. See note 3, above.

The epigraph originally provided for this talk was taken from William Roper's *Lyfe of Sir Thomas More, Knighte:*

To this Sir Thomas More myldly made answere, saying, Noe man livinge is there, my Lordes, that would with better wyll doe the thinge that should be acceptable to the Kinges highnes than I, which must needes confesse hys many-folde goodnes and bountifull benefittes most benignlye bestowed upon me.

I, too, have had "manyfolde goodnes and bountifull benefittes most benignlye bestowed upon me." See *The Constitutionalist*, pp. xi-xiii; Essay VI, notes 19, 20, above. See, also, Essay X, note 10, below.

X. Obscenity and Common Sense

1. This citizens' speech is adapted from a talk, "How to Begin to Think about Obscenity: Ends and Means," delivered April 24, 1965 before the Senate Club of Shimer College. The Notes were added subsequently. The Prologue and Epilogue were added at the time of first publication (in 1972).

Dozens of law review and other editors (between 1965 and 1972) found the talk well argued and yet unsuitable for publication in their particular journal: that is, it was regarded as most unfashionable (and not in the spirit of the new liberty) to say such things about the abuses of our liberty and literacy as may be found in this talk. But, then, it may be the fashion and duty of a few to be unfashionable. See, e.g., Essay I, notes 3, 4, Essay IX, above.

The quotation in the Prologue with respect to Joseph Stalin has been taken from Svetlana Alliluyeva, *Only One Year* (New York: Harper & Row, 1969), p. 142.

"Obscenity" and "pornography" are used interchangeably on this occasion (although the former may be really the more comprehensive term as well as more of a problem).

See, for further examinations by the author of many of the points touched upon in the citizens' speech: *The Constitutionalist* (Essay I, note 1, above): e.g., c. 5, nn. 123, 125, 126, 132, 143, c. 7, nn. 34, 59, c. 9, nn. 8, 9; "Preliminary Reflections on the Pentagon Papers," *University of Chicago Magazine*, Jan.-Feb., March-April 1972 (reprinted 118 *Congressional Record* S11560 [July 24, 1972]; Essay XII, note 2, below); "Self-Government and the Mass Media," in *The Mass Media and Modern Democracy*, Harry M. Clor, editor (Chicago: Rand McNally, 1974); "On the Making of Stained-Glass Windows for Rockefeller Chapel, The University of Chicago," *Midwest Magazine, Chicago Sun-Times*, March 11, 1973, p. 12 (see *Hyde Park Herald*, Chicago, May 9, 1973, p. 24) (the author was a contributing designer of the "Works of the Mind Window" and of the "Graduate's Window"). See, also, Essays II, IV, V, VI, VII, VIII, above, Essays XVI, XVII, below.

See, also, for useful discussions subsequent to the 1965 talk: Leo Strauss, *Socrates and Aristophanes* (New York: Basic Books, 1966); Harry M. Clor, *Obscenity and Public Morality* (Chicago: University of Chicago Press, 1969); Walter Berns, "Pornography vs. Democracy: The Case for Censorship," *Public Interest* (Winter 1970); Joseph Cropsey, "Radicalism and Its Roots," *Public Policy* (Spring 1970); Alexander Bickel and others, "On Pornography: Dissenting and Concurring Opinions," *Public Interest* (Winter 1971); Irving Kristol, "Pornography, Obscenity, and the Case for Censorship," *New York Times Magazine* (March 28, 1971); Harry M. Clor, editor, *Censorship and Freedom of Expression: Essays on Obscenity and the Law* (Chicago: Rand McNally, 1971). See, as well: *Report of the Commission on Obscenity and Pornography* (New York: Bantam Books, 1970); Allan Bloom, "Interpretive Essay," in *The Republic of Plato* (New York: Basic Books, 1968); Leon R. Kass, "Making Babies—the New Biology and the 'Old' Morality," *Public Interest* (Winter 1972); Willmoore Kendall, *Contra Mundum* (New Rochelle: Arlington House, 1971), p. 544; "What Alternative Society?" (an editorial), *Daily Telegraph* (London), August 7, 1971, p. 10.

See, on pollution, nature, and the seeming verities of economics, the collection from which Essay VIII, above, is taken; cf. Plato, *Republic* 341c, 346; Aristotle, *Politics* 1257b4sq. See, on the natural limits of "gainful . . . commerce," Edward Gibbon, *Decline and Fall of the Roman Empire* (New York: Modern Library, n.d.), I, 788. See, for a review of recent litigation in the Supreme Court of the United States with respect to both obscenity and its commercialization, "The Supreme Court, 1970 Term," 85 *Harvard Law Review* 229 (1971); for a review of recent English developments, the series, "The Abuses of Literacy," beginning in *The Times Literary Supplement*, January 14, 1972.

The perennial (and, in a sense, natural) lure of the obscene is suggested by what should be the choicest ribald lines of their year:

> No one who sees us will deny
> It is the only way to fly.

The naughtier reader will be able to imagine the subject of the "poem" from which these lines are taken. The more prosaic will have to resort to the *New Statesman*, August 13, 1971, p. 196. Cf. Plato, *Republic* 408c-409e.

The lure of the obscene may draw ultimately upon the desire of the young to learn (i.e., to grow up) and upon the desire of the aging to be again young (i.e., to forget, in order to enjoy relearning what they have outgrown). Thus, Chaucer speaks of young men lusting "to study things prohibited." "Franklin's Tale," *Canterbury Tales*. And Juvenal describes erotic exploits which he says would rejuvenate

even the decrepit Nestor. *Satires* 6.326. Consider, also, Richard Scofield's observation (*The College*, St. John's College, September 1970, p. 15), ". . . I have come
increasingly to see that intellectual virtue in general, which is the goal of a liberal
arts college, requires, as a condition for its existence, that sentimental and moral
education without which we are barbarians, not fully human . . . [P]overty and
vulgarity of feeling, more than stupidity, put humane letters beyond the mind's
reach. . . ." (See "Epistle to the Barbarians," Essay IV, note 50, above.)

It should be kept in mind, in thinking about what widespread indulgence might
imply, that a remarkable lack of *political* self-restraint among respectable leaders
contributed in Greece to the coming of the colonels' tyranny in 1967. See Essay I,
above. Consider, also, what the contemporary recourse to obscenity might imply
about the soul of America: "As Steven Marcus has remarked, even the new
pornography that emerged in American mass entertainment and art could be understood as 'a form of pseudo-radicalism' tied to this sense of loss of moral authority
in the formal structure of society." William Pfaff, "Vietnam, Czechoslovakia, and
the Fitness to Lead," *New Yorker*, July 3, 1971, pp. 33-34. See Harry Kalven, Jr.,
"Introduction," *Contempt* (Chicago: Swallow Press, 1970), on "contemporary
tensions between decorum and justice." Or as a notorious Chicago pornography
peddler protested, upon being harassed by the police, "After all, this is still the
United States, and we still should fight for the things that made our country great."
Chicago Sun-Times, January 5, 1972, p. 16.

*The notes which follow, including the remainder of this first note, pertain directly
to the citizens' speech—that is to say, to the* Logos.

"Obscenity," George Orwell observed, "is a very difficult question to discuss
honestly. People are too frightened either of seeming to be shocked or of seeming
not to be shocked, to be able to define the relationship between art and morals."
Critical Essays (London: Secker and Warburg, 1954), p. 142. See note 12, below.

When we concern ourselves with the problem of obscenity today are we really
concerning ourselves, in a secular manner, with the now unfashionable but nevertheless politically vital problem of piety? See, e.g., *Exodus* 3:6; *Deuteronomy* 34:6;
Essay VII, note 6, above. Consider, also, with respect to piety, W. E. B. Du Bois,
Souls of Black Folk (Chicago: A. C. McClurg & Co., 1903), pp. 11-12: ". . . all in
all, we black men seem the sole oasis of simple faith and reverence in a dusty
desert of dollars and smartness." Cf. *ibid.*, p. 8: "To be a poor man is hard, to be a
poor race in a land of dollars is the very bottom of hardships." Cf., also, Anastaplo,
"Neither Black nor White: The Negro in America," in *Notes on the First Amendment* (Essay IV, note 28, above).

However offensive public obscenity may be, we should be careful not to bring
government and law into disrepute by relying upon force and the criminal courts,
in lieu of more appropriate social measures, to remedy (or would it be to mask?)
our most pressing deficiencies as a community. "After some lesser business they
discussed the reconstruction of the South . . . 'No one need expect me,' said
Abraham Lincoln, 'to take any part in hanging or killing these men, even the worst
of them. Frighten them out of the country, open the gates, let down the bars, scare
them off.' 'Shoo,' he added, throwing up his large hands like a man scaring sheep.
'We must extinguish our resentments if we expect harmony and union. . . .'" Lord
Charnwood, *Abraham Lincoln* (Garden City: Garden City Publishing Co., 1917),
p. 450.

2. Aristotle, *Nicomachean Ethics*, I, ii, X, ix. See Euripides, *Rhesus* 105; *Suppliant
Women* 160-162, 195sq, 334sq, 1227sq. See, also, notes 13, 25, below. Cf. Homer,
Iliad, III, 64-66 (where Paris instructs Hector about the gifts of Aphrodite). Cf.,

also, Aristotle, *Nicomachean Ethics* 1162a16sq, 1177a12sq. But see Gibbon, *Decline and Fall*, I, 50-53, on the effects of a people settling into and for their private lives.

3. Thus we see in the opening sentences of John Milton's *Areopagitica* a movement from the advancement of "the public good" to the promotion of his "country's liberty" as the primary duty of the public-spirited citizen. See, also, note 26, below. Are not both the mobs and the Caesarism diagnosed by the young Lincoln (in his Perpetuation Speech of 1838) generated by the liberty promoted by our regime?

4. *Leisy v. Hardin*, 135 U.S. 100, 158 (1890) (a dissenting opinion by Justice Gray, endorsed by Justices Harlan and Brewer). Cf. Montesquieu, *The Spirit of the Laws*, XXI, xx, "How Commerce Broke Through the Barbarism of Europe."

"The end of all political struggle is to establish morality as the basis of all legislation. 'T is not free institutions, 't is not a democracy that is the end,—no, but only the means. Morality is the object of government. We want a state of things in which crime will not pay; a state of things which allows every man the largest liberty compatible with the liberty of every other man." Ralph Waldo Emerson, *Complete Works* (Boston: Houghton Mifflin Co., 1911), XI, 540-41. See note 13, below. Cf. Averroes, *Commentary on Plato's Republic* 27.14sq.

5. July 13, 1787; *Documents Illustrative of the Formation of the Union of the American States* (69th Cong., 1st Sess.; Hse. Doc. 398) (Washington: Government Printing Office, 1927), p. 373.

See, also, the religion-minded Article 45, Pennsylvania Constitution of 1776 ("Laws for the encouragement of virtue, and prevention of vice and immorality, shall be made and constantly kept in force . . ."); note 1, above (on piety).

6. See, for example, Clarence Darrow's suggestion about the influence of Friedrich Nietzsche's writings on an impressionable college student. *The Plea of Clarence Darrow in Defence of Richard Loeb and Nathan Leopold on Trial for Murder* (Chicago: R. F. Seymour, 1924), pp. 77-86. Cf. Montesquieu, *The Spirit of the Laws*, XII, xii.

7. Plutarch, *Lycurgus*. Milton, in *Areopagitica*, explains that Lycurgus "sent the poet Thales [to Sparta] from Crete to prepare and mollify the Spartan surliness with his smooth songs and odes, the better to plant among them law and civility . . ." See, also, on Thales, his connection with Onomacritus, the central figure in the "history" of lawgivers found in Aristotle, *Politics*, II, xii. Consider the significance of the discordance at the end of Plato's *Crito*, a discordance which protects from rational examination the "argument" of the single-minded laws.

Gibbon, in his *Decline and Fall of the Roman Empire* (c. 1, n. 39), suggests, "There is room for a very interesting work, which should lay open the connection between the languages and manners of nations." See, also, *ibid.*, I, 33-35; Plato, *Laws* 656c-657c; *Prose Works of John Milton* (London: J. Johnson, 1806), I, pp. xi-xii; Kurt Riezler, *Man, Mutable and Immutable* (Chicago: Henry Regnery Co., 1950), pp. 94-109. (What is obscene, so far as language-in-itself is, may be somewhat arbitrary or conventional. But it is natural for men to have conventions. [See note 12, below.] And it is salutary for the human being to practise self-restraint by respecting to a reasonable degree the conventions citizens believe necessary.)

Whatever may be said about the legislation of morality, it should not be expected that the very best can be legislated but, at most, the conditions for the emergence of the very best. Consider, for instance, the compromise with the very best implied in Xenophon, *Cyropaedeia* 1.2.7 (describing criminal processes among the Persians for ingratitude). Such a compromise is reflected as well in the kind of statute assessed in *Beauharnais v. Illinois*, 343 U.S. 250 (1952).

Compare, in Plutarch's *Nicias* and *Marcellus*, the stories of the Athenian Nicias and the Sicilian Nicias: the former allowed superstition to paralyze him politically, the latter ingeniously put superstition to political use. See Essay II, note 28, above.

8. Harry Kalven, Jr., "Metaphysics of the Law of Obscenity," 1960 *Supreme Court Review* 1, 3-4 (1960).

9. *Ibid.*, p. 4. Compare the respect shown for conventions by ruthless leaders as divergent as those quoted in note 17, below. See, also, note 12, below. (Does ruthlessness mean a denial of nature and hence even greater reliance than usual on convention, on what happens to be decreed? Charlotte Bronte argued [in a preface to *Jane Eyre*] in opposition to those "in whose eyes whatever is unusual is wrong": "Conventionality is not morality. Self-righteousness is not religion.")

Is not too much made today of the qualification, "a voluntary audience" (or, as we often hear, "consenting adults")? What induces more and more adults *to* "consent"? And may not this undermine, by a kind of seepage, the entire community, without the community as such really having had an opportunity to consent?

Do not "consent" and "voluntary" imply that the consenter understands what he is doing? Compare the "consent" of the taste buds to foods which harm the heart. See Shakespeare, *Coriolanus*, I, i, 99-150.

10. Compare a nineteenth century appraisal of political offenders: "It may be expedient to prosecute political delinquency, even to the death, but certainly not necessarily on account of the moral iniquity of the accused. Amidst conflicts of opinion, each half of the community is seditious in the sight of the other. When governments are unsettled, it has often been doubtful, with the purest characters, whether treason itself was not a duty. The English revolution made traitors *in law* of men of the highest personal honour; nor was it till things got solid, by the subsidence of the loose matter connected with that event, that personal integrity and political innocence became the same. To see no difference between political and other offences is the sure mark of an excited or of a stupid head. . . ." Henry Cockburn, *An Examination of the Trials for Sedition Which Have Hitherto Occurred in Scotland* (Edinburgh: D. Douglas, 1888), I, 68. See note 26, below.

See, on licentious words, Plutarch, *Moralia* 28A (Loeb Classical Library edition); Aristotle, *Politics* 1336b5.

11. ". . . But let us not flatter ourselves that we shall preserve our liberty in renouncing the morals which acquired it." Jean-Jacques Rousseau, *Letter to M. d'Alembert on the Theatre*, in Allan Bloom (trans.), *Politics and the Arts* (Glencoe, Ill.: Free Press, 1960), p. 113. Does not a community's liberty depend on its morale as well as on its morals? See, on morale, note 21, below. Cf., in Plutarch's *Pelopidas* 18-19, the account of the Sacred Band.

See, with respect to the epigraph for this citizens' speech, Plato, *Republic* 466e, 537a; Aristotle, *Nicomachean Ethics* 1149a 35sq.; Dante, *Inferno*, xxx, 130-148; Charles Darwin, *The Expression of Emotions in Man and Animals* (Chicago: Phoenix Books, University of Chicago Press, 1965), p. 293; Orwell, *Critical Essays*, pp. 142-43. See, also, Charnwood, *Abraham Lincoln*, p. 13: "The words of [Lincoln's] political associate in Illinois . . . may suffice. He writes: 'Almost any man, who will tell a very vulgar story, has, in a degree, a vulgar mind. But it was not so with [Lincoln]; with all his purity of character and exalted morality and sensibility, which no man can doubt, when hunting for wit he had no ability to discriminate between the vulgar and refined substances from which he extracted it. It was the wit he was after, the pure jewel, and he would pick it up out of the mud or dirt just as readily as from a parlour table.' In any case [Charnwood continues] his best remembered utterances of this order, when least fit for print, were both wise and incomparably witty, and in any case they did not prevent grave gentlemen, who marvelled at them rather uncomfortably, from receiving the deep impression of what they called his pure-mindedness."

See, also, as a sample of the "incomparably witty" Chaucer (whose intelligence it is easy to underestimate), "The Franklin's Tale." The heroine's self-preservative instincts "unconsciously" move her from reliance upon a set of precedents which center upon death with honor to reliance upon a set of precedents which center upon survival with reputation (for which Odysseus' Penelope provides her the most welcome model). Indeed, this story reflects throughout the Epicurean inclinations (see lines 331-360 of the Prologue to the *Tales*) of the franklin who relates it.

Is it distinctive of modern man that he has "no ability to discriminate between the vulgar and refined substances" which he shapes to his purposes? Consider the spider in Jonathan Swift's *Battle of the Books*.

12. Edward Albee wrote, in a preface to *The American Dream* (New York: Signet Book, New American Library, 1961), p. 54:

Is the play offensive? I certainly hope so; it was my intention to offend—as well as amuse and entertain. Is it nihilist, immoral, defeatist? Well, to that let me answer that *The American Dream* is a picture of our time—as I see it, of course. Every honest work is a personal, private yowl, a statement of one individual's pleasure or pain; but I hope that *The American Dream* is something more than that. I hope that it transcends the personal and the private, and has something to do with the anguish of us all.

(Cf. *The Selected Letters of Gustave Flaubert*, Frances Steegmuller, editor [New York: Vintage Books, 1957], pp. ix ["No lyricism, no comments, the author's personality absent!"], 148, 165-166, 194, 266.)

It is not suggested here, of course, that Mr. Albee should have been prosecuted for anything he has published. Instruction would have been more appropriate. See Heraclitus, Fr. 15 ("Their processions and their phallic hymns would be disgraceful exhibitions, were it not that they are done in honor of Dionysos."); Ovid, *The Art of Love* (New York: Universal Library, Grosset & Dunlap, 1959), p. 160 ("the laws of modesty"); Moses Maimonides, *The Guide of the Perplexed* (Chicago: University of Chicago Press, 1963), pp. 432-36, 573, 604; Sigmund Freud, *A General Introduction to Psychoanalysis* (New York: Washington Square Press, 1960), p. 194 (on due regard for that which is "most intimate in the personality"); Bertrand Russell, *Why I Am Not a Christian and other essays* (New York: Clarion Book, Simon and Schuster, 1957), p. 173 (emphasis added) (". . . The conception of the obscene has its roots deep in human nature. We may go against it from a love of rebellion, or from loyalty to the scientific spirit, *or from a wish to feel wicked*, such as existed in Byron; but we do not thereby eradicate it from among our natural impulses. No doubt convention determines, in a given community, exactly what is to be considered indecent, but the universal existence of *some* convention of the kind is conclusive evidence of a source which is not merely conventional. In almost every human society, pornography and exhibitionism are reckoned as offenses, except when, as not infrequently occurs, they form part of religious ceremonies." See note 18, below, for the passage preceding this one.).

Also instructive is Flaubert's lament, "Ah! Ce qui manque à la société moderne ce n'est pas un Christ, ni un Washington, ni un Socrate, ni un Voltaire, c'est un Aristophane." Quoted by Ortega y Gasset, *Meditations on Quixote* (New York: W. W. Norton & Co., 1961), pp. 162-63.

13. Leo Strauss, *Natural Right and History* (Chicago: University of Chicago Press, 1953), p. 323. Mr. Strauss continues, in this passage, "[Edmund] Burke himself was still too deeply imbued with the spirit of 'sound antiquity' to allow the concern with individuality to overpower the concern with virtue." See, also, Strauss, *The City and Man* (Chicago: Rand McNally, 1964), pp. 97-98; Essays II, IV, above.

The transformed status in modernity of "individuality" is suggested by two

radically different conceptions of law. The orthodox ancient teaching can be said
to have been that whatever the law (in the broadest sense of "law") does not command, it forbids. See Aristotle, *Nicomachean Ethics* 1138a4-8. Certainly, one of the
critical purposes of the law was understood to be that of promoting virtue. On the
other hand, "[T]he prevailing view [today is that] State interference is an evil, where
it cannot be shown to be a good." Oliver W. Holmes, Jr., *The Common Law* (Boston: Little, Brown, 1881), p. 96. Francis Bacon remained enough of an "ancient"
to believe, "I am of his mind that said, 'Better it is to live where nothing is lawful,
than where all things are lawful.'" *Apothegms*, No. 69. See Aristotle, *Nicomachean
Ethics* 1094a27, 1103b3, 1109b33, 1113b22, 1130b8, 1130b28, 1178a8, 1179b31, 1180a33;
Politics 1253a2, 1253a19, 1276b16, 1280b5, 1293b3, 1309b31, 1328a17, 1329a29, 1332a33,
1335b13, 1337a1, 1341b33. Cf. Aristotle, *N. Ethics* 1141a29, 1143b33, 1145a10, 1162a16,
1177a12; *Politics* 1271b1, 1287b9, 1324b5, 1333b22. See, also, Leo Strauss, *The City
and Man*, pp. 30-31, 41-45; Harry V. Jaffa, "Aristotle," in *History of Political
Philosophy*, Leo Strauss and Joseph Cropsey, editors (Chicago: Rand McNally,
1963), p. 67; Laurence Berns, "Thomas Hobbes," in *History of Political Philosophy*,
pp. 362, 366; notes 2, 4, above. Cf. Thomas Jefferson, *Notes on the State of Virginia*,
Query XI (New York: Harper Torchbooks, 1964), p. 90:
> ... were it made a question, whether no law, as among the savage Americans,
> or too much law, as among the civilized Europeans, submits man to the greatest
> evil, one who has seen both conditions of existence would pronounce it to be the
> last; ... the sheep are happier of themselves, than under the care of the wolves. ...

Cf., also, Plato, *Republic* 343; *Fables of Aesop* (London: Penguin Books, 1964),
p. 44.

14. This appetite for novelty is reinforced by the shamelessness which modern democracy seems to encourage. (See, also, notes 16, 22, below.) It may be seen as well
in the emphasis we now place on the value of artistic self-expression. Thus, one of
Oscar Wilde's characters (*The Picture of Dorian Gray*, c. 19) assumes art to be
"simply a method of procuring extraordinary sensations." Consider the "unbounded
passion for variety" which Gibbon describes. *Decline and Fall*, I, 74.

Is not the identification of the artist with the bohemian life (or with the life of
the expatriate) essentially modern? See, for example, James Joyce, *Portrait of the
Artist as a Young Man*. Cf. Laurence Berns, "Aristotle's *Poetics*," in *Ancients and
Moderns*, Joseph Cropsey, editor (New York: Basic Books, 1964). Cf., also, note 7,
above, on Euripides' *Orestes*.

One sees all too often today the man of genuine talent descending to fabrication
of the merely shocking and sensational, thereby exhibiting the affliction which has
paralyzed his artistic sense. That is, whatever talent he does retain unencumbered is
employed to make something which is no more than ingenious. One can hope that
that which is deep within him remains untouched by such exploitation. When a
man of genuine talent sets out to shock, it is the polemicist or the sick man or the
hostile man in him who seeks expression, not the true artist. It is the "self," not his
art, which is thus mobilizing his talents. Such distortions are applauded by the petty
and the disenchanted—by those, that is, who were always beneath the vision he had
had and who sense he has now come down to their level. Do not most artists
depend on the guidance and discipline of a healthy community in order to do their
best work? Does not Plutarch (in *Pericles* 13.3) regard the Acropolis at least as
much Pericles' as Phideas' work (or, as we would say, "creation")? See note 20,
below.

See, on the lure of novelty, Homer, *Odyssey*, I, 351-352; Aristotle, *Nicomachean
Ethics* 1154b20-30; the exploits of the King and the Duke in Mark Twain's *Huckleberry Finn*. Cf. Aristotle, *Politics* 1336b27-36.

15. See, on the relation of temperance and prudence, Aristotle, *Nicomachean Ethics* 1140b12sq. See, also, Averroes, *Commentary on Plato's Republic* 32.24sq, 49.14sq, 86.23sq. Cf. *ibid.* 59.10-12.

It has been suggested that exposure to the most blatant obscenity can sometimes be therapeutic. Perhaps a physician's prescription could be made available in appropriate cases. But the healthy reader or the serious writer should not require more eroticism than what Homer says of Odysseus and Calypso or of Odysseus and Circe. See *Odyssey*, V, 225-227, X, 333-335. Cf. *ibid.*, XXIII, 300-309, 321-325, 333-337. See, also, *ibid.*, VIII, 266-369. Cf., also, Plato, *Republic* 607d. (The contemporary reader could well be diverted, from what is legitimate in what he seeks for in obscenity, to the restrained portrayals of modern love in the novels of Graham Greene and to the adventure stories of John Buchan and Geoffrey Household [stories which have their excitement heightened by portrayals of heroes who happen to be pursued both by the police and by evil men]. Cf. John Donne, "The Extasie.")

Compare the vantage point at which Jonathan Swift places the poet in "A Description of a City Shower." Compare, also, the unexpurgated poems of Catullus —"documents" which are valuable for mankind to have and perhaps to leave in the original Latin. (See, on Catullus, William Butler Yeats, "The Scholars." See, also, Ovid, *Heroides and Amores* [London: William Heinemann; Loeb Classical Library, 1914], pp. 506-508, with respect to *Amores* III, vii.)

16. Richard M. Weaver, *Ideas Have Consequences* (Chicago: University of Chicago Press, 1948), pp. 27-28. See note 22, below. The first chapter of Mr. Weaver's book, "The Unsentimental Sentiment," is particularly valuable for the student of the problem of obscenity. (Thus, one need not say, as is done in this speech, *"public* obscenity": that which would be obscene in public need not be so in private [as, for example, between lovers or between doctor and patient].)

The following announcement, posted by the "Management", has been observed on a law school bulletin board: *"Playboy* at the Law Club Store. Also various other 'mags' which may appeal to your 'prurient interest.' We know when we see it, and this is it." Cf. "the dreams all men carry in their loins" (John Vieners, "For Jan," in Paris Leary and Robert Kelly, *A Controversy of Poets* [Garden City: Doubleday, 1965], p. 480); "for this is a goodly thing, to listen to a minstrel such as this man is, like to the gods in voice" (Homer, *Odyssey*, I, 370-371); "This aptness of language is one thing that makes people believe in the truth of a story . . ." (Aristotle, *Rhetoric* 1408a20) (consider, for example, the language employed by Shakespeare's imprudent Brutus ["There is a tide in the affairs of men . . ."] to persuade Cassius against his better judgment as to where Brutus and Cassius should fight Antony and Octavius).

17. We should be reminded of the retort of J. P. Morgan to the associate who complained that Morgan was angry with him for doing in public what others did behind closed doors, "That's what doors are for!"

"It was Zhdanov who reported Stalin's observation on the book of love poems by K. Simonov: 'They should have published only two copies—one for her, and one for him!' At which Stalin smiled demurely while the others roared." Milovan Djilas, *Conversations with Stalin* (New York: Harcourt, Brace & World, 1962), p. 158. See, also, the next paragraph in the Djilas text.

And it was Nikita Khrushchev who protested, upon having can-can dancers thrust upon him in Hollywood in 1959, that "humanity's face is more beautiful than her backside." See note 9, above.

As obscenity becomes a commonplace among us, privacy necessarily becomes more and more of a problem?

18. *Regina v. Hicklin*, L.R., 3 Q.B. 360, 371 (1868). Cf. Judge Hand in *U. S. v. Kenner-*

ley, 209 Fed. 119, 120-121 (1913); Lord Birkett, in *Does Pornography Matter?*
(ed. C. H. Rolph) (London: Routledge & Kegan Paul, 1961), pp. 8-9. Lord Cockburn's opinion in *Hicklin* continues, at pp. 371-72, "Now, with regard to this work,
it is quite certain that it would suggest to the minds of the young of either sex, or
even to persons of more advanced years, thoughts of a most impure and libidinous
character. . . . I take it therefore, that, apart from the ulterior object which the
publisher of this work had in view, the work itself is, in every sense of the term,
an obscene publication . . . But, then, it is said for the appellant, 'Yes, but his purpose
was not to deprave the public mind; his purpose is to expose the errors of the
Roman Catholic religion especially in the matter of the confessional.' Be it so. The
question then presents itself in this simple form: May you commit an offence against
the law in order that thereby you may effect some ulterior object which you have
in view, which may be an honest and even a laudable one? My answer is, emphati-
cally, no. The law says, you shall not publish an obscene work. An obscene work
is here published, and a work the obscenity of which is so clear and decided, that it
is impossible to suppose that the man who published it must not have known and
seen that the effect upon the minds of many of those into whose hands it would
come would be of a mischievous and demoralizing character. Is he justified in doing
that which clearly would be wrong, legally as well as morally, because he thinks
that some greater good may be accomplished? . . . I think the old sound and honest
maxim, that you shall not do evil that good may come, is applicable in law as well
as in morals; and here we have a certain and positive evil produced for the purpose
of effecting an uncertain, remote, and very doubtful good . . ."

Obscenity cases presuppose and thereby reaffirm a community's dedication to a
good society, however vague, uninformed and even misdirected that dedication may
often be. It is such vagueness which sometimes puts a prosecutor in the awkward
position of having to urge a jury to reclaim and apply a standard alleged by him
to be *the* community standard. But, on the other hand, is it not unreasonable to
suppose that there was no good reason heretofore for virtually all communities
imposing restraints upon what may be said publicly about certain things? Consider,
for example, the quotation from Bertrand Russell in note 12, above, a passage
which is immediately preceded by his observation, ". . . Modesty, in some form and
to some degree, is almost universal in the human race and constitutes a taboo which
must only be broken through in accordance with certain forms and ceremonies, or,
at least, in conformity with some recognized etiquette. Not everything may be seen,
and not all facts may be mentioned. This is not, as some moderns suppose, an inven-
tion of the Victorian age; on the contrary, anthropologists have found the most
elaborate forms of prudery among primitive savages." *Why I Am Not a Christian*,
pp. 172-173. Consider, also, Shakespeare, *Macbeth*, V, i; Euripides, *Ion* 230-232.

19. *Smith* v. *California*, 361 U.S. 147 (1959), *Transcript of Record*, Supreme Court of
the United States, pp. 81-83. The principal book in question (which has long been
unavailable) was *Sweeter Than Life* (New York: Vixen Press, 1954) by Mark
Tryon (a pseudonym).

A useful discussion of *Smith* v. *California* may be found in William B. Lockhard
and Robert C. McClure, "Censorship of Obscenity: The Developing Constitutional
Standards," 45 *Minnesota Law Review* 5, 43-47, 103-108 (1960). The authors described the case as one in which the Supreme Court "added a requirement of *scienter*
for criminal prosecutions to the battery of constitutional requirements that the Court
had already established, and thus seemed to jeopardize the widespread use of abrupt
criminal prosecutions as a means of suppressing materials thought to be objectionable." *Ibid.*, p. 43. See note 24, below.

20. Or rather, "adverse" publicity emanating from whatever journals do notice such books can usually be depended upon to promote sales.

Is it not both selfish and dangerous for intellectuals to insist, without regard for the effect on the moral opinions of the community at large, upon every minority's right to "express" itself as it pleases? See Plutarch's *Nicias* and *Alcibiades*. See, also, notes 25, 26, below.

Is it significant that that which is a "duty" for the judge in *Smith* v. *California* is no more than a "job" for defense counsel? It should be noticed that defense counsel's concluding comment about "whims of fate" (does he mean "chance"?) suggests that the making and preservation of virtuous men are considered by him essentially beyond the control of human reason. See the opening passage of Plato's *Meno* and the closing chapter of the *Nicomachean Ethics*. See, also, note 23, below. Cf. the beginning of Plutarch's *Dion*.

It should also be noticed that the judge sometimes confused in his remarks a description of how someone is corrupted with a description of something which would contribute to the corruption of readers. The former kind of description may not corrupt readers. Indeed, it may even be salutary to be shown how someone *is* corrupted, especially someone for whom the reader can be taught to care. Consider, for instance, the sort of thing Gustave Flaubert uses to attract us to Emma Bovary: "Countrystyle, [Emma] offered [her future husband] something to drink. He refused, she insisted, and finally suggested with a laugh that he take a liquer with her. She brought a bottle of curaçao from the cupboard, reached to a high shelf for two liquer glasses, filled one to the brim and poured a few drops in the other. She touched her glass to his and raised it to her mouth. Because it was almost empty she had to bend backwards to be able to drink; and with her head tilted back, her neck and her lips outstretched, she began to laugh at tasting nothing; and then the tip of her tongue came out from between her small teeth and began daintily to lick the bottom of the glass." *Madame Bovary* (New York: Modern Library, 1957), p. 25. Cf. *ibid.*, p. 357. Cf., also, *ibid.*, pp. 216, 277-279, 369-370. See *Selected Letters of Flaubert*, pp. 136-137, 140, 148, 162-164, 170-171, 177-179, 181, 184. See, also, Willa Cather, *A Lost Lady* (New York: Vintage Books, 1972), p. 13 (on the captivating Mrs. Forrester).

Does the "liberation" of artists, with the attendant demands of the "market," make it likely that bad literature will tend to drive out good? Would a Flaubert, for example, be obliged, lest he be ignored as "too tame," to be much more "explicit" than even he thought would be good for his art? See the text at note 12, above. See, also, note 14, above. See, as well, Willa Cather, *On Writing* (New York: Alfred A. Knopf, 1949), p. 42.

21. To "care" about such matters is to seem (and perhaps even to be) somewhat naive. See Plato, *Republic* 414d. See, also, Hobbes, *Leviathan*, c. 10 ("To speak [to another] harshly, to do anything before him obscenely, slovenly, impudently, is to dishonor [him]."). May there not be in the deliberate (even gratuitous) affront of obscenity an assault upon the sense of honor of a concerned community?

Consider, on the relation of naïveté and caring, the 1904 letter of the revered University of Chicago football coach, Amos Alonzo Stagg, to the President of the University:

It is with the greatest pleasure and satisfaction that I herewith send you a check for $1000 as a gift to the University. It was just a year ago during my sickness, you will remember, that the thought of making this gift came to me. I was greatly depressed and worried by the spirit shown by our team in the Thanksgiving Day contest, and in casting about for possible helpful things, my mind went back to my own college days at Yale. The sweet chimes of Battell

Chapel has always been an inspiration to me, and I recalled the many, many times during the period of my training that that cheery, hopeful ten o'clock chime had led me to fall asleep with a quiet determination for a greater devotion to duty and to my ideals.

The thought came to me and filled me with the deepest satisfaction, "Why not have a goodnight chime for our own athletes? to let its sweet cadence have a last word with them before they fall asleep; to speak to them of love and loyalty and sacrifice for their University and of hope and inspiration and endeavor for the morrow."

Whenever, therefore, the Alice Freeman Palmer chimes are installed, it would be my wish to have a special cadence rung for our athletes who are in training —perhaps five to ten minutes after the regular chimes at ten o'clock.
University of Chicago Maroon, April 26, 1957, p. 5.

Consider, also, the implications of Prime Minister Jawaharlal Nehru's remarks, in a letter of June 28, 1959, to Shri Bimal Roy, "I am glad to tell you that I liked your film *Sujata*. . . . It is a good film with good photography, and the story is interesting. There is always a danger in films which have too obvious a moral purpose, to become dull. . . ." See Averroes, *Commentary on Plato's Republic* 32.24sq, 49.14sq.

22. "This failure of the concept of obscenity has been concurrent with the rise of the institution of publicity which, ever seeking to widen its field *in accordance with the canon of progress*, makes a virtue of desecration." Weaver, *Ideas Have Consequences*, p. 28 (italics added).

Two photographs in the May 28, 1965 issue of *Time*, at pages 22 and 28, are examples of such desecration. Such pictures, especially since they *are* related to political discussion, are (and should be) hard for the law to deal with. See note 26, below. Cf. the quotation from *Regina* v. *Hicklin* in note 18, above.

If the traditionally (and obviously) obscene should come to be considered illegitimate for the community to discourage, the more critical instances of harmful publication and display are not going to be addressed either. That is, permissiveness with respect to obscenity both implies and reinforces the opinion that the character of its people is not a proper concern of the community. That which is not believed to be a proper concern is not likely to be dealt with properly.

23. We would take more seriously the concern often expressed about the possible temporary discouragement of the public sale of an occasional good book (because of restraints upon obscenity) if we could believe that the truly great books we already have were being seriously studied among us. If serious programs of undergraduate study, of which St. John's College is probably the best in the United States today, were generally established, the problem of the effects on the community of a thoughtless toleration of obscenity would become (would have become?) trivial. (See Gibbon, *Decline and Fall*, I, 783-784.)

In any event, it is unrealistic to expect a people to *choose* the better over the worse without proper training. Such training is unlikely either to be available or to be taken seriously if it should become generally fashionable to believe that it is all "but a matter of taste" what one should like. (Does not "matter of taste" come down, in this sense, to little more than "matter of chance"?) Is it not also unrealistic to expect many parents (assuming *they* happen to be properly trained) to be able to train their children in how to make proper choices in the face of whatever corrupting effort may be exerted by "the mass media"? Such parents would be obliged to devote themselves fulltime to the task and to run the risk as well of appearing tyrannical (thereby undermining parental respect in youngsters who see themselves "deprived" of what others are permitted to "enjoy"). It is, upon considering such circumstances, that one becomes aware of how much the family depends on the community to legitimate and thus help establish the moral standards which particular parents may then be in a position to refine further. See note 7, above. (If community support is inadequate, the integrity of the family is further undermined as children are wooed by the more permissive parent at the expense of the more disciplined—and all in the name of "love.")

24. We assume that no informed student of these matters in the West today regards with favor a return to any systematic program of licensing and "previous restraint" of printed matter. One problem with "previous restraint" is reflected in George Bernard Shaw's 1899 comment, "What, then, is to be done with the Censorship [i.e., the licensing of plays for performance]? Nothing can be simpler. Abolish it, root and branch, throwing the whole legal responsibility for plays on the author and manager, precisely as the legal responsibility for a book is thrown on the author, the printer, and the publisher. The managers will not like this: their present slavery is safer and easier; but it will be good for them, and good for the Drama." "The Censorship of the Stage in England," in *Shaw on Theatre*, E. J. West, editor (New York: Hill and Wang, 1958), p. 79.

A serious due process question can arise from the deliberate harassment of publishers and booksellers resulting from governmental shopping among jurisdictions in which to bring prosecutions most inconvenient for defendants. See note 19, above.

25. See, on the political relevance of circumstances, Aristotle, *Politics* 1288b22.

It *is* possible that the best available means for reducing appreciably the appeal and hence the significance of obscenity among us today might be, as some advocate, to repeal (with the proper explanation) all laws relating thereto. (Cf. note 22, above.) But would such advocates concede the right and even the duty of the community to intervene if the experiment should clearly result in a distinct coarsening of public discourse or in a pervasive moral flabbiness? That is, we are obliged to return again and again to what may be for us on this occasion the key question, "What *is* it legitimate for the community to be concerned about?" What answer to this question is implied by the fact that we, as a community, rely upon considerable legislation and tax revenue in establishing and maintaining our public schools? Do we not exhibit by our constant activity as a community the opinion that it is cavalier and shallow to insist that everyone can or should be left alone "to mind his own business"?

Compare the observation that "English Literature towers high above English Drama [which is subject to licensing] because Literature is subject to no judgment but that of its natural masters, the authors." Shaw, "The Censorship of the Stage in England," p. 77. Who are indeed the "natural masters" of literature? The masters for one purpose (that is, writing) may not be the masters for another (that is, distribution within a community of what happens to be written). See, in Francis Bacon's *New Atlantis*, the regulation of the public use, as distinguished from the private development, of inventions (Essay VII, epigraph, above). See, also, notes 2, 4, above.

26. "For this is not the liberty which we can hope, that no grievance ever should arise in the Commonwealth—that let no man in this world expect; but when complaints are freely heard, deeply considered and speedily reformed, then is the utmost bound of civil liberty attained that wise men look for." Milton, *Areopagitica*. See note 10, above. The government cannot reasonably be regarded, in the typical obscenity case, as trying to suppress grievances or complaints against itself, something which we are properly suspicious of whenever we encounter any attempted suppression of political speech.

One good argument *against* official restrictions upon obscenity is that they might be extended to interfere as well with our indispensable (however occasionally un-settling) political discussion, especially if we have come to equate literary expression with political speech. Would it be an argument *for* moderate restrictions upon obscenity now if it should be shown that the repression eventually provoked by continued licentiousness is likely to threaten freedom of political discussion as well? Besides, does not effective political freedom depend upon a people with a sturdy moral character, something that preoccupation with sensual gratification (or habit-ual public discourse about it) makes highly unlikely? See note 11, above. Cer-tainly, it is not prudent to believe that such widespread changes in language, opinions and style as we have witnessed in our time will have no significant political effects. See Aristotle, *Politics*, VIII, v (on virtue consisting "in feeling delight where one should and loving and hating aright"). Nor is it prudent to ex-pect that there will be no massive public reaction (however uninformed and hence self-defeating) against the current licentiousness: a radical change of regime may even begin to appeal to some as the only way out of the swamp. But are not over-grown swamps better than the bleak wastelands of contemporary tyrannies, whether of the Left or of the Right? Cultivated lands are, of course, even better.

Prudence also requires us to have a due regard for Mr. Weaver's caution (*Ideas Have Consequences*, p. 101):

That the public as a whole misses the issue of the motion picture's influence can be seen from its attitude toward censorship. For what the public is recon-ciled to seeing censored are just the little breaches of decorum which fret bourgeois respectability and sense of security. The truth is that these are so far removed from the heart of the problem that they could well be ignored. . . .

We have, in this attempt to suggest and examine first principles, ignored the distinctively American problem of federal-state relations. Much is to be said for allowing considerable local control (and hence variations among localities) in such matters. See *Jacobellis* v. *Ohio* (dissenting opinion), 378 U.S. 184, 204-205 (1964). See, also, Anastaplo, "Freedom of Speech and the First Amendment," 42 *University of Detroit Law Journal* 54 (1964); "Due Process of Law—An Introduction," 42 *ibid.* 195 (1964); "Closing Argument before the Committee on Character and Fit-ness," 19 *Lawyers Guild Review* 143 (1959). See, as well, *In re Anastaplo*, 366 U.S. 82 (1961); Essay IX, above.

XI. Canada and Quebec Separatism

1. Just as we can learn from Canada, Canadians have an opportunity to glimpse their future at our expense. A valuable study is George Grant, *Lament for a Nation: The Defeat of Canadian Nationalism* (Princeton: D. Van Nostrand Co., 1965). See also, *The Constitutionalist* (Essay I, note 1, above), c. 3, nn. 22, 28, c. 9, n. 1. See, as well, note 4, below.

This May 1971 report is a sequel to an article by me, "Canada and the Dilemmas of Decent Men," which was prepared for the *Chicago Daily News* (where it was published, in an edited version, on November 26, 1970) and which has been re-printed in its entirety in 116 *Congressional Record* E11057 (January 2, 1971). My November 1970 article includes this observation by way of "background" (at p. E11057),

. . . No Canadian government is in the position (no matter what its parlia-mentary majority) to "repeal" the two hundred years of history etched deep in the French-Canadian soul, a soul scarred by memories of having been conquered by the British and subjugated thereafter to essentially alien political and economic forms. What the government *can* do is to moderate from time to time French-Canadian separatist sentiment, but that sentiment will remain and will flare up whenever other grievances accumulate. The government is not likely to be able to do enough to eradicate such sentiment without either surrendering the entire country to French-Canadian rule (and thus promoting English-speaking separatism, of which there are already significant traces in the Western provinces) or simply forcing a thorough assimilation of French Canadians (beginning with the gradual elimination of the use in Quebec Province of French in the schools and government of the Province). English-speaking Canadians do see the government as already surrendering to the French Canadians, even while the French Canadians see themselves as already being subject to a program of forced assimilation.

2. See, for a study of Canadian law on these matters, Herbert Marx, "The Emergency Power and Civil Liberties in Canada," 16 *McGill Law Journal* 39 (1970). (I have found Professor Marx, of the University of Montreal law faculty, most helpful during my Quebec explorations.)

The use made in the October crisis of the War Measures Act is described in my November 1970 article (at p. E11058):

The principal exceptional powers currently being exercised by the Canadian government are the powers to search and arrest without warrants and to hold citizens a maximum of three weeks without charge. . . . According to the Montreal police, four hundred and forty-seven persons have been arrested in the course of the two thousand raids conducted by them since October 16. Of these, sixty-four remain in custody with fifty-one of them now indicted on such charges as seditious conspiracy.

The War Measures Act permits the federal government to exercise several other exceptional powers, including comprehensive censorship, control of prices and wages, and strict supervision of movement in and out of the country, but these have not been made use of (except for some restrictions placed upon radio and television). . . .

3. See *The Constitutionalist*, Appendix D. See, also, on the claims of governments that they are better informed than private citizens can ever be expected to be, the lecture quoted from at pages 744-745 of *The Constitutionalist;* Essay XII, note 2, below. See, as well, Essay XII, note 3, below.

4. My inquiries into Canadian federalism and the Quebec separatist crisis were prompted, in part, by my interest in American constitutionalism and by my experiences in Russia, Eastern Europe and Greece. See Essay I, above. The problems of the French Canadians bear upon, although they *are* different from, the problems and hence the prospects of Negroes in the United States. Cf. Pierre Vallieres, *Negres Blancs d'Amerique* (Montreal: Editions Parti Pris, 1969).

5. The following observations about the "two ways of life" are included in my November 1970 article (at p. E11057):

These discrepancies [in the unemployment rates described in note 6, below] are partly due to such factors as the superior schooling of the English-speaking and their much greater willingness both to devote themselves and their capital to commerce and to move from one part of the continent to another in search of employment (a willingness facilitated for them by their fluency in the language which dominates North American business). The competitive inferiority of the French Canadians is also partly due, it should be added, to the refusal of their ecclesiastical and political leaders of the past two centuries to prepare them for industrialized modernity. The French-Canadian way of life (with its roots in the France *prior* to the French Revolution) has emphasized much more than that of its English-speaking competitors (who include most of the immigrants, for they learn English, not French, upon arrival in Canada) the value of the family, of land and of tradition. Indeed, the thoughtful man is obliged in Canada more

than are we in this country, to face up to the serious appeals of two contending
sets of opinions about the nature of the good life, each of which does have much
to be said for it.

These observations may not take sufficient account of the chronic unemployment
problems in the English-speaking Maritime provinces. It is true, however, that when
a French Canadian leaves Quebec, he does leave his homeland: he finds it very
difficult to live as a French Canadian in Vermont (where a number have gone over
the years) or in other parts of Canada. See Essay XV, section vi, below.

6. My November 1970 article includes the following information (at p. E11057):

> The immediate grievances which today excite separatist sentiment to the point
> of explosion among French Canadians include the considerable unemployment
> which Quebec Province is now suffering. That province, with little more than
> one-fourth of Canada's 21,000,000 population, has 40% of the unemployed of
> the country. (The Canadian rate of unemployment in 1969 was 4.7%, that of
> Quebec Province was 6.9%. These rates are thought to be even higher this year.
> We, in the United States, are quite troubled today by an unemployment rate of
> 5.6%.) And, to make this recurring grievance even more bitter, virtually all the
> unemployed in Quebec Province are found among the 70% who are the French-
> speaking inhabitants of that province, not among the province's English-speaking
> inhabitants. This means that one French Canadian out of eleven in Quebec
> Province is now out of work.

> Should not Canadians be as receptive to American capital as Americans should be
> to Arab oil capital? Does not such capital, so long as it conforms to the laws of the
> land, tend to promote local prosperity and employment, no matter what its
> source? See, for measures designed to curb the influence of the American press
> (and, eventually, business?) in Canada, 121 *Congressional Record* S3002 (March 4,
> 1975).

7. See, on the continuing French-English debate in Quebec, *Christian Science Monitor*, August 2, 1974, p. 2; *Chicago Sun-Times*, August 6, 1974, p. 16. See, on the
Canadian response to immigration, *Chicago Tribune*, December 3, 1974, sec. 3, p. 17.

> Things do seem to have calmed down in Quebec in recent years but that may be
> due to such temporary influences as the Olympics Games construction program
> and the general (temporary?) retreat by radicals in North America and Europe.
> Even so, it may still be true that the only interesting Canadian politics is in Quebec.
> Certainly it is true that the Canadians continue to impress the American student as
> a sensible people.

> Such sensibleness was relied upon in the concluding remarks of my November
> 1970 article (at p. E11058):

> > One can hope that our Canadian friends pursue a more responsible govern-
> > ment policy than that evident in Chicago both during the Democratic Conven-
> > tion in 1968 and during the "Conspiracy Trial" prosecution following upon the
> > official blunders of Convention Week. Even more is at stake in Canada than
> > there was here in Chicago. Thus, a distinction must be made between firmness
> > and harshness. It takes considerable nerve for men in authority to sit and wait
> > out a crisis, relying only on conventional police powers, on patient political
> > action and on the good will and the good sense of their fellow citizens. Such a
> > restrained course is more likely than dramatic emergency measures to help re-
> > sponsible shapers of opinion among French Canadians to appreciate and to pro-
> > claim in a statesmanlike manner the value for all Canadians of the moderation
> > which their united country is capable of even in a time of serious crisis. *Prudence,*
> > it is encouraging to remember, is spelled the same in French and in English. But
> > so, unfortunately, is *debacle*.

XII. Vietnam and the Constitution

1. Various of the points discussed in this essay are also discussed in *The Constitutionalist* (Essay I, note 1, above): e.g., c. 4, nn. 36, 49, 59, c. 7, n. 67, c. 8, nn. 150, 179, c. 9, n. 11. Also instructive are Anastaplo, "Military Men and Political Questions: What the American Can Learn from Greece Today," 117 *Congressional Record* E6129 (June 17, 1971); "American Constitutionalism and the Virtue of Prudence" (Essay I, note 1, above), e.g., n. 39; Essay XI, section ii, above; Essay XIV, section iii (point 4), below.

   See, on "insubordination," Morton Kondracke, "National Interest versus the right to publish," *Chicago Sun-Times*, March 24, 1975, p. 10; Essay XVI, note 11, below.

2. See, for my discussions of the Pentagon Papers controversy, "Preliminary Reflections on the Pentagon Papers," *University of Chicago Magazine*, Jan.-Feb., March-April 1972 (reprinted in 118 *Congressional Record* S11560 [July 24, 1972]); "Self-Government and the Mass Media," in *The Mass Media and Modern Democracy*, Harry M. Clor, editor (Chicago: Rand McNally, 1974).

   The first part of my "Preliminary Reflections" article includes (at p. 9) some observations on Machiavellianism which bear not only on the subject of this essay but also on the themes which unite the seventeen essays in this collection:

   > It is evident throughout the Pentagon Papers that influential civilians in the government fancied themselves not only tough-minded but scientific as well. . . . With the depreciation of the deliberative element in man—the transformation of the rational into the merely calculating—there has come a depreciation of that serious morality which depends upon reason. Morality, as our Vietnam officials saw it, was something which the public was saddled with, even crippled by: morality fetters one's ability to understand how things really work; it is something which reveals and insures a naive grasp of the affairs of this world. They themselves were liberated from such old-fashioned restraints. That is, they praised as "pragmatism" what would once have been recognized and hence condemned as "Machiavellianism."
   >
   > It was Machiavelli himself who observed that the people in their naivete do tend to be morality-minded in their concerns: while the nobles can be depended upon to want more and more, not caring how they get it, the people are content to be left with the little which is their own. Educated men recognized long before Machiavelli the limitations of public opinion to which I have referred; they considered it one of their duties to try to shape public opinion in a useful manner. But those men, in refusing to go along fully with the simple pieties and naive moralism of the public, did not consider themselves liberated from the demands of morality. Rather, they recognized themselves as best equipped and thereby obliged to serve and realize the very same ethical standards and aspirations which public opinion vaguely, fitfully (sometimes even erotically) but definitely pursues. [See Essay XVI, note 11, below.]
   >
   > But what happens in an age when the teachings of Machiavelli have prevailed, when they have ensnared the more gifted men? (See, on those teachings, Leo Strauss, *Thoughts on Machiavelli* [Glencoe: The Free Press, 1958].) The "educated" continue to recognize the limits, as well as the power, of public opinion (and hence public morality), but they themselves (unlike their predecessors) are not guided by anything really higher or finer. Instead, they become eminently cautious, if not even fearful, as they sacrifice principle and good judgment (to say nothing of the good itself) to the demands of ambition: Plato's Thrasymachus and then his Callicles become their models of sensible men. Thus, the sensible modern is not likely to be moved by anything but a morality keyed to success

and appearance. Indeed, he is apt to be persuaded that it is expected of him that
he should keep even natural compassion well in check. If there is to be, in such
circumstances, any significant ethical restraint upon the exercise of power by the
more gifted men, it *has* to come from the sentimental, even backward, public, at
least until Machiavellian man can be shown what he does and does not know.

It is the success of Machiavellianism (with its persuasion of bright men that
they *should not* be concerned about conventional morality) which helps legitimate the modern constitutional elevation of freedom of speech and of the press
in public life. For it is freedom of speech—which never had to have in ancient
.(that is, pre-Machiavellian) times the status it enjoys today—which can help the
public become as informed as it is capable of becoming. It is freedom of speech
(with all its risks and banalities) which makes it possible for the deepest moral
sense of the community, however crudely it may be expressed at times,·to make
itself felt in the conduct of foreign affairs. It is also freedom of speech which
permits and even obliges citizens in private life to speak on public affairs, those
private citizens who are as informed and intelligent (and sometimes even as
experienced) as the men who happen to be in high office. Thus, it is freedom of
speech and public opinion which help make it possible for us to live humane
lives in an age in which even the most respectable among the sophisticated and
ambitious have been so taken by Machiavelli as to permit themselves to do
terrible things with "a good conscience." . . .

The section of my article in which this passage appeared can be found as well in *The
Journal: Forum for Contemporary History*, June-July 1972, pp. 31-33.

See, for an exchange by Malcolm P. Sharp and me with Mr. Ellsberg, "Self-
Government and the Mass Media," p. 54.

3. See Essay IV, section vi, Essay V, e.g., n. 23. It remains in our interest, of course,
to keep up with what is happening elsewhere in the world. Thus, there is merit
(is there not?) in the following description by the Central Intelligence Agency of
its "mission" (as seen in a flyer distributed in March 1975 to college students):

The primary goal of the national intelligence effort is to provide the facts and
estimates which are needed in the formulation of national security policy and
action. This involves continuous review of overseas trends and developments
which have a bearing on the security interests of the United States. The work
encompasses a variety of talents and many areas of knowledge; its importance
places a heavy premium upon the character and abilities of those who engage in it.

See, for a rather gloomy analysis of and forecast about what is happening elsewhere,
Walter Laqueur, "The Gathering Storm," *Commentary*, August 1974, p. 23. One
can, nevertheless, take *some* comfort from the realization that Mr. Laqueur's appraisal of the situations one *does* know something about (e.g., Greece, at p. 30)
seems somewhat uninformed. (I doubt, for example, that Mr. Papadopoulos could
"have won free elections hands down" at any time during his seven years in power.
Mr. Laqueur concludes his assessment of Greek affairs with the observation that
"there is no ground for optimism about [the] likely successor" of the colonels'
regime—and it is evident throughout his analysis that he did not anticipate the
obvious Karamanlis solution which was resorted to by the Greeks even as his
article was going to the press. Cf. Essay I, notes 2, 7, above.)

My "Preliminary Reflections" article opens with this reassurance about constitutional government in the United States:

I gave to the wife of a friend a few years ago, on the occasion of her naturaliza-
tion, a bronze plaque depicting the stratagem employed by Odysseus to rescue
his men from the cave of the blinded but still deadly Cyclops: it shows, of course,
a man lashed to the underside of a ram. I explained that my gift illustrated a

fundamental principle of constitutionalism which Americans should take to heart, a principle which helps decent citizens avoid despair and curb desperation. The principle is that "there's always a way out": that is, there are legitimate means provided within our constitutional system for dealing as a people with each of the dangers we are likely to face and with the various inequities we should attempt to remedy.

"There's always a way out" goes well with another of our political principles, "Take it easy." See "American Constitutionalism," n. 33; Essay XIV, note 17, below.

The decisive critique to be made of the unhappy American role in the Vietnam War may be that available in an observation by Lord Cockburn, in *Regina* v. *Hicklin*, L.R., 3 Q.B. 360, 371-372 (1868) (see Essay X, note 18, above):

> . . . I think the old sound and honest maxim, that you shall not do evil that good may come, is applicable in law as well as in morals; and here we have a certain and positive evil produced for the purpose of effecting an uncertain, remote, and very doubtful good . . .

But see Harold W. Rood, "Distant Rampart," *United States Naval Institute Proceedings*, March 1967; 121 *Congressional Record* E1844 (April 18, 1975); *ibid.* E2134 (May 1, 1975). Cf. *New Yorker*, April 21, 1975, pp. 141-142; Howard Wriggins, Letter, *New York Times*, May 6, 1975, p. 38. "They just wanted the damn place more than we did." A senior military analyst at the Pentagon (quoted, upon the end of the Vietnam War, C.B.S. Television, April 30, 1975).

Malcolm P. Sharp and I prepared for newspaper publication in April 1975 an article, "The Promises Presidents Make," which includes these observations:

> How are we to understand such solemn promises as those said to have been made in 1973 by President Nixon to the Saigon government in furtherance of the Paris peace talks?
>
> These promises may have bound the President and any successor to present to Congress and to the American people whatever case could decently be made for continued economic or renewed military aid to South Vietnam. But secret promises cannot, unless put in the form of a duly ratified treaty, bind the government or people of the United States to do anything more than exercise its judgment about what should be done in the circumstances of the moment. The limited authority of the Executive with respect to international undertakings should be evident to anyone (in this country or abroad) who troubles to inform himself about long-established principles of American constitutionalism.

The complete text is in "American Constitutionalism" (Univ. Dallas), n. 15.

XIII. The Case for Supporting Israel

1. The Yom Kippur War was still going on when this essay was written and published. Some of the points discussed in this essay are also discussed in *The Constitutionalist* (Essay I, note 1, above): e.g., c. 4, n. 117, c. 8, n. 150, c. 9, n. 3. See, also, Essay I, note 7, Essay IX, sections iv, v, above, Essay XIV, section ii, below. Mimeographed copies are available of the talk I gave at a Chicago synagogue, February 10, 1974, "The Case for Israel: *Joshua* 24: 13; *Deuteronomy* 4: 6; 2 *Samuel* 12: 3."

2. See, on property, *The Constitutionalist*, p. 819; Essay VI, notes 19, 20, Essay X, Epilogue, above. See, also, Essay XI, note 6, above. "The Arabs brought their ancestral desert with them [to a once-fertile Palestine]." Nikos Kazantzakis, *Journeying*, Themi Vasils and Theodora Vasils, translators (Boston: Little Brown, 1975), p. 176. Cf. *ibid.*, pp. 174-181. See, as well, Essay XI, note 6, above.

See Louis Harris, "Oil or Israel," *New York Times Magazine*, April 6, 1975 (reprinted 121 *Congressional Record* S5338 [April 7, 1975], E1666 [April 10, 1975]). See, also, 121 *ibid.* H2673, S5843 (April 10, 1975), S5972 (April 15, 1975). Cf.

Senator Charles H. Percy's well-publicized criticisms of Israeli policy for intransigence and undue caution, 121 *Congressional Record* S7025 (April 29, 1975). But see *Fables of Aesop* (London: Penguin Books, 1964), pp. 9, 20, 27, 58, 83, 95, 131, 98, 121, 136, 174, 180, 213.

"They consider it a most just cause for war when a people which does not use its soil but keeps it idle and waste nevertheless forbids the use and possession of it to others who by the rule of nature ought to be maintained by it." Thomas More, *Utopia* (New Haven: Yale University Press, 1964), p. 76.

3. See Leo Strauss, "Quelques remarques sur la science politique de Maimonide et de Farabi," *Revue des Etudes Juives*, C, p. 1 (1936); "Farabi's *Plato*," *Louis Ginzberg Jubilee Volume* (New York: American Academy for Jewish Research, 1945), p. 357 (see, also, *Persecution and the Art of Writing* [Glencoe: The Free Press, 1952]). Cf. David J. Elazar, Letter to the Editor, *Chicago Tribune*, June 19, 1975.

This essay was first published on the day of Mr. Strauss' funeral in Annapolis, Md., October 21, 1973. See Anastaplo, "On Leo Strauss: A Yahrzeit Remembrance," 67 *University of Chicago Magazine* 30 (Winter 1974). (The proper name index to Mr. Strauss' works anticipated in *The Constitutionalist* is not yet ready for distribution.)

XIV. Impeachment and Statesmanship

1. Even worse than indictments proved to be the publication of the taped White House conversations, an act of remarkable political folly. See "American Constitutionalism and the Virtue of Prudence" (Essay I, note 1, above), nn. 3, 9, 33, 56, 64; Essay V, note 23, above, note 17, below. See, also, Anastaplo, Book Review: Charles Goodell, *Political Prisoners in America*, *Book Week/Chicago Sun-Times*, July 8, 1973, p. 1. Cf. *The Constitutionalist* (Essay I, note 1, above), c. 8, n. 169.

Also foolish was the *release* of the candid photograph of May 14, 1975 showing the premature (and sophomoric?) Oval Office jubilation in connection with the *Mayaguez* rescue. E.g., *Chicago Sun-Times*, May 16, 1975, p. 1.

2. See Anastaplo, "Impeachment: Playing With Fire?" *University of Chicago Maroon*, Nov. 30, 1973, p. 2; abridged, *Chicago Sun-Times*, Dec. 9, 1973, sec. 1-A (the weekend after the *Sun-Times* had itself come out for impeachment) (reprinted in 119 *Congressional Record* E7595 [Nov. 29, 1973], E7672 [Dec. 1, 1973], E8185 [Dec. 22, 1973]). I refer in that article to "those mischievous tapes which (for all the fuss which has been made about them) are not likely to do much more than confirm our worst suspicions about the way Richard Nixon has always conducted his political affairs." I myself expected Mr. Nixon to appear worse in the tapes than turned out to be the case—but he was obviously compromised enough to disillusion even those who had five times voted for him for national office. See notes 13, 17, below.

Was not Mr. Nixon too long in our political life? He became the William Jennings Bryan of his time—and Watergate was his Scopes Trial. Even so, are not "private" tapes "unnatural" and hence inappropriate evidence in *political* matters? Similarly, Hamlet would have done better for Denmark and himself had he not relied upon ghostly revelations. See *The Constitutionalist*, pp. 30-32. See, also, Essay V, note 23, above.

See, for a reluctant recognition of Mr. Nixon's foreign policy accomplishments, John Kenneth Galbraith, *A China Passage* (Boston: Houghton Mifflin Co., 1973), pp. 23-24, 34, 67.

I argued in my "Playing With Fire" article: "The time to have talked seriously about Presidential impeachment was during our ruinous involvement in the Vietnam war, not after a President's Secretary of State has been awarded the Nobel Peace

Prize. There is, after all, a limit to how seriously such crimes as burglary should be taken, even when they have been aggravated by an attempted obstruction of justice." See Essay XII, section vi, above. To what extent is Mr. Kissinger's present ineffectiveness due to our extended exercise in impeachment? See, also, note 10, below. (Of course, an attempted interference with the electoral process should not be taken lightly. But see Epigraph, Essay I, above.)

3. Are we not exhibiting "withdrawal symptoms" after the disturbing excitements of the 1960s? See Anastaplo, "What Can Be Said for the Nixon Administration?" *Chicago Tribune*, Sept. 22, 1973, sec. 1, p. 16. See note 11, below.

4. See *The Constitutionalist*, c. 7, n. 41. See *ibid.*, p. 825, on the *Rosenberg case*.

5. "The 1972 campaign for Nixon's re-election was conducted like a private war." *Milwaukee Sentinel*, Aug. 9, 1974, p. 18. See, also, Rowland Evans and Robert Novak, "Hate Toward 'Enemies' Destroyed Nixon," *ibid.*, Aug. 10, 1974, p. 16. "Anastaplo said [at St. John's College] that the passions behind the impeachment movement had exceeded 'the limits of rationality and had to be checked'—a situation he blamed on both the 'excessive fervor of the critics' and the 'shameless maneuvering of the President himself.' *Annapolis Evening Capitol*, May 1, 1974, p. 3. See "American Constitutionalism," nn. 33, 56 (on the beginnings of Mr. Nixon's troubles).

6. Robert Bolt, *A Man For All Seasons* (New York: Vintage Books, 1962), p. xxii. See note 16, below.

7. *Chicago Sun-Times*, Jan. 28, 1974, p. 10. A comment upon this essay by the politician referred to, Abner J. Mikva (who is now in Congress again), was published in *Chicago rap*, May 20, 1974, p. 1.

8. See Essay XII, note 2, above, for citations to my discussions of the Pentagon Papers controversy.

9. *Time*, Dec. 24, 1973, p. 68. One would have thought that Mr. Nixon would be, after his "close call" in 1952, scrupulously clean about his financial affairs. But, it seems, central to his character and hence his career (*for good* as well as for bad) was a certain opportunism. Has he not been throughout essentially a political chameleon? George Meredith once observed, "We are betrayed by what is false within." *Book World/Chicago Tribune*, August 11, 1974, sec. 7, p. 1. And Heraclitus observed (Fr. 119), "A man's character is his guardian divinity." "He isn't 'Chet' Arthur anymore," an old political crony remarked sadly about Chester A. Arthur in 1882, "he's the President." *Book Week/Chicago Sun-Times*, March 23, 1975, p. 1.

Even so, it should be recorded (at least for the historian to consider) that there simply may not have been in the country at large the concern about Mr. Nixon and the Watergate misconduct which was expressed in intellectual and political circles, despite the extensive coverage of all this in the mass media. Thus, I travelled by bus, in mid-June, 1974, from Chicago to Santa Barbara, California (with stops in Cheyenne, Salt Lake City and Las Vegas). *Not once* during this week of travel did I overhear people even refer to the impeachment controversy—and one does overhear a lot of conversations on buses. Nor did I have the impression that the public's anger or shame inclined it to be reticent. All this is central to the long-run effect of what may generally come to be regarded as a vendetta by liberals against a somewhat successful "conservative" leader with "human" failings. Magnanimity *is* called for on all sides for the good of the country. See Essay IX, note 11, above, notes 15, 17, below.

"Kermit Eby and I discovered, upon exchanging impressions during the worst days with Senator Joseph R. McCarthy, that the groups of midwestern small-town businessmen which we had been meeting with were far less excited about the Senator's 'revelations' than were newspapermen, lawyers, and university faculties."

The Constitutionalist, c. 8, n. 131. The modern intellectual, by and large, does not seem to me to recognize his duty to promote moderation. (This is true of intellectuals both of the Left and of the Right.) That duty is addressed in both the "theoretical" and the "practical" halves of this book. The sporadic loose talk about the Kennedy assassinations, as well as about "repression," is a case in point. See, e.g., *The Constitutionalist,* c. 8, n. 135. See, also, Essay XII, note 2, above.

10. See Plato, *Republic* 414. Is the Kissinger "cover-up" now becoming unravelled? Contributing to the Secretary's difficulties today are the State Department failings in Cyprus (which followed in turn from the insistent American and Greek-American miscalculations about Greece since 1963). See Essay I, note 5, above.

11. See Anastaplo, Book Review: James M. Burns, *Roosevelt: The Soldier of Freedom, The Critic,* Jan.-Feb. 1971, p. 71. See, also, "Other abuses of power," *Chicago Tribune,* Feb. 4, 1975, sec. 2, p. 2.

Edward V. Hanrahan, the talented Cook County State's Attorney who got entangled in the "Black Panthers" controversy, may be another case of an erratic leader who stood too long (and not simply for selfish reasons) by the misconduct of subordinates who overreached themselves. See *The Constitutionalist,* p. 323, c. 8, n. 74. A man more political and more ruthless than Mr. Nixon would have cut himself loose from his Watergate subordinates early enough to have saved himself. See note 3, above, note 12, below. (The 1963 Profumo Scandal also comes to mind.)

12. See, e.g., William W. Crosskey, *Politics and the Constitution* (Chicago: University of Chicago Press, 1953). Consider as well the observations by David Eisenhower, one of Mr. Nixon's sons-in-law (*Chicago Tribune,* Sept. 5, 1974, p. 17):

[Those who became entangled in Watergate were] not so much a gang of felons that were out to subvert the Constitution, but by and large people who walked into and indulged in accepted practices within the unwritten rules of executive D.C. which had developed over four years . . . Maybe it was the personality of Richard Nixon that inspired it. But in either case, I don't think the individuals involved are on a par with Herman Goering, Joseph Goebbels, Rudolph Hess. . . . It's just not the same thing. Someone's ox is going to get gored . . . to check the unbridled expansion of executive authority, and it turned out to be ours. That's the way it goes.

Was one of Mr. Nixon's "sins" that of trying to make the bureaucracy behave itself—that is, of trying to subject it (like the military) to political rule? Be that as it may, there *has* taken place the past decade a salutary constitutional realignment with respect to the conduct of foreign affairs by the government of the United States, perhaps the most profound constitutional realignment in this country during this century. (The next decade may yet see a considerable reconstitution in the Soviet Union. That is to say, human nature continues to make its claims against the Russian tyranny.)

The report of the House Judiciary Committee on the impeachment of Mr. Nixon may be found at 120 *Congressional Record* H8967-H9109 (August 22, 1974). (The three articles of impeachment recommended by the Committee are at *ibid.,* pp. H8967-H8968.)

13. Consider the problem posed by Glaucon and Adeimantus in Book II of Plato's *Republic.*

I observed in my "Playing With Fire" article (which was prepared in October 1973) (note 2, above):

Resignation would be, of course, the simplest of the three prudent settlements I have listed. But this action may be more self-sacrificing than Mr. Nixon is capable of—unless he should become even more depressed than he has sometimes appeared to have been in recent months. Were Mr. Nixon selfless enough to resign for the good of the country, it might be argued by his more cynical critics, there never would have developed around the White House the grasping attitudes which have spawned the present general distrust of the President. I, however, do not consider his resignation unthinkable. Certainly, he could well resign if he *should* happen to be impeached by the House of Representatives. Mr. Nixon's resignation was on August 9, 1974. This was within a fortnight after the approval of articles of impeachment by the House Judiciary Committee.

14. See, e.g., "Confidence is Ebbing in White House Ability to Control Inflation," *Wall Street Journal*, July 16, 1974, p. 1. See, also, Essay VI, note 20, above.

15. See Anastaplo, "In Defense of Forthright Decency: The Pardon of Mr. Nixon," *Hyde Park Herald*, Chicago, Sept. 9, 1974; abridged, *Chicago Tribune*, Sept. 30, 1974, sec. 2, p. 6. See, also, Anastaplo, "An Amnesty on Discussions of Amnesty?" *Chicago Tribune*, Feb. 25, 1973, sec. 2, p. 2; reprinted in 119 *Congressional Record* H3280 (May 2, 1973). Cf. I. F. Stone, "Mr. Ford's Deceptions," *New York Review of Books*, Nov. 14, 1974, p. 3; also, 120 *Congressional Record* H10529 (Oct. 11, 1974). See, as well, Essay IX, note 11, above.

The continued imprisonment of the harassed, anti-war nurse, Jane Kennedy, remains a scandal. She seems, by all accounts I have seen, a decent woman.

16. I do have some reservations about this passage, as about the career and arguments generally of Thomas More, which need not be developed here. See, e.g., the discussion of conscience in Essay VI, note 39, above.

17. *The Utopia of Sir Thomas More . . . With Roper's Life of More*, George Sampson, editor (London: G. Bell and Sons, 1910), pp. 239-240. See *Fables of Aesop* (London: Penguin Books, 1974), p. 28.

It was, perhaps, only natural that Mr. Nixon "had" to go once he (and others) had permitted matters to deteriorate as far as they did in the Summer of 1974. Consider, e.g., the editorial comment, "The moral cynicism that runs like a dark thread throughout the transcripts is shocking." *Dallas Times-Herald*, May 5, 1974, p. 2B; "The case is complete," *Chicago Tribune*, Aug. 7, 1974, p. 20; "Nixon—a political failure," *ibid.*, Aug. 9, 1974, p. 10; James J. Kilpatrick, "My President lied and lied," *Chicago Daily News*, Aug. 9, 1974, p. 10; notes 1, 5, 13, above. (Be that as it may, Mr. Nixon should have been disposed of politically in 1968, if not much earlier, not in 1974.)

Consider, also, as a contribution to political moderation, the conclusion of my letter in the *Washington Post*, Dec. 5, 1973, p. A31 ("American Constitutionalism," n. 33) (see Essay XII, note 3, above):

. . . Some of Mr. Nixon's crowd have long seen foreign subversion lurking behind every domestic dissenter. Some of his critics, on the other hand, now manage to see an incipient dictator even in a President who is very much on the run. Both camps of extremists should be counselled, along with the American people and the American press, to *"take it easy"*—a most salutary prescription for the perpetuation of constitutionalism in the United States.

We hear more and more that Mr. Nixon came close to "cracking" under the intense, and unprecedented, pressures of his last months in office. Did it really make sense for the country to run the risk of subjecting him to such a test? To what end?

Certainly, we cannot count upon being as fortunate as we may have been on this occasion the next time we permit things really to get stirred up. Even so, the long-run effect of *this* adventure remains to be seen. See, e.g., Essay XI, section ii, above, on the dangerous folly of using a sledgehammer to smash a peanut. See, also, note 9, above.

Consider, as well, Malcolm P. Sharp and George Anastaplo, "The Promises Presidents Make" (Essay XII, note 3, above): "Was not the repudiation of the Versailles Treaty by the Senate in 1919 one of the great moments of American constitutionalism, with the same consequences for good as well as for ill as the execution of Charles I by the English in 1649? Any foreign government or people which neglects, in extended dealings with American public servants, to take due account of the Constitution of the United States invites self-deception and disappointment." See *Fables of Aesop* (London: Penguin Books, 1964), p. 175.

XV. Race, Law, and Civilization

1. Cicero, *Republic*, I, xvii. Many of the points discussed in this essay are also discussed in *The Constitutionalist* (Essay I, note 1, above): e.g., pp. 239-253, 310-311, c. 5, nn. 43, 126, c. 6, n. 50, c. 7, nn. 36, 77, 81, 95, c. 8, nn. 5, 9, 171, 177. See, also, Anastaplo, "Neither Black nor White: The Negro in America," in *Notes on the First Amendment* (Essay IV, note 28, above); "American Constitutionalism and the Virtue of Prudence" (Essay I, note 1, above), pt. 4, sec. 4 (also, n. 61); Essay V, section vii, Essay VI, section iii, Essay X, Epilogue, Essay XI, note 4, above.

2. See, e.g., Anastaplo, "One Introduction to Confucian Thought," 66 *University of Chicago Magazine* 21 (Summer 1974).

3. See *Deuteronomy* 4: 6; Essay V, section vii, Essay VI, notes 33, 51, Essay IX, above, Essay XVII, note 15, below. I do not consider Christianity separately since it did not develop independently of philosophy. See, e.g., the opening verses of the *Gospel of John*. See, also, "American Constitutionalism," nn. 20, 61.

4. See, e.g., *The Constitutionalist*, c. 7, n. 21. Cf. Moses Maimonides, *The Guide of the Perplexed*, III, 25-50.

5. Technology, on the other hand, may be "counterproductive," despite its material bounty: the resulting insulation of ourselves from nature may be philosophically deadening as may be the lack of significant contact with one another which technology promotes and permits. See, on the *polis*, *The Constitutionalist*, c. 7, n. 35; Essay VII, section iv, above. See, also, Essay V, note 17, above.

6. See Plato, *Timaeus* 22b; *The Constitutionalist*, c. 9, n. 2; Essay II, note 45, above. See, also, *ibid.*, p. 807. Cf. John Collier, *The Indians of the Americas* (New York: W. W. Norton, 1947), pp. 15-17; Willa Cather, *Death Comes for the Archbishop* (Melbourne: William Heinemann, 1938), pp. 187, 207-209, 263-264. See, also, Friedrich Nietzsche, *Thus Spoke Zarathustra*, pt. I ("On the Thousand and One Goals").

7. Edna St. Vincent Millay, "Euclid alone has looked on Beauty bare." See, also, John Keats, "Ode on a Grecian Urn"; *The Constitutionalist*, c. 5, n. 126; Essay VI, note 44 (point 5), Essay X, Epilogue, above.

8. See Jacob Klein and Leo Strauss, "A Giving of Accounts," *The College* (Annapolis: St. John's College, April 1970), p. 1. See, also, Essays IV, VI, VII, above.

9. Strauss, *What Is Political Philosophy?* (Glencoe: The Free Press, 1959).

10. Consider the exchange with Alexandre Kojève, Leo Strauss, *Tyranny and Wisdom* (Glencoe: The Free Press, 1963). See, also, Essay IV, note 47, above. George Orwell's *1984* suggests that such a tyranny would not be relieved by Homeric poetry and the like.

11. This was quite evident in an extended interview of Elijah Muhammad (of the Black Muslims) I conducted (with Merv Block, then of Associated Press), February 12, 1973. See, for "the world's best hope," Essay III, section v (end).

12. The shouting down of unpopular speakers, especially in academic communities, should, it seems to me, be firmly dealt with. See, e.g., *The Constitutionalist*, pp. 329, 635; Essay IX, note 1, Essays XII, XIV, above.

13. See Strauss, *Liberalism, Ancient and Modern* (New York: Basic Books, 1968), p. 3.

"Culture," which seems to mean today that set of authoritative opinions which happens to guide an association, is used as loosely as "philosophy": e.g., "a struggle between two philosophies of deterrence." Editorial, *Wall Street Journal*, June 12, 1974, p. 18. Cf. *The Constitutionalist*, c. 7, n. 77; Essay VII, n. 7, above. One must take account of such usages even while one discourages them. See, e.g., *ibid.*, c. 8, n. 171 (on the use today of "black" for Americans of African descent); *ibid.*, c. 7, n. 189 (for an editorial change to "black man" from my intended "man of color"). (I reserve for another occasion my discussion of the materials I have been collecting on the significance of "black" and "white," especially in the English language. It suffices here to mention this as a problem. Consider the observation by "Bricktop," the celebrated 80-year-old Negro entertainer: "All my life, if you called someone 'black,' you had to fight them." Studs Terkel Show, WFMT, Chicago, May 7, 1975.)

14. Of course, if one take cultural relativism seriously (that is, if one regards seriously an opinion about things which denies the sensibleness of seriousness), then one should not have a bad conscience, perhaps not even any conscience at all—unless one surrenders to the existentialist desire to take seriously the *one* set of standards upon which one has somehow settled. See, on conscience, Essay VI, note 39, above.

15. See "American Constitutionalism and the Virtue of Prudence" (Essay I, note 1, above); Essay VI, notes 19, 20, Essay XI, note 7, Essay XIV, note 17, above. Mimeo-graphed copies are available of a paper I prepared for the Center for the Study of Democratic Institutions, June 19, 1974, "The Instructive Prudence of Abraham Lincoln's *Emancipation Proclamation*."

16. See Anastaplo, "The Declaration of Independence," 9 *St. Louis University Law Journal* 390, 402, n. 24 (1965).

17. See *Sommersett's Case*, 20 S.T. 1 (1772). See, as well, the discussions of slavery (directly or indirectly) in *The Constitutionalist*: pp. 149-150, 154-155, 175-176, 239-254, 431, 473-475, 489, 511-512, 563, 579-580, 584-585, 600-603, 623, 645, 652-654, 670-671, 674-675, 679-680, 710-713, 726-732, 736, 740, 779-780.

   Would British abolitionism (in the 1830s) have provided the American colonies (if not yet separated) a baser ground for independence than could be resorted to in 1776? Contemporary Rhodesia comes to mind.

18. See Essay XVI, note 2, below.

19. See Herbert J. Storing, editor, *What Country Have I? Political Writings by Black Americans* (New York: St. Martin's Press, 1970), pp. 85, 92, 93, for W. E. B. Du Bois' comments on "triumphant commercialism" and on B. T. Washington. Cf. Essay V, note 17, Essay VI, notes 19, 20, above.

   Mr. Storing's anthology is most useful and his introduction to it thoughtful.

20. The Yankees do have, in the "long run," the advantages (including the commercial resources) of the New York market. See, on the effects of commerce, Montesquieu, *The Spirit of the Laws*, XX, i-ii; "American Constitutionalism," nn. 6, 51.

   Hank Aaron elected to finish his playing career with Milwaukee (an American League team). ("The emergence of blacks as superstars in sports is reflected in their salaries. *Ebony* points out that nine out of the ten highest paid athletes are blacks and baseball players. Their combined salaries total more than $3 million yearly." *Chicago Sun-Times*, May 26, 1975, p. 46.)

21. Elmer Gertz, *To Life* (New York: McGraw-Hill, 1974), p. 93. "Chicago attorney Earl L. Neal on Wednesday became the first black president of the University of Illinois Board of Trustees. . . . He remembers going into a restaurant for a sand-wich while at the U. of I. [from which he graduated in 1949] and being ordered to eat it outside after the sandwich was put in a paper bag. 'That was my first experi-ence with segregation,' he once said. 'Young people today gasp when I tell them

about it.'" *Chicago Sun-Times,* March 20, 1975, p. 3. (Cf. Essay IX, section ii, above.) Consider, also, a survey on "the number of black Americans holding elective office" in the United States: the number has increased 152% since 1969, but that is still only one-half of one percent of the 522,000 elective offices in the United States for a minority which comprises 11.1% of the country's population. *Ibid.,* April 24, 1974, p. 6. Even so, is not the rate of growth encouraging—or, at least, not discouraging? See Ellis Cose, *Chicago Sun-Times,* April 23, 1975, June 13, 1975.

22. 117 *Congressional Record* E10208 (September 28, 1971) (from *Crisis*). See, also, Essay XI, section vi, above.

"My point is that the Negro American writer is also an heir of the human experience which is literature, and this might well be more important to him than his living folk tradition." Ralph Ellison, *Shadow and Act* (New York: Random House, 1964), pp. 58-59.

It is well to remember Frederick Douglass' rebuke to his people: "We are imitating the inferior qualities and examples of white men, and neglecting the superior ones." Storing, *What Country Have I?* p. 42. And, then, conscience-ridden intellectuals make matters worse by condoning, if not even imitating, the inferior imitations. See, also, William Faulkner, *Intruder in the Dust* (New York: Vintage Books, 1972), pp. 155-156.

23. Indeed, they even seem to endorse here the linguistic theories of Alice's Humpty Dumpty (which they quote at Storing, *What Country Have I?,* p. 168).

24. Hobbes and Machiavelli come to mind. See, on Hobbes, Essay VI, notes 23, 33, 35, above; see, on Machiavelli, Essay XII, note 2, above. Compare the end of Aristotle's *Nicomachean Ethics* and its transition to the *Politics;* also, Essay IV, above. See, on Malcolm X, *The Spectator,* July 13, 1974, p. 49.

25. The Thomas L. Heath edition of Euclid (in the Dover Publications edition) is an invaluable as well as an entertaining aid.

Axioms, it has been noticed, are "propositions worthy of acceptance." *The College* (St. John's College), July 1974, p. 3. "[T]hey say that even an ass knows that the straight way to a point is shorter than the one round a corner." E. N. Lee and A. P. Mourelatos, editors, *Exegesis & Argument: Studies in Greek Philosophy* (Atlantic Highlands, N. J.: Humanities Press, 1973), p. 430. See, also, *ibid.,* pp. 427-430. Cf. Galileo Galilei, *Dialogues Concerning Two New Sciences* (New York: Dover Publications, n.d.), p. 162, where both the arbitrariness of definitions and their dependence somehow on nature are indicated:

> Although I can offer no rational objection to this or indeed to any other definition, devised by any author whomsoever, since all definitions are arbitrary, I may nevertheless without offense be allowed to doubt whether such a definition as the above, established in an abstract manner, corresponds to and describes the kind of accelerated motion which we meet in nature in the case of freely falling bodies.

Cf., also, Ludwig Wittgenstein, *Philosophical Investigations* (New York: Macmillan, 1968), p. 230e: "If the formation of concepts can be explained by facts of nature, should we not be interested, not in grammar, but rather in that in nature which is the basis of grammar?"

See Essay VI, notes 40, 44 (point 4), above. See, also, Essay X, notes 12, 18, above. Cf. Marvin Jay Greenberg, *Euclidian and Non-Euclidian Geometry* (San Francisco: W. H. Freeman & Co., 1974), pp. 57, 122, 131, 250-256. But see, *Basic Writings of Saint Thomas Aquinas,* Anton C. Pegis, editor (New York: Random House, 1945), I, 804-806, 827-829; Anaxagoras, Fr. 21a: "Appearances are a glimpse of the unseen." See, also, Democritus, Fr. 125.

26. See Essay IV, Epigraph, above. See, also, Essay VI, sections v, vi, above. See, as well,

Aristotle, *Metaphysics* 980a21 sq., 981b13-23 ("This is why the mathematical arts were founded in Egypt; for there the priestly caste was allowed to be at leisure."), 982a1-982b11.

XVI. Citizen and, Human Being: Thoreau, Socrates, and Civil Disobedience

1. See, on the significance of music (in the modern sense) for the proper education of the soul, Plato, *Republic* 398b-402d, 404e, 410a-412b, 424b-d, 620a, *Laws*, 654d-656c, 659c-e, 667b-c, 670d-671a, 700a-e, 701a-b, 798e, 812b-813a, 967e, *Crito* 50d-e. Compare, in Plato, *Crito* 43b10 ("discordant") and 54d2-5. See, also, note 8, below.

   Various of the points discussed in this essay are also discussed in *The Constitutionalist* (Essay I, note 1, above): e.g., c. 5, n. 11, c. 7, n. 45, c. 8, nn. 37, 70, 122. See, also, Essays I, II, IV, VI, IX, above. See, as well, *The Correspondence of Sir Thomas More*, E. F. Rogers, editor (Princeton: Princeton University Press, 1947), pp. 514-532.

   See, for a community-minded alternative to Thoreau's individualism, a Greek Orthodox prayer (*The Services for Holy Week and Easter Sunday* [Brookline, Mass.: Greek Orthodox Theological Institute Press, 1952], p. 45):

   O Heavenly King, strengthen our faithful kings, establish the faith, pacify the heathen, give peace to the world, protect the welfare of this city, place our departed fathers and brethren in the dwellings of the just, and of Thy goodness and mercy receive us also with our penitence and thanksgiving.

2. It should be noticed that had Thoreau, in his radical attack upon the Union, succeeded in persuading his fellow citizens of Massachusetts and of the North, it would have meant abandoning Southern slaves to complete control by a sovereign Confederacy which not only would then have been entirely slave but which would have been left free to strengthen slavery both by extending it to Cuba and Latin America and by reviving the foreign slave trade. This would have been comparable to critics of American military involvement in Vietnam withdrawing completely from all organized political activity in the United States. See the text at note 18 in Essay XV, above.

   Thoreau's antislavery rhetoric was indeed useful, but primarily because citizens such as Lincoln knew how to adapt it to political use in persuading freedom-minded citizens to save the Union rather than to permit the Slave States to go their own way.

   Consider (as support for Thoreau's approach?) the report by a diplomat (Henry J. Tasca) who was the American ambassador when the colonels fell in July 1974 (Essay I, note 7, above): "I do not agree . . . that the Turks brought back democracy to Greece. The junta was finished. They were through. It was the total lack of cooperation, the passive resistance of the Greek people that did it." *Hellenic Chronicle*, May 29, 1975, p. 1. Mr. Tasca was not always this sensible about Greece.

3. See Edwin Muir, "The Animals," in *Collected Poems* (London: Faber and Faber, 1960), p. 207. See, also, Essay VI, note 44 (point 5), above.

4. See Anastaplo, "The Declaration of Independence," 9 *St. Louis University Law Journal* 390 (1965); Essay IV, note 34, above; note 17, below. See, on adaptations to circumstances, Essay VI, notes 19, 20, above.

   It is often said that the citizen has the right to disobey whatever law happens to offend his conscience. But what assurance is there, for instance, that the punishment he may be willing to suffer for such disobedience can repair the damage done by his response to the promptings of a mistaken conscience? See, on conscience, Essay VI, note 39, above.

   It is also said that the citizen should be willing, even eager, to accept the punishment awaiting the deliberate lawbreaker. But may not the punishment awaiting the lawbreaker be part (perhaps even the most vital part) of the very law, or system of laws, which he is justly defying? See, e.g., *The Constitutionalist*, c. 7, n. 74.

5. Every discussion of a Platonic dialogue is, at best, an introduction. I say "introduction" because one can hope to do little more than examine the surface of such a dialogue or, perhaps, only to indicate what the surface is. I say "at best" because there are discussions, purportedly of Platonic dialogues, which are really about something else and can only mislead. See Plato, *Phaedo* 115e (cf. *Crito* 43b10); *Phaedrus* 274c-277a.

There is for us the problem of how to read a Platonic dialogue—and then there is also the problem of how to read a particular dialogue. The particular dialogue includes details peculiar to it that the reader must somehow notice and work from, details to which he must apply the general rule that nothing is there without a purpose. A good introduction may do little more than clear away the conventional opinions which can get in the way of Plato's effort to speak to his attentive and imaginative reader. See *The Constitutionalist*, c. 9, sec. 4; Essay II, above. See, as perhaps bearing on one's reading of the *Crito*, Plato, *Euthyphro*, *Euthydemus* 277d, 306d sq, *Republic* 327b, 449b, *Lesser Hippias* 370b-c, *Gorgias* 480d-e, *Meno* (Essay VI, note 51, above). See, also, note 16, below.

In this essay, *polis*, political community, and city are used interchangeably. See Essay XV, note 5, above.

6. See Leo Strauss, *The City and Man* (Chicago: Rand McNally, 1964), pp. 75-76, 79-80. See, also, Plato, *Protagoras* 334c-338e, *Gorgias* 457c-458b, 471e-472c, 474a-c, 505d-506c, 519d-e, *Laws* 722e-723d.

7. Cf. Plato, *Apology* 37a-b, *Statesman* 294bsq.

8. The discordant noise of the laws (see note 1, above, note 16, below) is likened by Socrates to that of the Corybantes, the priests who imitate the frantic "music" said to have been employed by the Curetes to conceal the crying of the vulnerable infant Zeus. (Was, that is, the truth concealed by the Curetes for the sake of justice?) Should the laws also be considered to be protecting by their overpowering noise something vulnerable but yet divine and worthy of such protection? See Essay X, note 7, above.

It should be noticed that there is a movement in the *Crito* from the many gods of the opening pages to the one god of the final sentence. The many gods would seem to include "the gods of the city" (*Apology* 24b-d), Zeus among others. See Plato, *Epistles* xiii, 363b. See, also, Essay II, section xi, above.

Socrates brings "on stage" not Justice (a single being) but the Laws (a multitude). See note 9, below.

9. We can assess Crito's judgment by noticing the disparaging reference he makes to the magnificent speeches recorded in the *Apology*. His concern for Socrates the friend and fellow citizen overpowers his respect for the noble and philosophical Socrates (for Socrates the human being?). Yet Crito does know Socrates well enough to anticipate difficulty in securing his assent to the escape plan. (Is Crito the oligarchic, elderly counterpart of the democratic, youthful Chaerephon? See Essay II, note 46, above.)

The laws (and city?) begin by speaking in the singular, perhaps as a tragic chorus (another "more refined 'many' ") does through its choragus. See, on the relation of poetry and politics, Laurence Berns, "Aristotle's *Poetics*," in *Ancients and Moderns*, Joseph Cropsey, editor (New York: Basic Books, 1964); Essay X, above.

10. See Plato, *Phaedo* 99a-b, 115c-d. See, also, *The Constitutionalist*, c. 9, n. 38; Essays VII, VIII, above, Essay XVII, below.

11. See Cicero, *De Officiis*, I, xli:

But no rules need to be given about what is done in accordance with the established customs and conventions of a community; for these are in themselves rules; and no one ought to make the mistake of supposing that, because Socrates or Aristippus did or said something contrary to the manners and established customs of the city, he may do the same. It was only by reason of their great and divine virtue that they had such license.

See, also, Plato, *Republic* 329e-330a; Aristotle, *Nicomachean Ethics* 1129b11-1130a1, 1130b18-21, *Politics* 1268b23-1269a29, 1280a9-23, 1276b16-1277b33.

12. The laws even claim they are like father and mother to Socrates (but only to Socrates as citizen?). Cf. Plato, *Republic* 413b-415a, 496a-497d. See note 16, below.

13. See Plato, *Republic* 499dsq; Plutarch, *Nicias* 538-539 (XXIII, 1-6); Essay II, notes 28, 31, 46, above.

14. Plato, *Apology* 31d-32a.

Socrates knows that he is at the age when men's powers can be expected to begin to fail. That his powers are still undiminished, however, is evident from the *Phaedo*.

It might be thought that Socrates' decision in the *Crito* was determined by his indications in the *Apology* that he preferred death to exile. But why did he take that position in the *Apology*? Does not that earlier decision suggest that something other than the kind of arguments made by the laws guides him in the *Crito*? (It should be noticed that neither philosophy nor Socrates' daemonic thing is invoked on this occasion. See Essay II, section xii, p. 28, above.)

15. Socrates refers to some of the arguments he relies upon in the *Crito* as having been established by him and his companions on other occasions. This, however, is not said by him about the arguments advanced by the laws.

See the concluding pages of Book I of Boethius' *Consolation of Philosophy*.

16. The ordinary city is magnified in the *Crito;* the city, and even the best city, is called into question in the *Republic* where justice is examined at great length with competent interlocutors. (See *The Constitutionalist*, c. 9, sec. 4; also, note 5, above.) It is this tension between the two attitudes, each of which has something to be said for it, which men must learn to cope with. (See *ibid.*, c. 2, n. 1.) Each attitude, pushed to its extreme, can be harmful: neither mere law-abidingness nor wholesale rejection of the laws is prudent. He who is to be able to balance one attitude against the other must devote himself to serious thought about the nature of man and of the political community, and about the form and conditions of excellence for each. (See Essay VI, note 44, point 1.)

In Socrates' cell on this occasion the principal natural senses of man are laboring under disabilities: too much "noise" and not enough light. In these circumstances, the "laws" (the very word, in Greek, means "conventions") are so bold as to identify themselves as at least as natural as one's father and mother. (See note 12, above.) They claim, in effect, to be as natural as the *polis* which makes (not generates) them. See Strauss, *City and Man*, pp. 14-15, 20.

One must wait until the "racket" stops to be able to listen to the voice of reason, to be able to think through the meaning of this dialogue. (See note 8, above.) Nor is the light adequate: on another occasion, under the sky of Crete, the laws are examined in detail by an Athenian and his companions at high noon, in a conversation which also begins at dawn. Plato, *Laws* 722c-d. See *Crito* 52e-53a. Cf. Plato, *Protagoras* 310a-311b, 361d-362a.

17. Similarly, do not Aristotle's arguments on behalf of that natural slavery which is both rare and unprofitable shake to its foundations that conventional slavery which can be both widespread and profitable? *Politics*, I, iv-vii.

We are reminded, by these arguments of Socrates and of Aristotle, of the qualifications and conditions found in the Declaration of Independence: the right of revolution is there so hedged in as to reinforce among American citizens respect for law and order. See note 4, above.

We are reminded as well of Heraclitus' exhortation (Fr. 44): "The people must fight on behalf of their law as though for the city wall."

See Plato, *Apology* 32a-e; also, the text at note 12 in Essay III, above.

XVII. On Death: One by One, Yet All Together

1. Professor May drew upon Elisabeth Kubler-Ross, *On Death and Dying: What the dying have to teach doctors, nurses, clergy and their own families* (New York: Macmillan, 1969). He is chairman of the Department of Religious Studies, Indiana University.

   Various of the points discussed in this essay are also discussed in *The Constitutionalist* (Essay I, note 1, above) and are referred to below. See, in addition, *ibid.*, pp. 30-31, c. 2, n. 39, c. 5, n. 126, c. 7, n. 3, c. 8, nn. 133, 185, c. 9, n. 31. See, also, Anastaplo, "The Daring of Moderation: Student Power and *The Melian Dialogue*," 78 *School Review* 474-478 (August 1970); "American Constitutionalism and the Virtue of Prudence" (Essay I, note 1, above), nn. 33, 51; Essay II, sec. xii, nn. 37, 39, 45, Essay VI, nn. 40, 44, Essay X, n. 11, above.

2. The attitude I am describing is not the serenity of men of faith. Such men, it may even be said, do not believe they face death. "When warned by the Duke of Norfolk that 'indignatio principis mors est,' [Sir Thomas More] coolly answered, 'Is that all, my lord? Then in good faith between your grace and me is but this, that I shall die today and you to-morrow." *Dictionary of National Biography*, XIII, 884. See notes 7, 11, below.

   I have had occasion to ask various people (including doctors) what in their opinion would be "the best death." The typical answer, "It is best to die while asleep," is revealing in that it displays neither curiosity about one's last moments nor any concern for an afterlife. That is, it seems that most men today (or, at least, many more than formerly?) would prefer to die unaware of what is happening to them!

   What good would it do, many would ask, for a man to discover what dying is like, to have one more opportunity to learn something about life, the soul and the body? Is not this really a question, in principle, about the good of *any* learning for the sake of understanding alone? That is, even the normal life span *can* be seen as but a moment when compared to eternity. See Essay VII, note 3, above.

   Was it not the Emperor Julian who said that he would "learn something even if he had one foot in the grave"? See Benedetto Croce, *An Autobiography* (New York: Books for Libraries Press, 1970), p. 77:

   > . . . To know and to have lost the power of learning, to be educated and to be unable still to improve one's education, is to bring one's life to a standstill, and the right name for that is not life but death.

   Cf. Edmund Wilson, *Upstate* (New York: Farrar, Strauss and Giroux, 1971), pp. 385-386:

   > As one grows weaker, one becomes more helpless, more lazy, and also more indifferent. . . . I have seen or sampled many kinds of experience . . . so that, not expecting any real novelty, I have no longer any curiosity beyond such as the satisfaction of which will keep me mildly amused while my faculties are gradually decaying.

   My father (1884-1957; see Dedication) was cheerful on his deathbed. See, also, Anastaplo, "On Leo Strauss: A Yahrzeit Remembrance," 67 *University of Chicago Magazine* 30, 32, 37 (Winter 1974). Sherlock Holmes observed: "Education never ends, Watson. It is a series of lessons, with the greatest for the last." Arthur Conan Doyle, "The Adventure of the Red Circle."

3. See, e.g., Plato, *Phaedo* 115b-116a. "People like the Gowries dont attach a great deal of importance to death or dying. But they do put a lot of stock in the dead and how they died—particularly their own." William Faulkner, *Intruder in the Dust* (New York: Vintage Books, 1972), p. 66. See, also, *ibid.*, pp. 89, 175-179, 219. See, also, Faulkner, *As I Lay Dying*, a peculiarly (perversely?) comic account of an attempt to give someone a proper (i.e., requested) burial. See, as well, Sophocles, *Antigone*.

4. The wide appeal today of Leo Tolstoy's *The Death of Ivan Ilyitch*, a rather superficial but passionate treatment of the subject, is indicative of modern tastes. See notes 14, 17, below. Consider, also, the emphasis on self, and on the reappearance of exact responses to similar stimuli years apart, as somehow the basis for "immortality" in Marcel Proust's *Remembrance of Things Past* (New York: Random House, 1934). See e.g., *ibid.*, I, 35-36, II, 1122-1123. Cf. *ibid.*, I, 543-545; *The Constitutionalist*, c. 9, n. 4; *New Yorker*, cartoon, July 24, 1971, p. 39. Is not what Proust takes to be a decisive conquest of time merely childish precocity degenerating into arrested development?

The thoughtful man realizes that the more thoughtful he is, the less likely he is to be unique ("individual"). That is, he realizes that "he" has been, as thinker, "here" "before" and that "he" will "return." Only the accidental and essentially superfluous is "individual" and hence vulnerable. Thus, the thoughtful man knows that what he has learned—what is correct and hence seems so wonderful about what he has learned—others, too, may investigate and learn as the centuries roll by. He knows, that is, that human reason may exist and develop as fully as has his own so long as human communities are preserved. See Essay X, notes 13, 14, Epilogue, above.

The thoughtful man also realizes that the distinctive ("personal") features of his "self" are, in the final analysis, impermanent and hence essentially unknowable and uninteresting. See Aristotle, *Nicomachean Ethics* 1139b18 sq., 1140b31 sq., 1141a20sq. See, also, *The Constitutionalist*, c. 3, n. 25, c. 6, n. 50, c. 7, n. 124, c. 9, nn. 30, 38, 39. Cf. G. W. F. Hegel *The Philosophy of History* (New York: Dover Publications, 1956), pp. 223-224. Even so, it may be pedagogically useful to make much of oneself, especially if one can suggest thereby the relation of deeds to words, of body to soul. (Consider the "framing" of the account of More's Utopia by meals immediately before and after.)

The quotation in the text is from Henry Thoreau, "Walking." See p. 213, above.

5. See *The Constitutionalist*, c. 8, n. 193, c. 9, nn. 32, 36. See, also, note 17, below.

See the funeral talk for Jason Aronson by Leo Strauss printed in Anastaplo, "On Leo Strauss: A Yahrzeit Remembrance," p. 38. See, also, Anastaplo "Mertha Fulkerson: Guardian of the Clearing," 117 *Congressional Record* H12557 (December 14, 1971). Cf. Anastaplo, "Emma Toft: Queen of the Peninsula," 120 *Congressional Record* E6228 (October 2, 1974); Essay VII, note 3, above.

I had occasion to make on March 6, 1975 the following remarks about Harry Kalven, Jr. (1914-1974):

This series of six weekly law lectures here at Rosary College, of which my talk tonight ["The Trial of Sir Thomas More"] is the conclusion, has been dedicated, as many of you know, to the memory of Harry Kalven, Jr., professor of law at the University of Chicago and a friend of this college. Mr. Kalven, who died last October, was to have given one of the lectures in this series.

Dr. Lawrence Freedman opened the inaugural lecture of this series by likening Harry Kalven to a jeweler, a craftsman who would hold people and arguments

up to the light to bring out the best in them. And when he found a gem of quality
—a man or woman, an argument, a turn of phrase—he would treasure it.

Among the jewels he treasured—and in this, as in several other ways, he was
like Thomas More, another man of sweetness and wit, serious about his civic duties
and born for friendship—among the jewels Harry Kalven treasured was his
family. In assessing many men of talent and distinction, the less said of their wives,
the better—especially if those wives are themselves so talented or so independent-
minded as to be inclined to resent their husbands' accomplishments. But in his
wife, a quite talented woman in her own right, Harry Kalven found a jewel, a
companion of many years who patiently listened to his always youthful speculations, who took pride in his triumphs, and who loyally ministered to him in his
afflictions. They enjoyed a companionship which could instruct their friends
(as Thomas More's life instructed *his* friends) in the satisfactions of a good
marriage. It is reassuring, at a time when women are desperately trying to "define
their roles," to be able to treasure the memory of the fruitful life Betty Kalven
shared with her husband.

The death, and even more the premature death, of such a man as Harry Kalven
affects, and affects deeply, all who had come to know and to depend upon him.
But his many writings and the generations of students he helped shape do
remain—as do, in the hearts of those close to him, the generous appraisals which
he had made of them and which leave them forever enriched.

Harry Kalven lives on in this form more surely, more vitally, than it is ever
given most men to live at all. I am reminded, in thus recalling him and the heartening influence he exercised in many crises, of the description in Shakespeare's
Henry V of the young king walking among the outnumbered English soldiers
in France the night before the fateful Battle of Agincourt:

> . . . O, now, who will behold
> The royal captain of this ruin'd band
> Walking from watch to watch, from tent to tent,
> Let him cry, "Praise and glory on his head!"
> For forth he goes and visits all his host,
> Bids them good morrow with a modest smile
> And calls them brothers, friends, and countrymen.
> Upon his royal face there is no note
> How dread an army hath enrounded him;
> Nor doth he dedicate one jot of color
> Unto the weary and all-watched night,
> But freshly looks, and overbears attaint
> With cheerful semblance and sweet majesty;
> That every wretch, pining and pale before,
> Beholding him, plucks comfort from his looks.
> A largess universal, like the sun,
> His liberal eye doth give to every one,
> Thawing cold fear. Then, mean and gentle all,
> Behold, as may unworthiness define,
> A little touch of Harry in the night.

(Mr. Kalven's opinions about obscenity are drawn upon in Essay X, sec. iii, above.
See, also, *The Constitutionalist,* p. 816.)

At the opposite pole from premature death, and also unnatural, is unduly
delayed death (that is, senility). Is the fear of senility a concealed (and, in a
sense, reasonable) substitute for the fear of death? That is, is not someone who
becomes permanently senile as much "departed" as someone who has died? It

should be evident that the serious burden here is upon the survivors, even more so than in the case of an obvious death. (Consider, in this connection, why the more humane Greek cities, in circumstances where the death of an infant seemed called for, preferred exposure to more direct means. See Essay IV, note 41, above.)

Professor Lloyd A. Fallers (1925-1974), who endured with remarkable fortitude over many years a debilitating disease which required elaborate operations, commented on this essay, "My own experience is that the greatest fear is of being kept alive in a basically *inhuman* condition—this is technically possible now." He particularly endorsed the paragraph at note 10 in the text, the third paragraph of section iv, and the final paragraph of this essay. He observed, with respect to the first of these three paragraphs, "Effectiveness also depends sometimes on a doctor's 'mechanistic' or 'impersonal' or 'inhuman' attitude toward his patient."

6. For example, one does not roll off one's bed while asleep. Consider how fragile and troublesome life would be if men did not have many unconscious or automatic tendencies toward self-preservation (such as breathing).

The thoughtful man does not deny the reality of pain, however much he may be able to ignore it; he takes reasonable precautions to avoid injury and illness; he makes vigorous efforts in an emergency to save his life or that of others. He is careful, that is, about his health and life, because he realizes (among other things) that certain people may be entitled to his services and that it is not good to permit others to commit an injustice by injuring him.

Nor does the thoughtful man deny that there is a significant difference between life and death and that it may be useful to develop in a community a sense of the sanctity of human life.

See, e.g., Plato, *Phaedo* 60b-c, *Apology* 34d, *Symposium* 220d sq. Cf. Plato, *Apology* 37e; Essay II, note 51, above. See, also, Aristotle, *Politics* 1278b23-31.

7. I can do little more here than mention the problem of how the soul, separated from the body, could "operate." "The body is loved by the soul, because without the body the soul cannot get sense-impressions." Philolaus, Fr. 22.

Consider the significance, for the subsequent discussion of the immortality of the soul in the dialogue, of the opening word of Plato's *Phaedo*. Consider, also, G. W. F. Hegel, *The Phenomenology of Mind* (New York: Harper & Row, Harper Torchbooks, 1967), pp. 337f, 390f, 413f; Hegel, *Philosophy of Mind* (London: Oxford University Press, 1971), pp. 32f; Jacob Klein, "Plato's *Phaedo*," *The College* (St. John's College), January 1975, p. 1; *The Constitutionalist*, c. 9, n. 38.

Consider, as well, these lines from William Wordsworth's "Tintern Abbey" (emphasis added):

> Therefore am I still
> A lover of the meadows and the woods,
> And mountains; and of all that we behold
> From this green earth; of all the mighty world
> Of eye and ear,—both what they half create,
> And what perceive; well pleased to recognize
> *In nature and the language of the sense*
> *The anchor of my purest thoughts*, the nurse,
> The guide, the guardian of my heart, and soul
> Of all my moral being.

"The spirit [soul] desires to remain with its body, because, without the organic instruments of that body, it can neither act, nor feel anything." The *Notebooks of Leonardo da Vinci*, J. P. Richter, editor (New York: Dover Publications, 1970), II, 287 (#1142). See, also, *ibid.*, II, 288 (#1147), 306-308.

8. Does the contemporary attitude about the "mystery" of death depend in part upon the fact that death is necessarily hidden (because of our technology) from the sight of most people today? Cf. *The Constitutionalist*, c. 7, n. 59 (on the solemnity of the autopsy room); also, note 17, below.

Old people's homes have also been subjected to criticism. But is not considerable reliance on old people's homes (which should, indeed, be better supervised by the community) to be expected in a society as mobile as ours, especially one with so much greater a proportion of old people than ever before in the history of the race? Are we willing to hobble such a society? (See note 9, below.) Many of us now live in large cities. Do we in our active years want to revise radically our lives now so as to make *our* lives as very old men and women more agreeable? Sentimentality about such matters may conceal the fact that there often are for men only hard choices, choices between alternatives which have something to be said for each of them as well as against each of them.

9. I suggest, furthermore, that our fundamental concern should really be with modern technology and the kind of life (including specialization and compartmentalization) that it permits and hence encourages—but I realize that modern men are not prepared to make the substantial material sacrifices which would accompany the salutary dismantling of their technology. See *The Constitutionalist*, c. 7, nn. 35, 122; Essays VII, VIII, X (Prologue, Epilogue).

The problem of nature (which is, in effect, denied by contemporary subjectivity and existentialism) is central to this entire discussion. See *The Constitutionalist*, c. 7, n. 77, c. 9, nn. 20, 38; Essays IV, VI, above. The natural should be distinguished, however, from the typical. Do not Socrates' concerns and activities in his last days of life provide a plausible model of how a man about to die should conduct himself, especially in circumstances where his "work" is done? See Essays II, XVI, above. Should we not say that the better a community is, the smaller the gap will be between the typical and the natural? Cf. note 17, below.

10. Similarly, the thoughtful man is not likely to be willing to concern himself with the many mundane problems necessary to be dealt with by the conscientious ruler. See Plato, *Republic* 520a-b. Cf. *ibid.* 473c-d. See, also, *The Constitutionalist*, chap. 9, sec. 4. Consider, as well, what may be the special case of Maimonides: were not his medical skills subordinated to other (political? philosophical? religious-rhetorical?) concerns?

I notice, in passing, the kind of confusion which can follow upon the use of such terms as "helping professions." If the attention of the medical profession is shifted from "healing" to "helping," special problems arise: for example, may a doctor (as doctor) kill his pain-ridden dying patient (in order to *help* him and his family)? Consider the distinctions made by Dr. Leon R. Kass in his paper, "Man's Right to Die" (35 *The Pharos of Alpha Omega Alpha* 73, 76 [April 1972]):

. . . However, in recent years, some people have questioned the validity of the distinction between allowing to die and deliberately killing, pointing out that both discontinuing the antibiotics and adminstering deadly poisons equally result in the death of the patient. That the outcome is the same is not to be denied. But the two acts are descriptively and morally different. First of all, the intention is different. In the one case, the intent is to desist from engaging in useless 'treatments' precisely because they are no longer *treatments*, and to engage instead in the positive acts of giving comfort to and keeping company with the dying patient. In the other case, the intent is indeed to directly hasten the patient's death. Secondly, the agent of death in the first case is the patient's disease, in the second case, his physician. . . .

Neverthless, it may be true that the notion of a death with dignity encompasses under *some* conditions (e.g., protracted untreatable pain) a direct hastening of one's death. It may be an extreme act of love on the part of a spouse or friend to administer a death-dealing drug to a loved one so in agony. But this is indeed a delicate matter, if we wish to insure that the hastening of the end is never undertaken for anyone's benefit but the dying patient's. . . . As one doctor put it, if mercy-killings were legalized tomorrow, doctors must not do them. Doctors must not kill.

Consider, also, Kass, "A Caveat on Transplants," *Washington Post*, January 14, 1968, p. B-1; "Averting One's Eyes, or Facing the Music?—On Dignity in Death," 2 *Hastings Center Study* 67 (May 1974).

11. The problem of deception is intimately related to the problem of justice and social harmony. See Plato, *Republic* 389b sq., 414b sq., 432b sq., 460a sq. Cf. Aristotle, *Nicomachean Ethics* 1096a11 sq., 1101a21 sq. See, also, *The Constitutionalist*, c. 2, n. 1, c. 8, nn. 135, 195, c. 9, nn. 25, 26; the discussions of rhetoric in "American Constitutionalism."

12. The cosmetic effort has extended even to the name of what was once called the "undertaker" and even the "gravedigger." See the description of the undertaker in chapter 27 of Mark Twain's *Huckleberry Finn*. See, also, Plato, *Gorgias* 462d sq.

It should be recognized, however, that undertakers often do help urban families, overwhelmed by the fact of death, to carry on with routine everyday affairs.

13. See, on the idea of progress and its implications, *The Constitutionalist*, c. 9, n. 3. See, also, Essays VII, VIII, XV, section iv, above; notes 4, 9, above.

14. Sentimentality and an emphasis upon self-expression go hand in hand. See *The Constitutionalist*, p. 313, c. 7, n. 124, c. 8, n. 193. See, also, Essay X, above; notes 2, 4, above.

15. See, on Martin Heidegger, Strauss, *Liberalism, Ancient and Modern* (New York: Basic Books, 1968), pp. 235, 237, 256; Anastaplo, "On Leo Strauss," p. 38; *The Constitutionalist*, c. 2, n. 7, c. 8, n. 139, c. 9, n. 19; Essay V, notes 12, 13, 22, above.

The anguish that moderns feel because of the fact of death draws upon and transforms the sentiments which permeate ancient drama, sentiments which (when properly used) make genuine tragedy so fresh and ennobling. And even today, the necessity of facing up to death permits and sometimes encourages ordinary people to be more open to the dignified and to the noble than they might otherwise be. Cf. Essay VI, note 40, above; note 17, below.

Consider the suggestion in Laurence Berns' "Aristotle's *Poetics*" (in *Ancients and Moderns*, Joseph Cropsey, editor [New York: Basic Books, 1964]), n. 23:

Thus the *Poetics* would appear to be that book of Aristotle's which comes closest to dealing with one of the key questions of Martin Heidegger's thought: the question, stated in non-Heideggerian terms, of how fear, tragedy, and natural piety contribute to the establishment of the mood, or disposition, out of which philosophy develops.

See the text at note 3, Essay XV, above.

See, on tragedy, death, and comedy, some of my concluding remarks from a talk, "Comedy and Death: An Introduction to *Huckleberry Finn*" (University of Chicago, May 17, 1975):

One problem, then, with Mark Twain's comedy—one might almost say, with American comedy—is that it makes tragedy unlikely among us—and without genuine tragedy, a great people of more-or-less democratic inclinations may be impossible. . . . Genuine tragedy depends on the noble. But the noble, which *is* to some extent based on conventions and which must be distinguished from the humane, is depreciated, if not undermined, by Mark Twain. . . .

Comedy, I have suggested, has appropriated among us the materials, if not the proper place, of tragedy. Perhaps this is inevitable, or at least highly likely, in a young country: that is, tragedy may require a settled country, while comedy is more appropriate for or at least more likely among a people still on the move. Thus, comedy depends more on, or is more likely to be characterized by, particularity, change, and the topical. And yet does not even it rely upon enduring community standards if the incongruous behavior portrayed is to be seen for what it is?

The depressed status of genuine tragedy among us may have contributed to our peculiar interest in and yet immature avoidance of death. There are two sober, not unrelated, ways a people (not the philosopher) may come to terms with death, the way of organized religion and the way of tragedy. To deal with death as Mark Twain does—in the context of stories which are largely comic in their language, in their evident intention, and in their effects—is not to deal with it properly: nature can be depended upon to assert herself against such unnatural experiments.

This inevitable self-assertion by nature means, among other things, that death is for us both something of an "obsession" and yet inadequately faced up to. Thus, Huck Finn can say at the outset of his recollections that he takes "no stock in dead people"—not realizing, it seems, that the long story which he is about to narrate (and which he already knows) is filled with death and dying.

Not to take stock in dead people is likely to mean, in practice, that the new is made too much of. Perhaps it also means that an emphasis is likely to be placed on self-preservative utilitarianism, even as death is not given its due. Certainly, it makes it difficult to make sense of the choices before us—for it is difficult for a people to have a meaningful future if it does not have its roots in a vital past, a past shared with its dead. . . . Without roots in a vital past, comedy loses its fruitfulness, especially when a style such as Mark Twain's is inherited by men less talented than was he. And even Mark Twain, we are told, died an embittered man. . . . See note 3, above; also, Preface, para. 1, above.

16. It is well to remember that there is what modern men (unduly sensitive to the possibilities of significant unconscious repression) would consider suspiciously little about dying itself in such comprehensive ancient treatises on the conduct of one's life as the *Nicomachean Ethics*. Aristotle's principal concern is with how one should live. He does recognize that death may be hastened (and that this is sometimes to be regretted) if one lives one way rather than another, but he also recognizes that this is sometimes unavoidable. See note 6, above. See, also, *Luther's Works (Table Talk)*, Theodore G. Tappert, editor (Philadelphia: Fortress Press, 1967), LIV, 65, 225-228, 429-430.

17. But the generality of men today, it should never be forgotten, do feel differently. Most men will endure all kinds of things (all kinds of dying) in order to avoid death. (Cf. note 15, above.) Thus, I have been told, an old Irishman said upon reading an account in the *Chicago Sun-Times* (December 30, 1970, p. 24) of this essay upon its delivery at an A.A.A.S. Convention, "I don't care *what* he says. I'm going to go out crying anyway." To which my response was, "More power to him!"

See *The Constitutionalist*, c. 6, n. 43; Essay VI, notes 19, 20, Essay I, note 1, above.

Index